THE BOWHUNTER'S
HANDBOOK
2nd Edition

M.R. James

©2004 Krause Publications

Published by

krause publications
An imprint of F+W Publications, Inc.

700 East State Street • Iola, WI 54990-0001
715-445-2214 • 888-457-2873
www.krause.com

Our toll-free number to place an order or obtain
a free catalog is (800) 258-0929.

Library of Congress Catalog Number: 2004094034

ISBN: 0-87349-850-X

Designed by Gary Carlson

Edited by Dan Shideler

Printed in United States of America

Dedication

With love to Janet and the James Gang: Jeff, Sandy, Kevin, and Laura; Dave, Norma, Marc, and Cady; Dan, Karen, Scottie, and Tyler; Cheryl and Madalyn Grace. Heartfelt thanks for understanding my frequent absences from James family events — and the restless stirrings in my hunter's soul.

Acknowledgments

I offer a tip of my camo cap to good friends G. Fred Asbell, Dave Holt, Dr. Dave Samuel, and Dwight Schuh for their gracious support of this writing project. Their expert bowhunting advice and knowledge, as well as the use of their names, make this book more complete and credible.

Thanks, too, are due professional photographers (and my huntin' buddies) Judd Cooney and Fred Burris, whose exceptional wildlife photos add the perfect visual touch at the beginning of each section and chapter.

Special kudos go to the talented *Bowhunter* magazine staff and to the generous men and women of the archery/bowhunting industry, whose technical information, product photos, and critical advice contributed much to the completeness of this book. Specific heartfelt thanks are due my former partners at Blue J, Inc., Publishers, Don Clark, Steve Doucette, Bob Schisler, and Fred Wallace, who know exactly what it is not just to have a dream but to live it!

Finally, sincere thanks to the countless hunting companions, guides, and outfitters, who at one time or another over the past 40-plus years, have joined me in conducting the necessary "field research" for this and my other writing projects.

About the Author

For more than 40 years M. R. James has successfully bowhunted big and small game across most of North America. Perhaps best known as the Editor/Founder of *Bowhunter* magazine, James actually launched his long outdoor writing career in the mid-1960s, well before originating his own bowhunting magazine in 1971. Today this award-winning author, editor, and public speaker often leaves his mountainside home in northwestern Montana, logging tens of thousands of miles each year, to share advice and bowhunting adventures. In addition to authoring half a dozen popular books and thousands of magazine features and columns, James conducts how-to seminars and appears as a regular guest on outdoor televison shows and in hunting videos. He continues to serve *Bowhunter* as the magazine's Founder/Editor Emeritus.

Inducted as the 54th member of the Archery Hall of Fame in 2003, James was honored for his many bowhunting accomplishments and his widespread influence on the sport. A Senior Member of the Pope and Young Club, official measurer, and former officer, he was editor of the P&Y record books published in 1975, 1993, and 1999. He also is a Life Member of the Professional Bowhunters Society, an organization he first joined in 1965. In 1998, the publishers and editors of *Petersen's Hunting* magazine named James one of hunting's 25 most influential personalities. In 1999, the Outdoor Writers Association of America (OWAA) presented James with the organization's distinguished Excellence in Craft lifetime achievement award for his extraordinary writing/editing career. He has been a columnist and Bowhunting Advisory Council member for *North American Hunter* magazine for over 25 years.

An admitted whitetail hunting addict, James still has found time between deer hunts to collect a majority of the recognized North American big game species. Several dozen of his trophy-class animals are listed in the Pope and Young bowhunting records, while a handful of truly exceptional animals have earned Boone and Crockett Club recognition.

Contents

SECTION I. Expert Techniques

SECTION II: Expert Strategies

Preface

"SO YOU WANNA be a better bowhunter?" This bluntly intriguing question launched the First Edition of *The Bowhunter's Handbook* published in the spring of 1997. And if your answer today is as positive as initial reader reaction was to that original edition, then this newly revised and updated volume is definitely the book for you. Regardless of your past bowhunting success, or the lack of any positive results, the following chapters can help you become the best bowhunter possible.

Take time to thumb briefly through these pages. Note each chapter's heading. Study the photos. Do these things and it should be obvious that there's much more here than basic bowhunting advice. True, there's plenty of elementary guidance for those folks just getting started, but this is a book for all bowhunters and especially those who are genuinely interested in self-improvement. No matter your hunting experience or personal choice of archery tackle, from home-crafted bows (selfbows) or the finest recurves and longbows to the very latest contemporary compound bows with a full array of modern accessories, this book contains plenty of essential how-to information complemented with time-tested recommendations. This information and instruction combines to create a complete graduate level course in successful bowhunting.

M.R. JAMES

The Bowhunter's Handbook was originally written for intermediate and advanced bowhunters: serious-minded men and women who wanted to sharpen their hunting and shooting skills, as well as widen their personal bowhunting horizons. It was created through the collective effort of recognized experts who rank among North America's best bowhunters, men and women with decades of proven ability. In short, it was a book designed cover-to-cover with a single purpose in mind: to educate and inform all readers, novice or expert, in understandable, no-nonsense words, while answering every possible question any bowhunter could ask.

That was then. This is now, and the enlarged, improved Second Edition copy you're holding enhances the original *Handbook* contents. So read it. Learn from it. Follow its tips. Practice its suggested techniques. Because if you do, there's no real reason why you, too, can't become an incredibly effective and consistently successful bowhunter.

Bowhunting's ABCs are still covered, of course, since archery fundamentals, from selecting the best equipment possible to developing the proper shooting form and technique necessary for depend-able accuracy, build the foundation for success. But beyond learning the physical aspects of drawing and releasing an arrow, you will come to understand the critical mental aspects of bowhunting. You'll discover how to build and maintain shooting confidence even under incredible moment-of-truth pressure; the necessity for proper bowhunting practice; how to hone your stalking and still-hunting skills; and proven methods of hunting and harvesting every species of game.

What more could any serious bowhunter need to know? Well, maybe a little.

For one thing, there is the knowledge that no how-to book, regardless of how complete in scope and content, is a substitute for firsthand, in-field bowhunting experience. All readers must clearly understand that in order to derive the greatest possible benefits from this book, they must invest time and effort beyond just turning its pages. This book is a starting point, a convenient reference source. It is not a magical shortcut to bowhunting fame and fortune and accomplishments. As most successful hunters already know, the harder they work, the more effective they become. Keep that truism firmly in mind as you read and digest this book's content.

People who know me will readily attest that I am a true toxophilite, someone who considers bowhunting and archery to be a full-time way of life rather than a part-time hobby or weekend pastime. For the record, my participation in National Field Archery Association tournaments started in the late 1950s, and I've been a serious bowhunter since the early 1960s, tagging my first whitetail in 1963. Then in mid-1971 my life changed forever when I helped to launch what would grow to become the most widely-read and respected bowhunting magazine ever published. Over the past three-plus decades, my name has appeared at the top of the *Bowhunter* magazine masthead. For additional details about my bowhunting curriculum vitae, flip back to the "About the Author" blurb printed on the inside of the front cover.

Admittedly, getting to know and befriend America's top bowhunters, from the late Fred Bear to modern-day legend Chuck Adams and other instantly recognizable men and women, to little known but tremendously talented and successful hunting archers that I've met in every part of this wide continent, has been a personally gratifying side benefit of my lifelong involvement in archery and bowhunting.

G. FRED ASBELL

DAVE HOLT

DR. DAVE SAMUEL

DWIGHT SCHUH

Fortunately for the readers of this revised book, G. Fred Asbell, Dave Holt, Dr. Dave Samuel, and Dwight Schuh – talented writers, veteran hunting companions, and my close friends – have generously agreed to lend their imposing credentials and vast experience to this writing project. Together, our combined archery/writing background represents nearly 175 years of successful bowhunting experience.

For the benefit of anyone not acquainted with the credentials of this impressive team, a short introduction of each contributor is appropriate:

G. Fred Asbell, an Illinois native who grew up in Indiana and lived much of his adult life in Colorado, now resides in Michigan. One of the nation's top traditional bowhunters, Fred served as *Bowhunter* magazine's Hunting Editor from 1980 to 2000. He was President of the Pope and Young Club from 1984 to 2000 and is the author of two popular books on instinctive shooting and one on stalking and still-hunting. A serious bowhunter since the early 1960s, he's taken a variety of big game trophies from grizzly bears to mountain goats. Today he serves on the staff of *Traditional Bowhunter* magazine.

Dave Holt, a longtime Colorado resident, has been the *Bowhunter* magazine technical guru since 1990. Widely recognized as one of North America's foremost authorities on modern bowhunting tackle and one of the most consistently successful bowhunters alive, Dave travels widely across North America in pursuit of multiple species. He also spends several months each year bowhunting and outfitting in Africa. An equipment perfectionist and author of the classic archery book *Balanced Bowhunting*, Dave has collected an impressive assortment of record book animals from two continents in a career that now spans over 40 years. An updated Second Edition of *Balanced Bowhunting* was published in early 2004.

Dr. Dave Samuel of West Virginia, a retired university professor and wildlife biologist, also has bowhunted extensively in Africa and North America. He has served brilliantly as *Bowhunter* magazine's Conservation Editor since its first issue appeared in 1971. He is an internationally recognized authority on methods to effectively combat the antihunting movement. Dave also is the author of the acclaimed 1999 book *Know Hunting*, an in-depth examination of the truths, lies, and myths about the role hunters play as wildlife conservationists. Dave has earned countless awards and honors for his leadership in pro-hunting, pro-conservation efforts.

Dwight Schuh of Idaho is the man I handpicked to succeed me as *Bowhunter* Editor. Hired in 1995 after a successful, award-winning career in outdoor writing and editing that dates back to the early 1970s, Dwight is the author of several popular books on bowhunting for deer and elk, as well as the comprehensive and best selling *Bowhunter's Encyclopedia*. He has tagged most of North America's big game species, along with a variety of African game. Much in demand as a seminar speaker and a frequent guest on various bowhunting videotapes and television shows, Dwight now handles all editorial duties for *Bowhunter* magazine.

As I mentioned previously, my bowhunting career started in earnest in the early 1960s. Through more luck than skill, I tagged my first Pope and Young record book whitetail in late November of 1963. Back then such successes were relatively rare, often meriting a small town newspaper write-up and grip-'n'-grin hunter/buck photo. While famous bowhunters such as Howard Hill and Ben Pearson and Fred Bear had regularly brought home game, most of us ended our deer seasons in the 1950s and 1960s with more memories than meat. More often than not we defined "success" in terms of game seen. Actually getting a shot was an exception to the bowhunting rule. And tagging a deer...well, that heady feat put any successful hunter in some pretty select company. Woodland wisdom of that mid-century era said the average bowbender could expect to spend an average of six to seven hunting seasons afield before arrowing his first deer.

Times have changed, thank goodness! Today's North American bowhunters are blessed for the most part with healthy and expanding game populations, very generous bag limits, and lengthy archery seasons. Additionally, never before in the history of bowhunting has there been such a selection of quality gear or such an availability of how-to-do-it, where-to-go information. Look around you. There's no shortage of helpful material from instructional seminars, books (such as this one), magazines, and videotapes. This indeed is the Golden Age of Bowhunting!

Regardless, despite all of the readily available information and technological advantages found in modern tackle, accessories, clothing, optics, footwear, treestands, calls, etc., bowhunting itself generally remains difficult and challenging. Despite being the best-equipped, best-informed bow and arrow deer hunters in archery history, the national success rate at the beginning of the 21st century runs somewhere just over 22%. True, in a handful of states about half or more of the bowhunters get their venison, but in other areas of the country only a tiny fraction of the licensed hunters manage to score. Regardless, consider that across North America today an average of only two out of 10 bowhunters end their season with meat in the freezer. That stark fact underscores the inherent difficulty of pursuing deer with sticks and strings. Again, that suits most bowhunters just fine.

What, some people wonder, would possess bowhunters to invest so much time in the woods with the odds stacked against them? The stock response from any serious bowhunter is "If you have to ask, you probably wouldn't understand." Truth be known, many bowhunters are converted riflemen and shotgunners who started seeking new hunting challenges. By handicapping themselves with one of the oldest weapons known to man and venturing into fields and forests to confront wary game on its home turf, they quickly discovered challenge aplenty.

The venerable Fred Bear, a man who singlehandedly did more to promote and popularize modern-day bowhunting than anyone else, explained it best. Indeed, "Papa" Bear spoke for thousands of veteran bowhunters when he observed that hunting with the bow and arrow offered "...all the basic thrills of hunting and very little killing. To me, the greatest thrill of bowhunting is in the stalk, in being in the woods, and the companionship. The kill is last."

But it was bowhunting pioneer Dr. Saxton Pope who perhaps perfectly captured the essence of bowhunting with the following words written nearly a century ago: "Today there is no need to battle with the beasts of prey and little necessity to kill wild animals for food; but still the hunting instinct persists. The love of the chase still thrills us and all the misty past echoes with the hunter's call.

"In the joy of hunting is intimately woven the love of the great outdoors. The beauty of woods, valleys, mountains, and skies feeds the soul of the sportsman where the quest of game only whets his appetite. After all, it is not the killing that brings satisfaction; it is the contest of skill and cunning. The true hunter counts his achievement in proportion to the effort involved and the fairness of the sport."

Generally, making a bowhunting kill is seldom easy. It's not enough to slip close to ever-alert wildlife, remain undetected, overcome feral senses far superior to man's, and then bring a hunting bow to full draw. Each bowhunter, to fill a season's tag, must also control heart-pounding emotions with an animal standing short yards away, pick an exact spot on that animal's chest, and then accu-

rately deliver a well-honed steel hunting head to its intended target. Such is the ultimate challenge – and the unparalleled personal satisfaction – of successful bowhunting.

Bowhunting is not for everyone, of course. Far too many people in today's I-want-it-now, success-oriented society demand immediate and tangible results. They apparently cannot grasp the idea that, as Fred Bear and Saxton Pope suggested, it is the total experience, the quest itself, that matters most. Even some hunters who are quite successful with firearms lack the patience and commitment that archery hunting demands. Still others apparently are unwilling to accept the perceived stigma of failing far more than succeeding. It's only after tasting the sweet elixir that even an infrequent bowhunting kill brings, that we can fully understand and appreciate the profound truth of the words of Pope and Bear.

If you are a serious hunter who will accept and understand that "bowhunting success" is basically a state of mind complemented by an occasional reality, you already are well on your way to reaping all of the benefits this ultimately challenging sport has to offer. But if you are someone who can define "success" only in terms of bloodied arrows and trophies sprawled on the ground, you're in the wrong sport for all the wrong reasons.

Page through any handy dictionary and check the definition of the word "challenge." I doubt that you can come up with any synonym that better sums up the appeal and substance of bowhunting. The mere thought of someone picking up a bow and arrows, then heading into nearby woods and fields in search of wary and elusive game, is enough to cause many people to shake their heads in admiration, wonder, and even disbelief. Yet every year over 3 million optimistic modern-day bowhunters do exactly that. They eagerly pick up their hunting bows, willingly forsaking modern firearms, and participate in a centuries-old seasonal confrontation between predator and prey.

If you are someone who is undaunted by long odds and imposing challenges (and I suspect that you are if you're reading this book), start now to properly prepare yourself to follow in the footsteps of bowhunting greats such as Maurice and Will Thompson, Dr. Pope and Art Young, Ishi and Will Compton, Roy Case, Howard Hill, Fred Bear and Glenn St. Charles, Ben Pearson and Jim Dougherty, and the other true trailblazers who created and passed along the legacy we now admire and enjoy.

But don't neglect to walk the same trails taken by your peers. By following in the boot tracks of today's most successful bowhunters, those talented men and women whose well-documented exploits contribute much to our rich and living heritage, you can avoid the trial-and error pitfalls of past decades. Finally, take comfort in the fact that there are knowledgeable bowhunters who will gladly share their expert insights and advice, who will answer questions and suggest solutions to common problems – either real or imagined – on virtually every bowhunting topic there is. Really, personal growth and individual improvement are what this book is all about.

Now, read on!

M. R. James
Whitefish, Montana

Section I

Expert Techniques

Chapter 1
Take Your Game To the Next Level

SOMETIMES YOU HAVE TO SMILE to keep from crying. Ask any veteran bowhunter and it's likely he or she can tell you a story that goes something like this: they personally know or have heard of some beginning bowhunter who buys or borrows a bow, gets a hunting license, heads for the woods on opening day, stumbles around in the dark, gets hopelessly lost, and finally sits down on a stump or log to wait for daylight — then promptly arrows a big buck that just happens to wander by. That novice bowhunter then says something to the effect that, "What's so tough about hunting with a bow and arrow?"

It happens. I've heard and seen various versions of this same ol' "bowhunting's easy" scenario for over 40 years.

Back in my native Illinois, campfire gossip has it that one of the biggest record book bucks ever was shot by an excited fellow in a tree stand who released prematurely, when his elbow accidentally bumped a limb just as he was drawing his bow. Seems the arrow wobbled away and thumped the whitetail in his hip, penetrating only a few inches — but just enough for the sharp broadhead to sever the deer's femoral artery. That big buck tipped over within a matter of seconds. Cynics speculate the lucky hunter was more surprised than the unlucky deer.

And I know for a fact of one monster Colorado muley that was tagged by a "bowhunter" who was so hung over after a late-night celebration of a buddy's birthday that the next morning — well after sunup — he'd stumbled 50 yards or so from camp before plopping down to wait for his world to stop spinning. When he opened his bloodshot eyes moments later, there stood one of the biggest bucks on the mountain. Unbelievably, that deer hung around long enough for the guy to fumble an arrow onto the string and somehow manage to get off a shot. He center-punched that huge buck and later joked that he thought he'd been shooting at a whole herd of bucks instead of a single deer.

At such times it may seem there ain't no justice. But I suspect that, in spite of such oft-told tales of a few one-shot wonders, actual occurrences such as the ones I've mentioned here are relatively rare. Although luck — both good and bad — plays an undeniable role in any hunting situation, those people who depend more on luck than skill to succeed most often are going to return home empty-handed. Rightfully so.

In his excellent book *Balanced Bowhunting*, Dave Holt correctly comments: "Bowhunting big game animals is a difficult challenge, even for the most experienced hunters. If you put in time and effort, however, the shot opportunities will come. How you handle those opportunities is the bottom line. To be at your very best, you should begin preparing long before the season opens."

If you're new to bowhunting but have experience with firearms, it's likely the transition will either be relatively easy or extremely difficult. A hunter who already is used to prowling our continent's fields and forests has a definite advantage over those who seldom venture from concrete sidewalks or suburban yards. And if that same experienced hunter knows how to locate and identify game, then set up an ambush or ease close enough to make a killing shot, he or she already has the hunting skills and abilities that are fundamental to bowhunting success. Only the weapon — and the yardages — are different.

When you're ready for new hunting adventures, you'll know it. Bowhunting is a challenging undertaking — regardless of whether you're afield close to home or half way around the world.

Big game like this wide-racked whitetail, and small game such as the Rio Grande gobbler, are waiting to challenge any hunter. Are you ready? Proper practice and understanding of your equipment and ability are necessary.

Often, it's this need to get close to game — or concern that perhaps they can't — that troubles hunters who favor firearms but are toying with the idea of taking up the "stick and string." Why wait for a point-blank shot or try to slip within 30 yards of a buck when you can tip him over at five to 10 times that distance with a flat-shooting, scope-sighted, centerfire rifle? Why waste so much time setting up a close shot when it's not really necessary? Unfortunately, some non-bowhunters just don't get it.

I can't count the number of times I've had some some rifleman walk over to admire a buck or bull I've arrowed, ask how close he was when I shot, and then react with incredulity. "You got *that* close to him?" is a common comment. "How'd you do that?" By being patient, for one thing. By watching the wind and taking great pains to remain unseen and unheard, for another. And when I ask, "Have you ever tried to slip up on a big buck (or bull)?" the usual answer is always the same. "No." There's no need so why try? Take the first good shot that presents itself and get it over with.

Frankly, most folks with this attitude will never understand the heartfelt satisfaction of facing a new and difficult hunting challenge. Or know the fulfillment found in getting spittin'-close to game animals — thwarting their keen senses — and remaining undetected long enough to draw an arrow and make the killing shot. The words of Will Thompson, a bowhunting pioneer who fought for General Lee in the Civil War and later took up archery hunting, explained it this way:

"No one can know how I have loved the woods, the streams, the trails of the wild, the ways of the things of slender limbs, of fine nose, of great eager ears, of mild wary eyes, and of vague and half-revealed forms and colors. I have loved them so that I longed to kill them. But I gave them far more than a fair chance. How many I have missed to one I have killed."

Those words, written in the late 19th century, are as timely and meaningful to serious modern bowhunters as they were over

100 years ago. They should not be regarded as some elitist's put-down of hunters who choose to use firearms and take game with long-distance shots. Neither, I'm convinced, is his comment a public apology for the fact that killing game animals with the bow and arrow is an integral part of bowhunting. Any hunting, for that matter. To paraphrase famed bowman Fred Bear, we may not go hunting just to kill something, but we do kill as part of hunting. And no hunter — regardless the choice of weapon — should ever feel the need to apologize for a fair-chase pursuit that results in taking an animal's life. That's gospel from the Book of James.

While all deer hunters dream of tagging a nice buck, the fact is only about two out of every 10 bowhunters will fill their tags. Bowhunting "success" should be measured in close encounters and shots almost made, not just kills.

In truth, most modern bowhunters launched their hunting careers using firearms. And many continue to enjoy guns as well as bows. Some surveys I've seen show that as many as 80 percent of bowhunters also hunt with firearms. Some of these two-season hunters bowhunt only to pass the days until it's time to head afield with a favorite deer rifle or slug-loaded shotgun. They're simply scouting the woods for local game concentrations. But others become so fascinated with bowhunting — and its inherent challenge — that their firearms soon begin to gather dust.

Like many former gun hunters, I quickly discovered exactly how challenging bowhunting could be. And after a season or two, using a firearm seemed downright easy by comparison. If I shot at something with a gun and it didn't drop, I was shocked. Bowhunting's not like that. While I still own several rifles and shotguns and occasionally hunt with them, it's just not the same — and never will be the same again. All serious bowhunters know exactly what I mean.

Beginners and experienced hunters alike need to clearly understand the responsibilities that go with hunting game animals. These creatures deserve our complete respect and admiration. If your exhilaration after making a clean kill isn't

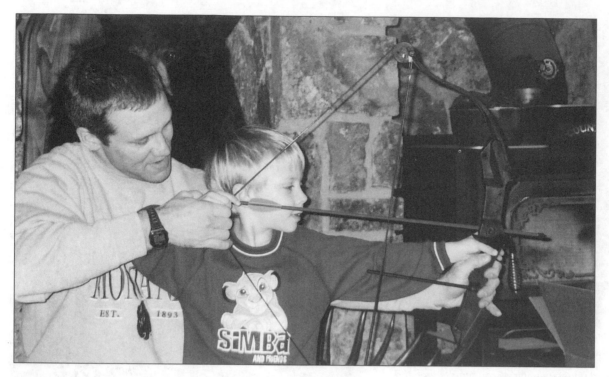

Some parents make sure an interested youngster gets the proper tackle and training to become a bowhunter — if that's the child's choice. Classes offered by the National Bowhunter Education Foundation are a great starting point.

tempered by at least a slight twinge of remorse and appreciation for the animal, you're missing the substance of our great sport. Further, in this modern age with dwindling interest in hunting — combined with constant public scrutiny and ongoing opposition by a tiny but well-financed group of vociferous hunter-haters — we owe it to all other hunters, landowners, the public, the animals we pursue, and ourselves to be the best hunters we can possibly be. Here's how:

• An excellent starting point is enrolling in a bowhunter education course. In some parts of the country, attending such classes is mandatory if you want to purchase an archery hunting license. Regardless, it's time well spent. Even veteran hunters can learn something from the volunteer instructors and the detailed materials provided by the National Bowhunter Education Foundation. For the name of the NBEF contact in your state or province, write or call NBEF Headquarters.

• Never venture afield without first honing your shooting skills. Proper practice not only gives you the proficiency necessary to hunt game animals, it soon teaches you your personal limitations. It also teaches what your equipment will and will not do.

Scouting during the summer months can help you locate game and plan where to begin your hunting season once opening day rolls around. And while you're at it, practice, practice, practice.

Bowhunting has changed dramatically — from camo to hunting gear — since the 1960s when M. R. James tagged this small whitetail. Most folks agree that things have never been better.

Learn your effective shooting range and don't exceed it. Practice shooting at unknown distances, preferably at 3-D animal targets without visible aiming points. You must learn to pick a vital spot on the animal's body, not rely on a bull's-eye or aiming dot commonly found on many practice targets.

- We bowhunters, at times, are our own worst enemies. Most physical injuries — as well as those spiritual injuries that damage the image of hunters and hunting — are usually self-inflicted. It's common sense to treat shaving-sharp broadheads with due respect. Don't walk around alone, or near a hunting buddy, with an arrow nocked unless you're in the final stages of a stalk and ready to shoot. A fall or slip could result in a nasty cut — or much worse.

- Handle broadheads respectfully and with extreme care. Always use a special broadhead tool to remove or tighten hunting heads and to replace dull blades. Make certainly your quiver completely covers the sharp heads on your hunting arrows. Never wear back, hip, or belt quivers while riding horseback or on an ATV. Ditto for climbing in and out of trees. Any accidental tumble could turn into a disaster. Also, when field dressing arrow-killed game, always account for all broadheads and blades before reaching into the animal's chest cavity. Watch your knife blade, too.

- Understand that you're not alone in the woods. Carrying a small light to and from your stand in the darkness will alert other hunters — perhaps even poachers — to your presence. Shots taken at shadowy shapes have killed bowhunters. No game animal is worth dying for or worth taking a foolish shot that could end up injuring someone. If you're worried about your light alerting deer or other game, use a red lens or filter to foil the animals' night vision.

- Don't climb fences, trees, or any structure while carrying your

It makes no difference whether you favor a stickbow or compound bow, the bottom line is you must learn to shoot it accurately. Also, keep in mind that game animals have little appreciation for proper shooting form. You must learn to shoot while standing, kneeling, and sitting.

Shooting at game animals is far different from shooting at targets. The sight of a big black bear standing 15 yards away can start any hunter's heart pounding.

bow. Keep both hands free. Use a climbing belt getting in and out of your stand. Use a haul line to raise and lower your bow and other equipment, and never hunt from any elevated stand without wearing a safety harness or belt. Be especially careful in wet or cold weather. More about tree stand savvy may be found in a later chapter dealing with that important subject.

- When hunting alone, always let someone — a huntin' buddy or family member — know where you'll be and what time you expect to return to camp or home. Consider adding a cell or satellite phone to your pack. Accidents can happen to anyone, no matter how careful they are. It's wise to be prepared. Always.
- Obey all game laws. Observe the rules of fair chase. Treat your fellow hunters as you wish to be treated — bowhunting's Golden Rule — and refuse to hunt or hang around with anyone who breaks hunting's written and unwritten laws.
- Obtain permission to hunt private property and then treat it as you would your own. Don't litter, leave gates open, or endanger livestock or equipment. Don't bring guests without first obtaining the landowner's permission. Never drive through planted fields or across soft ground where your vehicle could get stuck or leave ugly ruts.
- Respect the rights of non-hunters. Understand that loud, boisterous displays in public places — restaurants, stores, gas stations, airports, or public parks and campgrounds — can be downright offensive. Camo face paint and blood-stained or scent-doused camo clothing can be real public turnoffs, too. Ditto for drinking in public places, something that serves to reinforce the image of the boozing, loud-mouthed hunter that the antis love to point at as typical of today's "sportsman."
- Treat game with due respect. Stiffened, bloody carcasses with lolling tongues and gaping body cavities have no place on motor vehicles cruising public streets and highways. Take time to clean up excess blood before transport. Consider covering the animal's body with a tarp or game bag.

- Vow to only take shots that will result in a quick, humane kill — or a clean miss. If you wound any animal, do everything within your power to recover and tag it. Get help, if necessary. Never give up until you're absolutely positive the animal cannot be found. And when you fail to recover any game animal, don't brag about hitting it. "I stuck one" is the most thoughtless, disrespectful, and stupid thing any bowhunter can say.

Learning and Improving

In reality, the day we stop learning is the day we die. And the day a serious-minded hunter stops learning or trying to improve himself as a hunter — or naively believes he already knows all there is to know about his tackle, about the animals he hunts, and about himself — is the day he starts to stagnate. We must always strive to reach the next level of excellence.

On the matter of learning to bowhunt, Dave Holt compares it to putting together a picture puzzle that is composed of big and small pieces.

"The large pieces go together very quickly at first, but then progress slows. At times you become frustrated. Then one day you recognize a beautiful picture taking shape before you. After savoring your success, you realize there are many small pieces necessary to complete the puzzle. Bowhunting fits that mold because it provides enjoyment and occasional success to the beginner, while providing that same enjoyment plus a continual challenge to even the most experienced hunter."

Being able to shoot accurately and consistently is based on good mechanics complemented by rock-solid mental conditioning. This, in turn, builds confidence. Each ingredient is an integral part of bowhunting success. Each ingredient is present in every one of today's best bowhunters.

In my younger days, I played a lot of baseball — from Little League to my early college years — and I often compare hitting a ball with shooting a bow. Think about the mechanics this way:

More and more women are proving bowhunting isn't only for men. Tammy Koenig of Wisconsin is one of the country's top female bowhunters.

Learn to read the signs left by the game you hunt. This whitetail rub was not made by a spike or forky. It's a sure sign there's at least one "shooter buck" hanging out nearby.

Every batter possesses a certain amount of natural hand-eye coordination and physical strength. Every hitter adopts a comfortable batting stance. When he's in the batter's box, he relaxes and concentrates on picking up the ball as it leaves the pitcher's hand. He instantly judges the speed and movement of the ball, then swings and tries to make contact, or he takes the pitch. Each bowhunter — like each baseball player — has a different level of natural ability. Each has a slightly different stance. Each relies on hand-eye coordination and strength. Each relaxes and focuses on the target, then takes the shot — or passes it up. The similarities are evident.

While this book does not go into any detail about the ABCs of shooting a hunting bow (I'm assuming that each reader is already proficient with his bow of choice and wants to learn to be a better bowhunter), I will touch on shooting basics from time to time. The point I'm making with the baseball/bowhunting analogy is — or should be — quite obvious. To become successful hitting a ball or arrowing a buck, you begin with the fundamentals and your God-given talent. You work hard to develop your skills. And

if you're good enough and work hard enough you can reach the next level. You can improve. Believe it! Let's say you already shoot your tuned hunting bow fairly well. Your arrows fly straight and true at normal bowhunting yardages. You tear up the practice range and you dutifully work to tighten your groups. This is good. But it's not enough to guarantee bowhunting success. As already suggested, there's more work to be done. Much more.

Big game animals have little appreciation for perfect shooting form. In fact, at times it seems as if they'll intentionally do everything possible to offer you only difficult shots. For example, unless you can shoot as well while kneeling, leaning, or sitting as when standing erect, you're not really ready to bowhunt. Unless you're completely comfortable — and accurate — when shooting down from elevated stands or at steep uphill angles, you're not fully prepared and your weaknesses will cost you dearly at some point in your hunting career. Count on it!

Physical preparations completed, you must turn your attention inward. It's impossible to overemphasize the important role your mind plays in attaining consistent bowhunting success. The reason? Most successful bowhunters agree that shooting a bow is at most only 10 percent physical — and at least 90 percent mental! Chew on that for a moment.

Once good personal shooting habits are ingrained to the point that drawing and releasing each arrow becomes almost automatic, it's time for you to work on shooting well under pressure. This is what separates the successful bowhunters from the pretenders and wannabes.

Early in my hunting career, I happened to bump into a fellow from my hometown archery club. He'd won a state target archery championship earlier in the year, and frankly, could shoot circles around me on our club range. But at the time we met he was grousing over the fact that he'd just missed a big whitetail — standing broadside at less than 30 yards! I also could name one Olympic archery gold medalist who missed a gimme shot at a buck during his initial hunting season. How could such good archers miss easy shots? Simple. Their shooting form certainly wasn't to blame. The source of their problem could be directly traced to the area located between their ears.

There is a huge difference between releasing arrows at inanimate targets and flesh-and-blood animals. The pressure each shooter will feel is different, too. Likely, some excellent target archers will never be good bowhunters because they can't cope with the mental aspects of killing an animal. They can puncture paper or foam all day, but somehow they can't bring themselves to cause an animal's death. That's fine, if that's the way they feel. They probably should stick to targets and leave hunting to the hunters. Regardless, don't believe for an instant that accuracy isn't as important in bowhunting as in target shooting. Chances are if you can't consistently hit the kill area of your deer target under ideal shooting conditions, you likely won't fare well in the deer woods when an animal finally steps out within good arrow range. It takes shooting ability — *and mental discipline* — to become a successful bowhunter.

If you're human, the mere sight of a big-racked buck should be enough to cause your heart to start to pound, your breath to come in short, panting gasps, and your knees to turn to Jello. Believe it or not, these physical reactions are perfectly normal; they've afflicted hunters since the dawn of time. Actually, they're the physical manifestations of an emotional malady commonly known as either "buck fever" or "target panic." Entire books have been written on this subject, but suffice it to say that controlling your emotions — beating back feelings of panic — is entirely mental.

"The way I learned to control my own buck fever was to make it more important to shoot the arrow correctly than it was to fill my tag," says Dave Holt.

Another veteran bowhunter I know says he convinces himself he's not going to take the shot at a nearby animal, he's simply going to come to full draw and hold of a spot behind the buck's shoulder. Only when he's rock-solid on target and perfectly calm does he "change his mind" and let the arrow fly.

Personally, I simply ignore the animal's eye-grabbing headgear and focus my total attention on the exact spot where I want my arrow to hit. Nothing else matters until I'm locked in. Only after I'm on target do I shift mental gears and consciously strive to make a perfectly smooth release. Fortunately, more often than not, my shots fly true.

Catching a fleeting glimpse of a wall-hanger whitetail like this one can make any hunter anxious to get a second look — preferably standing broadside at 20 yards or less.

All of these mental techniques work and work well. If you have a different "system" that works for you, use it. Or maybe you'll want to try another method — or combine several methods — in order to remain calm while making the shot. Really, whatever works best is what's truly important. As the sage once said, "If it ain't broke, don't fix it."

But should the need for a shooting fix arise, by all means try something else. Nothing is more frustrating — and devastating — to any bowhunter than to succumb to panic when the moment of truth arrives.

So what else can be done?

Two shooter's aids more comonly identified with target archery — the clicker and mechanical release — can sometimes help a bowhunter beat the buck fever/target panic problem.

A clicker, or draw check, audibly signals the shooter when to release. They can help. First, a clicker helps you relax and focus complete on the target without worrying about making the release. Second, clickers denote a shooter's exact draw length for every shot. Third, they require the shooter to maintain good back tension, which produces a better release. Bowhunting clickers, such as the Clickety Klick, are mounted on the upper limb of any type of bow, stickbow or compound, and attached to the bowstring by a lightweight cord. The metallic click created by the spring steel device is not loud enough to frighten nearby game, although some bowhunters use tape to mute the slight noise. These devices help any shooter control panic and improve accuracy.

Oregon bowhunter Larry D. Jones, the nationally known game caller and a frequent huntin' buddy of mine, is a big fan of clickers, as are other serious but lesser known hunting archers. Larry routinely uses a clicker on his recurves, while compound shooter Dave Holt flatly states, "In my opinion, finger shooters must use a clicker to obtain the utmost accuracy, regardless of the type of bow they shoot." So whether improving your shooting skills or simply getting back on track after losing the mental ability to control your release, keep the clicker in mind for shooting consistency.

Mechanical releases may help, too, by allowing relaxation and focus without concern over when to shoot. Personally, I use releases for my compounds but shoot fingers with my stickbows. Many release users point to the fact that it's increasing back tension, not the conscious triggering of a release, that finally launches the arrow. Since the release comes as a surprise to the shooter, all the bowhunter needs to do is focus completely on the target without worrying about when to release. That will happen.

Naturally. When it's supposed to happen. So the next time the panic bug bites, try a release — or a new kind of release. You can always go back to a glove or tab once your problem goes away.

Remember, too, a heavy bow weight may contribute to target panic/ buck fever and poor shooting form. Try backing off your compound's draw weight — or switching to a lighter pulling longbow or recurve — until you regain control and your arrows are hitting on target once again.

"I blew the shot!" This all-too-common admission is repeated thousands of times each hunting season. And as long as bowhunters accept the annual challenge of pursuing animals with stickbows and compounds, arrows will fly off target. Most times shooting ability will be blamed, and in some cases that's true. However, before picking up a bow and heading back to the target range for more shooting practice, hunters should take a long hard look at the mental aspects of their game. Often, that's the weakest point in any bowhunter's attempt to step up to the next level of shooting — and bowhunting — proficiency.

Former baseball star Will Clark is one of many pro athletes who has discovered the "The Thrill" of bowhunting. The author made that same discovery over 40 years ago. That Illinois whitetail he's showing was arrowed on the 40th anniversary of his very first bowhunt in the Land of Lincoln.

Chapter 2
The Best Bow for You

WHENEVER I PAGE THROUGH books containing photos of pioneer bowhunters — from Saxton Pope and Art Young to Howard Hill and Fred Bear — I have to smile at the bows these legendary archers are holding. Of course, many contemporary bow-benders might have the same reaction if they took time to thumb the pages of old copies of *Bowhunter* magazine or the photo albums containing snapshots from my own early days in archery and bowhunting. One thing is immediately apparent: *times and equipment have certainly changed.* Those top-of-the-line stickbows and compound bows I once proudly carried now seem as ancient as the 1950-era autos I drove in high school. It's not that those old bows — or cars, for that matter — weren't effective and efficient tools for their day and age; it's just that when compared to modern models they're...well, obviously dated.

Kinda like aging bowhunters.

Back before I became conscious of the fact that being politically incorrect might offend some of my distaff readers, I routinely wrote that choosing a good hunting bow was akin to picking a girlfriend or wife — that what it all boiled down to was a matter of individual taste. Now that I've learned to tread on safer literary ground, I simply substitute cars and trucks for spouses when offering advice about selecting the best bow for you.

Think about it. Let's say you drive a Ford and I own a Chevy — or a Dodge, Jimmy, Toyota, or whatever vehicle you may care to mention. Each pickup mentioned has obvious stylistic differences and likely features a variety of similar options. But basically all of these trucks do exactly the same job. We buy and drive one pickup simply because it's the truck that we like and can best afford. Ditto for hunting bows. And when it comes to user satisfaction, one fact remains constant: *personal preference is what matters most.*

If you buy a certain bow because your good buddy or some famous bowhunter like Chuck Adams or Myles Keller endorses it, you could end up a very disappointed bowhunter. Choosing a bow usually doesn't work that way in bowhunting, any more than driving a particular make and model of motor vehicle will transform you into Jeff Gordon or Richard Petty. Neither will you become Chuck or Myles simply because you shoot a bow they use.

My point here is quite simple, really. Be realistic. Keep and open mind and trust your instincts. Shop around. And by all means check out as many bows as possible. Visit area pro shops, archery dealers, and sporting goods stores. Listen to what the guys behind the counter have to say, especially if they're knowledgeable and experienced bowhunters. But it's likely they'll push a certain brand or two, and that's okay. Hear them out. But whenever possible, shoot the bows that grab *your* attention and fit *your* pocketbook. Listen to what your hunting buddies say, too. But when it's finally time to plunk down your hard-earned money and pay for the hunting bow you'll carry afield, buy the one that *you* like best of all.

"Choosing a bow is a truly personal decision," Dave Holt agrees. "More than likely, the only point upon which we could all agree is that we want the best bow for the money. You should use the equipment that fulfills your needs and desires."

Underscoring exactly how personal bow selection is, Dwight Schuh quotes Tom Jennings, "Mr. Compound Bow" and an Archery Hall of Fame member: "Your bow is as personal as your toothbrush and jockstrap."

When a modern bowhunter heads afield, the choice of equipment has never been greater. Today's bows, arrows, and accessories are better than ever.

As with all subjective judgments, emotion will play some part in your ultimate conclusion. There's no way to escape it, and you shouldn't try. But while some hard-headed bowhunters have a "don't-confuse-me-with-facts-my-mind's-already-made-up" attitude, other savvy bow buyers have a much more practical approach to sorting out what's best for them during the decision-making process. They sort through the options, weigh the pros and cons, and eventually choose what's exactly right for them and the game they plan to hunt.

So, assuming you're willing to keep a tight rein on your emotions and have a reasonably open mind on the subject of modern hunting bows, what are the facts you need to know? How do modern recurves and longbows really stack up — no pun intended here — against today's compounds? What about Fast Flight strings? Are bow sights really necessary for hunting accuracy or can compounds be shot instinctively? Should I buy a one-cam compound? Two cams? Cam and a half? What about models with soft cams and speed cams? Should I even buy a costly new bow when I could do just fine with a less expensive used model? Whom do I believe? Whom can I trust?

The answers to these and other common bow-selection questions will be answered on the following pages and in a later chapter titled, "Bowhunting Add-Ons: What You Really Need." They should assist you in choosing the best possible hunting bow, or bows, for your money. In the meantime, however, remember that everybody, including I, has very different ideas when it comes to finding the perfect pickup truck, hunting bow   and wife. You alone must finally decide exactly which hunting bow is ideal for you, your physical abilities, and your individual tastes.

Over 80% of 21st century bowhunters use compound bows such as this Parker EZ-Draw model, which is fitted with a bow quiver, sights, peep, and string silencers. This compound is 33 inches long and weighs just over 3 pounds.

Putting Things in Perspective

When I first started shooting a bow in the late 1940s, I used crude selfmade kids' bows before gradually saving enough chore money to afford a store-bought youngster's longbow that probably pulled 20 pounds at my abbreviated draw. Then when I took up target archery, competing in NFAA rounds as a teenager in the late 1950s, I shot manufactured recurve bows made by Shakespeare (best known for their fishing tackle) and Ben Pearson, the Arkansas-based bow and arrow manufacturer. Each bow pulled between 40 and 45 pounds. In November of 1963, I shot my first whitetail buck with a Colt (better known for firearms) Huntsman recurve drawing 48 pounds at my 28-inch draw.

When the butt-ugly Allen compound came onto the bowhunting scene in 1967, I, like many others, was skeptical of this newfangled invention with its array of pulleys and cables. Its inventor, a Missouri bowhunter named H. Wilbur Allen, explained his bow's purpose this way: "All I was trying to develop was a bow that would get an arrow to a 10- to 25-yard target — a deer — before that target could move."

Consequently, Allen's invention signaled the dawning of Age of Speed in bowhunting. Regardless of the fact his compound model was faster than any of the recurves I was shooting, it wasn't until 1972 that I could bring myself to shoot one of the homely contraptions. My choice was a Jennings compound that was advertised simply as "The Fast One." I much preferred my Jennings to the original Allen model, which boasted of "knock-down power no other bow can approach." But wasn't the quietest bow ever made. I can recall teasing a buddy that his Allen bow sounded like a garbage can lid being dropped each time he released an arrow. That's hyperbole, of course, but you get the idea.

During a two-week late summer 1972 bowhunt in Colorado and Utah, I killed three muley bucks and summed up the performance of my Jennings compound with these words: "As a hunting bow, it is an

Production grade and custom made stickbows remain readily available. A visit to any well-stocked archery dealer or pro shop will reveal the latest models.

Montana bowman Ric Anderson favors the simplicity of a longbow while Iowa archer Ruby Custer opts for a compound. Obviously, both bows can produce the desired results for any deer hunter.

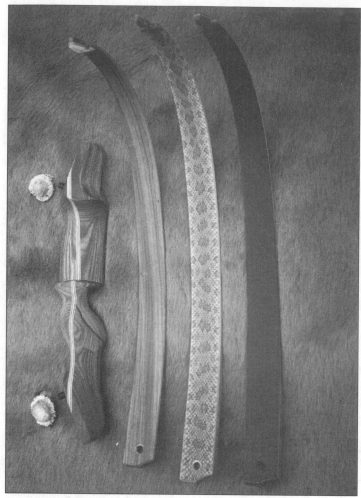

Takedown recurves such as this Schafer Silvertip offer a variety of limb looks and draw weights. These bows are easy to pack for travel and reassemble in moments upon arrival in hunting camp.

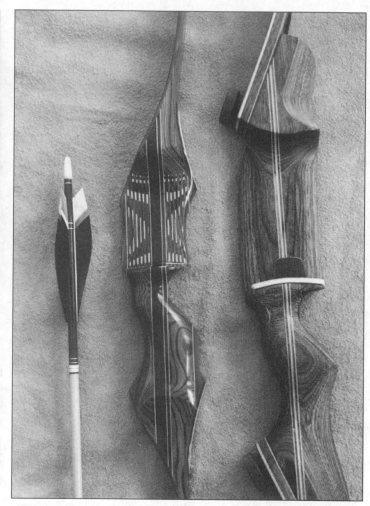

The beauty of custom-made recurves—such as this Choctaw model by Illinois bowyer Jerry Pierce and Silvertip takedown model by the late Paul Schafer of Montana—make these bows a true collector's item as well an efficient hunting tool.

amazingly fast, flat-shooting weapon. A compound bow also may well be the ugliest bow ever devised."

Although I wrote those words over 30 years ago, my opinion remains virtually unchanged. Early compounds were clunky and awkward and noisy and hard to tune, compared to the quiet grace of the longbow and recurve. But many shooters of the "traditional" bows couldn't quite get the hang of shooting them accurately. For too many, aiming was a matter of guesswork and good luck.

Enter the compound bow. You could pull it smoothly, feeling it relax comfortably before you reached full draw. Hey, compared to struggling with a stickbow, holding and aiming a compound was a snap, especially if all you had to do was to put a sight pin on the target. Your arrow flew just where it was supposed to — or darned close. In no time at all you were thumping arrow after arrow into that target butt. Instant results. Positive results. A perfect tool for contemporary, on-the-go people living in our fast-paced, success-oriented world.

Please don't misunderstand or take my words the wrong way. I'm neither a diehard traditionalist nor a pro-compound futurist. I'm just a serious bowhunter who's not missed a deer season in over 40 years. I've always shot all kinds of bows. Still do. Frankly, I don't really care which bow you choose to use — as long as you learn to use it well. That's the bottom line. As my old pal Fred Asbell often says, "Using a longbow or recurve should never be an excuse for

Longbows such as this St. Joe River model, handcrafted by Michigan bowyer Craig Potter, are becoming increasingly popular with bowhunters who have grown tired of tinkering with compounds and are looking for shooting simplicity.

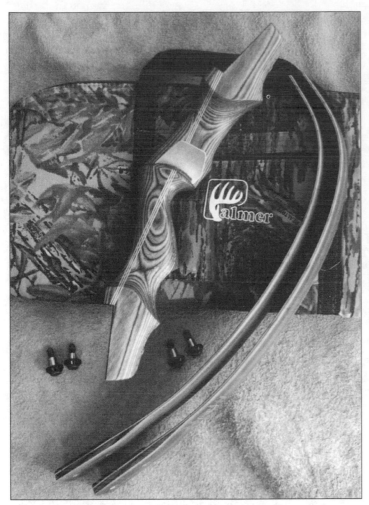

Takedown bows like this Mike Palmer recurve are easy to disassemble and carry. These bows are ideal for fly-in or pack-in hunts where space and weight are always at a premium.

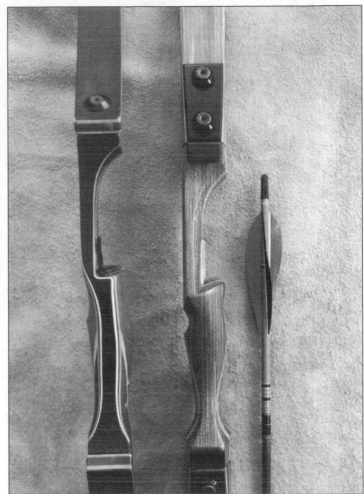

Takedown bows such as these recurves—a G. Fred Asbell Bighorn and a Mike Palmer Custom Carbon—require only an Allen wrench to remove the bolts connecting the limbs to the risers. They can be easily taken apart and reassembled within moments.

shooting poorly." Actually, despite having just drawn an overly simplistic shooting comparison between stickbows and compounds, I know for a fact it's as easy to miss a big buck with a compound as any longbow or recurve. Quite likely the single biggest edge a compound shooter has is the ability to remain at full draw longer — a definite advantage when that big buck or bull stops one step short of offering you a clear shot at the vitals. Everyone who has ever experienced the muscle-burning, arm-trembling agony of such inescapable bowhunting moments of truth, knows exactly what I mean. In such instances, the compound shooter invariably will be the last to let off in any face-to-face staredown with game. And no one I know will argue that this "hold-ability" isn't a distinct bowhunting advantage.

As do many people who regard bowhunting as an art form, I, too, have a bit of the romantic in my hunter's heart. That part of me resents the intrusion of science into archery. But in my mind, I'm also a pragmatic realist who accepts the fact that technology is an integral part of our modern world. In fact, I always have to smile when some chest-thumping traditional purist loudly proclaims that he'd never hunt with a compound, that real hunters use only "real bows."

In truth, modern longbows and recurves are much-improved replicas of the handmade tools crafted and carried by the bowhunt-

ing pioneers. While they resemble the bows of the past, they actually are composed of numerous space-age materials — fiberglass, plastics, acrylics, and epoxies, to name only a few. They're far more fast, accurate, and durable, thanks to modern technology.

Speaking of those who loudly damn technological advancements, how many of these indignant bow and arrow purists still ride a horse instead of driving a car or truck? How many take a bus or train or boat to some faraway hunting spot when they can arrive within hours by climbing aboard a jet? How many fashion their own clothing and footwear when Cabela's or Bass Pro Shops is a toll-free call away? To me, it's a bit hypocritical — if not downright two-faced — to be so particular about a hunting bow on one hand yet gladly embrace all other modern conveniences on the other.

Whatever new hunting bow you ultimately choose, for whatever personal reasons, the principles of using this ancient hand-held tool will be pretty much the same. Pick up any longbow, recurve, or compound and you still must use the strength of your arms, shoulders, and back to draw, hold, and release each arrow. You also must use your eyes and your mind to complement the other physical bow-shooting skills. And when you bowhunt, you always must employ the critical mental elements of self-discipline and self-control. It's true, even the best bow on earth cannot make you a successful bowhunter. Bows are mere tools; it takes the skilled hands of a hunter to give them life.

Following are a few hard facts about today's hunting bows as we begin our journey into and through the 21st century.

Longbows and Recurves

Bowhunting. That's the focus of today's traditional tackle, with relatively few modern bows being produced for target archers. So don't look for sight bushings, bow sights, and elevated arrow rests on most of today's stickbows. The hunting recurves and longbows being crafted now are mostly made for instinctive shooters who generally launch their arrows "off the shelf." They thrill to the sight of a feathered shaft in flight.

But as noted earlier, although the stickbows of the 21st century may look similar to their counterparts of the past, there are increasingly notable exceptions and differences. For example, modern longbows typically are somewhat shorter than they used to be, probably averaging around 64 inches. Some "longbows" are no more than 54 to 56 inches. Two-piece takedown models — most with male/female slide fittings — are becoming commonplace, too, as are longbow limbs with a reflex-deflex design (that bend away from the archer when the bow is unstrung). This new style, which was popularized by Montana bowyer Dick Robertson, generally provides a smoother draw and faster arrow, plus less hand shock. Fortunately, those three assets — smoothness, speed, and less shock — are found in a majority of modern longbows.

Such design changes offer definite advantages over the old straight-limb longbow look. Today's shooters even have the choice of a new locator grip, which features a slight indentation to comfortably fit the archer's hand. (Older longbows commonly had a straight grip configuration.) A final noteworthy modern option is the hybrid longbow, which looks like a cross between the longbow and recurve. These crossbreed bows have the straight limbs of traditional longbows, but their risers and grips look more like they belong on recurves. Some shooters prefer the look and performance of hybrids, feeling they blend the best elements of both bows.

Here's what traditional bowhunter G. Fred Asbell, himself a talented bowyer, says about contemporary longbows:

"Nearly gone from the archery scene a decade or so ago, longbows are back in vogue — strongly. And perhaps more so than the recurve, the longbow has benefited from a tip-to-tip updating/redesign by today's innovative bow makers. If you've been fascinated with the longbow's mystique but have been frightened away by horror stories of injured elbows and shoulders, and cautionary 'slower than molasses' comments, you should know you're getting info based on the longbows of yesteryear.

"Today's longbow is not the same creature," G. Fred continues. "Although appearance hasn't changed a lot, the handshock is mostly gone, and the speed has increased dramatically. Longer riser sections, which shorten the working limbs, are now in vogue. This increases arrow speed and adds weight to the bow's center, dampening vibration. People are shooting the longbow really well and enjoying it."

Longbows typically cost anywhere from a couple of hundred dollars to three or four times that amount. The fact is, there is an affordable production or custom-made longbow available to fit any hunter's needs. Generally, longbows are a bit less expensive than recurves. Most also are a tad bit slower, too.

A few words about draw length and bow weight are in order.

Most stickbow shooters will have a shorter draw length than those bowhunters who use compounds. In my own case, I shoot a 30-1/2-inch arrow from my compounds but 28-inch arrows out of my stickbows. The reason is simple: the compound bow relaxes its weight and is easier to hold at full draw than recurves or longbows. Also, the draw weight of my compounds averages 70 to 75 pounds; my stickbows average 55 to 60 pounds. Both types are effective for hunting most any North American game animal. As experienced hunters know, a tuned bow's kinetic energy is far more important than its draw weight or arrow speed. But proper shot placement is the key to consistent bowhunting success, regardless of the bow being used. More about this later.

Switching now to the subject of recurves, I've noted the hunting models come in a wide assortment of lengths, weight, and designs. There's no shortage of both production and custom models to fit every bowhunter's preference and price range. Personally, I dislike the ultra-short models. While they're easy to maneuver through brushy terrain, handle in a tree stand, or shoot from a ground blind, my own shorter bows stack more and have greater finger pinch than my longbows and lengthier recurves. Also, they usually don't have the in-the-hand stability that is necessary for consistent shooting accuracy. But there's no shortage of good recurves in my collection — averaging 58 to 62 inches, which is close to the national norm. Frankly, I love recurves and find them more fun to shoot than any bow I own.

Modern recurve bows range from spectacularly beautiful, intricately designed, handcrafted models to gracefully shaped yet mass produced bows, each with a price tag to match its creation process. Among many bowhunters, the three-piece takedown models are the most popular design. Typically, limbs are bolted to the riser with either one or two bolts, but boltless latching systems and slide-lock attachments are also available. Takedowns are ideal for the traveling bowhunter.

"Today's top-quality recurves will easily shoot arrows 185 to well over 200 feet per second (fps), matching the speeds of some com-

Pure instinctive shooters don't estimate yardage or use sight pins to hit their target. They simply focus on what they want to hit and release when things feel right. It takes considerable practice, but some top bowhunters swear this method is the best for bowhunting.

pound bows," G. Fred says. "Speed is desirable, as long as it doesn't come at the expense of stability. Stability and shootability are generally considered more important attributes for hunting bows."

To achieve greater speed, some bow manufacturers include carbon in their limbs. Others create bows built to withstand the limb stress caused by using Fast Flight strings. While it's true that Fast Flight bowstrings can add add an additional five to 15 fps to any bow's speed; they often are noisier and can cause limb damage — even breakage — in certain bows. Never switch to Fast Flight strings unless you know your bow can take the punishment. Check your warranty or call the manufacturer.

While on the subject of arrow speed, keep in mind that bows are rated by the ATA or Archery Trade Association (formerly called AMO, the Archery Manufacturers and Merchants Organization). An ATA speed rating is the speed of any bow set at 60 pounds of draw weight, 30 inches of draw length, and shooting arrows weighing 540 grains (five grains per pound of draw weight). This always should be the standard for comparing the relative speed of different hunting bows. Unless you are consistent in making equipment comparisons, it's much like comparing apples and pineapples — and it just won't mean very much.

For what it's worth, here's my personal opinion on the subject of arrow speed. I think far too many people get needlessly wrapped up

trying to milk a few extra fps out of their bows. It's accuracy, not arrow speed, that should matter most to any serious bowhunter. It was a wise ol' bowhunter who once remarked, "I'd rather hit the right spot with a slow arrow than miss it with a fast one."

Dave Holt accurately notes that the main benefit of a fast arrow "...is only paramount when we are shooting at unknown distances — both in 3-D and in hunting." And while Dave admits that fast, hard-hitting arrows are a definite advantage in bowhunting, he cautions, "Regardless of the other benefits, accuracy should always take precedent over penetration. Bows can be built for speed or accuracy, or they can be designed to compromise between the two. Basically, it's a give-and-take situation between speed and accuracy. Unfortunately, accuracy — particularly under the rigors of hunting — may have suffered. I believe too many bowhunters have focused on speed without realizing what it costs in terms of accuracy."

Summing things up: no one should ever underestimate the ability of a modern longbow or recurve user. True, it takes more commitment, practice time, and dedication to become deadly accurate with traditional bows, especially longbows; however, most archers willing to work at sharpening their instinctive shooting skills can develop surprising stickbow proficiency and results with proper practice. Want proof? Consider the fact that the two largest Alaskan brown bears ever tagged by bowhunters were arrowed by Monty

Matt McPherson revolutionized compound bow manufacturing during the early 1990s when he developed the one-cam concept. The Mathews SoloCam bows are among the best selling compounds available. M. R. James has used the XL model for several seasons — with excellent results.

Hoyt bows employ the cam-and-a half-system. Although the top and bottom wheels are identical in appearance, they're rigged differently from two-cam bows and offer a single power cable rather than two buss cables. Noted bowman Chuck Adams prefers a Hoyt Reflex for his worldwide hunting adventures.

The Martin Onza features a bridged riser that is offset to allow major wrist clearance on the bow hand. It's offered in several lengths from 40 to 32 inches and is available in both single- and two-cam systems. The Fuzion Cam allows draw length changes without relaxing the bow or changing its draw weight.

Browning and Dr. Jack Frost. Each giant world record bruin has a skull scoring 28 7/16 inches. Monty shoots a longbow while Jack prefers a compound. What really matters is that both bows — and the bowhunters — performed flawlessly.

Compound Bows

Simply stated, today's compounds are the sophisticated tools of the bowhunting trade. As most bowhunters know, they use an elaborate system of round wheels or eccentric cams and cables, working together in unison as the bow is pulled, to reduce (relax) any given bow's holding weight to a mere fraction of its listed draw weight. While early-day compounds of the late 1960s and 1970s had minimal letoff (my first compounds relaxed about 15 percent, if that), today's compounds commonly have holding weights amounting to 20 percent — more or less — of the advertised draw weight.

Visualize what this means. First, imagine using three fingers to lift 70 pounds of dead weight 28 to 30 inches off the floor, then holding it suspended there. How long before the finger-strain sets in and your arm begins to tremble from the tension? Not too long, probably, unless you're built like Governor Arnold. Next, imagine beginning to lift that identical 70 pounds off the floor, but most of the weight suddenly disappears. By the time you've lifted that dead weight to a height of 30 inches, you're holding only 14 pounds.

That's exactly what happens when you shoot a 70-pound compound bow with an 80 percent letoff.

Only a few short years ago, many compounds relaxed around 50 percent. The next plateau was 65 percent. Now the industry standard is 75 to 80 percent — with a handful of even higher letoff bows available. Back in 1997, McPherson Archery, for example, was running ads touting "the world's highest let-off!" — 86 percent. And most compound manufacturers readily acknowledge that the technology exists for bows relaxing up to 99 percent. But don't expect such bows to be marketed. Even compounds with 80 percent letoffs are somewhat touchy to tune and shoot accurately. My personal choice is a hunting bow with a 60 to 70 percent letoff, which I've found quieter, less finicky, and more forgiving to shoot. Bowmakers I've personally spoken with generally agree that ultra high letoff compounds are not in their marketing plans. Some believe we've already reached or are very near the practical limit for letoffs. Time will tell.

Speaking of high letoffs, the Pope and Young Club, North America's keepers of bowhunting records, once required a maximum compound bow letoff of 65 percent or less in order to enter animals in the record books. That 1988 rule changed as of January 1, 2004. Today all trophy-class game animals taken with any legal compound bow are eligible for the Club's records, regardless of the

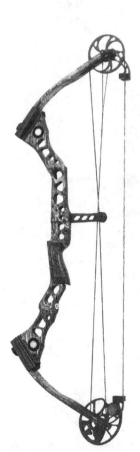

The Darton Magnum Extreme features an updated Controlled Power System (CPS) designed to reduce hand shock while shooting quieter and faster. It's just about 3 1/2 pounds and comes in 65 or 75% letoff. Interchangeable module allows draw length changes.

Looking like a cross between a compound and recurve, the ESC Oneida features unique riser-mounted cams. It comes in lengths of 43-46 inches and features Engineered Structural Composite (ESC) limbs made of super strong carbon composite material, which withstands extreme moisture and temperature change.

Renegade's Alpha-1 compound features a Flamethrower Cam to complement its proved EZ-1 Wheel. Its tip-to-tip length is 31-inches and mass weight about 3 1/2 pounds.

compound bow's letoff percentage. True, game taken with higher letoff bows will be designated with an asterisk in the records, but these outstanding animals are no longer being excluded from the P&Y listings, as was the case previously.

Besides the popularity and growing acceptance of high letoff, adjustable weight compounds, what else is new on the mechanical bow scene? Well, the quest continues for shorter, lightweight but rugged, quieter, and easier-to-tune bows. And faster bows, too. Let's look at bow length first.

Compounds with axle-to-axle lengths of only 30 to 32 inches exist today, but recent industry reports indicate the best sellers are 35 to 36 inches. Frankly, shorter bows typically require the use of a mechanical release. Finger shooters should consider using longer models in order to avoid finger pinch. Drawing short bows causes acute string angles, often making it difficult to maintain consistent finger pressure. This can adversely affect accuracy. Also, as with my short stickbows, I've found ultra short compounds somewhat touchier to shoot accurately, even when I use a release. I've noted they're a bit slower, too. My favorite compounds have an axle-to-axle length of 36 or 38 inches.

On a positive note, the mass weight of compounds has dropped drastically during the past decade and a half. Back in the late 1980s and early 1990s, my compounds — when fitted with a stabilizer, bow quiver, and full complement of arrows — weighed seven to eight pounds or more. Today my typical compound hunting setups weigh about half as much. The reasons? Bow re-design, new riser and limb materials, and improved machining techniques have all contributed to the gradual weight reduction of modern compounds. Of course, the recent trend to shorter and slimmer bows — with narrower grips eliminate hand torque problems — has affected compound mass weight as well. That's good news for today's compound shooters, since their hunting bows require less physical effort to tote afield. But even today's lightest compounds remain heavier than most longbow and recurve setups.

Modern compounds are quieter than earlier models, too. Remember my description of the old Allen compound sounding like a dropped garbage can lid? Well, that's certainly no longer the case, thanks largely to improved eccentric design, limb pockets, and built-in noise dampeners. Also, in 1999 the introduction of a simple but practical product called Limb Savers — soft rubber-like noise dampeners produced and marketed by Sims Vibration Laboratories — soon became common bow accessories. They truly are effective at quieting most hunting bows.

Earlier I referred to compounds as "butt-ugly," but I must admit that enough design improvements have been made over the years that I now consider them merely "homely." These high-tech ugly ducklings will never be beautiful swans; however, design engineers have worked hard to streamline and "pretty up" the compound's profile and overall appearance, covering limbs and risers with popular camo patterns.

Speaking of limbs and risers, split-limb and parallel limb models are relatively recent performance-enhancing improvements. They're increasingly popular and worth examination. Carbon and other modern materials — formed into various laminations — have definitely improved limb strength and performance. Risers come in straight, reflexed, and deflexed designs. They've grown lighter and stronger, thanks

Modern stickbows like this '04 Hoyt recurve are made of the very latest in modern materials, from limbs to riser. This ain't your daddy's stickbow!

Unveiled in 2004, the new Gyro-Tec compound bow from Hi-Tec Archery offers a patented Gimble System which allows the bow's handle to free float by pivoting horizontally and vertically with the natural twist of the shooter's wrist. The bow handle is set for true center-fire nocking, so the arrow has a straight path to its target. This bow carries a hefty price tag.

Short, lightweight bows specially made for youngsters and women are being made and marketed more than ever before. These bows typically have light draw weights but possess a powerful kinetic energy punch. Cole Eddie was 10 when he arrowed this record book black bear during a hunt with his dad, Dyrk.

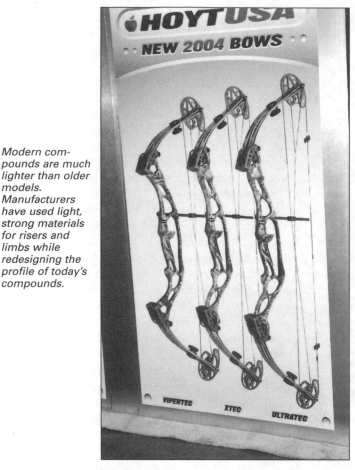

Modern compounds are much lighter than older models. Manufacturers have used light, strong materials for risers and limbs while redesigning the profile of today's compounds.

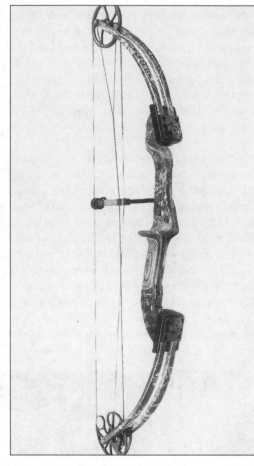

Split limb compounds came on the bowhunting scene during the 1990s. They helped reduce mass weight while enhancing shooting performance and speed.

largely to the crafting of forged aluminum. And just for the record, with straight-handled bows the upper and lower limbs extend in an almost direct line with the riser; reflexed bows have limb pockets in front of the handles; and deflexed bows have limb pockets located behind the riser.

As for design advantages and disadvantages, bows with straight and reflexed risers have a lower brace height and longer power stroke, facts that normally translate to increased arrow velocity. They also offer good balance in the bow hand following each shot. Deflexed bows, while not as fast, are typically more forgiving but tend to tip backward and require a stabilizer to maintain proper balance. I urge you to try each and choose whichever pleases your eye and best suits your shooting style.

Since 1992, when Matt McPherson unveiled his single-cam Mathews SoloCam compounds to the bowhunting community, tuning compound bows has become easier and easier. In fact, the trend toward easy-to-tune bows started back in the mid-1980s when manufacturers progressed from four-wheel to two-wheel models. But it wasn't until McPherson revolutionized bow technology — effectively eliminating the tedious synchronization tuning problems facing owners of two-cam bows — that things really changed. Single-cam bows — widely known not only for their ease of tuning but for staying in tune after initial setup — soon dominated the market. They remain king of the compound hill and are my personal choice. I, for one, consider one-cam bows to be the greatest single advancement in the history of compound bows. If you'd rather spend more time shooting than tinkering and tuning your bow, check 'em out.

Of course, It's impossible to mention one-cam bows without talking about speed. Again! I've already admitted my own bias about

the highly contagious "need for speed" illness afflicting many modern bowhunters. While I hope you'll grow immune to this bug's bite, I feel it is necessary to explain that compound bow speed commonly results from several factors: the design of the eccentrics (the more radical cams yield more speed); the bow's brace height (lower brace heights produce greater velocity); and bow design (reflexed or backset models are faster, as noted previously). There's also the matter of arrow weight, but that subject will be examined in detail in a following chapter.

Because speed sells — mainly by stirring exciting images in the mind of many male consumers — savvy bow companies stress how fast their bows shoot. While some sizzling compound models routinely crack the 300 fps barrier, an unimaginable feat only a few short years ago, the average is probably closer to 250 fps, give or take. And that ain't exactly slow! Still, whenever I encounter any speed freak who constantly tinkers to coax an extra fps or two out of his setup, I can't resist asking: "Do you really believe that buck standing 20 yards away cares if your arrow is traveling 230 or 280 or 310 fps?" I sure don't. All that matters to me is where my arrow hits, not whether it's trailing smoke at the time.

Lastly, there's the all-important subject of cost, and mostly the news is good for anyone looking for a new compound bow. Although there are high-priced models costing upwards of $1,000 available for folks who don't have to worry about budget-busting price tags, half that amount — or slightly more — can get you a top-of-the-line quality compound bow. Some deals offer a total package including a tuned-in, pre-sighted bow complete with an arrow rest, sight, string peep, silencers, etc. Some even throw in matched arrows and a bow quiver. Many manufacturers also offer lifetime warranties. Shop around but keep your checkbook or credit card pocketed until you've compared prices and found the best deal possible.

Compound bows are here to stay, despite being damned by some archery purists who detest these modern contraptions. Models that are easy to draw and hold remain the current rage. That advantage to many beginning bowhunters is obvious. As noted earlier, such bows are relatively easy to master. Shooting accuracy often comes much faster, too. This naturally appeals to many people. If you're one of them, do your homework, evaluate the pros and cons, and make an informed decision.

Final Considerations

Time was when draw weight was a critical consideration in choosing any hunting bow. Back in the early 1960s when my bowhunting career was in its infancy, I often wrestled with heavy-pulling bows during off-season shooting sessions — without much success, I must admit. It was mostly a macho thing, I guess. Saying that you were shooting an 80-pound stickbow meant you were a hairy-chested he-man, at least in the minds of some people who routinely overbowed themselves and stubbornly refused to admit they

Cam-and-a-half compounds have become popular with some bowhunters. This concentric idler wheel is found on certain Hoyt models.

couldn't handle such a heavy bow weight. Never mind the fact they risked a hernia each time they fought to pull the bow past half-draw — or hit the target butt two shots out of six. By golly, they were men!

Then in August of '65 I went mule deer hunting with a sweet-shooting Pearson Knight recurve pulling 42 pounds at my 28-inch draw. And on opening day of the Colorado season I proceeded to put a fiberglass arrow, tipped with a Bear Razorhead, completely through a buck standing broadside just over 40 yards away. My bruised male pride notwithstanding, I learned a valuable lesson that day in the Book Cliffs. Namely, I discovered that you don't really need a "man's bow" to let the air out of deer-sized critters. It's too bad other fans of heavy-pulling bows didn't have the same kind of eye-opening experience.

In following years I gradually shot heavier tackle, working up to stickbows averaging 60 pounds, plenty of weight for most big game I hunted — deer, pronghorns, black bears, elk, caribou, and such. My hunting compounds averaged 10 pounds more. And like many bowhunters afield during the 1970s, 1980s, and early 1990s, I smugly nodded in agreement when someone talked about the need for heavier pulling bows when hunting bigger game like moose, bison, muskox, and grizzly or brown bears. Little did we know.

We understand now that it's foot-pounds of kinetic energy — not a bow's poundage — that is all-important in bowhunting. Kinetic energy, a measurement based on an arrow's speed and weight, is

determined by multiplying the velocity of an arrow in feet per second times itself. Next, multiply that number times the weight of the arrow, and finally divide the answer by 450,240. The number you get translates to foot-pounds of kinetic energy. For you math majors, the formula is:

$$\frac{[(\text{Velocity squared}) \times \text{Weight}]}{450,240}$$

For example, let's say your arrow zips along at 250 fps. Squaring 250 gives you 62,500. Let's also say that your arrow weighs 450 grains, so multiply that number times 62,500. You'll come up with 28,125,000. Finally, divide that number by 450,240 and your answer will be 62.466 foot-pounds. Using the same formula, you can quickly determine the kinetic energy of your own gear. All you need to know is how much your arrow weighs and how fast it's flying. A handloader's grain scale and an archery store chronograph will provide those numbers.

What you can discover is sometimes simply amazing. For example, there are bows with draw weight of only 30 pounds that can deliver more kinetic energy than other bows pulling 60 pounds. Twice as much oomph? Well, it's true! Kinda shoots down the ol' heavy bow theory, doesn't it? More importantly, it underscores the need for change in those states with hunting laws based on the old minimum draw-weight standards.

Notably, kinetic energy testing is very good news for women and children who often cannot physically handle heavier-pulling bows. Many modern bows with relatively low draw weights can produce the foot pounds of energy necessary to efficiently and effectively drop big game animals. Recognizing this undeniable fact, and a marketing potential, bow manufacturers began creating and offering a wide selection of shorter draw bows that are ideal for interested youngsters and female bowhunters. Today, some legally licensed boys and girls — aged 10 and even younger — bowhunt and harvest deer under their parents' direction. Today, more and more women join the ranks of successful male bowhunters by tagging every species on earth, from grizzly bears to Cape buffalo. Such success stories — and the recent growth spurt in sales of youth and women's archery tackle — can be traced directly to bow-making advancements and the increased knowledge about how modern bows really work.

Following are a few suggestions you might consider when selecting a hunting bow that's just right for you:

- Keep kinetic energy — not draw weight — foremost in mind as you check out the various bow models and types.
- Look for a high-efficiency bow that feels right. Comfort and shooting confidence go hand in hand.
- If you opt to use a compound, don't go overboard on letoff. Remember that ultra-high letoff bows may be easier to draw and hold, but they're generally touchier to tune, keep in tune, and shoot accurately.
- Ditto for super-short bow models. And if you use bowsights, make certain the bow you're considering provides ample sight window space for adequate pin settings at your normal anchor point.

Remember, when selecting any hunting bow, you're investing in the future. Refuse to be rushed into making a decision. Check out and shoot as many bows as possible before settling on the one that your head, heart, and bow hand all agree is the best one for you. Chances are, you'll make the right choice.

Chapter 3
Straight Talk On Shafts

DECISIONS. DECISIONS. DECISIONS. Choosing the correct hunting arrow — a shaft that's just right for you and your hunting bow — is the most critical decision that you will ever make as a bowhunter. Why? No other single piece of bowhunting gear — from bows to broadheads, tree stands to camo clothing — is as important to your shooting and hunting success. While using a good, well-tuned bow is important, selecting and using just the right hunting arrow is an absolute must.

Exaggeration? Hardly. It's a fact of bowhunting life. For an arrow to fly straight and true to its intended target, several factors must be present in each individual shaft. These components include proper straightness, stiffness (or spine), balance, and weight. To find the most consistently reliable, durable, best penetrating, and accurate arrows for you and your hunting needs, take a close look at what's now available to 21st century bowhunters.

Aluminum Arrow Shafts

Despite what some people think, aluminum arrows are nothing new. It was the late James D. "Doug" Easton, the man recognized for setting the standard for material consistency in mass manufacturing arrows, who produced the first aluminum arrow shafts back in 1939. Doug had been making custom bows and cedar arrows since 1922. Frustrated by years of trying to perfect footed wooden arrows and the lack of consistency and uniformity in the cedar shafts, Easton set out to find a superior alternative arrow material. He wanted something that would solve the problems inherent in all wooden shafts. His solution, the aluminum shaft, forever changed the face of target archery and bowhunting.

Aluminum arrows remain a favorite choice of many modern archers and bowhunters. They provide amazing consistency in both size and weight. Manufactured to precise specifications and exacting standards, aluminum shafts are readily available in literally dozens of sizes, offering various diameters and wall thicknesses to meet any need. Moreover, these anodized metal shafts are impervious to moisture and never rust or warp. They're quite affordable, too, typically less costly than custom wood and most carbon arrows. Without question, there is an aluminum arrow of the exact spine and weight for every hunting bow ever made. And whether you want delicate, lightweight shafts created to generate maximum speed or heavy, durable shafts designed for delivering optimum hard-hitting energy and penetration, there's an aluminum shaft that's exactly right for you.

Frankly, choosing the right arrow is not always easy. To begin, you must decide what you want. Assuming one of several arrow sizes will provide the accuracy you demand, what is most important to you? More speed? Deeper penetration? Both? Here's where you must begin to sort through various options and settle on the shaft that best fills your needs.

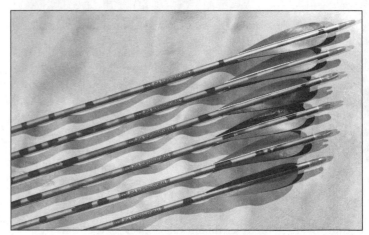

Aluminum arrows have been around for over half a century. Today's hunters have a wide selection of metal shafts to fit any bow and any need.

Reducing arrow weight typically increases speed and flattens trajectory. Yet heavier arrows generally provide deeper penetration. Which is best? Only one person has that answer. You. If you opt for speed, look for shafts with a large diameter and thin wall. All aluminum arrows have a four-digit number that provides this diameter/wall thickness information at a glance. Diameters are measured in 1/64-inch increments; thicknesses of the shaft's outer wall are measured in 1/1000-inch increments. This means a 2215 arrow shaft, for example, has a diameter of 22/64-inch and a wall thickness of 15/1000-inch. It's easy. Really.

M. R. James shoots both aluminum and carbon shafts and routinely collects game with both styles. He knows that choosing a quality hunting arrow is perhaps the most important decision a bowhunter can make.

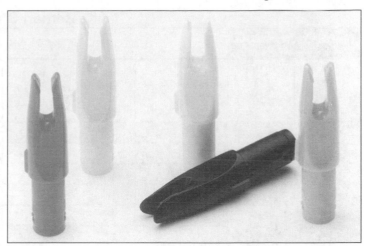

Nocks should fit the string comfortably, not too loose or too tight. Some experimentation will help you decide which nocks are just right for you and your hunting arrows.

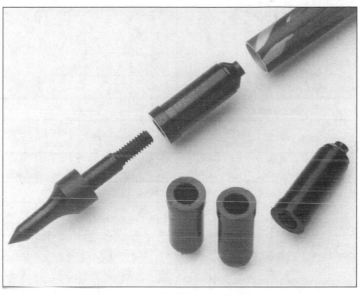

Screw-in field points and broadheads make switching from practice points to hunting heads a breeze. Most bowhunters using aluminum shafts favor the convenience of screw-in broadheads.

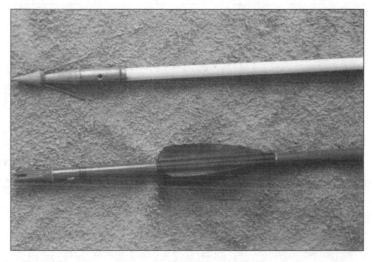

Heavy bowfishing arrows require rubber fletching—or none at all since most shots are made at close ranges—and barbed heads to hold the fish on the shaft until it can be retrieved.

Generally, larger diameters and thicker walls translate to a greater spine or stiffness. Shaft length affects the spine, too. Longer shafts are not as stiff as short shafts, even if diameter/wall thickness is the same for both. Broadheads likewise affect shaft stiffness. Heavier hunting heads will reduce an arrow's spine — causing it to flex more in flight — than lightweight broadheads.

Keep in mind that all arrows bend in flight. No arrow flies perfectly straight from the instant of release until it buries itself in its target. Slow motion, high-speed film capturing arrows during release and flight have shown this dramatic, side-to-side flexing, which is known as "archer's paradox." While you cannot actually see this shaft oscillation with the naked eye, it is always present. As you let the string slip away from your fingers, the bow string pushes your arrow forward. But the force of release causes the tail end of the shaft to flex to the left (if you're a right-handed shooter) and wrap around the riser as it crosses the arrow rest. As the arrow clears the bow, its tail flexes back to the right, then back to the left, and so on.

If the shaft is properly spined, your arrow flies true. If adequate stiffness is lacking, obvious wobble or fishtailing will be apparent and poor flight is the end result. Using a release aid normally (Text continued on page 32)

Beman Shaft Chart

BEMAN ARROW SIZE SELECTION CHART

COMPOUND BOW – Release Aid Calculated Peak Bow Weight - Lbs. Medium Cam	Single or Hard Cam	22.5 / 23" / 23.5	23.5 / 24" / 24.5	24.5 / 25" / 25.5	25.5 / 26" / 26.5	26.5 / 27" / 27.5	27.5 / 28" / 28.5	28.5 / 29" / 29.5	29.5 / 30" / 30.5	30.5 / 31" / 31.5	31.5 / 32" / 32.5	32.5 / 33" / 33.5	RECURVE BOW Weight - Lbs. Finger Release
27-31	22-26	A	A	B	C	D	D	E	F	G	H	I	22-26
32-36	27-31	A	B	C	D	D	E	F	G	H	I	J	27-31
37-41	32-36	B	C	D	D	E	F	G	H	I	J	J	32-36
42-46	37-41	C	D	D	E	F	G	H	I	J	J	K	37-41
47-51	42-46	D	D	E	F	G	H	I	J	J	K	L	42-46
52-56	47-51	D	E	F	G	H	I	J	J	K	L	M	47-51
57-61	52-56	E	F	G	H	I	J	J	K	L	M	N	52-56
62-66	57-61	F	G	H	I	J	J	K	L	M	N	N	57-61
67-72	62-66	G	H	I	J	J	K	L	M	N	N		62-66
73-78	67-72	H	I	J	J	K	L	M	N	N	N		67-72
79-84	73-78	I	J	J	K	L	M	N	N	N			73-78
85-90	79-84	J	J	K	L	M	N	N	N				79-84
91-96	85-90	J	K	L	M	N	N	N					85-90

Group A					Group B					Group C					Group D				
Size	Spine	Model	Weight Grs/Inch	Weight @29"	Size	Spine	Model	Weight Grs/Inch	Weight @29"	Size	Spine	Model	Weight Grs/Inch	Weight @29"	Size	Spine	Model	Weight Grs/Inch	Weight @29"
1000	1.000	Flash	5.6	162	900	0.900	Flash	6.4	186	750	0.750	Flash	6.2	180	750	0.750	Flash	6.2	180
1000	1.000	Energy	5.7	165	900	0.900	Energy	5.8	169	780	0.780	Energy	6.3	183	690	0.690	Energy	6.3	182

Group E					Group F					Group G					Group H				
Size	Spine	Model	Weight Grs/Inch	Weight @29"	Size	Spine	Model	Weight Grs/Inch	Weight @29"	Size	Spine	Model	Weight Grs/Inch	Weight @29"	Size	Spine	Model	Weight Grs/Inch	Weight @29"
630	0.630	Flash	7.0	202	630	0.630	Flash	7.0	202	570	0.570	Flash	7.2	209	520	0.520	Energy	7.1	206
600	0.600	Energy	6.9	201	570	0.570	Flash	7.2	209	520	0.520	Energy	7.1	206	460	0.460	Energy	7.3	212
					600	0.600	Energy	6.9	201	530	0.530	Hunter	7.4	216	490	0.490	Hunter	8.4	242
										500	0.500	Hawk	7.1	206	470	0.470	Hunter	8.3	241
										500	0.500	ICSH/V	7.3	211	500	0.500	Hawk	7.1	206
										500	0.500	CAMO	8.0	233	500	0.500	ICSH/V	7.3	211
															500	0.500	CAMO	8.0	233
															460	0.460	Matrix	8.8	255

Group I					Group J					Group K					Group L				
Size	Spine	Model	Weight Grs/Inch	Weight @29"	Size	Spine	Model	Weight Grs/Inch	Weight @29"	Size	Spine	Model	Weight Grs/Inch	Weight @29"	Size	Spine	Model	Weight Grs/Inch	Weight @29"
460	0.460	Energy	7.3	212	460	0.460	Energy	7.3	212	410	0.410	Energy	7.6	220	360	0.360	Energy	8.3	241
490	0.490	Hunter	8.4	242	410	0.410	Energy	7.6	220	380	0.380	Hunter	9.1	264	360	0.360	Hunter	9.3	268
470	0.470	Hunter	8.3	241	400	0.400	Hunter	8.6	249	400	0.400	Hawk	8.1	235	340	0.340	Hawk	8.8	255
500	0.500	Hawk	7.1	206	400	0.400	Hawk	8.1	235	400	0.400	ICSH/V	8.4	244	340	0.340	ICSH/V	9.3	270
500	0.500	ICSH/V	7.3	211	400	0.400	ICSH/V	8.4	244	400	0.400	CAMO	9.1	264	340	0.340	CAMO	10.0	290
500	0.500	CAMO	8.0	233	400	0.400	CAMO	9.1	264	400	0.400	Matrix	9.5	276	340	0.340	Matrix	10.4	301
460	0.460	Matrix	8.8	255	400	0.400	Matrix	9.5	276										

Group M					Group N				
Size	Spine	Model	Weight Grs/Inch	Weight @29"	Size	Spine	Model	Weight Grs/Inch	Weight @29"
360	0.360	Energy	8.3	241	300	0.300	ICSH/V	9.5	274
330	0.330	Hunter	9.4	273	300	0.300	CAMO	10.1	294
340	0.340	Hawk	8.8	255	300	0.300	Matrix	11.0	318
340	0.340	ICSH/V	9.3	270					
340	0.340	CAMO	10.0	290					
340	0.340	Matrix	10.4	301					

Size – Indicates suggested shaft sizes.
Spine – Spine of arrow size shown (static).
Model – Designates arrow model.
Weight – Listed in grains per inch.

Energy = ICS Energy
Hunter = Carbon Hunter
Hawk = ICS Hawk
ICSH/V = ICS Hunter and Venture
CAMO = ICS Camo Hunter, TreBark and Classic
Matrix = CarbonMetal Matrix

Easton Shaft Chart

Main selection chart — Column groups:
- COMPOUND BOW – Release Aid, CALCULATED PEAK BOW WEIGHT – Lbs. (Medium Cam / Single or Hard Cam), Point Weight 75 / 100 / 125 / 150 grains
- CORRECT HUNTING ARROW LENGTH (23"–33")
- RECURVE BOW, Finger Release, ACTUAL PEAK BOW WEIGHT – Lbs., Point Weight 75 / 100 / 125 / 150 grains
- MODERN LONGBOW, Finger Release, ACTUAL PEAK BOW WEIGHT – Lbs., Point Weight 75 / 100 / 125 / 150 grains

Point weight ranges: 75 = 65–85, 100 = 90–110, 125 = 115–135, 150 = 140–160.
Arrow length header (top / bottom): 22.5–23.5 = 23", 23.5–24.5 = 24", 24.5–25.5 = 25", 25.5–26.5 = 26", 26.5–27.5 = 27", 27.5–28.5 = 28", 28.5–29.5 = 29", 29.5–30.5 = 30", 30.5–31.5 = 31", 31.5–32.5 = 32", 32.5–33.5 = 33".

Med Cam 75	Med 100	Med 125	Med 150	Single 75	Single 100	Single 125	Single 150	23"	24"	25"	26"	27"	28"	29"	30"	31"	32"	33"	Rec 75	Rec 100	Rec 125	Rec 150	LB 75	LB 100	LB 125	LB 150
										A	B	B	C	C	D	E							41-46	38-43	35-40	32-37
									A	B	B	C	C	D	E	F							47-52	44-49	41-46	38-43
40-44	37-41	34-38	31-35	35-39	32-36	29-33	26-30		A	B	B	C	C	D	E	F	G	H	35-39	32-36	29-33	26-30	53-58	50-55	47-52	44-49
45-49	42-46	39-43	36-40	40-44	37-41	34-38	31-35	A	B	B	C	C	D	E	F	G	H	I	40-44	37-41	34-38	31-35	59-64	56-61	53-58	50-55
50-54	47-51	44-48	41-45	45-49	42-46	39-43	36-40	B	B	C	C	D	E	F	G	H	I	J	45-49	42-46	39-43	36-40	65-70	62-67	59-64	56-61
55-59	52-56	49-53	46-50	50-54	47-51	44-48	41-45	B	C	C	D	E	F	G	H	I	J	J	50-54	47-51	44-48	41-45	71-76	68-73	65-70	62-67
60-64	57-61	54-58	51-55	55-59	52-56	49-53	46-50	C	C	D	E	F	G	H	I	J	J	K	55-59	52-56	49-53	46-50	77-82	74-79	71-76	68-73
65-69	62-66	59-63	56-60	60-64	57-61	54-58	51-55	C	D	E	F	G	H	I	J	J	K	L	60-64	57-61	54-58	51-55	83-88	80-85	77-82	74-79
70-75	67-72	64-69	61-66	65-69	62-66	59-63	56-60	D	E	F	G	H	I	J	J	K	L	L	65-69	62-66	59-63	56-60	89-94	86-91	83-88	80-85
76-81	73-78	70-75	67-72	70-75	67-72	64-69	61-66	E	F	G	H	I	J	J	K	L	L	L	70-75	67-72	64-69	61-66	95-100	92-97	89-94	86-91
82-87	79-84	76-81	73-78	76-81	73-78	70-75	67-72	F	G	H	I	J	J	K	L	L	L	L	76-81	73-78	70-75	67-72	101-106	98-103	95-100	92-97
88-93	85-90	82-87	79-84	82-87	79-84	76-81	73-78	G	H	I	J	J	K	L	L	L			82-87	79-84	76-81	73-78	107-112	104-109	101-106	98-103
94-99	91-96	88-93	85-90	88-93	85-90	82-87	79-84	H	I	J	J	K	L	L	L				88-93	85-90	82-87	79-84	113-118	110-115	107-112	104-109

Group A
Size	Spine @ 28" Span	Model	Weight Grs/Inch	Weight @29"
1813	0.874	75	7.86	228
1716	0.880	75	9.03	262
780	0.780	Rdln	6.30	183

Group B
Size	Spine @ 28" Span	Model	Weight Grs/Inch	Weight @29"
1913	0.733	75	8.34	242
1816	0.756	75	9.27	269
690	0.690	Rdln	6.27	182

Group C
Size	Spine @ 28" Span	Model	Weight Grs/Inch	Weight @29"
2013	0.610	75	9.01	261
1916	0.623	75	10.05	291
3L-18	0.620	A/C/C	7.47	217
600	0.600	Rdln	6.92	201

Group D
Size	Spine @ 28" Span	Model	Weight Grs/Inch	Weight @29"
2113	0.540	75	9.30	270
2016	0.531	75	10.56	306
3-18	0.560	A/C/C	7.82	227
500	0.500	CA,KIN	CAWT	CAWT
3-28	0.500	A/C/C	8.11	235
520	0.520	Rdln	7.09	206

Group E
Size	Spine @ 28" Span	Model	Weight Grs/Inch	Weight @29"
2212	0.505	SS	8.84	256
2114	0.510	SS,75	9.86	286
2115	0.461	75	10.75	312
2018	0.461	75	12.28	356
3-28	0.500	A/C/C	8.11	235
500, 460	0.500, 0.460	CA,KIN	CAWT	CAWT
520	0.520	Rdln	7.09	206

Group F
Size	Spine @ 28" Span	Model	Weight Grs/Inch	Weight @29"
2212	0.505	SS	8.84	256
2213	0.460	SS,75	9.83	285
2115	0.461	75	10.75	312
2018	0.464	75	12.28	356
3 28	0.500	A/C/C	8.11	235
500, 460	0.500, 0.460	CA,KIN	CAWT	CAWT
520	0.520	Rdln	7.09	206

Group G
Size	Spine @ 28" Span	Model	Weight Grs/Inch	Weight @29"
2312	0.423	SS	9.48	275
2215	0.420	SS,75	10.67	309
2117	0.400	SS,75	12.02	348
2020	0.426	75	13.49	391
3-39	0.440	A/C/C	8.58	249
400	0.400	CA,KIN	CAWT	CAWT
460	0.460	Rdln	7.32	212

Group H
Size	Spine @ 28" Span	Model	Weight Grs/Inch	Weight @29"
2215	0.420	SS,75	10.67	309
2314	0.390	SS,75	10.67	309
2117	0.400	SS,75	12.02	348
2216	0.375	75	12.02	348
3-49	0.390	A/C/C	8.83	256
400	0.400	CA,KIN	CAWT	CAWT
410	0.410	Rdln	7.60	220

Group I
Size	Spine @ 28" Span	Model	Weight Grs/Inch	Weight @29"
2413	0.365	SS,75	10.40	302
2314	0.390	SS,75	10.67	309
2315	0.340	SS,75	11.67	338
2216	0.375	SS,75	12.02	348
3-49	0.390	A/C/C	8.83	256
400	0.400	CA,KIN	CAWT	CAWT
410	0.410	Rdln	7.60	220

Group J
Size	Spine @ 28" Span	Model	Weight Grs/Inch	Weight @29"
2512	0.321	SS	10.28	298
2413	0.365	SS,75	10.40	302
2315	0.340	SS,75	11.67	338
2219	0.337	SS,75	13.77	399
3-60	0.340	A/C/C	9.45	274
340	0.340	CA,KIN	CAWT	CAWT
360	0.360	Rdln	8.31	241

Group K
Size	Spine @ 28" Span	Model	Weight Grs/Inch	Weight @29"
2512	0.321	SS	10.28	298
2514	0.305	SS,75	11.33	329
2317	0.297	SS,75	13.38	388
3-71	0.300	A/C/C	9.92	288
300	0.300	CA,KIN	CAWT	CAWT

Group L
Size	Spine @ 28" Span	Model	Weight Grs/Inch	Weight @29"
2514	0.305	SS,75	11.33	329
2613	0.265	SS	11.49	333
2317	0.297	SS,75	13.26	385
2419	0.268	75	14.55	422
3-71	0.300	A/C/C	9.92	288
300	0.300	CA,KIN	CAWT	CAWT

Carbon & Kinetic Shaft Weights (CAWT)
Size	Spine	Kinetic Grs/In	Kinetic @29"	ST Axis Grs/In	ST Axis @29"	Hardwoods Green HD Grs/In	Hardwoods Green HD @29"	Obsession Grs/In	Obsession @29"	Epic Grs/In	Epic @29"	LightSpeed Grs/In	LightSpeed @29"	Excel Grs/In	Excel @29"
500	0.500			8.10	235	8.02	233	8.02	233	7.03	204	6.53	189	7.10	206
460	0.460	9.45	274												
400	0.400	10.20	296	8.95	260	9.12	264	9.12	264	8.17	237	7.41	215	8.12	235
340	0.340	11.04	320	9.53	276	10.01	290	10.01	290	9.00	261	8.16	237	8.80	255
300	0.300	11.64	338	10.69	310	10.14	294	10.14	294	9.14	265				

Size – indicates suggested arrow size.
Spine – spine of arrow size shown (static). See page 9 for correct Epic spine.
CAWT – Refer to Carbon & Kinetic box (left) for specific model and weight.
Color Designation for Aluminum Arrows – Within each box the aluminum arrows are color-coded.
☐ = lightest and fastest.
☐ = medium weight offering good speed and durability.
☐ = heavier weights for excellent durability and penetration.
☐ = aluminum/carbon and carbon.

Note: Shaft Weight at 29" is shown on our Arrow Selection Charts. To determine weight at your shaft length, multiply your actual shaft length by the grains-per-inch (gpi), not including point, insert or UNI Bushing.

SS	XX78 Super Slam Select and Super Slam (7178-T9 alloy)
75	XX75: Platinum Plus, Legacy, Camo Hunter, GameGetter, GameGetter II (7075-T9 alloy), Quattro and Yukon
A/C/C	Aluminum/Carbon/Composite
Rdln	Redline
CA	ST Axis, Realtree Hardwoods Green HD, Mossy Oak Obsession, Epic, LightSpeed, Fuxel
KIN	Kinetic

Suggested shaft sizes were determined using 100-grain points. See "Variables" on left side of page.

USING THE HUNTING ARROW SELECTION CHART

1. Once you have determined your Correct Hunting Arrow Length and Calculated or Actual Peak Bow Weight, you are ready to select your correct shaft size:

1.A Compound bows. In the "Calculated Peak Bow Weight" column (left-hand side of the CHART), select the column with the type cam on your bow, then the column with the point weight you use. Then locate your Calculated Peak Bow Weight in that column.

1.B Recurve bows and Modern Longbows. In the "Actual Peak Bow Weight" column (right-hand side of the CHART), select the column with the bow type and then the point weight you use. Next, locate your Actual Peak Bow Weight in that column.

2. Move across that bow weight row horizontally to the column indicating your Correct Arrow Length. Note the letter in the box where your Calculated or Actual Peak Bow Weight row and Correct Hunting Arrow Length column intersect. The "Shaft Size" box below the CHART with the same letter contains your recommended shaft sizes. Select a shaft from the CHART depending on the shaft material, shaft weight and type of shooting you will be doing.

For larger game, you should use heavier shafts.

(Text continued from page 29)

decreases archer's paradox, allowing you to shoot arrows of a lighter spine than is possible when using fingers. Release-shot arrows flex slightly — up and down.

Check the accompanying Easton aluminum shaft selection chart and you'll notice several possible shaft sizes for your bow's draw weight and personal draw length. For example, when I shoot one of my 70-lb. single-cam compounds at my 30 1/2-inch draw, I prefer a 2315 or 2317, although I can get equally good flight with other sizes, including 2514s and 2413s. Shooting various shaft sizes, comparing performance, and settling on the one arrow size I liked best gave me exactly what I wanted. Such experimentation will work equally well for you, too.

Before moving on, a caveat about arrow selection seems to be in order. In their continuing quest for speed, a few archers apparently can't resist the temptation to shoot extremely lightweight arrows, including ones lighter than those recommended by bow manufacturers. This is unwise. No one I know would intentionally dry-fire a bow, because they know releasing the string with no arrow in place can cause limb stress — and possible damage — to any bow. They also know that, in a few cases, bow breakage has injured shooters, some seriously. Yet the speed freaks obviously think nothing of using ultra-light arrows, which in fact is the closest thing to dry-firing a bow there is. My advice to you: Never use arrows lighter than the industry recommendations. Ever!

Carbon Arrow Shafts

Carbon arrow technology began to influence archery early in the 1980s. Back then two engineers working in Lyon, France, formed Beman Archery with a stated goal of producing world-class target and hunting arrows from carbon fibers. Since the day Beman was founded, the world of archery and bowhunting has never been the same.

Although these shafts were slow to gain favor, today they're a favorite of many bowhunters and commonly outsell aluminum in some areas. Actually, lots of modern bowhunters — including traditional archers who prefer hunting with stickbows — have discovered carbon, which is commonly called graphite. Its strength,

durability, and resilient properties make carbon shafting especially appealing. Advertised as offering "greater speed, flatter trajectory, and increased penetration," carbon arrows are here to stay.

Their popularity began to soar in the 1990s, appealing to folks wanting tough, light arrows that delivered consistent accuracy (to the best of any shooter's ability). Randy Ulmer, a professional shooter and one of the nation's top bowhunters, has this to say about carbon:

"The advantages of carbon arrows far outweigh the disadvantages. Carbon arrows are stiffer than an equivalent-weight aluminum arrow, so you can shoot a lighter arrow out of the same bow. Stiffer is better. It has been my experience that stiffer shafts group better than the shafts recommended by the charts, especially when I'm shooting broadheads. A stiffer arrow transfers more of its energy into penetration, rather than flapping around on impact as a weaker-spined arrow is prone to do.

"If you don't want to shoot a lighter arrow," Randy continues, "try shooting a carbon arrow that weighs the same as your aluminum arrow. I predict you'll group better with broadheads than you ever have, simply because the arrow is stiffer.

"A couple of other advantages carbon arrows have over aluminum: They are less reflective, which is a big advantage in sunny weather, and their small diameter causes less drag through air and tissue, giving them flat trajectory and deep penetration. One of the few drawbacks in the initial purchase price. They can be expensive. On the other hand, carbon arrows are more durable than aluminum arrows. You may find that carbons prove less expensive in the long run because a dozen carbon arrows may last as long as two or three dozen aluminum arrows."

Even some diehard stickbow shooters have forsaken wood to climb aboard the carbon-arrow bandwagon. While most compound shooters tout speed and flat trajectory as their primary reasons for switching to carbon, traditionalists have discovered the super-stiff shafts to their liking for two different reasons. First, carbon arrows typically come off recurves and longbows cleaner, and therefore recover faster in flight than either wood or aluminum arrows. Second, penetration — as Randy Ulmer suggested — is consistently better when carbon shafts are used. Also, any long-armed

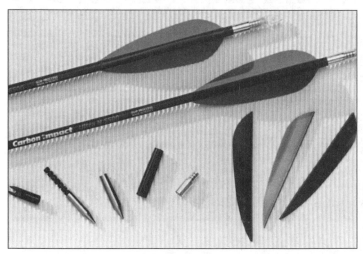

Some modern bowhunters—including a growing number of stickbow shooters—like the benefits offered by carbon arrows. Stiff, strong and lightweight, carbon shafts such as these from Carbon Impact are gaining in popularity, although aluminum arrows remain the top choice of today's bowhunters.

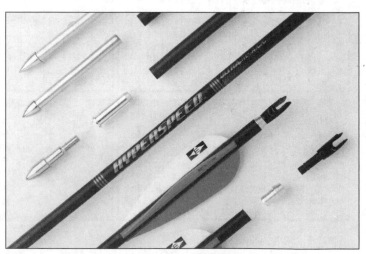

Easton's A/C/C HyperSpeed arrow pushes the limit for lightness—and speed. They are 45 to 60 grains lighter than equivalent A/C/C shafts and are designed for 3-D archers and field shooters to help reduce range-estimation errors. Easton advises shooters to have their bows checked by authorized dealers to avoid damage and personal injury.

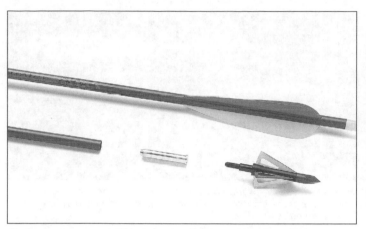

Carbon arrows are stiffer than aluminum arrows of equivalent weight. Shaft stiffness can improve arrow flight with broadheads and tighten groups. More and more modern bowhunters are using these graphite shafts.

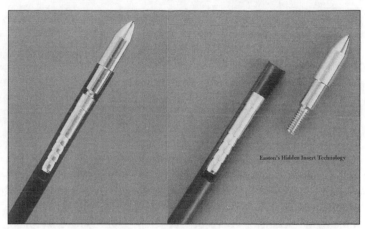

Here's an inside look at Easton's Hidden Insert Technology. Such advancements have made outserts and overfit nocks unnecessary. These improvements benefit bowhunters.

bowhunter who favors larger broadheads should find carbon to his liking. See the accompanying Beman chart fpr available sizes.

Regardless of bow choice, carbon arrows deserve consideration. In recent seasons I've used them as frequently as my favored aluminum shafts — with excellent results. They offer excellent flight characteristics and proper arrow performance, which, in fact, is every shooter's concern. Yet another option are the aluminum/carbon/composite arrows — such as Easton's A/C/C shafts with aluminum cores wrapped in layers of carbon fibers, or the Beman Carbonmetal Matrix, which combines the strength of carbon with the precision of aluminum — now available nationwide. These are the most expensive of all arrows.

Costly, precision-crafted all-carbon arrows may be worth the price differences, just as costly carbon/aluminum combos are snatched up by bowhunters who don't fret over budget restrictions. And for budget-minded folks there are economy-grade, lower-priced carbon hunting shafts are being made and sold at prices comparable to aluminum.

Besides cost, a few other drawbacks to carbon shafts do exist. One is an image problem, which is gradually being overcome. But these arrows do appear flimsy — even fragile — to hunters used to shooting larger diameter wood or aluminum shafts. They're not, of course, but their soda-straw look does take some getting used to. Another problem is the fact that these shafts sometimes explode when hitting a hard object. And unlike slightly bent or creased aluminum shafts that can be straightened and reused, carbon shafts are either straight or broken. All damaged carbon arrows must be pitched. Immediately.

Before shooting carbons, it's wise to check them for nicks, cracks, dents, or any sign that may indicate weakness. Additionally, carbon arrows sometimes shatter inside animals after impact. Breakage can leave sharp carbon splinters that should be located and removed. Any questionable meat should be discarded and care should always be taken during field-dressing chores to avoid hand injuries caused by the sharp fragments.

Inadequate rest clearance has been another frequent complaint. If you prefer a shoot-through rest, special steps are necessary to make sure the fletching on each arrow is perfectly aligned to slip between the support arms of your arrow rest. Even if you shoot a recurve or longbow and use a rug rest on your bow's shelf, you'll have to use

feather fletching and make certain there is an adequate groove between the rug and sight window. Otherwise, you won't be happy with the results.

In the early days of carbon, the small diameter of the shafts required screw-in adapters called "outserts" at one end and slip-over outsert nocks at the other. These arrows had abrupt edges that caused shooting problems when they snagged or hung up on certain arrow rests. Fortunately, today's carbons have nocks that slip directly into the shaft at one end and precision-fit screw-in broadhead or target point adapters at the other.

While I was an early-day skeptic of carbon arrows, I've changed my mind as the arrows have gradually improved. Consequently, I'd urge any serious bowhunter to stop by a favorite archery dealer or pro shop and check them out. Ask questions. Buy or borrow two or three arrows matched to you and your bow. Give 'em a try and judge for yourself how they perform compared to your current wood or metal arrows. You then can decide whether to switch or stick with your old favorites. I, for one, welcome the additional option in quality arrow shaft material.

Wood Arrow Shafts

Don't let anyone fool you. People who claim that few modern bowhunters use wooden shafts have never spent much time in traditional hunting camps or at summer gatherings of stickbow shooters. And while wood arrows — once the only available choice for archers and bowhunters — can claim only a small fraction of the modern arrow market, they've not vanished from the 21st century archery/bowhunting scene. Far from it.

G. Fred Asbell, an admitted romantic and traditionalist who delights in handcrafting his own hunting arrows, once shot aluminum religiously but now prefers wood over other arrow materials. He notes their stability, their forgiving nature, their warmth, their quietness — both leaving the bow and while carried in the woods — their feel, and their smell. Fred speaks for a legion of traditional bowhunters when he says:

"I like wood arrows because of the tradition and because, as bowhunting gets more and more sophisticated, I find more comfort in the romance and the very basic beauty of what was. It doesn't really have anything to do with what is better. I admit I enjoy being able to splinter a wood shaft against a rock or tree. It seems fitting and proper that arrows break rather than bend. And I guess the smell of the busted wood is part of it also. The fact that I can nurture my love for the romance of bowhunting — and still shoot an arrow as good as any that can be made — is particularly pleasing to me."

Dave Holt, known for his technical expertise and use of modern hunting tackle, adds: "Wood is an excellent shaft material. I sometimes use wood arrows for stump shooting and small game hunting."

A lack of uniformity is the major problem in matching wood shafts. By its very nature, wood varies widely in density and weight. There's also the problem of straightness. And spine. If wood arrows interest you — and they should if for no other reason than comparing them to arrows made of other materials — be prepared to take some time tracking down a set of properly matched shafts. While it can be both challenging and frustrating, you just may find the effort worthwhile.

"But I shoot a compound," someone is sure to say. "You can't shoot wood arrows from compounds."

Custom-made wood shafts like these handcrafted for the author are expensive, but worth the extra cost to many shooters when perfectly matched and spined to specific hunting bows. Despite what some bowhunters believe, wood arrows can be shot from compounds. Note the fletching's helical twist for maximum broadhead control and accuracy.

Wrong! Whoever started that old wives' tale didn't know his fir from his ash. If the wood shafts are spined for your bow's draw weight and matched to your draw length, there's absolutely no reason why you can't shoot wood from a modern compound bow. I have. Dave Holt has. Many other bowhunters have — and do. The only caveat I'd offer is the same one that applies to carbon: Check wooden arrows before and after each shot, no matter what bow you're using. Looking for cracks, dings, or weak spots is common sense. It may help you detect shafts that could break, split, or break upon release, injuring the shooter's bow hand. That kind of accident can happen with stickbows, too.

Here's a novelty—takedown wood arrows. Designed for backpack bowhunting, the shafts can be disassembled for easy carrying and reassembled in the field.

Having just mentioned stickbows, I should note that matching wood arrows to longbows is generally more critical — and sometimes more difficult — than with recurves. In fact, you'll likely find a much wider selection of arrow spines and weights when matching shafts to a recurve. Undoubtedly, that's due to the fact that longbows are not center shot and and recurves are. Arrows shot from longbows are not pointed directly at the target, but off to the left (for right-handed shooters). Regardless, properly spined arrows will wrap around the bow handle, straighten themselves, and fly straight to the target. This seemingly puzzling occurrence is the basis for a term mentioned earlier in this chapter, "archer's paradox." But enough about history. A couple of other problems with wood should be noted.

In addition to using bright red and yellow fletching on all of his hunting arrows, the author prefers a fluorescent dip on the tail end of each shaft for greater visibility in flight.

Wood can and will warp if the weather is wet, a problem you won't find in aluminum and carbon. Like aluminum, wood arrows can be straightened, but it takes time and experience. Also, wood arrows typically are more short-lived than other materials. Repeated shooting is believed to eventually weaken the spine.

Besides the famed Port Orford cedar, virtually every type of wood has been used by arrowmakers at one time or another — Norway pine, Douglas fir, Western larch, maple, white pine, white ash, yellow birch, ironwood, cherry, and on and on. Even compressed wood shafts were made by placing cedar blocks under tremendous pressure and then dowelling the blocks into shafting. Such wood material carried a steep price tag. And although unmatched low quality wood shafts can be bought for little money, the top-of-the-line, well-matched wood arrow sets are quite expensive, often costing more than a dozen premium carbon or aluminum arrows.

Frankly, I shoot few wood arrows these days, and when I do I mainly use a longbow or recurve. That's a personal preference, not a commentary on which shaft material is best for any given bow. The reason I don't shoot wood much is that, despite owning dozens

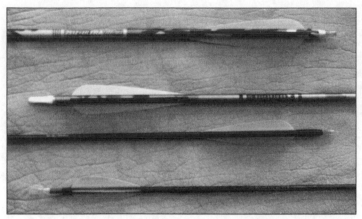

Hunting arrows with straight fletching and broadheads can be difficult to control. The author always uses shafts with offset or helical fletching for pinpoint hunting accuracy.

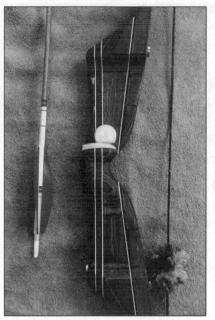

If you're shooting arrows off the shelf instead of using an elevated arrow rest, you must use feather fletching. When the author shoots this Black Widow takedown, for example, he uses matched wood arrows with five-inch fletching and a moderate helical twist.

of sets of customized wooden arrows, most are true works of art, almost too handsome to shoot. Many are footed shafts and tapered shafts — each dipped and beautifully crested, with brilliant fletching gracing the finished shaft. Footed shafts, incidentally, are made by inserting a piece of hardwood into the lower end of the shaft to increase shaft strength and durability. Tapered shafts are designed to improve arrow flight and reduce fletching wear, having eight inches or so of the nock end tapered from 23/64- to 5/16-inch.

Nocks must always be properly aligned. Crooked nocks affect accuracy, causing arrows to fly erratically. A misaligned nock is more of a problem than an improperly mounted broadhead. To check your nocks for straightness, hold the arrow loosely and blow on the fletch. Improperly mounted nocks will wobble noticeably as the shaft rotates. Heat and remove any faulty nock. Select nocks that snap snugly — but not too tight — onto the bowstring. If you shoot with a mechanical release, tighter is better. Arrows with loose-fitting nocks have a nasty habit of falling off the string at the worst possible time — like when a buck is standing just below your tree!

Arrow Fletching

Turkey feathers or plastic vanes? The debate about which material is best for bowhunting goes on and on. If you shoot arrows off the shelf, you must use feathers, of course. Use a good elevated rest and the choice is yours. The fact of the matter is both feathers and vane work well, and the ultimate decision should be left to the individual hunter.

Some shooters claim feathers produce greater arrow speed than shafts fitted with plastic vanes. It's true that feathered arrows do leave the bow faster; however, extensive testing by Dave Holt, Dwight Schuh, and other experts has determined there is very little difference in speed at common bowhunting distance of between 15 and 40 yards.

Other commonly debated topics concern fletching color and size, as well as helical, offset, and straight fletching. Some bowhunters — traditionalists and modern shooters alike — insist on using brightly colored, highly visible fletching rather than drab colors. They want to see their arrows in flight and pinpoint hits, something that can be difficult with some colors. Speaking of arrow flight, many veteran bowhunters shooting heavier arrows commonly use three five-inch vanes or feathers. Meanwhile, those who

favor lighter arrows often opt for three four-inch fletches to reduce weight and improve rest clearance. Whatever your personal preference, remember that bigger broadheads generally require bigger fletching to maintain control of the arrow as it zips toward its target.

Offset or helical fletching is another necessity for arrow control with many broadhead-tipped shafts. Upon release of an arrow, its broadhead will immediately compete with the fletching for arrow control. Unless the fletching is adequate, causing the hunting arrow to rotate smoothly in flight, the broadhead can wind-plane and force the arrow to veer off-target. Moderate helical fletching will adequately stabilize most modern broadheads and keep hunting arrows flying straight.

Carbon arrows, with their smaller-diameter shafts, present another problem. Since helical fletching won't work very well on carbon, I prefer to use fletching with a one- to two-degree offset. Speaking from long experience, I've never obtained consistently good arrow flight with straight fletching on broadhead-tipped arrows. I know, I know. Some hunters who use tiny, lightweight hunting heads — or mechanical broadheads — report good luck with straight fletching. Maybe so, but it's not for me. I'm not a big fan of either type of broadhead. I'll say more on this subject later.

If you're interested, experiment with various fletching configurations and sizes. Shoot arrows with your favorite broadheads mounted on their business end. That will quickly tell you what works and what doesn't. Always use what's best for you, your bow, and your shooting style.

Dave Holt prefers aluminum shafts with helical feather fletching. He explains: "I don't like plastic fletch on my arrows. Don't ask me to justify that statement; I can't. Often it just comes down to what we like. Your personal choices should be based on the points you consider most important."

Arrow Balance

Simply put, out-of-balance arrows don't fly worth a hoot. Ideally, you'll want a minimum of a 60-40 percent ratio with at least 40 percent of the total shaft weight on the broadhead end of your hunting arrow.

Flu-flu arrows are ideal for shooting at airborne targets and game birds. The shafts fly normally for short distances but are slowed by air drag on the oversized fletching, making arrow recovery easy.

Typically, flight problems arise only when there's too little weight in the front part of the arrow. It most often occurs if you're shooting a long arrow, an ultra-light hunting head, and vanes. Why? Keep in mind that any typical arrow's balance point is affected by a combination of factors, including the length and weight of the shaft itself, the weight of the fletching, and the weight of the insert and broadhead. The insert and broadhead combine to concentrate a good deal of weight in one place. Vanes, which are heavier than feathers, can change the balance point of any arrow. Ditto for long shafts that separate the opposing weights by a greater distance and magnify their effect.

If an arrow lacks sufficient weight at the front of the shaft, it cannot fly properly. Such out-of-balance arrows commonly puzzle shooters who often blame their bow for the erratic flight of arrows. A quick check of their arrows — keeping the 60-40 percent ratio in mind — could solve their problem and save them considerable consternation.

Arrow Quivers

Finally, before moving on to the subject of broadheads, we should briefly examine what's available for carrying hunting arrows into the field. In reality, there are three basic, popular styles of quivers used by modern bowhunters. These include the back quiver, the belt or hip quiver, and, finally, the bow quiver. Whatever your ultimate choice, always consider convenience, safety, and stability in making a selection.

Over the years I've used all types, but like a majority of modern bowhunters, I favor the bow quiver. While it does add weight to any bow, its convenience makes up for the extra poundage I lug around. All well-built models are rattle-free and durable, holding arrow shafts solidly in place in place with their broadheads protected under a hood designed to completely cover the razor-sharp blades. One- and two-piece models are readily available, some designed for easy removal once on stand. Although some hunters claim accuracy can be adversely affected by a bow-mounted quiver, most find no problems whatsoever. More about this in a later chapter.

Modern hip quivers likewise have sturdy broadhead hoods and individual shaft grippers. They are often favored by hunters who dislike the feel of bow quivers and believe they can get better accuracy shooting a perfectly balanced bow. If you want to give this type of quiver a try, make sure it's positioned so the fletching doesn't rustle against underbrush or interfere with normal movements as you walk along or draw your bow to make a shot. Check out the models that can be tied or strapped to your leg to prevent shafts from flopping around. The hip quiver — or a back quiver — is sometimes worn by hunters who routinely tote arrows in a bow quiver. But on extended backpack or backcountry hunts, they combine quiver types simply because they want to carry extra "ammo" along, just in case.

Back quivers — at least those worn by Robin Hood and Indian warriors — may be fine for movies and the target range, but they have absolutely no place in modern bowhunting. These quivers are noisy and dangerous — allowing arrows to rattle around and possibly fall out, creating a very real safety hazard. They also allow broadheads to rattle together in the bottom of the tube, quickly dulling sharp blades. If you want to try a back quiver, opt for the St. Charles-type which has a protective hood that covers the fletching and a foam-covered bar at the base to hold broadheads separate and solidly in place. Today, the Catquiver is perhaps the most popular back quiver available, offering padded shoulder straps and small packs that are part of the quiver itself. These little pockets are ideal for carrying a rain suit, survival gear, or extra bowhunting accessories for making emergency repairs in the woods.

Again, check out any and all quivers that catch your eye. Put 'em to the test where it counts, in the field. Then choose what's best for you and the kind of hunting you do most.

Veteran bowhunters like Bill Krenz of Colorado knows it's important to check arrows after each practice session. Cracked, dinged, or split shafts should be discarded immediately. Shooting damaged shafts can be dangerous if they break or explode when the arrow is released.

Chapter 4
Broadheads: On the Cutting Edge

WHENEVER ANY BOWHUNTER asks me what broadheads I use, my answer is always the same: "Sharp ones."

That's not really a flippant comment. It's the truth — and the sharper the better. Of course there's more to broadhead selection than the blades' sharp edges, but my point — pardon the pun — is this: the keenness of any hunting head is absolutely critical. Dave Holt sums up things nicely with this bit of sage advice: "Shoot the broadhead you like as long as it is razor-sharp, strong, and does not affect your arrow flight or accuracy."

Honestly, over the decades there have been many excellent designs and brands available to bowhunters, although most broadheads generally came in one of two basic designs — fixed blade or traditional-style heads and replaceable-blade heads. Within the recent past a third type — the mechanical-blade or open-on-impact broadhead — has burst on the modern bowhunting scene. Some industry reports estimate that as many as four in 10 bowhunters now use mechanical heads.

On one Texas bowhunt, the author used three modern broadheads to make one-shot kills (from left): the Barrie Ironhead, the NAP Spitfire and the Phantom 125.

To do its intended job, any broadhead — whatever its design — must penetrate hair, hide, and tissue. It also should create immediate and massive hemorrhage. No bowhunter should ever release a hunting arrow at any game animal unless the broadhead is as sharp as a surgeon's scalpel. Regardless, because arrows kill by hemorrhage, few arrow-hit animals drop on the spot — with brain or spinal hits being exceptions. Most run off to die on their feet or in nearby beds. Since massive blood loss causes a loss of consciousness and death, the more bleeding the broadhead causes, the better. Because few animals fall within sight, a tracking job is normally required. Good, easy-to-follow blood trails make a recovery much easier. And each blood trail begins with a razor-sharp broadhead. It's the best insurance for inflicting a quick, humane death.

Any examination of today's broadheads should begin with a brief look back at the evolution of hunting points. No one knows which Stone Age arrowmaker first bound a sharpened point onto a wooden shaft. What is known is that single act forever changed the effectiveness of the bow and arrow as both an implement of war and an efficient hunting tool. Previously, crude shaft tips were scraped to a sharp point with stone implements, then hardened over open fire pits. While these sharpened sticks could puncture the bodies of wild beasts, eventually causing death in some cases, the use of chipped stone points — with true cutting edges — changed history forever. These shaped points penetrated easily, severing tissue and internal organs alike, creating immediate hemorrhage and lethal wounds. Primitive man, the hunter, had just taken a tremendous evolutionary leap.

Modern man, the hunter, can look back at the dawn of bowhunting and fully appreciate the impact of this historic discovery. Subsequent refinements down through the centuries — the eventual use of bronze, copper, iron, and steel points for hunting and warfare alike — all contributed to the design and development of contemporary broadheads.

Bowhunting pioneers of the early 20th century — Saxton Pope, Arthur Young, Will "Chief" Compton, and others — crafted their own hunting tackle including bows, arrows, and hunting heads. Broadheads were made from any available metal. Discarded steel saw blades, for example, were one source. Metals were hand-cut and

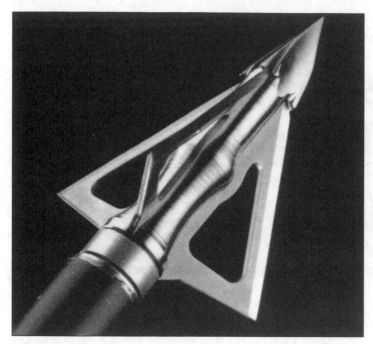

Several years ago Barrie Archery introduced its first titanium replaceable blade broadhead. The author has taken dozens of big game animals with the Rocky Mountain T-125.

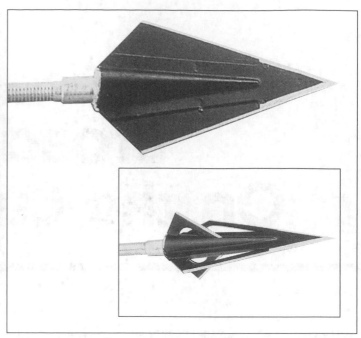

Magnus makes quality-constructed traditional heads. Bowhunting tests show that 3- and 4-blade broadheads cut more area than 2-blade heads.

hand-shaped, then finished with a grindstone and file. Slotted ferrules were made from metal tubing, bullet jackets, and similar objects, each pinned, soldered, welded, or otherwise attached to the steel blades. These sturdy homemade heads were all two-blade design. They varied greatly in size and weight; however, they served their purpose surprisingly well.

Although the very first American broadhead was offered for sale in an 1878 mail order catalog, it wasn't until the 1920s that commercially manufactured hunting points became widely available. Between that decade and the end of the 1990s, well over 1,000 different broadhead designs were produced. Many of these heads were made for direct sale to the bowhunting public. In recent years, the most popular heads have been replaceable blade models weighing 100 to 125 grains, with a cutting diameter up to 1 1/4 inches.

Modular Broadheads

In 1972 a Connecticut machinist and bowhunter named Dick Maleski forever changed commercial broadhead design and marketing when he introduced a new non-traditional broadhead. Maleski's Wasp broadheads featured a machined aluminum ferrule, hardened steel tip, and three modified Schick Injector razor blades held in place by steel locking rings. These new heads were immediately and enthusiastically accepted by bowhunters who demanded shaving-sharp heads. In fact, the new design started a tidal wave that swept over the broadhead industry. Soon similar designs and models appeared, including the Super-S heads from Duke Savora, Razorbaks from Andy Simo, Rocky Mountain Razors from Bob Barrie, and Muzzy multiple blade heads from John Musacchia, Sr. These and other razor-insert style heads have dominated the archery market since the 1970s. They remain the 21st century's most popular hunting heads.

Modular heads usually have exceptionally strong chisel or cone tips and multiple stainless steel, pre-sharpened blades. They're popular for their in-flight accuracy and ease-of-use convenience. And for any bowhunter who has ever had trouble sharpening traditional-style heads, they're a real godsend.

Blades can and should be replaced following each shot. Although pre-honed at the factory, each cutting blade still should be checked for sharpness before use. If it can't shave hair, it's not sharp enough. Whenever necessary, touch up the edges with a file, stone, and leather strop — or special ceramic sharpening tool — before heading afield. Remember, too, simply carrying broadheads around in a quiver can dull them. This is especially true if the arrow you remove and nock is the one you extract each time you're on stand. Keep blades sharp! Always!

Over the years I've hunted using several popular brands with excellent results, I might add. My own preference is for three- or four-blade heads weighing between 100 and 125 grains, with a slight bias toward the heavier end of that range. I dislike the tiny, lightweight, low-profile modular broadheads. These have a relatively small cutting diameter and tiny blades with minimal cutting surfaces. They're not my idea of a perfect broadhead. More about this later.

Mechanical Broadheads

Despite what some modern bowhunters believe, fly-open broadheads — each designed to open on impact — have been around in one form for more than half a century. Lately, however, some manufacturers have found eager buyers for modern-day mechanical broadheads. The Spitfire, Scorpion, and Shockwave from New Archery Products; the Wasp Jak-Hammer SST; the Rocket Sidewinder and Steelhead; the Rocky Mountain Revolution and Snyper; the Game Tracker Silvertip; and the Vortex Pro Extreme and Mini-Max heads are representative of mechanical broadheads. Seems these and other mechanical marvels are everywhere.

Little wonder. Expandable hunting heads, with their blades folded back into the ferrule, not only resemble field points but fly just like target points. They're widely recognized for delivering pinpoint accuracy. When the arrow strikes its target, the blades open and cut like conventional broadheads, often creating massive wounds because the cutting diameter of some open-on-impact models is wider than conventional heads. At least that's how it's supposed to work.

Referred to as "gimmicks" by some bowhunting historians and broadhead collectors, older fly-open heads were notorious for failing to perform as planned. Horror stories abounded about mechanical heads bouncing off broadside animals and glancing off quartering game — and I've seen it happen myself. While modern versions are of much better quality and usually perform as intended, lingering problems exist. Their very design means individual moving blades are less sturdy and stable. They're illegal in some hunting areas and unwelcome in many hunting camps. It seems guides and hunters love 'em or hate 'em. It also seems that when they work, all's well. But when they fail, they fail miserably.

As far as penetration is concerned, I agree with the general statement that expandables do not penetrate as well as fixed-blade broadheads, all things being equal. Frankly, some models don't work well because of the angle of the blades and size of the cut they make. Heads designed to chop a wound of about one and one-half to two inches wide simply don't have the penetration potential of normal heads that slice tissue. Also, the design of mechanicals means upon entry the open blades can twist or break more easily than fixed-blade heads. Regardless, some mechanicals perform quite well, thank you, and more improvements — with a resulting increase in popularity — are certain in the coming years.

I've field tested several brands of mechanical heads and have yet to experience broadhead failure. Regardless, I know others who have had difficulties. Quite candidly, I much prefer conventional broadheads that I know are going to perform flawlessly, shot after shot, time after time. Moving parts can and do fail. If you want to experiment with expanding broadheads, compare the various heads and select those that are quality-built. Also, use only bows that generate enough kinetic energy to ensure sufficient penetration — and wait for broadside shots at stationary animals. Me? I'll limit their use to small game, varmints, and gobblers.

Fixed Blade Broadheads

Long a favorite of many serious bowhunters, these traditional cut-on-impact hunting heads usually have a single blade of strong, welded steel. Often this blade's dual cutting edges are complemented by two auxiliary "bleeder blades," which either are stamped from the primary blade inself or are inserted into a slot in the ferrule. The cutting edges must be sharpened before and after use. Zwickey's famed Black Diamond Delta or Eskimo, the Muzzy Phantom 125, and Bear's Razorhead are familiar examples of these broadheads.

Traditional broadheads are widely hailed for their strength and penetrating ability, but there are drawbacks, too. Some are hard to sharpen. A few have in-flight stability problems. And some models with vented blades can whistle audibly in flight.

Like many long-time bowhunters, I prefer these heads over all others, although I frequently hunt with replaceable-blade, modular heads, too. For the record, my two all-time favorite fixed blade heads are the Rothhaar Snuffer and Phantom 125. The former is a

New Archery Product's Andy Simo (left), who unveiled the popular Razorbak and Thunderhead broadheads, recently introduced the Nitron, NAP's latest replaceable blade head.

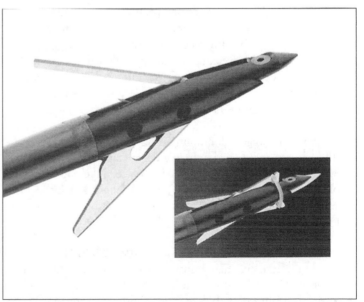

Mechanical blade heads have been around for decades, but today's open-on-impact heads are increasingly popular. They typically fly much like field points used in pre-hunt practice.

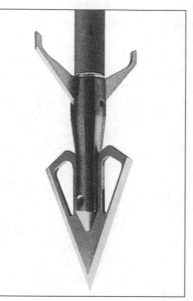

Here are samples of three popular hunting heads, each a different style. The Montec 3-blade is a cut-on-contact point, the Game Tracker a combination head that's both cut-on-contact and expandable, and the Muzzy replaceable blade head is one of the most-used broadheads around.

super-strong three-blade design available in several weights, including the 125-grain model I use. The Phantom 125, as its name suggests, also weighs 125 grains, but features a single piece ferrule and a patented locking system for its secondary bleeder blades. It's a truly tough, true-flying head that requires only touching up with a ceramic stick to maintain its lethal edge. And I've always enjoyed the prehunt ritual of sharpening my Snuffers with a file, oiled stone, and leather strop.

Whichever type and model you settle on, check each broadhead-tipped arrow for straightness and proper head alignment before shooting. Spin the arrow on its tip, keeping an eye on the spot where the head and shaft meet. If there's an obvious wobble, the arrow won't fly properly. Make sure all of your hunting broadheads are properly aligned. If they're not, replace them.

Broadhead Attachment

Broadheads may be attached to hunting shafts in one of two ways. Most modern heads come complete with screw-in adapters that easily fit into the threaded inserts of hollow aluminum and carbon shafts. The screw-in attachment system makes mounting or removing any broadhead a breeze, but that threaded part of the adapter is one possible weak point that may allow the arrowhead to bend or snap on impact. If you ever encounter this problem, consider switching to tapered shafts and glue-on heads. Regardless, to avoid nasty cuts, always use a wrench or tool when mounting or removing heads.

For wood or swaged aluminum arrows broadhead ferrules without the adapters are slipped onto five-degree tapers at the point end of each shaft and glued or cemented in place. Take pains to make absolutely certain the broadhead is perfectly aligned with the shaft. Otherwise, the head can wobble in flight, hurting both accuracy and penetration.

Other Selection Considerations

Size is always a popular hunting camp topic of conversation, whether it deals with big antlers or big hunting heads. When discussing broadheads, both the cutting width and number of blades must be considered.

Does a larger broadhead automatically translate to better blood

This NAP Thunderhead caused massive bleeding on a record book buck tagged by M. R. James. That's a chunk of lung tissue expelled from the exit wound.

trails? Not necessarily. No one will say that shot placement doesn't matter. Nor will any savvy bowhunter deny that some smaller multi-blade heads have more cutting surface than some large two-edged heads. I, for one, maintain that using a larger head is always an advantage if your accuracy and penetration are not adversely affected. Simply put, I want to deliver the best-flying, deepest-penetrating, and most damage-inflicting broadhead I can find. If pinpoint accuracy could be guaranteed with each and every shot, I'd consider smaller heads with minimal cutting surface. But animals aren't stationary targets. They have a disconcerting habit of doing the unexpected — such as taking a step just as you release. In such cases bigger is better. Size does matter.

If you use a larger head, you'll need to make certain that your arrow's stiffness and fletching are adequate to maintain in-flight control. Never use a large hunting head on an ultralight or a straight-fletched arrow. You won't be happy with the results.

As already mentioned, there are three broadhead point designs — conical, chisel, and cut-to-tip. Since point shape directly affects penetration, it's worth briefly reviewing which works best and why.

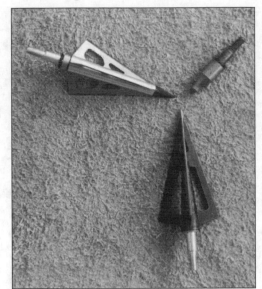

Practice points and broadheads may not fly the same. The time to find out is well before the hunting season begins.

One of the best practice points ever made is the Judo point from Zwickey Archery. The spring-arm design keeps arrows from snaking under grass or burrowing into the weeds and leaves.

For years, many bowhunters — including this writer — insisted that cut-on-contact broadheads had supreme penetrating capabilities. Next came chisel-tip heads, trailed by round or conical points. That order of penetration potency was pretty much accepted as gospel by bowhunters. Then precise, strictly controlled tests using all three point types — conducted in a variety of target materials including meat and hides — revealed some very interesting facts. Dave Holt and engineer Norb Mullaney, among others who conducted closely monitored penetration tests between blade-to-tip broadheads with heads with central-column tips, found very little actual penetration differences — less than half an inch when all other test factors were equal. Dave explains:

"I'm not trying to discredit quality blade-to-tip heads — they are great. Their performance over the years leaves little doubt about their effectiveness. On the other hand, I seldom see central-column heads given their due. It doesn't take a mechanical engineer to realize that the central-column design is generally superior superior in strength and more resistant to bending than the blade-to-tip broadhead designs. Again, in both testing and hunting situations, I have been unable to find more than a small difference in penetration between point designs when all other factors are equal."

So many variables exist in hunting situations that it's easy to see why misconceptions about broadheads arise. A few years ago during a Texas bowhunt, I shot a tall-tined buck at just under 20 yards. The arrow, tipped with a Phantom 125 blade-to-tip broadhead, blew through that broadside buck and disappeared in the brush. A day later, using the same 70-pound hunting bow, I arrowed a large thick-hided feral hog using an arrow tipped with a central-column Barrie Rocky Mountain Iron Head replaceable blade broadhead. The shaft penetrated the hog's chest as he stood broadside less than 20 yards away, but the head didn't exit the cartilaginous shield on the big boar's opposite side.

The buck ran perhaps 60 yards before folding; the big boar died nearly 100 yards away. Which style and model of broadhead performed more effectively? In each case the animal died within seconds and was easily recovered. Judging the results based solely on penetration would be patently unfair in this example. Besides, deer are smallish, thin-skinned animals; wild boars are large, tough-skinned critters. The Barrie Iron Head likely would have completely penetrated my whitetail, and the Phantom may or may not have exited the far side of the hog. I'll never know, not that it matters. My point is, despite each shot resulting in a quick, clean kill, I could have drawn apparent but erroneous penetration conclusions between the two broadhead types had I failed to factor in all pertinent information. I would suspect that similar hunting scenarios have added to the widespread misunderstandings and misinformation about broadheads.

The bottom line — based on precise testing and comparable bowhunting situations — is that conical and chisel point tips consistently penetrate as well or nearly as well as cut-on-impact broadheads, at least with ideal shots taken when the animal is broadside and unmoving. My personal recommendation: Select and use a sturdy, dependable head that flies and penetrates well, creates a lethal wound, and suits your personal hunting needs.

Other Heads

Although broadheads are mandatory for big game bowhunting, practice points and small game heads are — or should be — found in every bowhunter's arrow box.

Field points are ideal for routine target practice; however, Zwickey's four-pronged Judo points are best for stump shooting because they do no snake under grass or skip off into the weeds. Judo points may be used for smaller game, too, although small blunts made of metal, plastic, or hard rubber are typically favored.

And just because you practice with 125-grain field or Judo tips doesn't mean your 125-grain broadheads automatically will fly the same or hit at the same point on your target. Mechanical points may come close but should be checked, too. In fact, you shouldn't hunt with any head that you haven't practiced with! This doesn't mean shooting at game with your dull practice broadheads, either. You know what I mean.

To find out point-of-impact differences between practice points and broadheads, if any, you must shoot and check your respective arrow groups. If obvious differences exist, try to determine why and attempt to correct the problem. Ideally, you want your practice arrows and hunting arrows to hit the same spot on any target.

More important to bowhunters, of course, is knowing exactly where their broadhead-tipped arrows will fly. As you begin serious pre-hunt practice, it's smart to shoot only broadheads. Keep your shooting skills sharp throughout the hunting season, too. Once the actual hunt starts, some bowhunters don't practice much if at all. Smart bowhunters avoid getting rusty by practicing daily, even if it's simply taking a practice shot or two before climbing down from their tree stand.

In my own case, I always carry at least one Judo-tip or blunt in my bow quiver. Since my hunting and practice arrows have the identical impact point, I can maintain my shooting edge by launching occasional shots during lulls in my hunt. And I'm one of those guys who rarely climbs out of any elevated stand without first shooting at a nearby leaf, grass clump, or rotten stump.

I always insert that practice arrow nock-first upside down in my bow quiver. This prevents me from accidentally grabbing and nocking a practice shaft if I get the opportunity to take a quick follow-up shot at missed or wounded game. It's disconcerting — and embarrassing — to find yourself drawing down on a big game animal and suddenly notice a Judo point or blunt on the business end of your arrow.

Literally thousands of different broadheads have been produced over the years, providing ample opportunity for collectors such as the late Floyd Eccleston. This Michigan collection is among the most complete in North America.

So What's the Perfect Broadhead?

I've already confessed which broadheads I prefer — and why. Before moving on, it's important to pass along some food for thought and meaty suggestions that can help you narrow your own broadhead choice.

- **Avoid broadheads with a cutting width of less than one inch.** Small, low-profile heads can do the job if you make a perfect shot every time. But few bowhunters I know, even the pros, have that ability, and it's when you've made a marginal hit — as the animal reacts unexpectedly — that you'll fully appreciate a wider head.
- **Choose a broadhead with at least three to four blades.** Heads

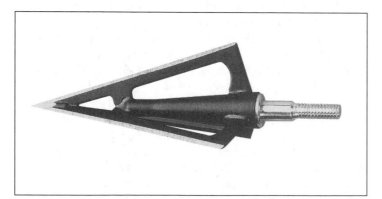

Invented by Ohio bowhunter Roger Rothhaar decades ago, the Snuffer has long been a favorite of the author. It's now produced by Magnus and is available in weights up to 160 grains.

with only two cutting edges may be strong and penetrate well, but they're often difficult to shoot accurately. Even when they are on target, two cutting surfaces rarely have the internal cutting potential of three- and four-blade heads. First, it's much easier for a two-blade broadhead to miss an artery or vein than multi-blade heads. Second, wounds created by two-blade heads can close or become plugged more easily. Since you always want the best blood trail possible, opt for heads that will produce the most hemorrhaging, inside and out.

- **Avoid oversized, heavy broadheads that will lose trajectory and fade in flight.** Just as I urge you to avoid the tiny, super-light broadheads that require pinpoint accuracy to do their job — and barely exceed the 7/8th-inch width minimum required by most states — don't go to the opposite extreme. For my money, a perfect broadhead does not weigh less than 100 grains or more than 145 grains. Given a choice, I'll take a 125-grain head every time.
- **Always select a smooth-edged broadhead.** Those heads with burrs or serrated cutting edges may look wicked but their looks are deceiving. Hair, tallow, and meat can clog the ragged edges, slowing penetration and cutting potential. You want blades with edges that look like grandpa's straight razor — and are every bit as sharp.
- **Go with a proven winner.** There are many excellent broadheads available today — one to suit any bowhunter's individual needs. Shop around and shoot as many heads as possible, by all means. But don't skimp on quality to save a dollar or two, and don't fall for passing broadhead fads or gimmicks. Buy and use brand-name hunting heads that have a long record of consistent success. You won't be sorry.

Chapter 5
Bowhunting Add-Ons: What You Really Need

IN TRUTH, all you really need to go bowhunting is a bow, some broadhead-tipped arrows, and your fingers. Of course, you should have some kind of quiver, too, since it'll make carrying your arrows easier. It's also a good idea to have some kind of protection for your shooting fingers — usually a glove or tab. Finally, you'll likely need an armguard to prevent those painful forearm scrapes and bruises (armguards also keep the sleeve your camo shirt or jacket from snagging on the bowstring when you shoot). Those are the basic necessities, really. Attend some hunter education course, add hours of shooting practice, buy a hunting license, and it's quite likely your home state or province will consider you a "bowhunter."

A simple hunting bow and arrows are all you really need to take up bowhunting. But there are certain practical add-ons that you'll want to check out.

There's surely much more to it than that. Many veteran bow-benders point out that the respectful term "bowhunter" must be earned, not bestowed. There may be instant coffee, instant relief, and instant gratification (at least according to some ads for groceries, acid indigestion, and swingers), but there ain't really no such thing as an instant bowhunter.

Of course, the manufacturers of a whole host of modern archery products don't want folks to stop spending after purchasing the few practical and basic items mentioned in the opening paragraph. Their success depends on convincing you that a vast assortment of optional bowhunting accessories should be part of your personal list of "must have" archery products.

Actually, optional accessories may or may not help you become a better-prepared, more effective bowhunter. Following is a brief but critical examination of seven of these purely elective bowhunting aids:

Bowsights

Most bowhunters who shoot compound bows use sights. That's a fact. But one additional fact is that there's absolutely no reason why a compound user cannot shoot his or her bow instinctively. And quite effectively, thank you!

Pompous critics pooh-pooh instinctive shooting, pointing to the fact that good sight shooters can "shoot circles" around barebow shooters. That's likely true if you're talking about shooting tight groups at known distances. But critics often confuse target archery with bowhunting, which have about as much in common as tennis and ping pong. In many cases, bowhunters don't know the exact distance to their target. Furthermore, how important are two-inch, four-arrow groups to a bowhunter who typically has one chance — one arrow — to take home a trophy?

Don't misunderstand. Accuracy is critical to any shooting success, and a bowsight admittedly can help a shooter focus full attention on the target. But highly proficient instinctive shooters — like stickbow shooter G. Fred Asbell and compound shooter Judd Cooney, for example — not to mention hundreds of others, have proved the shoot-by-instinct method works and works well for bowhunting. Fred's best-selling instinctive shooting books, videos,

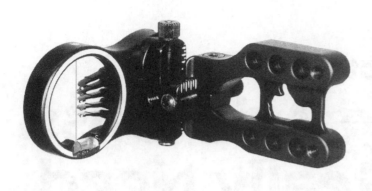

Most compound shooters use multi-pin sights and sight in their hunting bows at typical ranges from 10 to 40 or 50 yards. Knowing the exact distance to the target is critical for sight shooting success.

Single-pin sights—either fixed in position for close-range shots or adjustable for any reasonable yardage—are preferred by some bowhunters. This Sightmaster one-touch adjustable model offers convenience and simplicity.

Good bow sights are sturdy with adequate protection for the pins. They also allow fine-tuning adjustments vertically and horizontally. This makes finding the correct elevation and alignment relatively easy.

Many bowhunters favor sights with fiber optic pins that make zeroing in on the target simpler. This bow sight also contains a level to insure proper alignment.

and jam-packed how-to seminars, have taught many thousands of archers and bowhunters the essentials of this ancient technique.

Regardless, easy-to-pull-and-hold compounds are ideal for sight shooters, especially beginners who must learn to concentrate on an exact spot while mentally reviewing a complete checklist of shooting steps — drawing, anchoring, aiming, releasing, and following-through. Absent is the muscle-tiring strain of holding a heavy-pulling stickbow at full draw and waiting for that big buck to step into a shooting lane under a treestand. And if you believe you shoot better with bowsights than using the point-and-shoot method of a pure instinctive shooter, there are some things you should know to help you face the bewildering array of bowsight choices available today.

Without question, multiple-pin sights are the most popular of all the sighting devices now in use. These easily mount to the bow with screw-on or dovetail brackets. Most have four or five adjustable pins with bright pinheads of varying colors, typically set at 10-yard increments. Once the pins are sighted-in, it's important that they do not move. Consequently, select and use sights with sturdy pin guards. These guards will prevent pin damage or misalignment during normal field use — or in the event of accidental slips and falls. Most

good sights come already enclosed inside rugged plastic or metal frames. If your pins are unprotected, buy and install a pin guard before heading to the woods. Sooner or later, any exposed sight pins are going to cause you problems. That's a promise.

Single-pin sights are favored by a few bowhunters who refuse to shoot beyond 20 to 30 yards. Really, some ultra-fast bow and arrow setups do not require multiple pins at shorter yardages. Another one-pin option that allows shots at longer ranges is found in the moveable models, which can be easily adjusted — some with one-finger control — for any reasonable bowhunting yardage.

The weaknesses of sights are evident in common bowhunting excuses such as "I couldn't see my pin" or "I picked the wrong pin." Again, for bow sights to be most effective, shooters must know the distance to their target. Having sight pins on your bow is no guarantee that you'll hit what you're shooting at. Also, avoid tiny pins that are difficult to see in typical low-light woodland condtions. Fiber-optic, fluorescent, and electronic sights can solve the visibility problem; however, keep in mind that the use of any electronic device attached to your bow or arrow will disqualify your animals from the Pope and Young records. Also, some so-called lighted sights are illegal in certain parts of the country. Always check local

A recent innovation in bow sights is seen in the "stacked pin" alignment from Steel Tech. This setup provides additional pin strength.

Pendulum sights involve a single moveable pin that when sighted in adjusts automatically to take all guesswork out of judging distance. The author has used pendulum on several successful deer and bear hunts.

hunting laws before investing in any electronic sighting device.

One more single-pin possibility — which certainly solves the problem of which pin to choose when that big-racked buck wanders under your stand — is the calibrated pendulum sight. Once sighted-in, it adjusts automatically as you raise or lower your bow — and is on target at usual tree stand yardages. I've taken several whitetails and black bears with a Keller Pendulum Sight — the granddaddy of all "automatic" sights — and can attest to its dependability and accuracy. These devices compensate for distance, tree stand height, and bow poundage and are dead-on up to 30 yards. All you do is pick a spot and aim. The pendulum sights I've used are a bit noisy to shoot, but can be easily quieted. About the only serious problem you may encounter with these sights occurs while hunting in uneven terrain, as when your stand is on a sidehill or in a depression and you need to take an uphill shot. But for flatland tree stand hunting they're tough to beat. And although the Keller sight comes equipped with a pin light, removing the tiny battery or the battery/light tube itself makes the sight non-electronic within a matter of seconds.

Crosshair sights with multiple crosswires or single wires are another popular choice with bowhunters. When properly adjusted, they are very accurate and almost automatically provide the correct windage. This means if you know the yardage to the target and select the proper crosswire, your arrow should be dead-on, hitting just where the crosshairs are being held. Of course, the same can be said of pins. It's a personal thing.

Several other sighting devices exist — electronic dot sights and laser sights, as well as fiber-optic sights, rifle-bar sights, and rangefinder sights, to name a few — but most have little practical application for bowhunters. Dot sights and laser sights, for example, are expensive and are better suited to firearms than bows and arrows. Rangefinder sights, in which horizontal bars of varying sizes are "fitted" on broadside game, do not take into consideration the size differences between antelope and elk, for example. Of these options, only fiber-optic sights, which gather available light and channel it to the sight pin tips, have many supporters within the bowhunting ranks.

One recent innovation in bowsights is the vertical inline sight, such as the Trophy Ridge Matrix or Nitro Xtreme models. These sights offer excellent visibility and strength, The vertical alignment of the steel pins can help with pinpoint accuracy, too. The fiber-optic pins are easy to see during dim lighting conditions.

While I shoot my stickbows instinctively, I do use sights on my compounds and prefer multi-pin models that allow me to shoot accurately at distances out to 40 yards or slightly beyond. I welcome the challenge of getting close to game and releasing arrows at normal bowhunting yardages. Ninety-plus percent of the shots I take are under 30 yards.

Again, sights are an unnecessary but very common add-on used by hundreds of thousands of modern bowhunters. Frankly, I've found them hard to beat when shooting at known distances. On the other hand, shooting a bow well without even thinking about yardages is what makes instinctive shooting so appealing to many bowhunters.

Rangefinders

Since knowing the exact distance to any animal or target is critical for consistent sight-shooting success, many bowhunters now carry commercially manufactured rangefinders. While early models of these amazing optic devices were large and awkward to use in common stalking and still-hunting situations, the newer compact laser rangefinders are small and easy to handle. They provide almost instant info that takes the all the guesswork out of estimating yardages.

Lately I've used a Bushnell Yardage Pro while stalking Wyoming elk and mule deer, as well as British Columbia bison. But most often I employ that same easy-to-use one-button rangefinder from my tree stands while hunting whitetail deer and black bears. It's a big help in keeping me from spreading my scent around. I used to pace off distances around the stand before climbing aboard. These days, after getting into my tree, I simply focus my rangefinder on a nearby stump, log, rock, bush, or whatever natural marker is handy. Instantly I know the yardage. And that's very good information to have when a big buck or bruin finally ambles into view.

Laser rangefinders work by sending out an invisible infrared energy pulse that reflects off a chosen target. The beam then bounces back to the rangefinder, which instantly displays the distance to within a yard or so. There also are models which use a system of mirrors to produce double images of a target. Focusing the split images until they merge produces a readout of the exact yardage. I have a well-used dial-operated Ranging model that employs this particular rangefinding technology. Besides my own Bushnell and Ranging models, I've used Nikon and Leica rangefinders that combine yardage-measuring with monocular magnification. Prices start at less than $100 and top out at several times that amount.

Based on my own hunting experiences, I now know that

rangefinders can be used on bedded, browsing, or slowly moving animals, as well as distinctive landmarks near stands and blinds. While I'd rather be reaching for an arrow than a rangefinder, there are certain times when I'm still-hunting or stalking that I check out yardages. Rangefinders have helped me put some good animals on the ground. They just might help you, too.

Always check game laws before using any electronic distance-calculating devices. Technically, they may be illegal to use in hunting areas where the law prohibits lights of any type from being focused on game animals. Trophy-class animals taken with the aid of laser rangefinders are eligible for the Pope and Young records. The Club bans electronics attached to a bow or arrow; however, this rule does not apply to other legal electronic devices.

Mechanical Releases

Over the past decade-plus, mechanical release aids have gained widespread acceptance and popularity with many serious bowhunters. It's been estimated that today three out of every four bowhunters favors releases over fingers. So exactly what's good and bad about releases? Let's take a look.

Increased accuracy and shooting consistency are usually cited as the basic benefits. It makes sense, too. When you grip a bowstring with the meat end of three shooting fingers, getting a smooth, identical release shot after shot is somewhat difficult. A hand-held

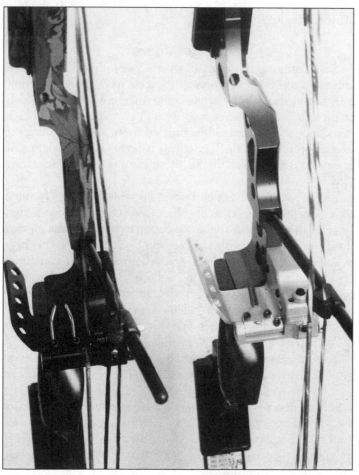

Overdraw systems are favored by speed-conscious shooters who want to use a short, light arrow. They can increase bow speed, but typically are noisier and usually require the use of a mechanical release.

release, however, touches the string at one small contact point, and it requires only a light touch on the release trigger or button to send the arrow on its way.

When shooting with fingers, the bowstring rolls over the finger-tips as muscle tension is relaxed; triggering a release propels the string and arrow forward in a relatively straight line. View any videotaped slow motion replay of an arrow being shot and you'll see that a finger release actually causes the string to move slightly to the left (for right-handed shooters, to the right for lefties). Consequently, the finger-shot arrow begins its journey by moving sideways instead of directly forward. A release can help to eliminate this particular problem.

Also, many expert shooters insist that for pinpoint accuracy each release should come as a complete surprise. Rather than opening your shooting fingers when your mind screams Now!, you should slowly apply pressure — much like squeezing the trigger of a rifle — until the shot is made.

Obviously, fingers work fine for today's archers, just as they have for many centuries — although some ancient Asian archers used a type of release devices ages ago. Chuck Adams, perhaps the most successful bowhunter alive, shoots fingers. So did the late, great Fred Bear and Howard Hill. And some mechanical release critics delight in noting that a release can be noisy, awkward to use, get lost, or fail at exactly the wrong moment. They chortle over the fact that releases can be adversely affected by cold and wet weather, by dust and dirt. For ease of use and overall reliablity, they proudly note that nothing beats fingers. One finger-shooter I know once remarked astutely, "My fingers never get lost or fail me. I'll take 'em over a release any day of the week."

But if you decide to try shooting with a release, I'd urge you to test several and decide for yourself how well or poorly they work for you. You need to understand that it often takes some practice to become proficient. It'll likely require setting up and tuning your bow from scratch, too, depending on your personal shooting style. Although some folks — including some very knowledgeable bowhunters — claim you can't shoot the same bow with fingers and then switch to a release and maintain your accuracy, I've not found that to be the case. I own several hunting bows that I can mix and match — fingers or release — without any tinkering and without any obvious problems.

Speaking of problems, I discovered years ago that a release can help a shooter overcome a common shooting malady — target fever (alias "buck fever"). At certain times in my decades-old shooting career, I've found myself unable to lower my bow arm and lock-in on a target, whether hunting or practicing. I'd catch myself holding high and then dropping my arm at the instant of release. The result, of course, was a total disaster. I was lucky to hit the ground two out of three shots! And it seemed that no matter how hard I tried, I simply couldn't bring my sight pin to bear on what I wanted to hit. Then one day I slipped on a release. Voila! As if by magic — or some giant magnet — my pin would center a target every time. And after shooting with a release for a short time, I found I could go back to fingers without missing a beat. Finger shooters should keep this in mind if and when they're bitten by the target panic gremlin. And current release shooters may beat buck fever by switching to a different type of mechanical release. Releases can help. That's the truth.

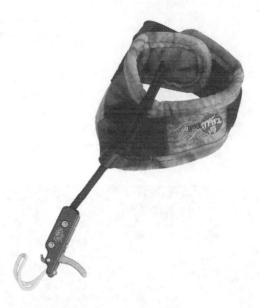

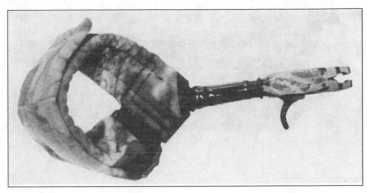

Caliper releases are common, clamping around the string just below the arrow nock. Releases generally provide a cleaner release than that of finger shooters

Wrist releases like this T.R.U. Ball model are held in place by Velcro and the hunter's grip. Shots are triggered with a squeeze of the forefinger. Note the cord that fits around the bowstring until the shot is made.

Another popular type of release is held solely by the fingers as the bow is drawn. Contact with the bowstring is minimal and the arrow is released by touching a button with a thumb or finger.

Release selection should never be a problem, either. There are two basic styles — finger-held and wrist strap releases — that have found wide acceptance with bowhunters, but there are dozens of different makes, models, and price ranges. I use and like the Winn Free-Flight caliper-release that yokes to my wrist and is triggered by my index finger. Scott, T.R.U. Ball, Tru-Fire, Cobra, Winn, and other companies offer dozens of choices. Most are reasonably priced with many choices available for less than $100.

You can also find dozens of releases that attach to the bowstring with rope loops, ball bearings, rotating and pivoting holding devices, as well as calipers. Already noted is the fact that releases commonly come with triggers or buttons — and back tension releases are yet another option. For anyone suffering from target panic, Dave Holt suggests a release that you trigger with your little finger rather than a thumb or index finger. This, he offers, will reduce jerking or punching the trigger. My own advice is to try several different styles and models before plunking down any cash. If and when you find one you like, buy a back-up and keep it handy, just in case. People who learn to rely on mechanical releases are pretty much lost without one.

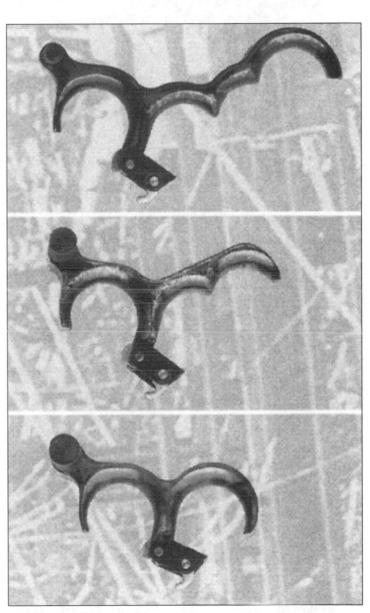

Back tension finger releases — drawn and held by two, three, or four fingers (as shown) — are triggered automatically when the shooter's back and shoulder muscles are in proper position for ideal shooting form.

47

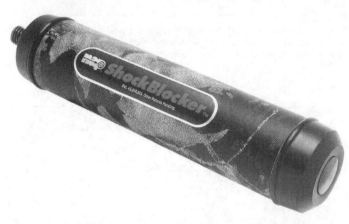

Unlike the long stabilizers seen on bows used by target archers in competitive shooting, such as the Olympics, hunting stabilizers are much shorter, usually measure less than a foot.

Michigan bowhunter Tom Nelson is one of many successful bowhunters who favors a stabilizer to give his bow proper balance. That's a buck he killed in November of '03.

Stabilizers

Do you really need a stabilizer on a hunting bow? Probably not. But will a stabilizer on a hunting bow help? Yes. Here's why.

Stabilizers built for bowhunting do several things — add weight, provide better balance, and absorb vibration. Unlike the ultra-long stabilizers you'll see on some target bows, some measuring several feet in length, hunting stabilizers are short, stubby rods typically less than a foot long. They conveniently screw into a threaded accessory hole in the bow's riser, located below and in front of the grip.

The additional weight is intended to help stabilize a bow and improve accuracy by eliminating handle torque. With lightweight target bows, a stabilizer offers obvious benefits; however, a heavier compound bow — often mounted with a bow quiver and its complement of half a dozen or more arrows — is by comparison plenty heavy to start with. Adding as much as another pound just doesn't make much sense to some folks who have tote around all that dead weight from daylight to dark. They usually consider their bows stable enough, thank you very much. But others, especially those who try to coax as much speed as possible out of their bows, know the steadier the bow the better the accuracy. Besides, stabilizers help to dampen bow noise, too, and that's a plus with most any hunting bow.

Balance is another matter. Ideally, a bow should remain in the upright position or tip forward at the moment of release. If your bow already does this, and many do, a stabilizer is not really necessary. On the other hand, bows with deflexed risers — where the limb pockets lie behind the handle — usually tip backward sharply when shot. A stabilizer can solve that problem in a heartbeat.

Finally, by serving as a shock absorber, a stabilizer not only mutes bow noise, but it also can reduce hand shock and absorbs vibrations that eventually may damage a compound's limbs or handle. Compounds with speed cams often benefit from a stabilizer.

Bow Noise Dampeners

Some of the newest and best noise dampening products to burst on the bowhunting scene in recent years are the energy-absorbing devices offered by Sims Vibration Laboratory. These unique, simple products reduce bow noise and vibration — and are worth a close look by serious bowhunters. They're on all of my own hunting bows.

Made of rubber-like material called NAVCOM, these accessories reduce high frequency sound by up to 30 decibels. They also provide better bow stability shot after shot, and help prevent the wear and tear on bow parts that repeated shooting can cause.

LimbSavers attach directly to any bow's upper and lower limb (and there is a model for split-limb bows, too). In addition, Sims makes an adjustable modular stabilizer system, stabilizer enhancers designed to reduce noise up to 50 percent, and a cable dampener

Here's the author's hunting setup. His Mathews compound is equipped with sights, stabilizer, bow quiver, wrist sling, plus noise-dampening LimbSavers and string silencers.

device that fits onto any compound's cable-guard system. There are Mini LimbSavers which attach to sights and bow-mounted quivers — even stickbows — to help kill vibration and noise, and even bowstring silencers called Leeches.

Other companies have followed Sims' lead and now offer similar noise dampening products. I urge you to check out and use one or more of these practical, inexpensive vibration and noise-killing products.

Peep Sights and Other String Accessories

Having already mentioned bowstring silencers, it's natural to proceed to a brief review of string accessories. We begin with string peeps, which serve as a rear sight and complement any bowsight setup.

There's no doubt that peeps will promote good eye-to-pin alignment with any target, be they flesh, foam, or paper. Instead of looking past the string at a sight bead, you look directly through the bowstring and pick up the sight tip before bringing it to rest on your target. Many sight shooters I know claim that using a string peep will improve accuracy, and I would agree based on my own experience with peeps.

If the peep sight is properly mounted to perfectly align with your eye — and if it does not move up or down the string by even a fraction of an inch — it can improve shooting consistency and accuracy. Unnoticed slippage once cost me a big whitetail and taught me to always make sure the peep cannot move. Other nightmare stories abound involving shots missed or lost because of peep problems. "It

was too dark...the peep didn't rotate like it should...there was a drop of rain (or snowflake) blocking the hole." This list of excuses goes on and on.

Time was when I avoided peeps due largely to numerous horror stories I'd heard. I now use them more times than not because they do help me focus on the exact spot where I want my arrow to hit. I'd encourage you to try them for yourself — and decide for yourself. Some people love 'em and others detest 'em. If you do opt to add a peep to your bowstring, look over the various types: free-floating, self-aligning, and horizontal peeps. I'd recommend the hole be at least 1/8-inch. Mine are 1/4-inch.

Kisser buttons, plastic or rubber devices which fit the string and touch the corner of your mouth when you draw the bow, are intended to guarantee a consistent anchor point shot after shot. Although some bowhunters swear by them, I don't believe they're necessary and I never bother. Try them if you like.

As far as I'm concerned, both nocking points and string silencers are far more important than peeps or kissers. Silencers reduce game-alerting bowstring twang. I prefer the rubber noise dampeners commonly called "cat whiskers" or "spider-legs," although some of my hunting bows have silencers made out of yarn and thin strips of beaver pelt. The only problem I've had with the yarn or fur occurs on wet days when releasing an arrow results in a sudden faceful of water spray. I generally place two silencers on each bowstring, one near the top and another toward the bottom. These devices are very inexpensive and easy to install.

Nocking points are critical to shooting success. I prefer the metal clamp-on nock sets and often wrap string serving or dental floss around the bowstring to prevent any slippage. When I use a release, I often place a rubber O-ring or eliminator button below the nock set to act as a cushion between release aid and arrow nock. This prevents an arrow from falling off the string after the bow is drawn but let down without an arrow being released.

Another way to ensure that upward pressure from a release doesn't inadvertently push the arrow nock loose is to use a rope loop or or a commercially made metal string loop in place of a nocking point. Your release clips directly onto the loop, not the string, eliminating several problems including string wear and dropped arrows. Another plus already mentioned but worth repeating is the fact it places the release directly behind the shaft, pushing the arrow straight ahead and helping create good broadhead flight.

Purely optional accelerator balls or "speed balls" fit on the string and are plugged by advocates who say they help silence and speed up a bow at the same time. Generally, I've found that most bowstring attachments will slow arrow speed by a few feet per second. If you want to know the truth, buy or borrow a chronograph and check it for yourself.

Arrow Rests

While many common arrow rests have remained basically unchanged for decades, certain 21st century technological advancements are worth noting. For example, the Whisker Biscuit from Carolina Archery Products has gained favor with some serious bowhunters in recent years. Its original design was circular with synthetic fibers completely encircling either a carbon or aluminum shaft, cradling it in place for perfect arrow alignment shot after shot. This original design now has been improved with tapered entry slots for faster loading and minimal fletching friction.

Some savvy bowhunters eliminate bowstring twang simply by attaching short pieces of yarn. When the bow is repeatedly shot, a "puff ball" appears and quiets any hunting bow.

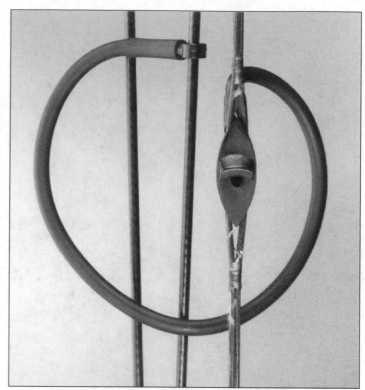

Self-aligning string peeps like this Fine-Line model act as a rear sight for bowsight users by providing good eye-to-pin alignment. If a peep is used for bowhunting, the hole should be large enough to allow easy viewing of the target.

G. Fred Asbell, like a majority of traditional archers, disdains the use of sights and a stabilizer. He does favor a bow quiver and often uses string silencers.

The Whisper Disc from Golden Key Futura is similar to the Whisker Biscuit but utilizes foam instead of bristles within its circular disk. Another recent technological improvement is represented by Golden Key's Power Drop arrow rest. This model is only one example of the new fall-away rests that have become the rage in recent seasons. Such innovative rests fall away upon release, providing unobstructed fletching clearance as the arrow leaves the bow. Some models utilize cords, tubing, and springs which "cock" the rest as the arrow is drawn into shooting position. Others simply stay in position and fall away as the shot is made. Look for other tackle improvements in the near future.

Final Thoughts

Obviously, there are many other bowhunting add-ons you may want to examine and consider. Overdraws are still popular with some bowhunters who like to shoot short, lightweight arrows in order to get even more speed from their compounds. Although I don't like 'em and won't use 'em, you should collect the facts, try them or examine them for yourself, and decide what's best for you.

Targets are a good investment, too. Burlap bags, foam blocks, and lifelike 3-D animal targets (often with replaceable cores for the vitals) can be easily handled and set up anywhere it's safe to shoot. Some are made for practice points only and others for broadheads. Other targets handle both types of heads. Regular practice keeps shooting skills sharp, so it's good to invest in one or more targets.

Bow carriers — both hard and soft protective cases — are certainly a worthwhile investment, too. Ditto for a good fanny pack or daypack. And don't forget a skinning knife, either. Finally, how about a tackle box for such items as a bow square, nock pliers, string

Laser rangefinders have become a regular part of many sight-shooters' gear. These compact devices give instant — and accurate — distances to any game animal or target.

Portable targets make practice possible almost anywhere. Some are designed only for practice points while others handle both field points and broadheads.

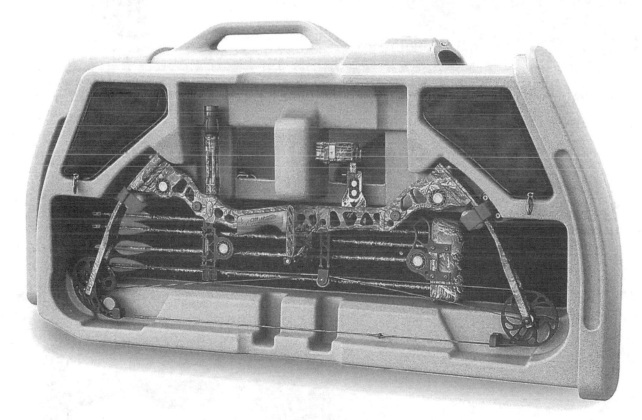

Hard bow/arrow cases are ideal for the traveling bowhunter. And in some hunting areas bows must be cased while in any motor vehicle. These cases are a good investment and help protect gear during transport.

wax, broadhead wrench, head-puller, and other handy items? Of course, if you enjoy tinkering, there's always a need for a bow press, arrow straightener, fletching jig, and...well, you get the idea. This list, like that pesky Energizer bunny of TV commercial fame, just keeps going and going and going. Better get your personal wish list started. Today!

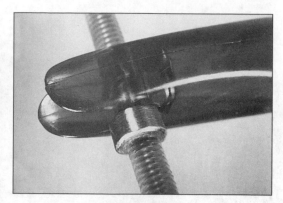

A nocking point must be placed at the proper position on every bowstring.

The Sims LimbSavers are made of rubber-like material and are attached to the bow limbs to help reduce noise. They work well and are widely popular with many modern bowbenders.

The Quick Shot Whisker Biscuit is yet another arrow rest gaining widespread favor with bowhunters. This slotted model prevents shafts falling off the rest and allows shooters to load their arrows quickly.

Drop-away arrow rests like this one from Golden Key-Futura have become popular in recent years. Contact with the shaft is maintained while a bow is drawn; however, upon release these rests fall out of the way of the arrow's fletching. This provides a cleaner release and truer arrow flight, advocates claim.

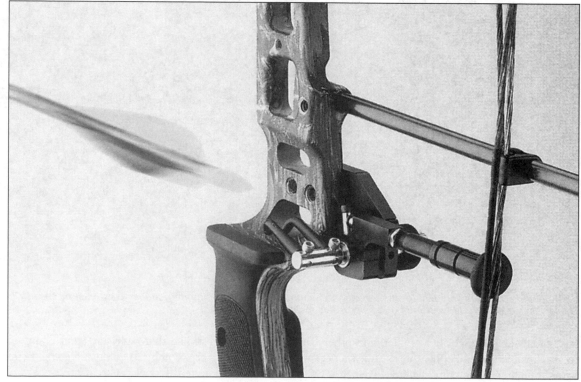

Chapter 6
Hunting Strategy: Making the Shot Happen

A NORTHWESTERLY WIND gusting across the freshly picked Illinois cornfield bore a mid-November bite. My nose was leaking like a kitchen faucet as I squinted into the teeth of the icy breeze and hunkered deeper within my warm camo, scanning the edge of the field for telltale movement. During the past 45 minutes I'd already seen two distant bucks bird-dogging meandering does, but at this moment nothing was moving except the rattling cornhusks and rustling oak leaves.

Most any bowhunter would be pleased to put this big whitetail on the ground. But how a hunter handles pressure makes the difference between success and failure afield. For consistent success, you must make the most of each chance you get.

It was early afternoon, cold and overcast. I was huddled 20 feet up in an oak tree, just inside a long finger of mature timber that overlooked the picked field and a wooded, brushy ravine. Within easy bow range two good deer trails opened into the cornfield. A fresh rub glistened whitely on a sapling beneath my stand; I also could see a newly pawed scrape under a drooping oak limb off to my right. This was a great-looking spot, and with the pre-rut finally kicking into high gear, I calculated that with luck and patience I'd soon get my chance to draw on a good buck.

Forty long years had passed since I first matched wits with Illinois whitetails. Deer were as rare as grizzly bears in Wabash County back then (the state's entire deer herd was guesstimated at maybe 30,000 animals). So when the 1962 deer season rolled around, a friend and I had headed south to Pope County's Shawnee National Forest. It was an unforgettable hunt.

On the very first morning I'd watched a buck make his way up a hardwood rise. At the time I was crouched beside a faint game trail that threaded among the white oaks and shagbark hickories, finally disappearing into a sandstone cleft in the high ridge behind me. I remember gripping my Pearson recurve and trembling, my pulse hammering like a pileated woodpecker drumming on a hollow snag.

By some miracle the approaching eight-pointer didn't see me. When he stepped behind a thick-trunked oak, I began my draw. Unexpectedly, the deer stopped less than 20 yards away. Only the tip of his glistening nostrils showed, and I could see his black nose sorting out the morning scents. My heart plummeted with the sudden realization that the friendly cross-slope breeze was now touching the back of my neck.

Whoosh! I jumped at his explosive alarm snort and watched the buck whirl and bounce gracefully downhill, his snowy tail waving goodbye. That memorable encounter sparked a passion that still burns brightly after so many intervening deer seasons.

Refocusing my attention on the empty cornfield, I was shocked to see a buck nosing along the corn rows maybe 60 yards away. Fumbling for my binoculars, I could tell at first glance that his wide rack was far more impressive than any I'd seen during the past week. Where this buck had come from was anyone's guess. More important, he was there — and slowly angling my way.

A flash of movement to my right tore my admiring gaze from the big whitetail. A doe was moving past the scrape at the field's edge and entering the timber on a trail that led directly under my stand. She already was less than 20 yards away. And when I glanced back toward the buck, he was trotting toward me, neck extended, grunting as he came.

Promptly forgetting my binocs, I reached for my bow instead. As the doe moved under my tree, the buck was already cutting into the timber on a second trail just over 15 yards away. Horsing my bow to full draw, I focused on a broad shooting lane just as the buck entered the opening. Hurriedly locking my top pin on his moving shoulder, I voice-grunted in hopes of stopping him. No such luck. His total attention was on the doe. And in another few steps he'd be screened by brush.

There was a *crack!* and puff of drifting hair as my arrow blew through his chest. The buck instantly veered to his right and crashed headlong through a tangle of briars...

If I've learned nothing else over the four decades between those two long-ago whitetail shooting opportunities in the Land of Lincoln — with one buck escaping untouched and the other piling up less than 150 yards from my stand — it's this: in bowhunting there's precious little time or margin for error in most close-range encounter with deer and other big game animals. In short, when you recognize any good chance for success, you must take it — or fail.

Experience and talent help, of course, but there's more to it, something natural, instinctive. Years of hunting and hundreds of thousands of practice shots — including shots at moving targets at point-blank range — have built my confidence to the point I can perform in any pressure-packed bowhunting situation. Does that mean I never fail or miss a shot? Of course not. But it does mean that more often than not I can make the shot happen — and that's an ability shared by every successful bowhunter I've ever met.

I like to say that I go on autopilot when I find myself under pressure. All the practice shots I've taken have made shooting a bow a subconscious act. I do not have to even think about drawing, holding, aiming, releasing, and following through. It just happens. One moment I'm wholly focused on the animal, waiting and watching for the opening I need. Suddenly my arrow is on its way. And I can't begin to tell you the times I've been surprised — shocked, really — to see my colorful fletching appear against an animal's side. I'd somehow made the shot — subconsciously, automatically. That should be your goal, too. G. Fred Asbell sums it up this way:

"Bowhunting requires shooting without thought; a draw, anchor, and release that is automatic. Not necessarily a speedy movement — it might be slow and deliberate. But there is no room for conscious fundamentals when shooting at game. Your complete concentration is on the animal and everything else should be habit.

"The bowhunter must form and practice positive shooting habits," G. Fred maintains. These habits need to be simple enough so when confronted by game the shot is made without being conscious of the shooting mechanics. Howard Hill, whose shooting feats have never been duplicated, was a stickler on form — he preached it constantly. But he kept it simple, too. There was a simple draw and positive anchor with each shot. Nothing more, nothing less. But when he shot coins out of the air, it was total

Dave Holt knows how to handle pressure-packed confrontations with trophy bucks. He regularly tags record-book whitetails like this fine example.

concentration on the coin; the draw, anchor, and release were automatic."

Newcomers, who are far more concerned about hitting a life-size deer target than dimes tossed in the air, may pick up a bow believing that such total concentration on a target will never happen. They'll always, it seems, need to think about drawing and releasing an arrow. But just as they once learned to field and throw a baseball as a droopy-drawered Little League youngster, they did learn — and over time they either improved to the point that fielding and throwing the baseball became automatic or they ultimately gave up the sport. Bow-shooting is no different.

Dwight Schuh recalls stalking and killing his very first buck in southeastern Oregon some 30 years ago. His description of the shot — and his feelings afterward — perfectly illustrate what I'm talking about:

"He started feeding again. In painfully slow motion, I drew, found the anchor, and thought about aiming. But somehow, the arrow was invisible and the deer was only a blur, and I was wondering when the deer would spook, but he continued to feed, and then the arrow was gone.

"And then the bow was down, and I saw the buck charging away uphill. No arrow. Had I missed? The buck turned and sprinted downhill, and then I saw it. In the middle of his chest, on the opposite side, was a huge splotch of blood. The buck ran full speed, maybe 75 yards, then as if his back legs were going too fast they ran out from under him and he crashed over backwards. I stood frozen for many minutes, watching the deer, watching for movement, but

(Above and below) There's a world of difference between shooting at targets and the real thing. Live bucks have a way of making some hunters forget everything they know about shooting a bow.

Good bowhunters practice until shooting a bow becomes automatic, something done without conscious thought or effort. In hunting, your complete focus should be on the animal and where you want your arrow to hit.

there was no movement. The deer was dead!"

Kneeling beside his first deer moments later, Dwight remembered the months of shooting practice.

"I started in April and shot nearly every day until August. In addition, I hunted small game such as ground squirrels and marmots, since shooting at live animals is different from shooting paper targets. After a few months of this, it felt great to know it was more than luck when the arrow went where I wanted it.

"I was no Howard Hill, but my confidence had increased immeasurably. Not only had I learned to place my arrows, but shooting had become automatic, so that when I drew on that first buck — even though the deer, the bow, the arrow all practically disappeared in the excitement — everything worked! Shooting had become such an automatic process that I diidn't have to think about it."

Veterans who already know how to shoot understand exactly what Dwight meant — and what I'm saying. They already possess the shooting basics and want only to zero-in on the aspects of shooting at game that will result in consistent success. For my money, and that of many top bowhunters, there's nothing like stump shooting and small game hunting to prepare you for the real thing. As G. Fred Asbell notes:

"Stump shooting can be done almost anywhere. An open field, a nearby woods, a drainage ditch, anywhere you won't be shooting at the same target over and over. Usually you only get a single shot at an animal while hunting, so practice making the first shot count. Practice to such a degree than you only shoot one arrow at any target.

"A target is anything that pleases your imagination. A leaf, a clump of weeds, a discarded beer can (carry it out of the woods after you've finished perforating it!), merely a shadow will do. But you should change it with each shot; vary the distance each time.

"Try all types of unorthodox shots. Shoot under low-hanging branches and through holes in brush. You'll learn where you can and can't shoot — how an arrow acts when it leaves your bow.

"Kneeling is different from standing to shoot. I do a lot of still-hunting and most of my shots are from my knees. I think the same is true with other bowhunters, but you don't see many people practicing that way. Assess your hunting needs. Think about the kind of hunting you do and practice accordingly.

"Are your shots mostly from elevated stands? Do you stalk game? Maybe you do a lot of both. Practice what you need. Forget the 50-yard shots if you're whitetail hunting in heavy bottomland timber. Learn to hit exactly where you aim, up to 30 yards or so, out of a tree stand."

Long-Range Shooting

Some folks advocate long-range practice, citing the effectiveness of modern bowhunting tackle and the shooting opportunities that exist beyond 40 yards. In part, I agree with the benefits gained by honing your long-range shooting ability. Most notably, you can develop sufficient shooting skills and confidence that shots taken at typical bowhunting yardages — 10 to 40 yards — will seem almost easy by comparison. And there may be times when a follow-up shot at wounded game is necessary if you can't get close and want to end it quickly. Those are legitimate reasons for long-range practice sessions. But I strongly disagree with those unthinking few who routinely practice long-range arrow-lobbing at game animals.

One top bowhunter I know advocates long-range target practice, but then cautions against taking such shot at live game unless the shooter is "fully capable" of hitting the animal every time. Frankly, that's a cop-out. Show me any beginner capable of hitting the eight-inch kill area of a 3-D target at 60 yards or more and I'll show

you someone who likely believes he can do the exact same thing when shooting at a real buck or bull. And perhaps he can, but no one — including the best bow shots on earth — knows with certainty he can hit what he's aiming at every time.

I've said it before but it's worth repeating: Hitting the animal is not your goal; hitting the animal in an exact spot that will result in a quick, humane death should be your only goal. More than a bowhunting goal, it's an obligation. Animals can and do move, often when you least expect it. A perfectly aimed arrow released from the fastest bow still isn't fast enough to travel 50 to 60 yards — and center both lungs — before a browsing deer takes a single step or two. And when you're shooting long-range at an eight-inch kill area, you don't have much margin for error. An arrow that misses the chest cavity by mere inches can result in a wounded, unrecovered animal — and other black mark against bowhunting.

Distance also magnifies your mistakes. Most shots at targets are static, made under mostly ideal conditions without the need for

M. R. James took this Idaho bruin several decades ago. When his chance for a good shot came, he took it. The black bear was dead within seconds after the broadhead struck.

G. Fred Asbell notes you'll likely only get one chance at an animal — so you need to make your first shot count. Fred tagged this Indiana whitetail in 1975.

When the author shoots at game, he never thinks about missing. Ever! His full focus is on releasing the perfect arrow. With experience, the rest takes care of itself.

If you want your next deer hunt to end with you and a buddy dragging a big buck out of the woods, you must learn to ignore the deer's headgear. Pick an exact spot and make the shot.

haste. With animals, there's usually the pulse-drumming excitement of the moment combined with the uncertainty of what's going to happen next — often compounded by the problem of not knowing the exact distance. All this adds up to the pressured bowhunter facing an entirely different situation from that of someone calmly taking long-range practice shots. This is exactly why I'm not impressed by people bragging about making long shots on game. I know that generally more luck than skill was involved in putting their animals on the ground.

One field study by the late Dr. Robert Jackson of the University of Wisconsin-LaCrosse, found that experienced bowhunters hit and lost more animals than hunting newcomers. A bowhunter himself, Bob Jackson told me he believed the veteran hunters took longer shots because they thought they could hit the animal — and all too often they did, just not where they intended. On the other hand, beginning hunters either missed entirely or failed to take the shot because they lacked confidence. Confidence is good, but overconfidence can cause problems. My advice to any bowhunter is to think twice before taking those extra-long shots at game. Again, it's not the same thing as shooting at stationary targets. Not the same thing at all. The animals we hunt deserve better.

So exactly what bowhunting ranges are most common for the continent's big game species? Let's take a brief look at some recent findings compiled and reported by the Pope and Young Club, keepers of North American bowhunting records. These averages, gleaned from information collected over the years from thousands of successful bowhunters, represent only trophy-class animals. It's likely, however, they also reflect a nationwide norm for each species listed.

- **Whitetail Deer** — Nearly 80 percent of the trophy bucks are killed from hunters in elevated stands. Three-fourths are tagged at less than 30 yards, with the majority of trophies arrowed between 10 and 19 yards.
- **Mule Deer** — About six of every 10 big muley bucks are tagged by stalking, with another 20 percent taken by still-hunting. Almost 75 percent are shot at less than 40 yards, with nearly one-third of these killed at distances of between 30 and 40 yards.
- **Other Deer** — Many Columbia blacktails — perhaps 30 percent — are shot between 30 and 40 yards, with the vast majority of bucks arrowed well under 40 yards. The average shot on Sitka blacktails is even closer with most bucks taken between 20 and 30 yards. Most Coues whitetails are arrowed between 10 and 20 yards, with all but a mere handful killed at ranges under 40 yards. Stalking is the most popular means of taking each species.
- **Pronghorn Antelope** — About half of the trophy bucks are shot from ground blinds, with one-third taken by stalking. Over half are killed at less than 39 yards, with one in four bucks shot at 20 to 30 yards.
- **Elk** — Stalking is the most common hunting means, with calling second, accounting for nearly 70 percent of the bulls taken. Some 70 percent are shot at under 40 yards with most — nearly one-third of the trophy bulls — killed between 20 and 30 yards.

Half of the black bears killed by bowhunters are arrowed at less than 20 yards. The author shot this Saskatchewan giant at 12 yards.

- **Black Bears** — Some 70 percent of the big bruins are shot over bait, with over half of these arrowed at less than 20 yards. Less than 10 percent of the bruins are taken with shots of 30 yards or more.
- **Other Bears** — Most Alaska brown bears and grizzlies are taken while stalking, and most are shot at less than 40 yards; a majority of kills occurs between 20 and 29 yards. Most grizzlies are killed standing 10 to 19 yards or 30 to 39 yards away. Polar bears, usually stalked or bayed by sled dogs, are commonly shot at ranges of between 30 and 40 yards.
- **Caribou** — Perhaps half of the record book bulls are taken with shots between 20 and 40 yards, with another 20 percent killed at less than 20 yards.
- **Cougar** — Nine of every 10 record-book lions are shot with the help of hounds. Over half of the shots are under 20 yards with another 30 to 40 percent taken at ranges between 20 and 30 yards.
- **Moose** — Stalking accounts for over half of the trophy-class bulls, with calling and still-hunting a distant second and third, respectively. About 70 percent of the bulls are shot at under 40 yards, with most moose killed while standing 30 to 40 yards away.
- **Sheep and Goats** — Eighty percent are shot while stalking, with well over half tagged at less than 40 yards. In fact, one in four mountain goats is killed at under 20 yards.
- **Bison and Musk-Ox** — Stalking is the primary hunting method, with most bulls of each species shot at distances between 30 and 39 yards — and only rarely are bulls killed with shots more than 40 to 50 yards.

Such statistics dramatically illustrate the fact most top North American big game trophies are arrowed at typical bowhunting distances of 40 yards or less. That's certainly well under the 50- to 60-plus ranges a handful of people cite as "reasonable" bow shots.

Again, this is not to say that animals can't be killed at longer ranges. An arrow can kill an animal standing 350 yards away, if that's how far your hunting bow can lob an arrow off some mountainside. Of course, for that to happen your sharp broadhead would have to find the critter's vitals — which is necessary no matter what

Jan Perry, California's "Lady Bowhunter," stands barely 5 feet tall, but has arrowed everything from bison, blacktails, and black bears to this hefty gobbler. She knows total concentration on the target pays off for any hunter.

Getting close to big game animals isn't easy at ground level. Most whitetails are tagged by hunters in elevated stands — at distances of less than 20 yards.

the distance of your shot. Alas, there's the rub with long-range arrow-flinging. Even though modern bows with matched arrows are capable of pinpoint accuracy at amazing distances — when shot from machines under ideal conditions — its a fact that men aren't machines and most hunting situations aren't ideal. Remember that the next time you're tempted to lob an arrow at some unsuspecting animal standing halfway to the next county. You might accidentally kill it — but chances are far greater you'll miss or wound it. That's true no matter how well you can perforate paper or foam targets.

Final Considerations

Years ago many "bowhunters" didn't spend a great deal of time shooting in the off-season. With the approach of another deer season they'd dig out and dust off their tackle and practice by flinging arrows at some backyard target. Come opening day, they'd head for the deer woods, ready or not — with largely predictable results.

Serious bowhunters have always spent a lot of time shooting their bows, and today a majority of bowhunters I know shoot their bows year-round. Besides hunting small game, varmints, and rough-

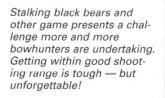

Stalking black bears and other game presents a challenge more and more bowhunters are undertaking. Getting within good shooting range is tough — but unforgettable!

fish, there are 3-D shoots and indoor/outdoor leagues, weekend archery tournaments and jamborees, interactive video practice systems — a virtual plethora of bow-shooting possibilities designed to keep your shooting eye keen and your shooting skills sharp when you're not hunting.

Actually, no modern bowhunter worthy of the name ever tries to hone his bow-shooting a few short days or weeks before hunting season rolls around. It's totally irresponsible to head afield without complete physical and mental preparation — and that ain't going to happen overnight! Take whatever time is necessary. Don't rush things, ever. You — and certainly the game animals you hunt — will be far better off for doing things right. And that means a complete, proper, and patient approach.

Practice should be fun, beneficial, not a jaw-clenching endurance test that leaves you worn out and frustrated. If you're like most of us, you'll probably be tempted to overdo practice sessions a bit as hunting season draws near. Don't. Too much practice can be as bad as too little. What sometimes happens when you push yourself too hard is you get tired and fall into bad shooting habits. This can quickly wreck your shooting ability and destroy your confidence. Quite often the harder you work at solving the problem, the worse things become.

Keep in mind it's perfectly normal to have good and bad practice sessions. I know, for example, that one day all my arrows seem to be laser-guided missiles that fly unerringly to the target. The next day those very same arrows seem to have a mind of their own, resisting my best efforts to control them. It happens. And when it does, accept it. Don't fight it. Personally, when I'm shooting well

(Above) Minnesota bowhunter Rob Evans took this whopper whitetail not far from his home. The 160-inch buck easily made the Pope and Young records. (Below) M. R. James has been an official measurer since 1978. He's being assisted in the process by Dr. Dave Samuel and the successful bowhunter. Trophy-class game animals of each species may qualify for record book entry if they exceed established minimums. Whitetails must score at least 125 inches.

I like to keep my eye sharp and my muscles tuned with light practice sessions. I'll often stump-shoot no more than a dozen or so arrows each day — or maybe every other day. Often I do a lot more walking than shooting, taking plenty of time between shots and never releasing more than one arrow from the same spot or same shooting position. I also fight the urge to do too much shooting as the time for my hunt draws near. And the instant I find myself falling into some shooting slump — and slumps happen to everyone — I simply hang up my bow for a day or two and don't even think

about practicing. I've discovered that by the time I pick up my bow again, I'm usually back in the shooting groove just as if there'd never been a problem. Try it for yourself sometime. It sure works for me.

Finally, I can almost guarantee that with time and experience you'll eventually realize that the moment has come when you can focus fully on an animal and take the shot without any conscious effort or thought. And believe me, that magic bowhunting moment is worth waiting and working for.

Chapter 7
Advanced Performance Tuning

STICKBOW OR COMPOUND? Diehard traditionalist or futurist? Whatever hunting bow you choose and how you feel about bowhunting tackle, you should realize that all bowhunters and their tackle share one thing in common: *A properly tuned hunting bow makes our tackle — and us — better.* Tuning, in truth, is the only way we can get the top performance from our selfbow, recurve, longbow, or compound.

Why? Only well-tuned bows provide consistently good arrow flight to complement our shooting skills. Good arrow flight, in turn, spells improved accuracy and better penetration — admirable and desirable goals for all serious bowhunters. So whether you tune it yourself or rely on the know-how of your favorite archery dealer, make sure your hunting bow has been tested and properly adjusted before you carry it afield in search of game.

Time was, before the advent of the compound, most fine-tuning was done by target archers whose need for pinpoint accuracy during tourney competition is critical for high scores. Many bowhunters simply yanked back and turned loose, because in those days, frankly, far too many folks gave little thought to how their bows performed. As long as they could be drawn and shot without arrows wobbling on the way to a target, that was good enough. Besides, way back in B.C. (Before Compounds), when all hunters were carrying stickbows, so-called "tuning" was fairly simple. It mainly consisted of establishing a nocking point, checking and adjusting the bow's brace height by twisting the string, and finally making sure the arrows were matched to the bow and shooter. Simple, huh?

But times, equipment, and attitudes have changed drastically since the mid-1960s. Not only do modern compounds require more pre-hunt attention to detail, today's bowhunters are typically a more hands-on, equipment-savvy group. They're also more demanding

Stickbow or modern compound, it makes no difference. Each will do the job for the modern bowhunter. But any bow needs to be properly tuned before being used.

Any hunter shopping around for a new bow will find no shortage of makes and models. Whatever a person's individual choice, it's critical the arrows fly straight and true. Tuning is the basis for proper field performance.

61

than ever before, wanting peak performance from their tackle. They realize the importance of straight-flying arrows where one shot can make or break a hunt — or in some cases the entire season.

So no matter your choice of a modern hunting bow, you need to know that tuning is generally a three-step process that's not really complicated (but can be challenging to some folks whose mechanical prowess is limited to uncapping a beer bottle and manning the television remote). Such people are better off seeking assistance from a pro shop employee or a knowledgeable hunting buddy. For others, it's a routine matter to set up any new bow, shoot it, make the necessary adjustments, re-shoot it, and then head for the deer woods with a bow that's in near-perfect tune.

To get started, about the only thing you'll need is the same tackle you'll be hunting with later. Your attention will focus mainly on the bow, string, arrows, and arrow rest. However, if you'll be shooting with sights and a mechanical release, you should tune your bow with these common add-ons already in place. Using the same anchor point for tuning and hunting is only common sense. If you change your shooting style or any gear — such as an arrow rest or shaft size — before opening day rolls around, you will have to tinker with the bow some more before you go hunting. It's critical to know that your arrows are flying straight and true. When that big buck steps out of the shadows, there's little margin for error.

Even after you've got your hunting bow in proper tune and it's delivering your arrows right where you're aiming, you'll still want to periodically check the tuning and make necessary adjustments. Once your bow is set up, it won't take much time and is well worth the bother. Briefly, here's what you need and what you need to do.

Stickbow Tuning

There are three areas of concern when tuning a stickbow — the brace height, the nocking point, and your arrows.

"Probably the first and most important item to consider on a recurve or longbow is the brace height, or fistmele," says G. Fred Asbell. "This is the distance in inches from the string to the bow when the bow is strung."

Since brace height affects arrow flight, arrow speed, bow noise, and bow stability, its importance is obvious. So your first step in tuning should be to set the brace height according to the manufacturer's recommendation, typically six to seven inches.

You can adjust your bow's brace height by using a longer or shorter string. Another easy option that achieves the same result is twisting or untwisting the string. You do this to eliminate poor arrow flight, bow noise, and excessive vibration (often caused by low brace height). Fred offers this advice:

"Personally, I start by bracing any bow as low as I can, low enough so that I am getting bad arrow flight and noise. Then, I twist up the string until everything clears up. For me, that's often where I get the best performance from my bow.

"If you don't want to mess around with all the adjusting and experimenting, twist the string to obtain maximum bracing. A higher brace height will often make your bow quieter and automatically eliminate most arrow flight problems. But expect your bow to pull harder and probably shoot slower.

"You will also probably get more speed from your bow at the lower brace height. How? Simply stated, the brace height of your bow determines how long the string 'stays with' or keeps pushing

A paper tuning rack is commonly used to check in-flight arrow straightness. Some shooters consider perfect arrow flight to be more critical downrange than immediately after leaving the bow.

your arrow. The lower your brace height, the longer the string stays with your arrow. I feel this is very desirable with heavy hunting arrows."

The next step in stickbow tuning is finding the proper nocking point. This is a critical but simple procedure that guarantees your arrow will be positioned in exactly the same place on the string with each shot you take. The result will be consistent arrow flight.

If you have a T-square or bow-square handy, begin by placing a temporary nock locator on the bowstring — a piece of tape works well — between 1/8- or even 1/2-inch above a direct line from your arrow rest or shelf to the string. Despite what some people claim, there is no one correct height to locate a nocking point. You must shoot arrows to find where they fly best from your stickbow. It well may be at the 1/8-inch mark — but it could be 1/4- or even 1/2-inch up the string. Go too high and you'll see your arrows flop or porpoise. Drop back a bit until they're flying straight and true. Then clamp a permanent nocking point in place on the string. Properly matched hunting arrows — whether wood, aluminum, or carbon — should fly well without additional supplements.

Speaking of hunting arrows, matching shafts to your bow and draw length is the final stickbow tuning consideration. Check a shaft selection chart or visit your nearest archery shop for assistance, if needed. Finding shafts for center-shot recurves is usually a snap. Matching arrows to longbows, however, is sometimes trickier. The reason? Since longbows aren't center-shot, they require perfectly spined shafts that bend around the bow's handle on release, then recover to fly true to the target. Arrow straightness is an absolute must. While uniformity and straightness are rarely a problem with carbon or metal shafts, longbow shooters who favor wood need to pay special attention to finding and using wooden shafts that will give them wobble-free flight. Excellent wood arrows are available; finding them is not always easy.

Lastly, it's been said before, but it's worth repeating: If you shoot a stickbow off the shelf, you must use feather fletching. Vanes simply do not work. And G. Fred Asbell adds one final bit of advice for

TUNING COMPOUND & RECURVE BOWS

The first phase of tuning is to make preliminary adjustments to your equipment, nocking point and in/out position of the arrow, to correct the three most common arrow flight problems: Porpoising—vertical wobble, Fishtailing—horizontal wobble, and Clearance. NOTE: Install all accessories on your bow before tuning. Change only one variable at a time when tuning.

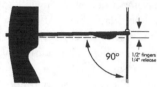

To begin, install a movable nocking point on the bowstring. (Clamp-on types are ideal.) Initially position the nocking point on the bowstring about 1/2" (1.3 cm) above square (fingers) or 1/4" (0.63 cm) (release). **Porpoising is caused by incorrect nocking point location and should be corrected first.**

Arrow Centering—Adjust the horizontal (in/out) position of the cushion plunger or arrow rest assembly so that the tip (center) of the arrow point is correctly aligned for your type of equipment.

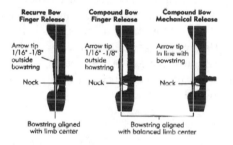

Recurve Bow Finger Release — Arrow tip 1/16"-1/8" outside bowstring. Nock. Bowstring aligned with limb center

Compound Bow Finger Release — Arrow tip 1/16"-1/8" outside bowstring. Nock. Bowstring aligned with balanced limb center

Compound Bow Mechanical Release — Arrow tip In line with bowstring. Nock.

Fishtailing occurs when the arrow leaves the bow with the nock end shifted to one side or the other and can usually be corrected by adjusting the spring tension on the cushion plunger, bow weight (if adjustable) or arrow point weight.

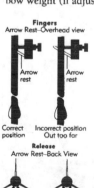

Fingers — Arrow Rest–Overhead view — Arrow rest / Arrow rest — Correct position / Incorrect position Out too far

Release — Arrow Rest–Back View — Correct–Good vane clearance / Incorrect–Poor vane clearance

Arrow rest—Adjust the arrow rest to provide good fletching clearance for your type of equipment. **Good clearance is absolutely essential for optimum grouping, consistency and accuracy.** The arrow and fletching should pass by the bow and arrow rest without making contact.

The Bare Shaft Planing Test can be used to correct Porpoising and Fishtailing, also check for Clearance using the spray powder test described in Easton's Arrow Tuning and Maintenance Guide.

Paper Tuning Arrow Test

The Paper Tuning Arrow Test is a good basic bow tuning method for all three types of shooting styles—Recurve with finger release (RF), Compound with finger release (CF) and Compound with release aid (CR).

- Firmly attach a sheet of paper to a frame type rack approximately 24" x 24" (60 x 60cm).
- Position the center of the paper about shoulder height with a target mat about six feet (1.5m) behind the paper to stop the arrows.
- Stand approximately six feet (1.8m) from the paper.
- Shoot a fletched arrow through the center of the paper with the arrow at shoulder height.
- Observe how the paper is torn.

 A. Tear A indicates good arrow flight. The point and fletching enter the same hole.
NOTE: Try the following instructions in order, one at a time.

B. Tear B indicates a low nocking point. To correct, raise the nocking point 1/16" (1.6mm) at a time and repeat the procedure until the low vertical tear is eliminated.

 C. Tear C indicates a high nocking point, Clearance problem or (for release aid) a mismatched arrow spine. To correct, lower the nocking point 1/16" (1.6mm) at a time until the high tear is eliminated. If the problem remains unchanged, the disturbance is probably caused by a lack of Clearance or (for release aid) a mismatched arrow spine. CR only—if no Clearance problem exists try:

1. A more flexible arrow rest blade or reducing downward spring tension on launcher rests.
2. Decreasing or increasing peak bow weight.
3. Reducing the amount the shaft overhangs the contact point on the arrow rest.
4. Using a stiffer arrow shaft.

NOTE: The following instructions are for right-handed archers. Reverse for left-handed archers.

Fingers

 D. Tear D indicates a stiff arrow for RF, CF archers. To correct:
1. Increase peak bow weight.
2. Use a heavier arrow point and/or insert combination.
3. Use a lighter bow string.
4. Use a weaker spined arrow.
5. Decrease cushion plunger tension, or use a weaker spring on "shoot around" rests.
6. CF only—Move the arrow rest to the right in small increments.

 E. Tear E indicates a weak arrow or Clearance problem for RF, CF archers. To correct:
1. Check for Clearance.
2. Decrease peak bow weight.
3. Use a lighter arrow point and/or insert combination.
4. Use a heavier bow string.
5. Use a stiffer spined arrow.
6. Increase cushion plunger tension or use a stiffer spring on "shoot around" rests.
7. CF only—Move the arrow rest to the left in small increments.

Release Aid

 D. Tear D is uncommon for right-handed, CR archers. It generally indicates that the arrow rest position is too far to the right or that there is possible vane contact on the inside of the launcher rest. To correct:
1. Move the arrow rest to the left in small increments.
2. Make sure the arrow has adequate Clearance past the cable guard and cables.
3. Make sure your bow hand is well relaxed to eliminate excessive bow hand torque.

 E. For CR archers, a left or high-left tear is common and indicates a weak arrow or Clearance problem. If a high-left tear exists, make sure you correct the nocking point first before proceeding further.
To correct:
1. Move the arrow rest to the right.
2. Make sure your bow hand is well relaxed to eliminate excessive bow hand torque.
3. Decrease peak bow weight.
4. Choose a stiffer spined arrow.

F. Tear F shows a combination of more than one flight disturbance. Combine the recommended procedures, correcting the vertical pattern (nocking point) first, then the horizontal. If you can't correct the arrow flight problem, have your local pro shop check the "timing" (roll-over) of your eccentric wheels or cams.

- Depending on the type of arrow rest/mechanical release combinations, it may be necessary for archers using release aids to make adjustments opposite from those described above.
- Once you have achieved a good tune at six feet (1.8m), move back six feet more and continue to shoot through the paper. This ensures that the tune is correct.

Knowing how to interpret the tears in a test paper can help you tune your bow to peak performance.

folks wanting good arrow flight out of their longbow or recurve:

"I'd insist on nothing but helical-fletched arrows. To me, a straight-fletched arrow is an abomination. With a broadhead on the end, it is difficult to shoot accurately under ideal conditions; under hunting conditions, they're mostly a joke. You're needlessly penalizing yourself."

There you have it. If you've set your brace height correctly, located the nocking point in the proper place, and are shooting arrows matched to you and your bow, you're ready for some serious shooting practice. Rest assured that the stickbow you're holding will perform to your expectations — and to your shooting potential.

Compound Tuning

As with tuning a stickbow, for most shooters there are three basic areas of concern when it comes to properly tuning a compound: Doing the initial setup, testing arrows with paper, and, lastly, making necessary mechanical adjustments to correct any problems. Admittedly, it's a bit more complicated. But before turning to the step-by-step procedures, let's begin by debunking a few long-held tuning beliefs that might just open a few eyes — including yours.

"Most of us automatically assume that exact tiller adjustments, precise cam synchronization, and other mechanical adjustments guarantee a perfect paper test," says Dave Holt. "And when that coveted bullet hole is achieved, we presume it means everything is perfect and our bow has attained the ultimate in accuracy. I used to think so, too, but today I would say that's not necessarily true."

To make his point, Dave cites the case of world-class archer Terry Ragsdale who in 1978 shot the first perfect score in the history of the Las Vegas indoor tourney. After returning home from his record-setting performance — trophy and prize money in hand — Terry put his perfect-shooting bow to a tuning test and discovered it was leaving a multi-inch tear in the paper. Terry said if he had

known about "the questionable arrow flight" before the Las Vegas shoot, he might have packed up and headed home. More about paper tears and what they mean to accuracy after Dave debunks a few more myths. He begins by asking:

"What is tuning, anyway? I don't know about you, but I have only two major concerns: reasonably good arrow flight and superb accuracy with my broadheads. Another primary consideration is clearance through the rest area. But even this important ingredient is just one of several checkpoints and adjustments all compound bows require during initial setup.

"If you set up a large number of bows, you will find that some are much more difficult to tune than others. And every so often you'll find one that refuses to provide satisfactory arrow flight. Such a bow can appear to have all its adjustments, including limb tiller and cam synchronization, perfect. To say this is a frustrating experience is an understatement. At one time, such encounters always left me searching for answers."

In Dave's search, he made a number of interesting discoveries. For example, in a 1990 technical video from Easton, slow-motion review of arrows leaving the bow proved most bows, including the popular single cam compounds, have a launch cycle that is less than perfectly level.

"Just as we thought the perfect paper tear to be the ultimate measure of a perfectly tuned bow, we also believed that perfect cam synchronization guaranteed a smooth launch. Now it appears that this is not the case. Recently, a few top-notch bow mechanics have found that some bows are more tunable when the cams are intentionally desynchronized. For problem bows, it sometimes helps to put slightly less string (less wrap) on the upper cam. Such an adjustment ensures that the first motion of the nocking point is upward and forward. This upward movement is not nearly as harsh as driving the arrow downward into the rest."

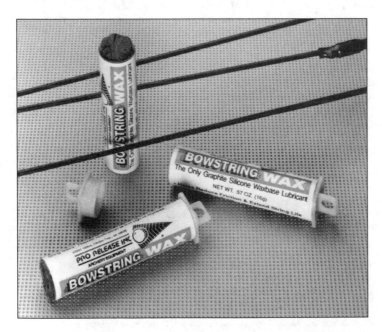

(Above) String wax helps protect and lubricate your bowstring. This wax from Pro-Release comes in an easy-to-apply tube and contains graphite and silicone.

(Right) To eliminate synchronization problems with eccentrics on their high-performance two-cam bows, Golden Eagle created user-friendly Xact Timing. By loosening a screw and rotating the timing device on one wheel or cam, the bow is brought into perfect synch.

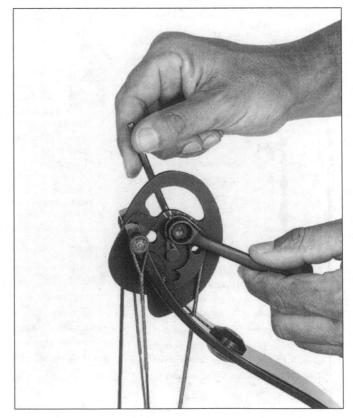

Need to work on your compound bow? You'll likely need a bow press. This self-standing Bracklynn electronic model makes relaxing the limbs of any compound bow as easy as pushing a button. Other bow presses are readily available.

A bow/arrow holder like this Handy-Stand can be useful for practice or tuning sessions.

"In conjunction with this theory, it is now acceptable to have the nocking point travel in a slight arc above the plane of the arrow during the launch cycle. This upward arc is definitely preferable to a nocking point that drops and remains below, or zigzags above and below, the horizontal plane of the arrow during the launch.

"To my knowledge, none of today's bows have a perfectly smooth (level) launch cycle and this includes the single-cam bows. But some bows do have less vertical travel than others. I believe bows that have the slight upward arc to their launch cycle are currently the most tolerant and tunable, although a perfectly level launch should provide the ultimate in bow tuning ability.

"Remember, most of today's well-tuned bows already shoot with extreme accuracy. But as top engineers work out smoother launch cycles, future bows may be even more tunable and tolerant of shooting style and arrow spine."

Dave Holt and a growing number of serious bowhunters no longer insist on a perfect paper tear (bullet hole) through paper at close range. "In fact," Dave notes, "some top shooters prefer a slight high left tear (for right-handed shooters)." Keep that in mind as you set out to tune your own hunting compound. Now here's the step-by-step tuning method recommended by Dave Holt:

1. Consult the arrow manufacturer's shaft selection chart to ensure that you select arrows with the proper spine for your setup.
2. Set the limb tiller at "even" while adjusting the draw weight to your specifications.

A workbench bow vice can hold your bow securely while you install accessories or make necessary adjustments and repairs. This handy device comes from C.W. Erickson's Mfg., Inc.

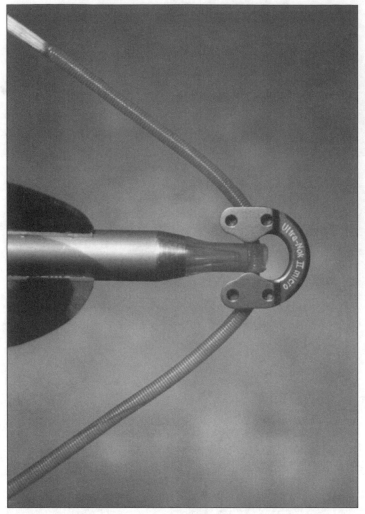

The Ultra-Nok bowstring attachment is designed to reduce serving wear and arrow pinching, while allowing a release to fit directly behind the arrow to increase speed and accuracy.

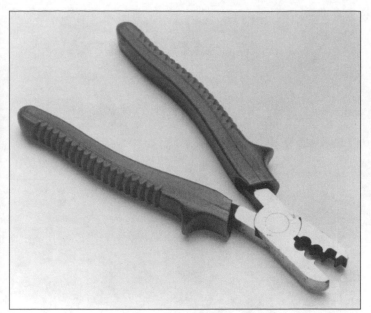

Nocking pliers like these from Game Tracker allow string nocks to be installed or removed without damage to the nock or bowstring. A precise nocking point ensures shooting consistency.

3. Adjust the bow to your exact draw length. Many bowhunters improve their shooting form by shortening their draw length up to one inch.

4. Verify the draw weight and tiller settings from Step 2.

5. Attach the arrow rest according to its instructions and adjust the center shot.

6. Install the nock locator on the string. Start with a setting between level to 1/4-inch high, but be sure to take into consideration the diameter of your arrow shaft. If you shoot with a release, use at least two nock sets to help prevent them from moving.

7. Spray powder (some deodorants work well) on the arrow rest and riser or on the shaft and fletching. Take a test shot and then check for fletch contact. Remember that minor contact from the shaft is inevitable.

8. Fletching contact with the rest can often be reduced by turning the nock slightly in one direction or the other. For this reason, it is best not to glue nocks onto new arrows until after you find out whether this adjustment is necessary.

9. Conduct a paper test from close range. Start by placing the paper three to four yards from the bow. Make sure the arrow completely passes through the paper before striking the back-

stop. Make adjustments to the center shot and nocking point as necessary. A slight high-left (opposite for left-handed shooters) tear of about 1/2- to 1/4-inch, in addition to the shaft and fletching, is acceptable at close range. "I prefer to have a near perfect bullet hole when I shoot through paper from 20 yards and beyond," Dave says.

Troubleshooting Your Compound

Should you experience tuning-related problems, try these 10 troubleshooting tips, making only one adjustment at a time:

1. If you experience a high nock tear, lower the nock locator or use a weaker launcher arm setting. For a low nock tear, do the opposite.

2. For right and left tears, change the center shot and/or adjust the spring tension in the cushion plunger.

3. When dealing with the arrow rest and nock locator, make the first adjustment a minor one. If that doesn't provide the desired result, make the second adjustment more significant. If there is no change after the second adjustment, go back to your original setting and try something else.

4. Reread the rest instructions carefully. The manufacturer may have included helpful hints.

5. By the nature of their anchor, some finger shooters induce an S-type curvature in the bowstring. Without using an arrow, draw the bow and use a mirror or have a friend look for string twist while you are at full draw.

6. If you have severe string twist, consider dropping the top or bottom finger as you reach full draw. Some of the nation's best shooters use this method to improve accuracy. Another option is to try a release aid.

7. Adjust the poundage up and down to see whether either change achieves the desired results.

8. Release shooters should consider using an eliminator button.

9. Consider using feather fletching — it is more forgiving.

10. Experiment with shafts of different spines.

Setting up a hunting bow includes establishing a permanent nocking point. A bow square and a clip-on nock are handy for finding and marking the proper location.

Be aware that low brace height, short axle-to-axle length, radical cams, overdraws, and high arrow speeds make all bows more difficult to tune. You should also remember that an improper hand position on the grip can cause torque and ultimately affect the bow's tune. Your hand position must be in the correct location, and it must be consistent.

Other troubleshooting ideas include looking at wheel synchronization and limb deflection. Checking for these conditions usually requires the assistance of a skilled bow technician.

When your arrow exhibits a near-perfect paper tear for all distances beyond 20 yards, you can make subtle adjustments that may improve your bow's accuracy. But remember, the meaningfulness of an accuracy check is directly related to your ability as a shooter. Your shooting skills must be excellent to identify small changes in your bow's ability to shoot tight groups.

The following minor changes may improve your bow's ability to shoot accurately: nocking point location, center-shot adjustment, cushion-plunger tension, rest-launcher tension, tiller, snug-fitting nocks, perfectly aligned nocks, and spine (since slightly stiff arrows tend to group best).

"Once you feel your bow is properly tuned for field points, the next step is to shoot a broadhead through paper," Dave says. "Again,

I require a near perfect bullet only from 20 yards and beyond. At this point, you can compare the points of impact between broadheads and field points."

If your broadhead-tipped arrow hits above the field point group, try raising the nocking point. Lower it if broadheads hit low. If broadheads hit to the left of the field point group, move your rest to the right; move it to the left if your broadheads hit right.

"Now you are almost ready for opening day," Dave promises. "Once you have sighted-in, the next step is to conduct a broadhead accuracy test. This is not a point-of-impact test; it's an accuracy test to make sure that your broadheads group nearly as well as your field points."

Some people, including experts — claim broadheads and field points weighing the same will have the identical point-of-impact if your bow is properly tuned. Don't be surprised if this doesn't happen. Some pros also say a bow quiver and its complement of arrows make tuning difficult due to increased handle torque and inconsistent bow weight. Don't take that as gospel, either. Shoot and discover the tuning truths for yourself.

If you have an accuracy problem with your broadheads, try these final suggestions:

1. Make sure your broadheads and nocks are perfectly aligned with the shaft.
2. While conducting the accuracy test, closely watch your arrow groups. Make sure the same arrow is not always the greatest distance from your aiming point; if you find a bad arrow, replace it and start the test over
3. Try feather fletching. Not only is it more forgiving, but it provides slightly more control.
4. Try slightly smaller or vented-blade broadheads. High-quality, open-on-impact mechanical heads are another option.
5. Slightly reduce your draw weight.
6. Use helical fletching.
7. If you use three-fletch arrows and three-blade broadheads, try to align the fletching with the broadhead blades.
8. Be sure to check your arrow's balance point. Ten percent or more forward of center is best.
9. As a last resort, change to a less critical setup.

If you are satisfied with the results of your accuracy test:

1. Record your exact draw length.
2. Mark the limb bolts.
3. Record the nocking point height.
4. Record the distance from the bottom of the nock locator to the center of your peep sight (if used).
5. Record the exact axle-to-axle length (write this measurement on the limb tip near the axle with a permanent marker).

Properly tuning a compound bow is no mysterious or daunting procedure; it does take some time, but tuning is a necessary part of any compound user's pre-hunt preparation. Get to know your bow. Adjust it to eliminate problems and help it reach its maximum potential. In turn, your perfectly tuned bow will help build shooting confidence — and self-confidence can pay big dividends in the deer woods.

Finally, don't forget to re-check your bow's tune once or twice a year. An untuned bow is going to give you shooting headaches. Your accuracy will suffer and the wobbly arrows you shoot will not penetrate as well. These are problems no bowhunter wants or needs.

Chapter 8
Camouflage: Blend In And Score Big

A DEAD BRANCH popped like a pistol shot in the cold early morning stillness. Jolted, I stopped climbing and glanced sideways toward the nearby ridgeline. Suddenly, 50 yards above me, the unmistakable sight of a heavy and wideswept moose rack loomed against the lightening September sky.

"There he is!" I hissed, instinctively dropping to one knee.

Pulling an arrow free and fitting its nock to bowstring, I risked a quick peek downslope. Larry already had shrugged out of his backpack and was fumbling to free his video camera. Just below him Garry had belly-flopped onto the frosty Alaskan tundra. Not exactly the ambush scenario we'd plotted, but it would have to do. Ready or not, this particular rutting bull was coming in and looking to kick some butt.

The three of us — bowhunter, cameraman, and guide — were each camouflaged head to toe and glad of it. The bull finally strode onto the skyline and stood glaring down on us. Earlier, we'd seen a cow pacing on this same ridgetop and figured a bull might be nearby. We'd guessed right. He'd likely heard us walking and mistook us for some cow-stealing rival. As I crouched watching, my heart pounding, he lowered his head and slashed at a clump of dwarf willows with his massive antlers. Satisfied at last, he turned back to stare down toward where I was doing my best impression of a stunted spruce.

Streamers of gray-brown velvet dangled from his right antler tip. At least half a dozen points jutted from his right brow and almost as many sprouted from his left. His wide palms looked wide enough to cradle my down sleeping bag — with me inside! I had no question whether this was a legal bull; my lone doubts centered on what he'd do next and what, if anything, I could do about it. Then, as if reading my troubled mind, the three-quarter-ton giant grunted once and started walking downhill. Directly at me.

Here we go again, I remember thinking. Only the previous

The author was wearing face paint and Day One camo in the Apparition pattern when he arrowed this giant Alaskan moose at 16 yards.

October, on a northern Alberta moose hunt, I'd watched another red-eyed bull stalk within 16 yards before stopping to study me. He sensed I was there, but my camo prevented him from identifying exactly what I was. And when he finally turned, I quickly drew and drove an arrow through his lungs just before he stepped into the thick brush. Despite that comforting memory, I wasn't exactly thrilled at the prospect of having this Alaska-Yukon bull walk into my lap. Yet here he came. Under 30 yards now. And closing fast.

Abruptly the bull angled to his left, skirting a patch of chest-high brush. Somehow my bow was at full draw, swinging on the moving wall of dark hair, seeking out the distinctive hollow behind his heavy shoulder. Twenty yards. Eighteen. Another step and he was perfectly broadside, my top pin locked on his ribs. Magically, my yellow-white fletching appeared just where I was focused. Instantly the big bull lunged ahead, crashing downslope, splashing across an alder-lined creek. Ten yards up the opposite ridge he stopped to stare back toward where I knelt. I quickly fitted another arrow to the string even though I knew it wasn't necessary.

Seconds later the bull's rear legs turned to Jello. Then gravity took hold, pulling him over backwards. He toppled heavily onto the tundra with a ground-jarring thud, briefly struggled back to his feet, and immediately collapsed a final time. It was over as quickly as it had begun.

Lucky? Sure. But luck or no luck, I know one of the primary reasons I had tagged two record book bull moose in as many seasons was due in part to my camouflage. It had worked and worked well.

Camo Facts and Fallacies

Camouflage doesn't make you invisible. It won't magically prevent game from seeing or scenting you. But, used wisely and regularly, it certainly helps tip the odds in your favor at critical times when a hunter with no camo would be nailed in a heartbeat by keen-eyed critters whose survival depends on sensing and avoiding danger. If nothing else, it gives the well-prepared bowhunter additional confidence — and at times, confidence in yourself and your tackle spells the difference between hunting success and failure.

Although military-style camo has been around for decades — and found favor early on with some hunters who purchased camo clothing in military-surplus stores long before copies of those camo patterns were carried by sporting goods dealers — today's camo is made as much to catch the eyes of customers as hide the human form from the eyes of game animals. Undeniably, there's more than a mere grain of truth in Jim Crumley's assessment of today's hunting-specific camouflage clothing: "This is designer stuff — fashion."

Jim should know. Jim Crumley is the creator of Trebark camo and the man widely credited with starting the modern day camouflage

Time was when military surplus camo was all that was available to hunters. This photo of M. R. James was snapped in the early 1960s.

Jim Crumley was the man who started the modern day camouflage revolution when he developed the Trebark pattern. It was specifically designed for hunters in tree stands and woodland settings. Trebark is now a part of Mossy Oak.

clothing revolution. In the summer of 1980, a full-page ad in Bowhunter magazine introduced something new: "A specialized camo for the specializing bowhunter." Trebark was the first camo clothing designed by a bowhunter for bowhunting. Its black and tan bark-like pattern was ideal for tree stand hunters. Back then, Trebark pants and jackets sold for only $19.95 each and quickly sold out, but Crumley and his ad had launched a new multi-million dollar industry. By the mid-'80s Toxey Haas of Mossy Oak camo and Bill Jordan of Realtree had introduced patterns and clothing of their own. Soon these three brands captured about 90 percent of the camo market.

Dozens of other camo clothing name brands and patterns — some equally effective and a few sadly impractical — came and went. Today there's no shortage of camouflage attire for any possible hunting terrain and situation. I've tested many of the available camos on my own hunts, from Winona and ASAT knitwear to Natural Gear, Bushlan, Predator, Skyline, Backlander, Day One, Advantage, Sticks n' Limbs, King of the Mountain, and a whole host of others you may or may not have heard of. The list goes on and on.

In truth, all camo patterns work to some extent. But so do the traditional red-and-black plaid woolen outfits worn by some rifle hunters decades before the advent of blaze orange clothing. G. Fred Asbell often wears a plaid wool shirt, dark wool pants, and a battered felt hat on his bowhunts — and takes as many animals as anyone.

According to G. Fred, "It is probably unimportant whether you wear specifically patterned camouflage. A great fuss is made over camouflage patterns, but I am unconvinced that any one camo pattern is a great deal better than another. I would say that I think the smaller, busier patterns are fairly ineffective in most hunting situations.

"It seems to me that light reflection, tone, hue, and texture are much more important than the pattern itself," he continues. "And if you break up solids a bit, you have accomplished your goal. To my eye, it is more important that the material have enough texture to diffuse light. Take a piece of cotton — or cotton synthetic — camo and a piece of wool out into the sun sometime. Lay them on the ground or hang them on a bush in the sunlight. Then step back and take a look. What you will see is that the hard, smooth finish of the cotton or cotton synthetic material reflects light considerably more than does the wool. Under some conditions, the camo pattern is lost completely in the reflectiveness of the cotton fabric. The piece of wool is non-reflective because its fibers diffuse light. In complete shadow, either material will suffice, but in a mixture of sunlight and shadow, my eye tells me the wool is vastly superior. However, if you heavily print patterns on wool, as some have done, the printed areas reflect as much light as they would on any other material. This means, I guess, heavily printing a camo pattern on the surface of any garment can reduce its effectiveness dramatically.

"We are constantly amazed at how difficult it can be sometimes to see animals — deer, elk, moose, sheep — when they are practi-

Camo face paint is a viable option to a facemask or headnet. This young bowhunter is getting a hand from his father prior to their afternoon hunt.

Camo headnets and gloves complete any bowhunter's camouflage outfit. When calling game—or simply turning your head or raising a hand—you're less likely to be spotted if you cover all areas of bare skin.

The author credits his head to toe camo with allowing him to take this New Mexico record-book bull. Although caught in the open while crawling through a grassy mountain park, James simply lay down as the herd fed close, then he was able to make the shot.

cally right in front of us. We say they are 'well camouflaged' because we can't see them — yet they aren't multiple colors as we have known camouflage to be; they are predominantly a single color. Interesting.

"The truth is that you and I have difficulty seeing animals many times because they are covered with hair — and hair diffuses light — and because they are mostly standing still. These two things are more important than pattern will ever be."

Honestly, you can camouflage yourself quite well in checks, plaids, or a variety of muted colors. After all, camouflaging yourself simply means blending into the surroundings. And as Fred points out, most big game animals blend in quite well without any blobs and squiggles, limbs and leaf outlines so common in most modern camowear.

Arguments continue over how much color, if any, big game animals can see. Many researchers agree that most animals recognize some colors, namely blues, violets, and to some extent, yellows. At the same time, reds and oranges appear in various tones of gray, as do the greens, browns, and blacks commonly found in camo clothing. The eyes of all mammals have two types of light-receiving cells — rods and cones. Cones, which are more common in humans, perceive all colors, especially during daylight hours. Rods, on the other hand, are sensitive to low light conditions but weak on color perception. That's why big game animals have better night vision than hunters, and why they see colors differently than we do in the daylight hours.

More often than not when scent doesn't betray our presence, it's movement or our human shape that alerts wary game. I know that many times I've sat unmoving against a large stump or tree and had deer walk within mere feet of me without even glancing my way. On other occasions, in identical situations, I've brushed away a pesky mosquito and looked up to see a nearby deer locked on me like a bird dog on point. And all of us have topped some ridge or hill and paused to check our surroundings, only to have some critter bust out of cover below us like Satan himself had set fire to its tail. But I can guarantee you that it's the human silhouette, movements, or both — not color — that sends most critters crashing away.

Scent-containing camo is becoming increasingly popular with 21st century bowhunters. Scent-Lok clothing (shown) features odor-absorbing carbon layers that help contain telltale human smell. A wide variety of scent-blocking liners and camo outerwear are readily available.

"Camouflage your moving parts," I always advise folks in my bowhunting seminars. "It doesn't do a lot of good to wear a camo cap, shirt, jacket, pants, and boots only to leave your face and hands flashing around for the whole world to see. Dark-colored or camouflaged gloves along with camo face paint or a headnet complete the job camo clothing starts. And don't forget to camouflage your hunting tackle, either."

Fall sunlight glinting off a bow or quiver full of hunting arrows will alert game as fast as shining a signal mirror in their eyes. Time was when shiny bows and unpainted arrows were common because that's the way they were made. If a bowhunter wanted to camouflage his hunting gear, he had to do it himself. Fortunately, savvy manufacturers were quick to pick up on this potential problem. Today, they mostly offer hunting bows and shafts in a wide variety of dull, non-glare camo paints and popular patterns.

Back to the subject of camo clothing, matching colors and designs to your hunting area is important. For example, you shouldn't wear light brown, greens, and tans stalking a bull elk in the black timber; neither should you wear black and dark green clothing while crawling across the tawny prairie in hopes of getting within arrow range of a big pronghorn buck. The common sense mixing and matching of colors and patterns to suit your surroundings can pay off big time.

"Boy, you sure blend into those rocks," Wyoming photographer Fred Burris once remarked on a mountain goat hunt we shared. At the time I was wearing gray and black-streaked wool camo from King of the Mountain. "When you're not moving, I'd never see you if it weren't for your fletching."

That's a great testimonial. Here are a couple of others. On a whitetail hunt in the scrub oak tangles of southeast Texas, a still-hunting buddy commented how well my Bushlan and NatGear camo turned me invisible each time I paused to check my surroundings. And on a Wyoming hunt for prairie muley bucks, a guide complimented my ASAT (All Season All Terrain) camo outfit. Such comments from a hunting partner or guide can go a long way toward telling you how well your camo is working. If someone who knows I'm there has trouble seeing me, I know the animals I'm hunting will have trouble, too.

Covering Scents and Sounds

To my way of thinking, total camouflage means exactly that — including the covering of clothing sounds and scents as well. As long as you're breathing, scent control will be a problem no matter how odor-free you otherwise are. Each minute in the woods works against you, no matter how clean you were when your hunt started. And while I try to keep my carcass and clothing reasonably clean — often using scent killing sprays and wearing a Scent-Lok suit under my camo — I still monitor the wind and realize that animals have unbelievable scent-detecting ability.

Once I sat rock-still as a black bear approached an odoriferous bait pile, snatched a rotten beaver carcass in its mouth, then took

This is a caribou-eye's view of the author during a Newfoundland bowhunt. One stag walked within 3 yards of the motionless bowhunter — and moments later M. R. James arrowed a giant woodland 'bou from less than 20 yards. His head to toe Realtree camo played a major role in his success.

Whitetail guru Gene Wensel is one bowhunter who proves wool garments and plaid patterns work well in the deer woods. He tagged this whopper buck way back in '81.

off like a turpentined tomcat when the wind changed and he caught a whiff of me only 15 yards away. Imagine what kind of olfactory abilities it takes to sort through several layers of potent, nose-wrinkling odors and still be able to detect danger. That's what we're up against. That's exactly why I agree with frequent hunting partner Judd Cooney, who advises that in addition to wearing head-to-toe camo, all bowhunters in search of success should "keep the wind in your face, the sun at your back, and luck at your side."

Noise is another matter. In stalking and still-hunting situations, I steer clear of scratchy, rustling clothes that rasp like sandpaper on every leaf and twig they touch. Animals are quick to pick up such sounds, especially at close range. This is one reason my camo clothing favorites run toward wools, soft cottons, fleece, chamois, and other quiet synthetic fabrics. By the way, here's a favorite test of mine to determine exactly how quiet — or how noisy — your hunting clothes and gear are.

Before hunting from a tree stand, have a buddy stand below you in a spot where you figure you'll likely get a shot at a deer, bear, or whatever. Have him turn his back and close his eyes so he can't see any movements. After a minute or two, slowly raise your bow and come to full draw (not aiming at your companion, of course!) and see if he hears you move. If there's the slightest rustle of your clothing, the faintest scrape of your arrow against its rest, the slightest creak of the tree stand or its seat — anything at all that's audible to human ears — you can bet the family auto that any animal standing there will hear you, too. Make whatever changes in your attire or equipment that solves the noise problem before it costs you a shot at game! Wear quieter clothing. Change arrow rests. Tighten that stand. By the way, this same noise detection test also works well for stalkers and still-hunters standing at ground level. Try it for yourself. It just might open a few eyes — and ears.

(Above) The author has tagged a variety of big game species while sharing the woods with rifle hunters. When the law mandates that bowhunters must wear blaze orange vests and caps, M. R. James doesn't worry about it. Animals do not see colors the way humans do and most often are alerted to danger by movement, not the clothing the hunter is wearing.

(Right) The late Paul Schafer, one of this continent's top bowhunters, donned white sweats to stalk mountain goats during a late season snowfall. This big billy never saw him until it was too late.

Noisy footwear is another common problem that needs attention. Even if you hunt only from stands, you must avoid boots with hard soles that squeak or clunk each time you stand up or shift your weight. Some bowhunters I know go so far as to carry or install a small square of noise-muffling carpet to stand on. Carpet your stands or change your footwear. Do whatever's necessary to avoid any telltale sounds that might occur at inopportune moments. For ground-level hunters, many prefer thin-soled rubber boots over the heavy, cleated types. In early season and dry weather, lightweight athletic shoes designed for running or hiking may fit your needs. A few companies — Cabela's and Bass Pro Shops, for instance — list lightweight camo sneakers that work well when bowhunting. I've used the Silent Stalk sneakers with good results. Ditto for the Rocky Silencer sneakers. Both are fully waterproof and are affordable. The former comes in odor-blocking Scent-Lok and Supprescent models, too.

Some spot-and-stalk bowhunters wear fleece booties especially made for stalking. I've worn Baers' Feet for years while stalking elk and other mountain game. They work well except on steep or wet slopes. The Carlton strap-on Felt Sneaker is another option. On a recent hunt for Wyoming muleys and a few other occasions I've shucked my boots and completed the final stages of a stalk in my heavy hunting socks. This tactic works well at times, but keep an eye out for cactus, thorns, and other pointy things in your path. I prefer wearing at least two pairs of socks during this maneuver. When I'm ready to slip my boots back on, I simply peel off the dirty pair first and wad the grimy socks in my pack. Do whatever it takes. Masking sound is a part of the total camouflage package.

What about folks who wear eyeglasses? Sunlight glinting off the lens can grab an animal's attention as fast as a signal flare. That why most of my bespectacled buddies wear caps with bills or hats with brims that shade their glasses. If you can shoot without the cap or hat interfering with your draw, this is the simplest way to go. I've seen some sunglasses that come with a non-glare lens — and somewhere I saw glasses with a see-through camo pattern masking each eyepiece. Check around. Whatever it takes, right?

And while talking about the upper face, we mustn't forget the lower part, either. Some of us grow our own camo and wear it year-round, or at least during hunting season. As noted earlier, others prefer headnets and wash-off camo creams and pastes. If you opt for a headnet or a facemask, get in plenty of practice while wearing one. Avoid those with individual eye holes in favor of masks with a single cut-out space for both eyes. Imagine coming to full draw on the biggest buck you've ever seen and starting to aim — and seeing only the cloth flap that covers the bridge of your nose! I can guarantee you that's the last time you'll ever use a mask with separate eye holes — but by then it's too late. Let this be a word to the wise. Just don't ask me how I know so much about potential problems with headnets and facemasks. Sometimes I wish I didn't.

Overconfidence in camouflage can be a big problem, too. Be realistic. The stuff won't make you vanish — just as scent-blocking sprays and scent-suppressing clothing won't totally eliminate human odor. It helps but it ain't magic. I'm always amazed when I see some bowhunter perched in a fence row tree stand in late fall or early winter wearing some leafy pattern. Usually such folks are a dark blob against the sky, about as inconspicuous as a flamingo standing in a covey of quail. If there are no leaves left to blend in with, what else is there? That's right, there are tree limbs and sky.

So doesn't it make more sense to climb into a stand wearing light-colored winter camo? It's far better against a late fall or winter sky than the same dark green and brown outfit you'd wear earlier in the season

As for masking your smell, special clothing, sprays, soaps, and shampoos can help. I've seen how effective they can be when it comes to hiding human scent. But nothing totally hides you from keen-nosed game. I'm convinced animals still smell some trace of you, but they just don't realize how close you are. But that's just one man's opinion, not scientific fact. I can only pass along what my own experiences have been.

Just as you want to avoid being seen by the animals you're chasing, at certain times of year — especially if you're sharing the woods and fields with gun hunters carrying rifles, muzzleloaders, pistols, or slug-loaded shotguns — you want to be easily seen and identified by other hunters. That's why hunting laws often mandate that bowhunters must deck themselves out in so many square inches of blaze orange during big game firearms seasons.

So won't wearing hunter orange really handicap a bowhunter? Not really, unless he's hunting turkeys or waterfowl or other wildlife

Seasonal camouflage can help any hunter blend into his surroundings. The author has found this snow camo from Natgear to be effective for late-season hunting.

Lots of bowhunters routinely carry a daypack or fanny pack on their daily hunts. Many prefer camouflaged models, such as this Mountain Man Pack from Fieldline.

Scent-conscious hunters often use odor-control body soaps and sprays. Nature's Essence offers this Total Body Deodorant in addition to Natural Wash Soap and Ground Zero Scent Destroyer spray for clothing and equipment, plus various cover scents.

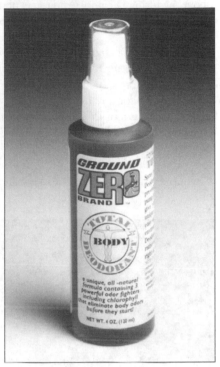

that can instantly detect certain bright colors. Despite what some folks claim, my own hunting experiences have proved that wearing a blaze orange vest and cap makes no difference at all in being visible to big game animals. Zip. Zero. Nada. While I've heard claims to the contrary, all I know is what I've seen with my own eyes — and what game hasn't seen with theirs. I've successfully hunted deer, moose, caribou, bear, and mountain goats while decked out in hunter orange (the lightweight mesh and cloth kinds, not the reflective and noisy plastic stuff). Here in Montana, for example, once the archery season ends in October, all bowhunters afield during the subsequent big game firearms season must partly dress in orange just like our gun-totin' counterparts. Not once have I ever seen my fluorescent cap or vest draw a deer's attention. Ever. Ditto for the other big game species I've hunted — and shot — while dressed like a partially camouflaged neon sign. Such firsthand experience leads me full circle to a commonly held belief I stated at the outset: Movements and the human shape are what give away hunters more than any other single factor, except maybe scent.

But if it'll make you feel better, and if it's legal where you hunt, check out the orange and black camo patterns offered by some clothing companies.

Finally, complete camouflage covers your attitude as well as your actions and anatomy. Think of it this way. If you want to blend in totally, you must avoid calling any attention to yourself. You must think and act like what you are, the ultimate predator. And that's something that comes hard to many people in today's hectic, fast-paced modern world.

G. Fred Asbell is right on the attitude-adjustment target when he talks about the need to step out of "man-ways." He explains how he does it:

"A friend of mine talks about 'woods-ways.' It's his name for

movement while hunting. He says it takes him a day or two of actual hunting before he begins to slow down, look a lot, and get into the feeling of hunting movements. I agree. It takes time to step out of the 8:00 to 5:00 hustle-up, beer-with-the-boys world and step into the quiet, easy-does-it, sharp-eyes realm of big game.

"Years ago, I found it impossible to leave work in a tear each evening, speed down the highway to my hunting area, jerk off my work clothes, pull on my hunting clothes, and then slip animal-like down a game trail. It's too much change, and it never worked. Moving too fast, making far to much noise, seeing only a gray winter woods and not the distinction of limb and bush, I'd not slow down until the sight of a deer in flight reminded me of why I was here. Crawling into a tree was the only way evening hunting after work could be productive for me.

"I work at thinking of myself as a predatory animal, psyching myself into observing and digesting every shadow, every detail around me. Sometimes, I even catch myself narrowing my eyes into slits as I imagine the prowling wolf might do. Sometimes, standing or squatting, unmoving, watching everything around me for a long time puts me into a proper frame of mind. And then sometimes I'm just a clumsy clod, with buckets for feet, who couldn't stalk a deaf, blind, and lame deer. On those days, I wisely look for a tree."

Dwight Schuh agrees with the need to make this mental transition, to slow down and flow with nature to avoid catching an animal's eye. The best camouflage made won't work if you're mentally unprepared to hunt. And speaking of the best camo, Dwight's choice is remaining absolutely motionless whenever possible. "Non-movement may be the best camouflage of all."

Looking to the Future

Some 21st century bowhunters probably look forward to a time when someone will make a potion or cream that when sipped or rubbed onto skin will turn people invisible. Or how about futuristic transport devices that are capable of safely breaking down your body's molecules in one place and reassembling them in another? Talk about the ultimate camo! And forget about spot-and-stalk. Spot-and-fly is the only way to go!

Unrealistic? Of course. Today. But right now, camouflage makers are talking about anatomically correct patterns that have photo-realistic detail for any hunting terrain or situation. There's even serious talk of photo-sensitive fabrics that change patterns and shades as the hunter walks from shadows into sunlight. In truth, nobody knows exactly what tomorrow's camouflage will be. As for what's available today, bowhunters have never had it so good.

Camo shirts, pants, jackets, and caps have become the "uniform" of most modern bowhunters. Patterns are offered to match any bowhunting area.

Dwight Schuh proved that he Predator design in this Day One camo outfit was very effective in fooling this Shiras bull he arrowed during an Idaho bowhunt.

In recent years "leaf camo" has become popular with some bowhunters.

Chapter 9
Tree Stand Savvy

I WAS WAITING for the big three-by- three blacktail to step into a shooting lane when I heard another deer walking in the crunchy oak leaves behind my tree stand. That wide-antlered three-pointer feeding past 20 yards away was a definite shooter, but he was still screened by limbs. With yet another deer now moving in behind me, I decided to wait and see what kind of headgear — if any — the new arrival was wearing.

My stand was fairly low in the moss-covered black oak. I dared not risk any movements until I was ready to raise my bow and take

the shot. Normally I would be still-hunting rather than perched in an elevated stand, but the California hills were tinder-dry and this August day and stalking conditions horrible. While I love spot-and-stalk bowhunting tactics for these diminutive coastal deer, I'm savvy enough to know what will work and what won't. That's why I was perched in a freshly hung tree stand.

The rustling grew louder. Seconds later a handsome four-by-three emerged less than a dozen yards to my right. His high, velvet-furred rack bobbed as he moved uphill toward the browsing

To be an effective tree stand hunter, you must learn to shoot at sharp, downward angles. This takes proper practice and plenty of it. Always wear a safety belt or harness when in an elevated stand.

A stand need not be high if the background hides the hunter's form. M. R. James shot a P&Y buck from this stand which is just over 12 feet off the ground.

77

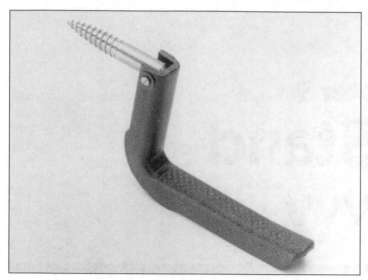

Screw-in tree steps like this single-fold Cobra model can help any bowhunter hang a portable tree stand in a hurry. Where legal, screw-in steps are a handy means of getting in and out of an elevated stand.

Strap-on tree steps and lightweight ladder sections are increasingly popular. The rope binders hold each unit securely in place without damage to the stand tree.

buck. Still I waited. The angle wasn't quite right. Neither blacktail knew I was near, and I'd be tickled to tag either animal. Both were no-brainer Pope and Young candidates.

Finally, with my pulse drumming inside my ears, I drew just as the second buck stepped into a shooting lane. He paused, perfectly broadside, staring back downslope. And then my arrow zipped through him. Both bucks instantly bounded away. Too late.

This memorable action perfectly illustrates how effective a well-placed tree stand can be. While some people point to bowhunting's steadily climbing success rate and blame technological advancements, namely the compound bow and various modern "gadgets," many veterans agree that most of the credit for any noteworthy increase bowhunting success should go to tree stands. It's estimated that eight to nine out of every whitetail tagged by North American bowhunters is arrowed from an elevated stand. And one-third or more of all Columbian blacktails reportedly are shot by tree stand hunters.

"Without a doubt," states Dave Holt, "more whitetails are taken from tree stands annually than by all other methods. But many hunters fail to harvest deer with any regularity. As in many other endeavors, the difference between success and failure often comes down to the little things — the details."

Conventional wisdom says that in many areas of the country bowhunting from elevated positions is undoubtedly the most effective and productive method of harvesting deer. It should be noted that other big game species — including bear, elk, and even pronghorn in certain watering areas — may also be successfully hunted from elevated stands. The basic advantages of this effective method include the following:

• A tree stand hunter almost always has a greater field of vision; approaching game is much easier to detect and evaluate. You'll not only see more animals, you'll usually get a much better look at them for a longer period of time.

• Climb only 10 to 12 feet into any tree and telltale human scent is maintained or dissipated at a level above where keen-nosed game animals normally detect human presence. Regardless, always situate tree stands so prevailing winds will carry your scent away from

any primary game trail or feeding area.

• Most game animals, unless tree stand hunting pressure is heavy, do not expect danger from above. While deer and other animals learn quickly, they frequently are vulnerable to this hunting method until one or more near-misses educates them.

• Any movements and sounds you'll make in readying yourself for the shot are usually minimal and often go unnoticed; the chances you'll alert game are slim — much less than when hunting at ground level.

• If undetected, any bowhunter perched in a tree stand often has the luxury of selecting the best possible shot, something that isn't always possible on the ground.

Of course, there are certain disadvantages, too. First, you have to select the proper tree and position your stand at the best height and angle. Next, finding and creating adequate shooting lanes can be puzzling or challenging to some. In addition, a few bowhunters simply are not cut out for the sit-and-wait hunting method, where patience and confidence in a single location are necessary ingredients for success. Finally, there is the ever-present danger of a fall. Safety harnesses and climbing belts or lines should be part of any serious bowhunter's tree stand gear. And never climb into or out of any stand while carrying your bow; use a haul line to raise and lower all hunting tackle. Finally, remember to take special care when getting in or out of a tree stand in cold or wet weather.

If you plan to be an effective tree stand hunter, you must practice shooting from elevated positions — preferably from the tree stand itself — before your actual hunt. Many bowhunters in trees tend to shoot high. Often subtle changes in shooting form may be to blame. For instance, you might lower the bow arm to take the shot, not bend at the waist, or hold your head and anchor point differently. One remedy is to take pains to maintain proper shooting form, always. This is relatively simple if the bowhunter will bend forward instead of trying to shoot down while standing erect. Despite what some may believe or claim, I've found that gravity has very little effect on arrows shot at steep downward angles, especially at short-range targets. Check it for yourself.

But sight shooters and instinctive shooters alike can fall prey to shooting difficulties when they find themselves shooting vertically if they've done all their pre-hunt practice shooting horizontally. Think about it. Problems are understandable if you do all your practicing on level ground. Even instinctive archers, who learn to focus on one tiny spot on a target and release their arrow when things "feel right," typically practice repetitive shooting drills from ground level. And gravity certainly does affect the trajectory of horizontal shots. So what's the problem and the cure?

Let's say that you practice faithfully until you're consistently able to hit the kill area of a McKenzie or Delta whitetail target at 30 yards. Whether you realize it or not, gravity is playing a role in arrow flight. If you're a sight shooter and have zeroed-in a 30-yard pin — or shoot bare bow and have learned to point and shoot accurately — you'll probably hit what you're aiming at when a live deer finally steps out in front of you 90 feet away. But when you're in a tree and shooting down at a foam or flesh-and-blood buck, gravity won't affect your arrow the same way. This is why pre-season practice from stands is so critical. Even if you know the exact yardage, your arrow likely won't hit where you think it will. And unless you do know where to hold when shooting down at game, you'll often miss entirely, or worse, get a poor hit.

Even if you never climb into a tree stand an only still-hunt or stalk game, you'll need to put in plenty of practice time shooting uphill and downslope. That's really the only way to imprint the effect of upward and downward arrow flight in your brain. Only through lots of practice will you become a consistently proficient

shot in much of this continent's uneven hunting terrain. Remember, the very same shooting principle applies any time you and your target are on a different horizontal plane. And believe it or not, gravity has little effect on uphill shots at common bowhunting distance of 40 yards and less. Aim accordingly.

Other conventional how-to advice always includes the suggestion to locate your tree stand near the junction of two or more well-tracked game trails. Stands overlooking feeding or watering areas may be likewise effective. Where baiting is legal, a stand hung near the food source can be deadly effective.

Try to select a tree large enough to break the human silhouette. Always be aware of your background and take pains to avoid being silhouetted. Game animals keep close tabs on their surroundings. They're quick to notice anything that's out of place or moves suspiciously.

Approach and enter your stand as quietly as possible. This is especially critical if your stand tree is near a bedding area. Keep in mind that most animals have acute hearing and carelessly crunching through dry leaves, cracking limbs underfoot, or clanging your bow against a metal stand is going to be noted. Count on it. Recently in Michigan I barely clinked my ring against my bow's cable guard. It instantly alerted a big buck standing less than 20 yards away.

Some veteran hunters actually still-hunt en route to their stands, slipping shadow-quiet through the woods. I know a good number of treestand deer and bear hunters who've gotten their animal before

Ladders specially designed for hunters typically break down into three- or four-foot units for easy carrying. When combined, they reach heights of 12 to 20 feet and are easy to use.

Permanent stands are both ugly and unsafe. With the variety of portable stands now available, there's no excuse for nailing boards to trees.

climbing aboard to begin an evening's hunt. Keep your eyes and ears open on the way to your tree!

How high is high enough? This common question has no easy answer since much depends on the tree and its surroundings. I've shot deer from stands not eight feet off the forest floor. I've also taken game from stands situated nearly 30 feet in the air. I'd say the average is found somewhere in between those two extremes. When setting up, consider the terrain, surroundings, prevailing winds, thermals, and the species being hunted. Hang your stand accordingly. Also, check out what Dr. Dave Samuel has to say on this same topic in the Q&A chapter later in this book.

I've frequently gone on record and mentioned my hatred of permanent stands. They're ugly, potentially dangerous, and even illegal in some areas. You can only hunt from them when the wind is right. They let every other hunter in the woods know where you're hunting (and when empty often lend themselves to being used by slob hunters too lazy or dumb to find their own hunting hot spots). And don't ever kid yourself, the game you're hunting will soon know you're around if you use the same stand site day after day. I could go on and on, but you get the idea. If you insist on building and using one, be sure you have the landowner's permission and always try to minimize nail or spike damage to the trees that support the stand platform. Roping a stand in place is one viable option, providing you use strong nylon rope and know the difference between a slip-knot and half-hitch. Compared to stands that are hammered and nailed in place, simple rope stands can easily be disassembled after the hunting season. If your permanent stand is not removed at year's end, carefully check it for signs of any deterioration before climbing aboard the following season.

But for me there's nothing like a good portable stand. I can't count the times I've hung and hunted from a stand only to see all the game activity shift to a spot only a short distance away. Moving a portable stand to where the action is takes mere minutes. And some of the deer I've arrowed have been tagged shortly after I've relocated my portable stand. As their name suggests, portables give you a mobility and flexibility unfound in the simplest permanent stand ever erected.

There's a wide selection of stands available, too. So-called climbing stands require some coordination and muscle power to get into position and can be used only in certain straight-trunked trees where low limbs won't interfere with getting the stand into place. Non-climbing stands that cinch to a tree with a chain, cable, or rope are a personal favorite. They generally require using multiple individual rope-on or screw-in tree steps. Strap-on ladder sections are another option, as are stout limbs if the tree offers natural steps that allow easy climbing. Once the stand is hung, I may leave it in place for several days or even weeks, depending on game movement or action. A ratchet-strap placed around the stand's base can add stability to most any setup, making the stand safe, solid, and unable to shift or slip.

Many ladder stands, tripod or quadpod stands, and similar structures aren't exactly portable. But they're not permanent, either. They can work well in brushy terrain when stand trees are few or non-existent. Tripod and quadpod stands are free-standing structures topped with a swivel seat. I've used several models on Texas hunts with good results. Ladder stands, often with a platform and seat on top, are designed to be leaned against suitable trees and strapped or chained in place. Always take special care securing

Ideally, the stand tree should be large enough to hide the human form. There also must be ample room to draw a bow and shoot in several directions.

these stands: climbing the ladder before the stand is anchored is risky.

Hinged tree-wedges, designed to fit in a tree's fork, and harness devices, which allow you to wait suspended above the ground, are other possibilities. And one obvious option in certain trees is sitting in the tree itself. I know of several such trees that are perfect for sitting or leaning comfortably during long waits for game. I used one such big cottonwood near the Arkansas River on a recent whitetail hunt in eastern Colorado. Whatever your ultimate choice of tree or stand, comfort is the key to waiting patiently. Choose a stand with a comfy seat that's both sturdy and quiet, free from creaks and groans — the stand's and yours, too!

Although it should go without saying, check to make certain there's ample room to raise and draw your bow, whether you're right-handed or a southpaw. Don't make the stand area look as though it was attacked by some berserk chainsaw-wielding logger. Keep necessary trimming to a minimum, if possible — creating adequate shooting lanes without going totally overboard. I always carry a small folding saw and ratchet-cut shears in my daypack for just this purpose. Consider carrying off the small limbs and branches that fall under your stand tree during trimming. Deer and other game may notice the changes and shy away. Some hunters even dab mud or camo paste over the white, newly cut limb stubs near their stand. This camouflages the freshly trimmed cut marks from sharp-eyed game. I've done it myself, on occasion — just in case.

Finally, if your stand doesn't come with a bow holder, it's always wise to make certain there's a handy place to hang your bow within easy reach. Perhaps a convenient branch will do. I often use a small screw-in bow hook. Holding a bow during long waits can become downright tiresome and uncomfortable. Whichever your choice, hanger or holder, just be certain you can reach your bow with minimum movement.

Advanced Tree Stand Techniques

Coloradoan Dave Holt is one of the most dedicated and consistently successful tree stand hunters I know. The game animals that he collects on his annual wanderings include many of record-class proportions. They serve as proof positive that he knows what he's doing when it comes to bowhunting from elevated stands. He claims it's not magic, that he merely applies both science and savvy to his approach. Next, Dave offers a baker's dozen tips for getting high to lay the animals low.

- First, don't get too dependent on any one bowhunting approach, including thinking that a tree stand is the only way you can be successful. Realize that each situation and setup is going to be different. Run the obvious through your portable hair-covered computer first. If it appears that a conventional approach will work, give it a try. But, if the situation screams for something radically

Safety-conscious bowhunters always wear a belt or harness when hanging a tree stand. Falls injure — and kill — bowhunters every deer season.

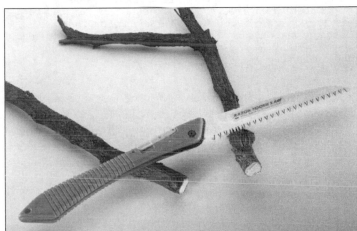

A folding saw like this Bracklynn model is ideal for trimming shooting lanes around your tree stand.

So-called climbing stands can quickly put a bowhunter high above the ground. They're lightweight yet strong. This Summit model comes with shoulder straps.

different or the traditional methods you try simply don't produce, change something. Some of my best maneuvers were born from failure. For example I shot one of my biggest bucks from a tree stand placed in a lone, dead tree. My hunting partner thought I was crazy, but that tree was the right place to be.

- One of my favorite statements is, "I hunt deer, not trees." Most tree stands are not adaptable enough to fit my needs. I have hunted whitetails in 12 states and seldom have found the perfect tree in the optimum place. I pick the location first and then make my tree stand fit the tree that offers the best opportunity — hence my preference for adjustable tree stands. If you find yourself looking for a tree that will accommodate your stand, consider who might be gaining the advantage.
- No matter what scent-control precautions you take, do your utmost to keep the wind in your favor. But also realize that you won't be successful in this endeavor 100 percent of the time.

(Above and right) Mississippi bowhunter Will Primos demonstrates the right and wrong way to rattle from an elevated stand in the fall woods after the leaves have fallen. Without a facemask, he'll be easy to spot by any buck drawn to the sound of the "horns." Donning a mask and using a rattle bag instead of real or synthetic antlers makes Will—and his movements—less obvious to any approaching deer.

• Hunting high adds the benefits of getting away with much more movement and often provides a scent advantage. On the negative side, it makes the shot a little more difficult, and the extra height makes some hunters uncomfortable. For those reasons, tree stand height should be a personal decision. I prefer to hunt above 15 feet.

• Equipment: for getting up and down safely, I like the Tree Hopper Drill and Bolt System Products' climbing belt, Easy Climb screw-in steps, rope-on ladders, and tie-on tree steps. Other important items include a quality-brand pruner, extension pruner, leather gloves, rubber gloves and boots, compass, and a powder bottle and down feathers for checking the wind. I also tie yarn on a few nearby limbs — it helps me keep track of the wind while I'm hunting. I use a notebook for recording which wind conditions will work best for each stand site. And last but not least, always use a good safety belt, or better yet, a harness.

• I insist on well-cleared shooting lanes; I often prune heavily (first making sure I have permission). The tie-on ladders not only work for placing a tree stand, they make reaching those shot-blocking limbs on nearby trees much simpler to reach.

• I put up lots of tree stands each fall. I have kept records and am convinced that the first time you hunt from a tree is your best opportunity, particularly if you are hunting mature bucks. Consequently, I move a lot and am not bashful about moving and pruning during the season. I have killed several Pope and Young-class bucks within 24 hours of placing a stand.

• Picking that final tree can be both fun and frustrating. I love fun-
nels, but most of the time they are not that obvious. When I find funnels with rubs and scrapes, it really gets me excited.

• I love letting the deer show me where to put my stand. When I'm hunting a new area, I like to put up an observation stand. If nothing is obvious in new terrain, I try to pick a tree where I might get a shot while making sure I can see plenty of the surrounding countryside. They say if you see a big buck twice in the same place, you should be able to get a shot. I don't wait — if there is going to be a second sighting of a big buck, I want him in bow range. Unless it's an unusual situation, I'll move in and hunt the big deer I spot from a distance as soon as possible — waiting only for a favorable wind.

• Think! Think about why you are picking a certain tree — consider your options. Think about how you are going to place your stand and tree steps, and use safe branches as steps. Consider how much trimming will need to be done. Walk a 360-degree circle around the tree before starting. Keep the steps close together; it's safer and quieter. Place a pull-up rope and make sure you there is a clear lane where you can quietly pull up your gear.

• Once a stand is in place, do your final trimming. Consider shots in all directions. If possible, shoot a few practice shots. This is the best way to ensure proper clearance of your bow limbs and elbow at full draw. At the very least, pull an imaginary bow and visually check for good clearance. I always try to leave a few short limbs for hanging my bow and pack. I like the bottom limb of my bow to be hanging about eye level, and I always keep an arrow on the string.

• Consider how you are going to approach the stand site. If necessary, clear a path. Do not allow any foliage to touch above your rubber boots. Try to make sure that your hands and clothing do not touch anything the deer might smell. I have had several deer track me — they all seemed to be smelling the flora I had brushed against. I once had a doe turn around and leave the area after smelling a barbed wire fence I had touched nearly three hours earlier

Finding a hot scrape in a primary breeding area is an open invitation to any savvy whitetail hunter to hang a portable stand downwind and wait for the scrape-maker to pay a return visit.

This riverside bear stand paid off with a record book bruin the day after this spot was selected.

Bowhunters have no shortage of tree stand makes and models. Prices range from about $50 to several times that amount.

A decoy situated near a hot scrape can draw nearby bucks when combined with rattling and calling sequences.

• Rattling, calling, decoying, and scents all work in conjunction with tree stands. I have used them all successfully, but they are not magic. Generally, I prefer to depend on nothing but my choice of tree stand locations. But at the right time, any of the above deer-enticing methods can make the difference between success and failure. They certainly should not be overlooked.

Final Thoughts From Above

Not only is wearing a safety belt or harness a common sense safety precaution, these strong straps can be used to your benefit. At times I've leaned out, away from the stand, to take a shot at a deer or bear passing directly under my tree, or standing in a position where a conventional shot was impossible. The harness or belt anchored me safely while I made the shot.

Learn to shoot while seated. Some bowhunters tend to play jack-in-the-box when they see a deer approaching, immediately popping to their feet to make the shot. Such pop-up movements have saved the life of more than one wily old buck. At times it's much better to remain seated, keep both eyes on the deer, and slowly reach for your bow. Should the buck happen to glance up, it's far easier to freeze a hand in place that your entire body. Even if you normally stand up to take a shot, knowing how to shoot well while sitting gives you an edge. I can guarantee you that at some time you're going to have to make a seat-of-the-pants shot or nothing — and it'd be a real shame if you didn't get the shot because you couldn't shoot from a tree stand seat.

Practice will eliminate embarrassing surprises, too. Shoot from the same stand you'll be hunting from, or one exactly like it. That's true even during your backyard practice sessions, too. Always check to make sure you have adequate bow limb clearance and can shoot while seated. Any time you have to struggle to reach full draw, you've got too much bow poundage. A bow should pull smoothly and easily whether you're sitting, standing, or leaning away from the tree at the end of a safety strap.

Shooting down at different angles and yardages will give you the knowledge you need to determine exactly where your arrows will hit. Remember, there 's a right way to take every shot, and it's up to you to learn what it is. Soon you'll have a feel for where your arrows will fly and you'll automatically adjust accordingly. And when that gray-faced, tall-tined buck finally steps into a shooting lane under your tree stand, you'll be ready to take your best shot.

A decoy placed along a field's edge can attract the attention of any passing buck.

Montana bowhunter Ron Nail arrowed this fine whitetail from a well-placed stand not far from his rural home.

Chapter 10
Stalking Smarts

I FOLLOWED MY SHADOW down the sage-dotted hillside, moving slower than was really necessary. A bracing September crosswind rustled the sagebrush around me, masking any slight sounds my lugged boot soles made as I felt my way closer, ever closer. My eyes swept the dry wash just below, seeking the telltale glint of tine tips that marked the exact location of the muley's bed. If he was still bedded here, I knew he already was within good bow range. All I needed was to spot him before he realized that danger was near.

M. R. James arrowed this P&Y muley in Wyoming after stalking the bedded buck.

More than a full hour had passed since I last glassed the buck in his shaded bed. He was lying nearly invisible in a shallow cut at the base of a Wyoming hill half a mile away. After branding his location in my brain, I tucked my binoculars away, dropped out of sight, and swung far to the left, getting the afternoon wind in my face. Then I circled unseen to approach the ridgeline above where the muley had bedded. But with the passage of time and change of prairie perspective, nagging doubts had crept in. With each careful downhill step I could not help but wonder: *Is the buck still here? Is this even the right hillside?*

Finally nearing the bottom of the sidehill, just above the shaded spot where the buck should be, I stopped amid the wind-stirred sage and carefully scoured my surroundings. Another step or two and the sinking sun at my back would cast my moving shadow across the dry wash, movement that would instantly alert any deer bedded nearby. But I still couldn't see antler tines poking from the shaded void below. Stalemate. So I simply sank to one knee, unsnapped an arrow from my bow quiver, and fit its nock to the string. The next move belonged to the bedded muley...if he was still around.

Minutes tick-tocked away. They dying sun melted into the high ridge above and behind me. Impatience was chewing on my gut. I almost had convinced myself that I was kneeling scant yards from an empty deer bed, that by now the muley I'd stalked was nibbling on some clump of bitterbrush further down the draw. I fretted that my hunt's final minutes were being wasted, that—

Suddenly the buck was standing broadside and rigid in his dusty bed at no more than a dozen yards. He was staring upslope, looking away from me, likely alerted by an eddying breeze with some hint of man-smell. Or perhaps it was some sixth deer sense that defies explanation. Somehow he hadn't seen me. Yet.

I eased my bow back and focused on the buck's ribs centered at the end of a narrow tunnel in the moving sage. I was vaguely aware of his whitish four-by-four antlers with clinging strips of dark velvet. Then my red

Stalking within good arrow range of animals like whitetail deer is difficult, but it can be done. The author is seen easing within 30 yards of a browsing whitetail and drawing for the broadside shot.

and yellow fletching disappeared through the gray buck's side. His death rush was short-lived. I rose and moved toward him, flooded with the satisfaction that a long and success stalk always brings.

"Stalking is one of hunting's finest words," explains G. Fred Asbell, whose 1997 book *Stalking and Still-Hunting: The Ground Hunter's Bible* perfectly explores all aspects of what many people agree is bowhunting's stiffest challenge and greatest thrill. "Stalking, hunting on the ground, is the very essence of hunting. Stalking embodies all that hunting is, all that it ever has been at its finest moment, all that it can be.... Man and animal, a head-to-head battle for survival. Instincts. Wit against wile.

"Stalking is the key ingredient in the imagery of hunting," Fred adds. "It is woodsmoke; it is wet leaves and fresh earth; it is the thump of the bowstring and the sound of feathers against the hand; it is sunrise and sunset; the small of damp wool and well-oiled leather; it is the morning rain against the tent; it is strong coffee; and it is the wind smelling of fall and then winter. It is the essence of what we do in the woods...it is basic to the primordial urge."

Also, for far too many modern bowhunters stalking is a lost art. In an age when most of us simply climb into a tree and wait for game to walk under us, many hunters will never know the excitement and elation that comes with getting down and testing their *hunting* skills — not just their *shooting* ability — against wary game. And to my way of thinking, that's a doggone shame!

Sure, stalking's tough. It's a given that you'll fail far more often than you succeed. But take it from Fred and me, nothing in bowhunting comes close to matching the heart-drumming exhilaration and throat-catching contentment that stalking can provide.

"Walk a little, look a lot" is great advice for any bowhunter who is stalking big game. Glassing distant animals, especially early in the day, can help plan how best to approach within shooting range.

Deer and other brush-loving animals are difficult to approach in heavy cover. Chances are they'll hear or see you long before you're close enough for a good shot.

Unless you try it for yourself, you'll never know exactly what — or how much of bowhunting — you're missing.

Start out by trying to stalk whitetails — or trying to sneak over the prairies looking for pronghorn antelope — and it's likely you'll wind up frustrated and empty-handed stalk after stalk. "Give me back my tree stand," a deer hunter might groan. "Put me back in a water hole blind," a pronghorn hunter might plead. Understandable reactions. Again, stalking such critters is hard. But it can be done. Understand, too, most other big game species — mule deer, elk, bears, caribou and moose, sheep and mountain goats — are routinely stalked and tagged by bowhunters year in and year out. So why not sample the challenge sometime? Why not join in on the fun?

"The idea is to use a skill when and where it fits and works best," Fred notes. "Tree stands, ground blinds, drives, stalking, and still-hunting all have a place in any hunter's bag of skills. Stalking and still-hunting can be an extremely valuable tool for you, regardless of how you prefer to hunt."

Good point. Following are some general comments about stalking, followed by specific instructions for becoming adept at what Fred calls "woods-walking."

Stalking Basics

Unlike still-hunting, where you slip along quietly hoping to bump into an animal somewhere nearby, stalking requires seeing the animal first — often at a distance — and then carefully working close enough to take a killing shot. Stalking doesn't rely on chance encounters between a hunter and game; it means first locating an animal and then sneaking within range. Obviously, stalking takes patience, skill, and more than a little bit of luck.

Since the benefits of total camouflage — the right kind of camouflage — have been detailed in an earlier chapter, I won't repeat them here. I'll simply note that stalking success depends largely on remaining undetected until you're in position for the killing shot. Camo helps. Enough said.

To begin your search for stalkable game, you'll likely need two things: good optics and open country. Locating a good vantage point is your first step. Find a spot where you can sit and glass. Get there early, preferably by first light, and look for game animals feeding or moving toward daytime beds. Be patient and painstaking. Let your binoculars or spotting scope cover the ground. Stay put until you've located an animal you want. Then watch him and study a way you might sneak close. Is he bedded or feeding? Is there adequate cover nearby? What about obvious landmarks you can use as reference points during your stalk? Can you approach close enough for a shot or will he need to move?

Think. Take your time. Resist the temptation to strike out cross-country until you've got a plan. Don't think your binoculars are only good for long-range use, either. I've carried a pair of 7x26 Bushnell Custom Compacts or Bausch and Lombs into the woods for years, and I use them constantly when still-hunting and stalking game. If you don't carry and frequently use a pair of lightweight optics for your own stalking efforts, you're needlessly handicapping yourself. Binoculars are great for peering into the surrounding shadows, checking out anything suspicious that catches your eye, and finding game standing or bedded in heavy cover. Don't leave home without 'em!

If an animal is bedded, you'll have one advantage. He'll likely stay put for hours, giving you ample time to move close. Just remember to keep tabs on the wind and take pains to be as quiet as possible. Remember, a bedded buck or bull might be resting, but that doesn't mean he's not alert. Often there's one or more companions bedded nearby, complicating things. Also, always make careful mental notes of his exact location. Once you've left your glassing point, everything is going to look different. If you're unsure — or careless — it's easy to blunder into bedded game. Pinpoint the bed sites, then slowly move in. You have to see the animal before it sees you or you're not likely to get the shot.

Luck always helps. I once watched a record-class Wyoming muley bed at the edge of an aspen patch just below a sage-covered sidehill. Since there was no way to get close by working through the trees, I knew I'd have to angle across the open hillside and work up on him from below. This was risky. Stalking downhill is almost always easier. Also, I knew he might see me the instant I stepped into the open. Or later he could smell me if the rising thermals reached his bedding site before I did. But this was really the only chance I had.

By the time I'd covered the mile or more to where I'd watched the buck bed down in the sage, nearly two full hours had passed. The early September morning was turning hot. I felt naked as I eased through the dusty, sun-cooked sage just below the timber's edge. Any second I expected that big buck to boil out of his bed and bounce away into the trees. But then I saw his tall, velvet-tipped antlers just ahead. By chance, he was facing away from me, relying on his sensitive nose to warn of any danger approaching from

A spotting scope can help a bowhunter save valuable time—and lots of steps—in checking and evaluating distant game. Montana bowhunter Stan Rauch is pictured glassing for mountain goats.

below. But by angling close, I'd managed to escape detection. Undeniably, lady luck had smiled on me that day, and moments later I shot him in his bed at 20 yards. But carefully planning and executing the stalk helped me take that buck, too. As some wise bowbender once remarked, "Seems the harder I work at hunting, the luckier I get."

When the animal is up and on the go, forget about trying to move in and catch him from behind. Either try to keep him in sight until he finally beds, figure out where he's likely heading and get there first, or ambush him somewhere between as he passes by. Stalking close is all it takes in some situations. The critter just might turn and head your way. You never know, so be prepared for all possibilities.

Elk, of course, are one animal you can stalk by sound as well as sight. As long as the bulls are bugling or the cows chirping, you can keep tabs on their whereabouts as you inch closer. In fact, you might not see the bull you're after until you're ready to take the shot. But stalking "blind" like this is a difficult way to tag an elk. This is especially true if there are cows or satellite bulls hanging around. Your chances of bumping into another animal are high. Spook one elk and you can kiss your unseen bull goodbye.

Whether stalking by sight or sound, you must keep the wind in your favor. An animal might check and disregard some slight movement you've made, but let him smell you and he's gone. Personally, I view the wind as a valuable ally as well as potential enemy. Given a choice, I much prefer

stalking game on days when the air isn't dead calm. Wind rustling the leaves can mask your approach as well as any unnatural sounds, although a gurgling creek or stream works well, too. If nature doesn't lend a hand, improvise. On one Utah deer hunt, I used the sound of a jet passing high overhead to close the distance between me and a bedded muley. And once in Ohio, I used the sound of nearby highway traffic to ease through the woods to within bow range of a whitetail browsing along a field's edge.

And always keep at least one eye open for natural travel routes

Horseflesh beats shank's mare for getting into the backcountry where elk, deer and other game can be sighted and stalked from a distance. Horses come in handy for packing out trophies, too.

After easing close to browsing and bedded game, a well-aimed arrow can be the perfect ending to a perfect day.

(Above) A powdery snow can help a bow-hunter move quietly; however, for safety's sake, an arrow should not be nocked until the shot is about to be taken.

(Left) Stalking gregarious animals like elk is difficult because there are lots of eyes and ears around to pick up any careless sound or movement you might make.

The author stalked and shot this tall-antlered Wyoming bull during a September bowhunt.

Missouri bowhunter Mark Petersen journeyed to Alaska where he stalked and arrowed this fine bull moose.

— a game trail, a sandy creekbed, stepping stones, or whatever — anything that can help you move quietly through heavy brush or noisy terrain as you try to get closer to game. A passing shower or fluffy snowfall can improve stalking conditions tremendously.

When conditions are dry or frigid, slow down even more. Noise is unavoidable at such times, and even the best woodsmen can't walk through brittle, ankle-deep leaves or crusty snow without making some noise. On a few days, it's best to admit that stalking conditions are against you and simply take a stand somewhere.

Learn to glance at the ground with each step. Avoid crunching through dry or frozen leaves, breaking brittle sticks, and kicking loose rocks. If you do make a noise, wait longer than usual before moving ahead. In elk country, a reassuring cow call or chirp can fool curious ears. On several occasions while stalking deer, I've grunted or blatted softly and stood unmoving for several minutes after breaking a dry limb underfoot.

Lift your feet higher than normal. Plant each foot cautiously, softly, feeling your way before putting your weight down. And if you believe you're moving slowly enough, slow down even more. As with most all forms of bowhunting, patience is truly a virtue.

Some bowhunters wrongly believe that once they've closed the distance to 50 yards, they can't get any closer and prepare to take the first available shot. Under some circumstances that may be wise — assuming you're

Sheep are known for their keen eyesight. Slipping within bow range of a nice ram like this Stone's sheep is rarely easy. But longbow hunter Nathan Andersohn of Colorado pulled it off during a British Columbia bowhunt.

Woods-Walking Mechanics

In his excellent book on stalking and still-hunting, G. Fred Asbell states the personal belief that, although many hunters are fascinated with the idea of being able to stalk animals effectively, few folks are willing to give it a serious try. I agree. That's a shame, too. Because with some time, practice, and determination, most people can learn to stalk game — and greatly broaden their bowhunting horizons.

So what do you do? First of all, simply watch people walk, Fred urges. You'll commonly see a heel-first, arm-swinging gait that resembles a soldier on parade. By comparison, only a few people make contact with the forward portion of the foot — usually the ball of the foot — and then shift the weight forward onto their toes. Whichever stride is used, it's okay for sidewalks and level ground. But it simply doesn't work well in the deer woods.

"Animals are born with the innate ability to move quietly through the woods," Fred states. "The reason for this is as simple as the fact that they have four legs and we have two. With two legs in contact with the ground at all times, balance is easily maintained and leg movements can be as slow and careful as necessary. With only two legs, when we step forward only one can remain on the ground. Therein lies the problem we must overcome."

Over decades of observation and practice, Fred has noted a specific technique he recommends for "woods-walking." Learn it yourself and your ability to move quietly over the ground and through the woods will improve tremendously. Here's how Fred explains it:

"The beginning, and the key ingredient, is changing your weight distribution. We humans walk by shifting our weight into each step as it begins to move forward, which creates an 'out-of-control' walking style. What we want to do is change that so we are keeping our weight on our back foot as the step forward is made. Let me say that again: We are changing our weight distribution so all of it is on the rear foot, and it remains there as one foot moves forward.

"Let's begin with the left foot as the rear foot. All of your weight remains on your back (left) foot, which remains on the ground as the right foot moves forward and touches the ground weightlessly. When the right foot, which is the forward foot, is touching the ground, then and only then is the weight shifted forward from the left foot to the right front foot. In order to shift your weight forward, you will need to consciously shift your body forward. This will bring your weight onto your (right) front foot, which will lift your (left) rear heel slightly off the ground. Now the (left) rear heel moves forward, weightlessly (because you've just transferred your weight to the right foot), and becomes the front foot. What was the weightless right front foot is now the weight-bearing rear foot. The left front foot comes to the ground, weightlessly, finds a soft place, and the weight is shifted to it. And on and on. Believe me, the technique is more difficult to explain that it actually is.

"The idea is to keep the weight well back on the rear foot until the front foot has been placed onto the ground. Because there is no weight bearing on the front foot, it can be placed on the ground gently and quietly.

"Do it like this. Stand straight with both feet close and about shoulder width. Your body weight should be over your legs and slightly back. (I think I tend to lean back slightly just before I begin moving.) Being aware that you are keeping all of your weight back, lift your weightless right foot abnormally high (there's a reason for this) and then bring it down carefully toward the ground. Twist the

M. R. James stalked close to this Texas whitetail and waited for the buck to move into an opening in the brush. One arrow at 20 yards dropped the whitetail.

deadly accurate and longer-than-normal yardages and indeed cannot work closer. But each stalk and each bowhunter is different. You alone know what you can and can't do, both stalking and shooting. Go with your gut instincts. In my own experience, I've often eased within 35 to 40 yards and sometimes even closer. One windy morning, with half a dozen big-antlered muley bucks bedded in the oak brush below me, I butt-scooted feet-first down an open shale slide to within 30 yards of the nearest buck. I later missed the shot when the deer finally stood — but I did get the shot.

Is it possible to get too close? Yes. And the closer you get, the greater the chance of being detected. When surprised at close range, most animals will blow out of the country, offering low percentage running shots or no shots at all. Once I'm within comfortable shooting range, I often won't try to get closer. I'll simply kneel and wait with an arrow nocked and ready. Sooner or later — unless the wind shifts or he hears something suspicious — the animal is going to stand up or move into a shooting lane. And when he does, I'm ready.

At times you can speed up the process by tossing pebbles or small sticks into the brush. Grunting can work, too. The idea is not to scare the critter, simply make him curious enough to stand and check things out. I've worked this ploy several times on stalks for mule deer, and I know it can work to perfection. But given a choice, I'll always opt to let an animal stand of its own accord. Take it from me, it's much easier to get a good shot at a completely relaxed animal than one that's on red alert after some unusual sound. This is especially true of older, hunt-wise bucks.

The collared peccary—or javelina—is ideal for stalking. That's the author hoisting a Texas pig arrowed by hunting buddy Larry D. Jones.

The author stalked and shot this tall-tined Texas whitetail on a January bowhunt.

foot slightly toward the inside and arch the big toe upward as you make ground contact first with the ball of your foot. The foot sort of 'feels around' on the ground, searching for a good place that won't make noise — and you can feel things with your foot (there is no weight on it, so it is easy to do). Keeping your body weight on your back foot throughout is what makes this technique work. If you vary your weight distribution, you will have problems. When you find a quiet place — and I might move my foot here and there for several seconds — the ball of the foot goes down easily and then the foot is rolled back level, bringing the outside of the ball of the foot onto the ground, toes still arched upward. Then the toes go down and the rest of the foot follows cautiously. Now with your right foot completely on the ground, with no noisemakers under it, your body weight is then eased forward onto that (right) foot.

"Once the weight is transferred to this foot, it now becomes the weight-bearing foot, and then the trailing foot, as the left foot is lifted high, is moved forward and placed weightless on the ground. Again, the idea is that the weight is always kept on the back foot, while the front foot moves forward and eases onto the ground, after

making sure that no twigs or crunchy leaves are under it. The exaggerated high lift of the front leg and foot is helpful in establishing the weight-back feeling, but it is also important because it brings your foot straight down through any tall grass or brush (as opposed to crushing it forward). The foot also makes less noise coming straight down on the ground rather than sliding forward into and onto things. Notice that animals most definitely go into this high-stepping gait when they are trying to be quiet.

"You must always work at making yourself go slowly. Moving too fast is a major obstacle to keeping your balance and controlling foot placement. There are times when moving quickly is important when stalking, but we already know how to move quickly. What is needed at this stage is very slow, controlled movement. In the initial stages of woods-walking, you need to always be cognizant of going slowly.

"Since this kind of walking doesn't come naturally to most of us, you'll have to spend a little time with it. Practice in front of a mirror, out in the yard, or just walking through the house. I find that doing it in front of a full-length mirror imprints what I am doing in my mind and makes it easier to slip into as the need arises. Being able to visualize yourself actually doing the woods-walk can be a big help to many people. It has helped me quite a lot.

"Bend the knee a bit and lean back slightly as you lift the leg high, almost like you are prancing, and then carefully bring it down. Keep the upper body completely motionless with the arms tucked in against the rib cage. You should work at shifting your body weight forward with no discernible movement other than a slight, almost undetectable, forward lean. Watch yourself. It becomes a gliding movement. It's not hard at all, but it is different. At any time in the movement, you should be able to freeze and move nothing — and not have to set the front foot down. The weight must be kept back and the upper body upright. It may take a little practice to feel comfortable with that, but it is the ideal we are seeking, and you can do it. You will quickly become aware of the value of good balance and to some degree, flexibility.

"What you are trying to do is to keep complete control of your feet and your body as you move forward. And you want to be able to freeze at any time in the movement and maintain complete control of your balance. Practice will hasten your ability to do that.

"When you feel comfortable with the mechanics of the woods-walk and can maintain your balance pretty well, go to the woods and give it a try. Start with a fairly clean and open area, perhaps a trail. Practice until you feel comfortable with it an then try a little tougher piece of terrain, 'tougher' being more uneven, more underbrush, more ground cover or rocks. You'll quickly see the importance of balance. The rockier, more uneven terrain will probably find you flailing the air with your arms in an effort to maintain balance. Go slowly and work at getting your balance under control before each step and movement."

Total self-control, in fact, is what gives any successful stalker the edge he needs to consistently get close to game. Whether you decide to try woods-walking or merely sneak along as best you can, you'll still need complete mental discipline and well-practiced physical skills if you hope to compete again an animal's senses. Stalking, in truth, may be the ultimate bowhunting challenge because it puts all of your hunting skills to the acid test. It's tough, sure. But if you don't try it, you'll be missing out on some of bowhunting's best moments — and the greatest of thrills.

Elk are visible, stalkable animals—at times. The author stalked this record-book bull by figuring out where the elk was going and getting there first.

Dr. Jack Frost spotted two bedded blacktails while stalking game in northern California. After edging close, he voicegrunted to get the bucks to stand and then arrowed this P&Y candidate.

Chapter 11
Still-Hunting Secrets

IT HAD RAINED the previous day and a cloudy, dark November sky held the threat of still more chilly precipitation. Walking was easy in the dampened leaves along the fence row, and I moved quietly, eyes probing the shadows. All at once a slight movement stopped me. Through a scrubby oak growth just ahead, a buck stepped into the open along a top of a dry ditch that ran toward me and then hooked away to my right. A tiny, elevated island of brush had been created by the meandering waterway. It was from this cover that the deer stepped, testing the wind.

The distance was perhaps 40 yards. A westerly breeze was angling across me, blowing away from the deer. After a long moment, he turned back into the thick brush. Breathing hard, I forced myself to move slowly through the screen of trees and down into the sandy ditch bed. It seemed to take forever as I stepped silently forward, stopped poised, and listened for agonizing moments before taking another careful step. I could hear the buck snapping twigs in the deep brush. Twice he grunted softly.

At last I was in position for a shot if the buck appeared again. Silently, suddenly he was there, standing 20 yards to my right. For the first time I could see his wide, heavy rack and rut swollen neck. But caught at an awkward shooting angle, I dared not raise my bow. The buck cocked its ears and looked directly at me, nostrils working to catch any telltale scent. Surprisingly, the big whitetail calmly turned away and walked back into the brush, grunting as he disappeared.

In the deepening evening shadows I shivered and watched,

Some wide-open spaces of the West lend themselves to still-hunting. Wooded areas and timbered ridges, for example, provide suitable cover for animals and hunters alike.

hoping to catch sight of him again. As if by magic he materialized to the left of the thicket, unmoving, standing broadside. There had been no sound or apparent movement. But all at once he was there. In the open.

I slowly raised my recurve, aimed, and released. The deer whirled and crashed headlong into the brush. Despite trembling hands, I somehow managed to nock another arrow. As the whitetail bounded into the open beyond the brushy island, I foolishly released a second arrow — and missed by several feet. But my first arrow had cut deep in his chest. Then he was gone, and I could only stand staring after him, dumbfounded by his strange actions. It wasn't until I started skirting the brush that a smallish doe exploded from the thicket and flagged away. At last I understood why the rut-smitten whitetail had acted so odd.

That was 1963. Admittedly, I had little knowledge of the whitetail rut — or of bowhunting, for that matter. I often hunted deer much the same way I still-hunted fox and gray squirrels in the bottomlands and woodlots of southern Illinois and Indiana. It stood to reason that the same slow-and-easy hunting technique would work just as well on bucks as bushytails. As it turned out, it did when Lady Luck smiled and handed me a gift-wrapped, rut-goofy Pope and Young buck. Is it any wonder that I'm still hooked on still-hunting? That once-in-a-lifetime encounter certainly involved more luck than skill. But I've learned a lot since '63, taking more than my share of big game with both feet planted firmly on terra firma. Still-hunting works. Believe it!

What It Is — And Isn't

Some folks don't understand still-hunting. They usually think it means going out into the woods and sitting still somewhere near where game might pass, or perhaps wait in a tree stand or ground blind for the chance to shoot. Or they may believe it's a synonym for stalking — which it definitely isn't.

Simply put, still-hunting is slipping through a hunting area on foot, easing along as noiselessly as possible, always alert for nearby game. On the other hand, stalking involves slipping close to animals you've already seen and know are there or somewhere close by. Still-hunters don't have the advantage of knowing where an animal is — or even if he's in the same corner of the woods. Frankly, that makes it tough.

So why bother? Well, for one reason some people simply aren't cut out for sitting in ambush for long periods of time, waiting for game to saunter past. They just don't have the patience it takes to stay planted in one spot. And while successful still-hunting certainly requires patience, walking slowly through the woods — pausing frequently to look and listen — it's far better than fidgeting in some stand for hours on end. At least when walking you'll burn nervous energy, as well as get to know the area as you cover the ground. That's a real plus for the still-hunter. Also, you can satisfy that mind-gnawing need to know what's over the next rise or beyond that next clump of brush. Finally, some terrain and some animals are made for still-hunting. Ignore such obvious opportunities and you'll miss out on an exciting and often highly effective means of taking game.

When and where does still-hunting work? It's been my experience that still-hunting can work at any time you're afield using any other hunting method. It may surprise you to know that during its 2001-2002 recording period, the Pope and Young Club reported just as many record book whitetails were arrowed by still-hunters as bowhunters waiting in ground blinds. Except for during the annual rut, the best times for any type of bowhunting are usually early and late in the day. The only difference between still-hunting and the most popular methods is instead of climbing into a tree stand or blind — or climbing to some high point to glass at the start of a spot-and-stalk hunt — you head into your favorite hunting haunts prepared to do some slow walking and lots of looking.

The key to still-hunting success is spotting the animal before it sees you. If you find yourself in a situation like this, your chances of getting a good shot are slim—or none!

Keep an eye open for quiet places to walk. Whenever possible, still-hunt or stalk game with the sun at your back. Solid rock, hard-packed or powdery dirt, sand, grassy areas, moss, carpets of pine needles are all naturals. As mentioned at the beginning of this chapter, I like to be afield after rain has dampened the woodlands, or when a fine mist or light snow is falling. Heavy rain or snow can drive animals to cover; light precipitation doesn't affect them. Such times are made for still-hunters.

Under certain conditions — and with certain species — you can spend an entire day slowly still-hunting a chunk of suitable real estate. Pronghorns and caribou, for example, come to mind as distinct possibilities. These animals may be up and about — or bedding in plain view — throughout the daytime hours. Each can be successfully still-hunted or stalked across certain parts of their home range (but seldom on the open prairie or treeless tundra unless the terrain is rolling and broken). Other species, sensing the approach of a storm — or immediately following a prolonged rain or heavy snow — are often up and about, actively feeding. I know I've taken several deer during the midday hours by still-hunting the approaching storm fronts when the animals sense bad weather ahead.

Brushy country that lacks adequate trees for hanging stands can be ideal for still-hunting whenever animals are on the move. All that's really necessary are numerous game trails, mixed with occasional open areas that allow you to move quietly. Thick cover limits your field of vision, but it's rarely a problem unless it keeps you from getting a clear shot if and when the animals finally are sighted. Other good still-hunting areas worth checking are those found in rolling and rugged country and heavily wooded terrain where long-range glassing isn't possible. As long as there are animals in the immediate vicinity, feeding or moving to or from bedding areas, fully camouflaged bowhunters always have a chance. All that's necessary — and this is usually the hard part — is catching sight of the critters before they catch sight of you.

Binoculars can be a still-hunter's best friend. They're great for checking out suspicious objects in the shadows or underbrush.

One successful Ohio still-hunter I know said he views himself as a mobile, one-man hunting blind. Dressed in quiet camo from cap to boots, he takes a slow, silent step or two, and then stands unmoving for long minutes at a time — sometimes taking an hour to cover less than 100 yards. Each time he pauses, he instantly becomes part of his surroundings. By moving into the wind and doing more watching than walking, he greatly reduces his chances of detection. The big antlers hanging on his trophy room wall easily convinced me that he has perfected the business of still-hunting, and I've always tried to follow his lead.

Remember, still-hunting won't work in country where the animals can spot you coming long before you're within arrow range. Again, the key to success is spotting the animal first. Otherwise, you're wasting your time while giving the game in your hunting a basic course in Human Detection and Avoidance 101.

How many deer do you see? A still-hunter must learn to look for parts of deer, not the entire animal. The doe at center is easy to see. But did you notice the doe and big buck (arrows) that already have you pegged?

A camouflaged still-hunter is, in effect, a portable blind. It's necessary to do far more looking than walking. Big game may overlook a stationary hunter, but will quickly pick up any movements.

Walking around with an arrow nocked is unsafe. An arrow should never be fitted to the string until the final stage of a stalk when a shot opportunity is imminent.

Still-Hunting Savvy

My old hunting buddy, G. Fred Asbell, is convinced that looking — really seeing — is the single most important skill you can develop as a bowhunter. "I've always believed that the hunter's eyes are his single most important asset," Fred says. "Your ability to see animals before they see you is more important than anything else. The hunter who chooses to hunt on foot — particularly the still-hunting bowhunter — must develop his eyesight to the fullest.

"Your ability to see animals, still or moving, is a skill you must work at constantly — and if you do, you'll get much better at it, and your ability to successfully hunt on the ground will improve dramatically."

Fred also calls still-hunting a state of mind. "I think it's important to get your mind tuned into sliding through the woods, undetected, and seeing everything. You must walk slower. You must psych yourself into adopting the predatory state of mind."

Fred's latest book, *Stalking and Still-Hunting: The Ground Hunter's Bible*, contains some of the best information and advice I've seen anywhere. The following facts and hunting tips can help you not only to grasp the basic problems faced by all still-hunters but tell you what to do about them.

- Understand that an animal's ability to see you first will be a much bigger problem for you when you have no specific idea where the animal might be. When you're still-hunting, you are trying to remain hidden, even through you do not know just where those eyes that might see you are located. With still-hunting, your ability to see the animal before he sees you is more important than anything else.

- Scout the area you want to still-hunt. Do it exactly like you'd look for a place to put up a tree stand. Look for signs of travel, feeding, and other activity. If the season is right, look for indicators like rubs and scrapes. It's easy to see where activity is the heaviest, and it's easy to see that activity is rarely, if ever, scattered across a given piece of terrain. It's almost always centralized in specific places through saddles, along creeks or bottoms, and in connecting draws of brush and trees. I try hard to find a feeding area and to figure out how the animals are getting into it and then back to where they lay up during midday. When you're still-hunting, I think you need a much more thorough knowledge of the area than when you're simply going to put up a tree stand.

- Move as little as possible, and always do it in short segments. There is a real tendency for still-hunters to become so engrossed in moving quietly that they move continuously. This is a major error in the technique. You should be stationary much more than you move. Over the years, this has been a difficult thing for me to do. I have a real tendency to move continuously, particularly if the footing is quiet and there are no animals visible. Eventually it dawned on me: A majority of the animals I'd seen in the woods — before they saw me — had been seen when I was stationary and the animal was moving. Considering how much better an animal's eyes are than mine, it has to follow that he will see me most of the time before I see him — if I'm moving and he is stationary. This is one of the reasons I think that trying to still-hunt through a bedding area is usually not a very wise thing to do. It is as sure a way as I know to spook animals. Unless you know specifically where an animal will be bedded and can stalk that spot, I'd not attempt it.

Okay, let's say you've moved slowly into the core of your hunting area. You're moving your eyes much more than your feet, pausing often to check out the surroundings for some hint of movement, some unusual shape or patch of color that catches your eye. Then you see a deer move. He's a nice buck, too. He's browsing in the brush just ahead of you, angling slightly away. There's no chance he'll feed into bow range unless he completely changes directions. You have to try to get closer to take a shot. Your still-hunt suddenly becomes a stalk. What should you do?

• Always try to move in a straight line toward any animal you see and stalk. If you are standing upright, keep your upper body motionless, arms in tight against your body, and move only your legs. Move slowly, letting your weight glide forward onto your front foot. When your movement is straight toward the animal, all of your motion will be hidden against your body and will be much harder for the animal to detect. Even when you are in cover, try to keep your body moving at the animal. Once you turn sideways to the animal, there is so much more motion visible because movement is outside the plane of your body. Think about an airplane coming straight toward you, versus an airplane mov-

ing left to right across the sky in front of you. Which is more difficult to see? Any left or right lateral motion will be much easier for the animal to pick up.

Are there things you can do — besides wearing total camo — that will help you to remain relatively invisible to the watchful eyes of animals you're hunting? Yes.

• Stay in the shadows. Avoid sunlit areas. There's no way you can move through bright sunlight and not be seen by any animal within seeing distance — particularly if he's in shadows himself. Your motion is highlighted to the max when you move in sunlight. People in advertising have known for years to put a spotlight on, or behind, something to make you aware of it, to bring it to your attention. We all talk about how well the deer themselves are camouflaged, how hard they are to see. All that goes out the window when you see them in a sunlit field. They might as well have strobe lights flashing on them. And you and I are much more visible than they are!

• Use all the available cover. I try to move from one piece of cover to another, always consciously trying to position myself so I can draw my bow, just in case. In typical whitetail country, there's no shortage of cover, and I will most often pick a place in the direction I am traveling and move to it. In Western mule deer and elk country, it is sometimes more difficult. I've had animals suddenly appear when I'm standing in the open. At times they'll not see me, or see me and eventually decide I'm not a threat and move on. But in such instances, you'll almost never be able to get a shot off.

Besides passing along common sense advice such as staying off the skyline and doing whatever's necessary to camouflage the human form, G. Fred Asbell notes that successful still-hunters and stalkers don't hesitate to get down — and sometimes dirty — to work into position for a shot. He explains his own thoughts on the

(Right and above) Still-hunting brush country for smaller game like wild boars and javelina is excellent practice for big game seasons. Hogs have good hearing and keen noses, making it a true challenge to slip within bow range while remaining undetected.

Stay in the shadows and avoid open areas. Notice how easy it is to see these deer moving across an opening in the woods. The same is true for hunters.

Still-hunting Southwestern brush country is sometimes rewarded by a close shot at game, like this javelina that the author tagged on a Texas bowhunt.

subject with these words:

"I do a lot of crawling, especially in stalking situations and probably more when I've after mule deer and elk rather than in whitetail country. That has nothing to do with the animal, but instead the type of country I'm hunting. Many times crawling is the only way to keep your silhouette behind cover, and sometimes it's simply a matter of shrinking your silhouette as low as possible.

"I'm surprised by the number of hunters I've met who are amused by the thought of actually getting down on their stomachs and crawling after an animal. I don't remember any stalk on mountain sheep or goats when I didn't, at some point in the stalk, end up on my belly. There's little cover above timberline where those guys live; you'll not often get near them unless you're willing to wear out a few belt buckles. But I'd hasten to point out that it is also very possible to crawl yourself into a situation with no cover and end up not being able to get a shot off."

Just as there are times when it's critical that you remain unseen and unheard, it occasionally pays to make the right kind of noise. Indeed, certain sounds can benefit any hunter. Many veteran bowhunters already tout the seasonal effectiveness of imitating deer grunts and elk talk, not to mention "horn" rattling. Such productive auditory aids can be used alone or to complement visual aids, like decoys. So what other sounds, if any, can benefit a hunter? For one, learn to walk like a deer.

Let's say you suddenly find yourself standing in ankle-deep dead leaves where each step you take sounds like an elephant tip-toeing through a brushpile. Or let's say you're walking through the dark on the way to or from your stand. You know game is in the area and you don't want to unduly alert them to your presence. Here's where

Trying to catch up with a moving bull elk is usually wasted effort. It's far better to intercept him as he moves between feeding and bedding areas.

If you see a deer approaching, it's usually best to let him pass by your hiding spot than to try to draw and shoot when he can see you raise your bow.

knowing how to "deer walk" can come in handy. Fred explains:

"Four-legged animals sound completely different than we two-legged critters. Animals instantly recognize the difference. You only have to hunt a season or two before your own ears can easily tell the difference between a buck coming through the woods looking for a doe and your hunting buddy heading over to meet you at an appointed time.

"Man normally walks in a steady, constant 1-2-3-4 cadence which goes step-step-step-step and so on. Each footfall follows the previous one. It's like a large, ticking clock — sounds evenly spaced, continuous, monotonous. Animals instantly recognize this distinctive walking rhythm.

"Animals, on the other hand, normally walk in two-step rhythms — step-step (pause), step-step (pause), step-step (pause). Obviously, this is one reason to learn how to move silently through the woods — or to try to make noise that sounds like a deer walking. Here's how you do it.

"Point your toes downward with each step, bringing them onto the ground quickly, in succession. Next, snap each heel down sharply. Create two distinct sounds, one made by the toe and one by the heel. Toe, heel. Pause for a second, then bring the other toe down, immediately followed by the heel sound. What you do is create the step-step (pause), step-step (pause) sound of a walking deer — the sound of four distinct steps. You do this by repeating the toe-heel (pause), toe-heel (pause) cadence as you walk. Since this is exactly how a four-legged animal sounds as it walks, other animals

When a buck hears you and spooks, but doesn't catch your scent, it's sometimes possible to stop him with a reassuring grunt or two from your deer call.

100

The author shot his first mule deer buck in 1965 while still-hunting in Colorado's Book Cliffs. Over the decades, he's successfully still-hunted and stalked dozens more, including this Wyoming wall-hanger. Moving slow and quietly are keys to success.

"It's pointless for me to tell you how well 'deer-walking' works. You'll have to try it for yourself. I use it often when walking to a stand or coming out. One season I was walking in the dark toward a ground blind I had set up the previous day when a deer snorted at me in the dark. I heard it bound away two or three jumps and then stop. I immediately began 'deer walking' while remaining stationary. I'd do it a few times, then wait a few seconds and do it again. In the half-light I could tell the deer — a doe — was standing there, listening. She later took a few steps my way, looked for a few more moments, and then turned and fed calmly away.

"One time in Iowa a buck spotted me. I hadn't heard him in the picked cornfield, but when I saw him he was staring at me from about 30 yards away. Since he didn't run, I figured he wasn't exactly sure what I was. It wasn't good light, and there was quite a bit of brush between us. Moving only my feet, I began walking like a deer and grunted a few times. The buck walked closer to investigate. I stopped and stood unmoving as he stared at me for several minutes before dismissing me and turning away. Unfortunately for him, he'd gotten too close and the end of season was near. I plunked him. Deer walking works."

Final Thoughts

Admittedly, there are times and places — with various species — when tree stands and ground blinds are far more practical than still-hunting or stalking. No one I know will ever argue that tree stand hunters aren't far more successful that bowhunters who hunt solely from the ground.

Regardless, keeping both boots planted on woodland soil — while challenging wary game animals on their home turf — is one personal test no serious bowhunter should ever ignore or refuse to try. To do so is to remain incomplete, unfulfilled. Honestly, there's a vast difference between shooting animals and hunting animals. One method is mostly passive, a waiting game; the other means is largely active, a quest for success. Both require patience and shooting skill; each is an efficient, time-honored hunting technique. Yet there's a definite difference in the hunting ability required.

Admittedly, choosing the proper ambush site, carefully hanging a stand or crafting a natural blind, and then waiting silently for an animal to appear, is challenging and satisfying. Yet nothing I've experienced in bowhunting can match the one-on-one, eye-to-eye thrill of meeting big game on relatively equal terms — and winning. But win or lose these up-close and personal confrontations, it guarantees the exciting moments will never be forgotten. Ever! Try it for yourself to discover exactly what I mean.

hearing this think another animal is walking along.

"Go outside, preferably in an area with a few leaves (so you can hear yourself). Practice this rhythm — toe-heel (pause), toe-heel (pause). Close your eyes and do it, listening carefully. Think about how a walking deer sounds. Think about the rhythm. In just a short time, you'll have the sound and the rhythm exactly right. Two fellas practicing it together works well. Turn your back and listen. You'll begin hearing a "deer" walking behind you."

Fred goes on to explain how this benefits a still-hunter:

"Deer may lie there and watch, or they may stand up to see who's coming, but they usually don't bolt instantly if the 'deer walk' is done correctly. It may just give you the chance for a shot. When a buck hears you and spooks but doesn't catch your scent, it's sometimes possible to stop him with a reassuring grunt or two from your deer call.

"I want an animal to hear a familiar sound and to stand up to investigate. I've had it happen several times. I've also had them just lie there, probably thinking I was another deer coming to bed down.

"It is so simple to do that it doesn't take you mentally away from the overall process of getting close and remaining undetected. And it doesn't put your body into contortions that animals are sure to spot. It's like learning to twitch a fishing rod as you reel in the bait. You've changed the way things are happening, but you're still ready to react when the opportunity arises.

Chapter 12
Letting Go: When and Where to Shoot

GOOD SHOOTING LIGHT was still long minutes away when the first shadowy shapes of feeding deer drifted beneath my stand. Concealed amid trailside junipers, I knew I was in an ideal ambush site. But pale dawn was once again slow in coming on this overcast November day. So I simply sat fretting, impatiently peering into the murky grayness, straining to see if any of those moving shadows wore antlers — big antlers! Unfortunately, it was impossible to tell.

I'd first seen *my* buck — or at least the wide-racked, tall-tined buck I hoped to tag — on the very first morning's hunt. At the time he'd been feeding slowly past a well-situated ground blind not far from where I now perched. He trailed a band of dainty does and small-racked bucks working downhill from daytime beds toward one of the ranch's many feed stations strategically placed among the cedars, live oaks, mesquite, catclaw, Texas persimmons, hackberry, elms, and blackbrush that composed this particular chunk of Hill Country real estate.

Truthfully, had I been hunting solo, I'd have eased to full draw at the first broadside opportunity; however, on this particular trip I was hunting primarily to get first-rate video footage for *Bowhunter* magazine's television show. So for the moment, as the camera hummed softly, I had only been able to watch, my heart jackhammering under my camo jacket. And by the time the cameraman had whispered, "Better take him," it was too late. The huge buck had already moved past the best shooting position in our blind's screened front window. As I tried to shift into position for the shot, my padded seat had creaked beneath me. Instantly all of the nearby deer — including the huge buck — jerked alert.

The big whitetail had known something was amiss, and seconds later he snorted and thumped away among the junipers. Not surprisingly, I hadn't seen him since.

That had been a few days earlier. Now, with time

running short but enough video already shot for a good show, I'd elected to hunt solo on my hunt's final day. I'd blown one chance at a true Hill Country monarch by waiting longer than I should have. I wasn't going to repeat that same mistake if lady luck gave me another close-range shooting opportunity.

Minutes ticked by. The rocky roadway, flanking junipers, and brush-furred hills around my stand began to take on a sharper resolution. The shadowy deer shapes transformed into individual does and yearlings. One small-antlered buck fed past. And then a

M. R. James tagged this record-class Texas whitetail in the final stages of his hunt. Much more than shooting accuracy played a role in his success.

big-bodied deer stepped into view off to my right. One look at his headgear told me my buck was back!

Even at 40-plus yards there was no mistaking that wide, dark, and tall-tined rack with its distinctive split brow tines. This deer dwarfed the other whitetails feeding nearby. There was absolutely no question I was looking at the boss buck of this particular section of Hill Country deer heaven. And he was slowly picking his way in my direction, feeding as he came.

Unfortunately, at this moment several does and fawns were standing practically beneath my stand. There was no way to ease my bow to full draw without being spotted or heard, so I simply sat and watched, trying to suck air through my camo facemask and ignore the staccato drumbeat of my thudding heart.

The buck gracefully jumped a fence and walked closer, quartering slightly toward me. He was perhaps 20 yards when I suddenly lifted my bow and drew it in one single fluid motion. On the periphery of my awareness, I sensed the closest deer scattering below me. But, as I'd expected, they quickly paused, uncertain but fully alert. By then it didn't really matter. I was already centered on the buck's chest.

He froze in midstride, standing perfectly broadside, his head with its crown of magnificent upswept antlers turned toward the wary but uncertain does. And in that final instant as my arrow flashed away and through his chest, I gave silent thanks I'd gotten a

second chance.

Sure, after four-plus decades spent prowling North America's deer woods, I know when and where to shoot accurately. It's learned experience combined with practiced shooting skills. Both factors are absolutely critical in almost any bowhunting success formula you can name. Here's what Dave Holt has to say on the subject:

"Accurate shooting alone doesn't guarantee success when hunting. It is only one of many challenges that must be handled correctly when you are staring that big buck in the eye and know this is the moment of truth. Putting your arrow in the right spot during a situation like that requires more than just shooting ability. Buck fever, range estimation, and trajectory can also cause you to miss that all-important shot. The weakest of these skills is often what determines your success or failure as a bowhunter."

As I do, Dave believes that it's critical that you know when to let go of the arrow and to shoot that same arrow at game to the very best of your ability. In other words, if you have confidence and concentrate on releasing a perfect arrow every time you take a shot, your accuracy and success rate will improve. That's a promise.

As mentioned, long experience has taught me precisely when to release and where to place each arrow. When that Texas whitetail froze broadside at under 20 yards, he sealed his fate because I already was at full draw and set to release. At that range he wasn't going to duck my arrow. All I had to do was to focus on correctly shooting my arrow, the final step in any successful bowhunt.

While each bowhunting opportunity you'll face differs somewhat, there are certain positive steps you can take to greatly increase your ability to consistently take game, under any circumstances.

When To Shoot

Deciding exactly when to release an arrow is perhaps the most profound judgment you'll ever make as a bowhunter. The outcome of your hunt — perhaps your entire season — hinges on that single factor. Consequently, every bowhunter must seek to answer the one all-important question: *When is the best time to shoot?*

At first glance, it may seem a no-brainer. You see an animal within good bow range and you shoot it. "Take the first good shot you get," is standard bowhunting advice. But exactly what constitutes a "good" shot? Since each bowhunter and each bowhunting situation differ, what's good for one hunter may be risky for another.

Knowing when to release an arrow is instinctive. Contributing factors always include your personal equipment choice, your shooting ability, your past hunting experience, your target's position and distance, and your personal ethics. Consequently, only one person — *you* — can decide if and when to take the shot.

A shot I didn't take serves as a perfect example of what I'm talking about. One November morning, I rattled in a big Montana whitetail, the kind of buck that most deer hunters see only in their dreams. On the prod and spoiling for a fight, he paused 35 yards in front of my tree stand and proceeded to demolish a slender sapling. More than once I was tempted to take the broadside shot as he worked over that hapless tree. But since I was carrying my longbow that day, I resisted the urge. True, the setup was ideal, but I knew in my heart that I'd be pushing my personal stickbow shooting abilities — 25 yards and under — if I released. To me, the risk of wounding such a magnificent animal kept me from raising my longbow. For G.

Concentrating on releasing the perfect arrow, shot after shot, will improve any bowhunter's accuracy. Once the basics of shooting a bow are mastered, bowhunting is mostly mental.

An instinctive shooter like Larry Streiff, former Records Chairman of the Pope and Young Club, relies on "feel" rather than estimating yardage and choosing the proper sight pin to accurately deliver his arrow to its target. Instinctive shooting is most common with recurve and longbow shooters.

Michigan bowhunter Tom Nelson is one modern bowhunter who favors a mechanical release and bowsight to shoot accurately at known distances, just like most modern bowhunters. That's a California blacktail he arrowed.

Proper practice develops good shooting form and pinpoint target accuracy. Most bowhunters hone their shooting skills on realistic targets situated in actual hunting terrain.

Deciding when to release an arrow is the most decisive judgment any bowhunter will make. The hunting tackle, personal experience, shooting ability, distance and position of the animal all enter into the ultimate decision.

Knowledge of big game anatomy helps any hunter properly place shots. Bowhunter education classes are an excellent place for beginners to learn such basics—and for veterans to augment their awareness.

Fred Asbell and more proficient stickbow shooters, the shot would have been a good one. For me, it wasn't — and I knew it. And while memories of that big whitetail still haunt me, I have never second-guessed my decision to pass up the iffy shot. Again, you and you alone must decide what is the best shot for you.

Properly preparing to take any bowhunting shot includes both mental and physical training. No responsible bowhunter ever ventures afield without at least a fundamental understanding of his hunting tackle, his personal proficiency, his quarry, and the relevant game laws for his hunting area. All the time spent preparing for the eventual moment of truth, when a game animal finally steps into view, is both necessary and worthwhile. When shooting your bow well becomes routine, you're ready to face the final challenge — as long as you understand your limitations and are committed to making a quick, clean kill every time you release a hunting shaft.

To help make the proper judgments, you should always keep these bowhunting facts somewhere in the back of your mind.

- Compared to any modern firearm, notably muzzle-loading rifles and slug-loaded shotguns, hunting bows are extremely short-range weapons limited to almost point-blank hunting distances. In fact, most bowhunting kills are made at distances of 30 yards or less. This means it's critical for you to get extremely close to game animals, remain undetected, and make an accurate shot. Remember, too, merely hitting an animal with your broadhead-tipped arrow is not your goal; hitting that animal in an exact spot that will result in a humane kill is what really counts.
- Hunting arrows are missiles that propel razor-sharp broadheads toward intended targets. The fastest hunting arrow is practically standing still when compared to the slowest bullet. Besides a lack of comparable velocity, arrows do not have the shocking power of bullets and are more easily deflected by leaves or small twigs — or stopped completely by heavy bones. This means it's essential for you to have a clear shooting lane, as well as a working knowledge of big game anatomy, before releasing your arrows.
- Sharp broadheads, of course, are the business end of hunting arrows. They typically kill by penetrating the body cavity sufficiently to sever major veins and arteries, creating massive internal hemorrhage or organ failure. Dull broadheads won't penetrate as well as sharp ones or create the blood loss necessary for quick kills.
- The savviest, most successful bowhunters always aim for the chest area when an animal is standing broadside or quartering slightly away. I'm convinced a double-lung hit is bowhunting's most deadly shot. Properly placed, a sharp head through the chest not only causes the lungs to collapse, but creates massive blood loss. The result, more often than not, is a short blood trail and speedy kill.
- Even at point-blank range, it's easy to miss large animals like moose or elk if you fail to pick an exact spot where you want your arrow to strike (remember the importance of releasing a perfect arrow?). All veteran bowhunters know that shooting at an entire animal is a sure-fire recipe for failure — but some forget that fact when a giant buck or bull swaggers into view.
- Aside from accidental brain or spinal hits, arrow-struck game animals rarely drop within sight, except in open hunting terrain. More often than not, fatally wounded game runs away, usually making it necessary for the bowhunter to follow a blood trail in

Animals have no appreciation of perfect shooting form. Successful hunters must take advantage of any shooting situation that might arise. The author was kneeling when he arrowed this Wyoming mule deer at just over 25 yards.

order to recover the animal (another case for using well-honed hunting heads). The time spent honing your tracking skills is another wise and necessary investment. Dwight Schuh calls trailing and recovering an animal "the final step in successful bowhunting." He's right.

- To wait or not to wait before taking up any blood trail depends on several factors: placement of the shot, weather conditions, and the presence of predators in the hunting area. When in doubt, wait at least 30 minutes — and keep absolutely quiet! Don't even walk over to check for blood or look for your arrow. The wounded animal might be standing or bedded just out of sight, listening and wondering exactly what happened. The slightest unnatural noise may send it crashing away in panic — and even hard-hit, mortally wounded animals can cover considerable ground if spooked. So don't ever rush things. Remember, too, that the key to always recovering your animals starts with a sharp broadhead on the business end of a well-placed arrow.

- Finally, never forget that it's your responsibility to recover each and every wounded animal. You owe the effort to yourself, your fellow hunters, and to the animals themselves. Ethical bowhunters will never abandon the search until the animal is found and tagged, or they are convinced the hit was in a non-vital area and the injured animal will fully recover.

Knowing exactly when to shoot — or when not to shoot — is accumulated wisdom that all prudent bowhunters develop over time spent in the woods and fields. Eventually, it will become as instinctive as drawing your bow, locking on target, and focusing on making the perfect release.

"Be sure or don't shoot," is my personal bowhunting motto. It's a credo adopted by every successful bowhunter I know. It should be yours, too!

Where To Shoot

Sensing exactly when to release an arrow is only half of the bowhunting success equation. To solve the how-to-achieve-consistent-bowhunting success quandary, it's equally critical to know just where to place your keen-edged broadheads. Frankly, it's virtually impossible to overemphasize the importance of proper shot placement.

For my money, there's no better or deadlier shot in bowhunting than a solid double-lung hit. But flesh-and-blood big game animals aren't staked 3-D targets. They not only have an unsettling knack

Well-placed arrows kill quickly and humanely by penetrating the animal's body, creating a massive hemorrhage and/or immediate organ failure.

Big game animals often appear unexpectedly. Bowhunters should learn to shoot accurately from any shooting position—standing, sitting, kneeling, crouching, etc. The author often shoots while seated in an elevated stand.

The author firmly believes a double-lung hit is the deadliest shot in bowhunting. This young buck went down within 30 yards. The results will be the same for the biggest buck or bull—a short blood trail and a quick kill.

for appearing and pausing where some pesky bush or handy limb hides all or part of their vitals, but they can and do immediately react to imminent danger. By the way, for most hunters, not even the most realistic foam targets can produce the supercharged emotional rush evoked by the mere glimpse of approaching antlers. With such potential distractions standing between success or failure, you must decide instantly whether to wait for an absolutely perfect shooting opportunity or release a potentially lethal arrow under less than ideal circumstances. As with deciding when to shoot, since each and every shot situation is slightly different, deciding where to place that shot is another judgment only you can make.

"Avoid all risky shots!" is no-brainer advice. But realize that every big game animal is vulnerable to a well-placed arrow that does not penetrate both lungs. Regardless, in examining all potentially deadly shots a bowhunter can take, it's important to know every fact — and every risk — involved.

Head and Neck Shots: Such shots may be good for big game gunners, but they're among the worst any bowhunter can take. Sure, if your broadhead accidentally severs the spinal cord or penetrates the brain, the animal is instantly dead or dying. Ditto when a razor-edged broadhead slices through the animal's windpipe or carotid artery. But a skull is composed largely of arrow-stopping bone. And the neck is mostly muscle. Head or neck shots might kill a big game animal, but usually they result only in non-vital hits and

This trophy-class Montana whitetail in the three-photo sequence demonstrates just how quickly a shooting chance can come and go. Once the buck senses danger, he immediately turns and moves off. An experienced bowhunter might get a shot as he quarters away. For most hunters, he'll be gone before they can draw and shoot. Believe it!

wounded, unrecovered animals. Dwight Schuh speaks for all knowledgeable bowhunters when he says, "Shoot at the neck of a rabbit or grouse if you want, but for Pete's sake don't shoot at the neck, or head, on any big game animal."

Rump Shots: Some well-known bowhunters, including the late Fred Bear and modern legend Chuck Adams, once advised shooting deer-sized animals in the rump. There's no arguing that a broadhead that cuts the femoral artery on the inside of either back leg will quickly kill the largest critter alive. But that artery is a tiny target. Miss by even a fraction of an inch and it's likely you'll merely bury your broadhead in the animal's hip or leg bone, leaving your arrow flagging from the animal's rump as it bounds away. Today the growing consensus is that butt-shots are risky and should be avoided under most circumstances. Adams now has joined the majority in urging bowhunters to always aim for the animal's chest when seeking a primary target. It's excellent advice.

Sometimes ground-level bowhunters may be tempted to drive an arrow lengthwise through an animal's body as it stands facing directly away. A sharp broadhead that enters beneath the tail and centers the pelvic arch can cut its way through intestines and stomach into the chest cavity, providing the bow has transferred enough kinetic energy to the arrow at the instant of release. On small-framed animals such as pronghorn antelope or certain deer, this shot can be very effective. Regrettably, the identical shot taken on larger game such as elk or moose often results in a gut-shot animal and a long, difficult tracking job that may or may not result in recovery. My advice? Avoid rump shots. And exercise extreme caution when shooting the tail end of smaller game, too. If you're close and unde-

Head and neck shots are a definite no-no for bowhunters. Patience may be rewarded moments later with a much better shooting opportunity.

from ambush with point-blank frontal shots, for the most part I avoid them. This is especially true when hunting larger game. Despite the temptation, I'd urge you to leave all such shots to the experts — people with the shooting skill and anatomical knowledge to put their arrow through an exact, perfect spot that will allow it to penetrate the vitals. For example, Chuck Adams killed his huge polar bear on Baffin Island in 1989 with a frontal shot under the white bruin's chin at 20 yards. A decade earlier, G. Fred Asbell quickly dropped a 1,500-pound British Columbia moose at 20 feet with an arrow striking the junction of that bull's neck and brisket. Despite his undeniable success, Fred perfectly sums up my own feelings about frontal shots with his candid admission, "I don't like them."

One final caveat: It's risky to release an arrow if the facing animal has you spotted and is alert to danger. The hottest-shooting 300+ fps compounds can't match the reflexes of alarmed game. If the animal moves the instant you release your arrow — and you can bet the family farm he's going to react to the noise or motion of your bow — even a well-aimed arrow can be off-target by the time it arrives a split-second later. Believe it!

Running Shots: It takes practice — and plenty of it — for a bowhunter to consistently hit the lung area of moving targets. Generally, it's easier for instinctive shooters to master this skill than bowhunters who use sight pins. For years, I've urged people to resist the urge to shoot at running game unless the animal is already wounded and may escape. Simply stated, very few bowhunters have practiced enough — or have the shooting skill — to attempt shots at running animals. Too many things can and do go wrong.

Walking Shots: Slowly moving animals passing beneath or close by your ambush site offer greater possibilities for success than shots taken at running game. Regardless, a stationary target is the best of all shooting options. Remember, a soft grunt, a low whistle, or the word "whoa" spoken aloud can often stop game in its tracks long enough for a killing shot, provided you're already at full draw and locked on your target. I limit all my walking shots to maximum distances of 15 to 20 yards.

tected, and the animal is calm, chances are good that if you're patient you'll soon get a shot at the animal's vitals. Chest shots are better shots. Always.

Frontal Shots: Head-on shots can be deadly on game animals if a sharp broadhead penetrates the heart-lung area. But that's a big "if." While I've taken several pronghorns and a handful of deer

Wouldn't you know it! Deer have an uncanny ability to pause with their vitals protected from a well-placed broadhead.

Frontal shots are risky. This small buck is already alert and ready to run. He'll be on the move by the time an arrow arrives.

(Left) Rump shots are iffy at best. Avoid 'em! Unless the femoral artery is cut or penetration is sufficient to reach the vitals, a wounded—and unrecovered—animal is likely. (Right) An expert bowhunter might be able to kill this buck with a perfect hit; however, he is in less than perfect position for a killing shot. Wait for a better opportunity!

Hitting moving targets takes practice—and lots of luck. Few bowhunters have the skill to consistently kill running deer. Resist the temptation!

Great body position, but... This buck knows you're there. He's looking you in the eye and ready to run. He'll explode into motion the instant you try to draw your bow or release an arrow.

A walking deer often can be stopped with a grunt or low whistle. A stationary target is preferred although slowly moving game can be consistently taken by experienced bowhunters.

Broadside and Quartering Shots: Broadside is best, some bowhunters insist, but I prefer the front leg of any broadside animal to be forward. If a deer is standing normally, for example, I take pains to place my arrow in or just behind the crease of the animal's shoulder. If the leg is back, I may wait for a better shot because it's possible to miss the lungs entirely because they're mostly hidden behind the shoulder. While a liver hit is possible, and deadly, lung hits result in quicker kills and shorter blood trails.

When an animal is quartering slightly away from you, it presents an ideal opportunity to angle your arrow through its chest and lungs. If you're on the same level, hold for an exact spot just below an imaginary horizontal line perfectly dissecting the body. If you're in an elevated position, hold low unless the animal is directly beneath you. Always try to envision your broadhead's diagonal path through the lungs and aim for the animal's off-shoulder.

Front-quartering shots are an entirely different matter. Place your arrow behind an animal's shoulder as he angles toward you and it's likely the broadhead will slice into the stomach and intestines. Frankly, that's a terrible spot to accidentally place an arrow, much less to do it on purpose. Wait and watch for a better shot. If you're in a tree, I'd also urge patience. A better chance may come when the animal quarters past or walks beneath your stand. Even if the ideal shot never materializes, it's better to watch game walk away than wound an animal with a poorly placed arrow. When hunting

(Above and left) Patience does pay. By passing up a broadside shot at this walking buck, a perfect opportunity arises when he pauses to relieve himself.

Front-quartering shots are questionable. An arrow behind the shoulder will penetrate the paunch and intestine. Bone and muscle can stop a sharp broadhead before it reaches the lungs.

A stationary broadside shot at an animal's chest is ideal, providing there is nothing to deflect the arrow before it reaches the target.

(Right) This velvet-racked whitetail is broadside and unaware of your presence. Do you take this shot? Why or why not? It doesn't take much—a single leaf, twig or weed—to deflect a well-aimed arrow. Be sure its flight path is clear or don't try the shot. (Below) An animal quartering slightly away is considered an excellent bowhunting shot.

from the ground, you can hold low on the chest, just in front of the near leg. While such shots into the crease between the shoulder and rib cage can be deadly (provided there's adequate penetration into the chest cavity), you already know my feelings about front-facing shots. If attempted at all, they are best left to the bowhunting pros who know exactly what they're doing.

The ultimate choices about releasing and placing arrows are yours and yours alone, of course. But for what it's worth, I'm convinced that if all bowhunters limited their shots to 30 yards or less and only took shots that would result in double-lung hits, wounded and unrecovered animals would become almost as rare as woolly mammoths in the deer woods. Whatever you decide, keep in mind there's no substitute for actual in-the-field shooting experience mixed with a healthy dose of common sense.

Chapter 13
After the Shot: Tracking, Recovering & Field-Dressing

TWO BUCKS EMERGED from a brush-choked cedar swamp to the left of my stand. They paused briefly in the evening dimness, scent-checking the gently eddying air currents. They finally angled slowly my way, moving almost noiselessly through a weedy opening in the darkening trees. One was a gangly yearling wearing a skinny three-point crown; the other buck was a burly big woods bruiser with at least 10 long tines jutting from his pale, thick-beamed rack. Watching the two approaching deer, I moved in ultra-slow motion to carefully lift my bow with its nocked shaft from a nearby hanger. Behind my camo-streaked face, a growing drum roll throbbed audibly within my temples.

As the bucks quartered closer, I followed their painfully slow progress through my bow's sight window. Over the pounding in my ears I finally could hear their hooves rustling among dead leaves. They were close, but the little buck shielded the 10-pointer's chest. I couldn't draw.

Finally, when the two whitetails walked past the cluster of dark pines that concealed my stand, they stopped and stood staring straight ahead, ears cupped. Turning my head slightly, I could see the

shadow shapes of deer moving through the trees across an old logging trail off to my right. A small group of does and fawns was browsing there.

Below me, the yearling stepped ahead, eyes still locked on the feeding deer. But the 10-pointer dropped his head to nose the ground. I instantly eased to full draw, anchored, and put my top pin low on his thick chest. But his near foreleg was back. So I waited, fully focused on making the shot. And when he finally stepped forward, my arrow blurred toward the exact spot I wanted it to fly.

The shadowy woods suddenly came alive with flagging deer. My buck blindly crashed in a half circle, heading back toward the cedar swamp. But he didn't make it. I watched him go down 40 yards away, powerful legs still flailing at the dry leaves and woodland duff. But soon he grew still, managing only to lift his head a final time. Then the weight of his beautiful, long-tined rack pulled it back to earth. My season was over.

That's the way it's supposed to happen. Even after over 40 years of bowhunting, I'm still amazed at the deadly effectiveness of a well-placed arrow. A carefully-honed hunting head can be instantly lethal. Even so, more often than not the fatally hit animal will not drop within sight. That means you'll need to follow a blood trail. And you'll need to be prepared. You owe it to yourself, the wounded animal, and all responsible bowhunters everywhere to do everything humanly possible to recover and tag each animal you hit.

Anti-hunters delight in claiming that bowhunters hit and lose at least half of the animals they shoot. They blame such outrageous hunting losses on everything from ineffective equipment (a definite lie) to a widespread lack of shooting/tracking skills (which may be true in some cases). They loudly proclaim that the woods are literally full of ani-

Hitting an animal is only part of the hunting equation. To be a successful bowhunter, you must also be able to track and recover wounded game.

Locating your arrow after any shot is a good first step. Even if you believe you've missed, take time to find out for sure. A bloodied or broken shaft is proof-positive that you've wounded the animal. Next, you must do everything possible to recover and tag it.

This Colorado record-book bull left little blood despite a mortal wound that quickly dropped him. Sure of a lethal hit, the author and a friend continued their search and soon found the big elk.

At times, hard-hit game bleeds profusely. But more often than not you'll need patience and a keen eye to unravel the blood trail and locate the animal. Perseverance is key.

mals left to die a slow, agonizing death by heartless, bumbling bowhunters whose insatiable blood lust inflicts horrible suffering on innocent woodland creatures. That's bull of a non-elk kind, but each unrecovered animal makes such outlandish claims more credible.

Undeniably, in all forms of hunting — whether scattergunning for upland game and waterfowl or using a big bore rifle on the earth's largest creatures — some wild game will be hit and lost. That's a sad fact of hunting life, no matter what the species or the weapon of choice.

In fact, research has proved that bowhunters are far more efficient that the hunter-haters want the public to believe. A 1990s' multi-year wounding study at Minnesota's Camp Ripley, the 53,000-acre military reservation near Brainerd — conducted by Jay McAninch of Wendy Krueger of the Minnesota Department of Natural Resources, along with Dr. Dave Samuel of West Virginia University — found that a maximum of 13 percent of wounded animals were unrecovered. That's a far cry for the 50 percent claimed by the antis — and it must be noted that not all of the injured deer died of their arrow wounds. A majority recovered fully. I suspect that's the case more often than not wherever bowhunters pursue deer.

Truthfully, few arrow-killed deer are ever found rotting in the woods after bow season ends. Immediately following archery seasons, routine examinations of thousands of gun-killed deer at check stations in multiple states — using metal detectors and careful visual examinations — have found very few checked animals with any evidence of an arrow wound. Perhaps more importantly, those few that had been wounded were generally in excellent health at the time of their death, having no lasting ill-effects from the broadhead wounds.

These findings are very important because vocal bowhunting critics equate "lost" game with "dead" game. Not true. Undeniably, a few animals do die of their wounds; however, a majority of arrow-hit animals don't die. They recover, undoubtedly wiser for the experience. And the reason for such a high recovery rate should be obvious. Researchers have found that a razor-sharp broadhead cuts cleanly, rupturing blood vessels around the wound. This creates a numbing effect with relatively little pain. If there is not sufficient blood loss — about one-third of the animal's total blood volume — or massive damage to internal organs, the clean, scalpel-like cut

115

The big buck that left this blood trail didn't run 50 yards before going down. This is the kind of trail that can result from a solid double-lung hit.

Here's an ideal tracking situation: snow and an obvious blood trail. The bull moose that left this sign dropped within 45 yards. Most trailing jobs will take more effort under less than perfect conditions

quickly heals. Chances of the wound becoming infected and causing a painful, lingering death — as hunter-haters claim — are slight.

Sadly, a few thoughtless "bowhunters" help to perpetuate the myth of uncaring ineptness with such public comments as, "I ain't got my deer yet, but I've stuck a couple." Such stupid, mindless remarks are sometimes outright lies. One two-year field survey found that only one out of four bowhunters who claimed to have hit a deer actually wounded an animal. Also, it seems some wannabe bowhunters cover their own ineptitude with fabrications in an attempt to impress listeners. And even in cases where animals are hit and lost, no ethical hunter ever brags about wounding shots or unrecovered animals. These sad instances are reason for silent shame and a vow to do better, not chest-thumping and bragging.

Any time you release an arrow at an animal, whether you think you've hit your target or missed cleanly, it is your ethical responsibility to follow up the shot with a thorough visual examination of the area where the animal was standing. First, always check carefully for any evidence of a hit, such as cut hair or drops of blood. Even if you're positive you missed, search for confirmation by locating your arrow and checking it for any trace of blood. When you can't find your arrow, conduct a painstaking search of the surrounding area. If tracks are present, follow them. Sometimes you won't find any blood sign until you've followed the animal's escape route for some distance. Only after you've looked long and hard — and are 100 percent certain the arrow missed — should you resume hunting.

Second, if you see the arrow hit or later find proof you've wounded the animal, prepare to start the second stage of your hunt — tracking and recovering the animal. Although each tracking job and blood trail will differ, depending on the species of game and

position of the hit, the following tips will increase your odds of eventually locating the animal and putting your tag on a well-earned trophy.

Tracking/Trailing Tips

You've just made the shot and you saw your arrow smack home. Your trophy instantly crashed away, quickly disappearing into the thick woods or dense brush. Now all is still — except for the wild thudding of your heart and your racing mind. What's next?

- First of all, try to calm down. Take a deep breath or two. Mark the exact spot where you took the shot and mentally note where the animal was standing. If you're hunting from a ground blind or tree stand, that part is easy; however, if you're still-hunting or stalking, take a careful look around you. It's especially critical to pinpoint the exact location just in case you later need to return to the scene to resume or begin your search from the very start. Many veteran bowhunters carry toilet paper, surveyor's tape, or some similar flagging material for this purpose. In a pinch, an extra arrow or two from your quiver will do nicely. Then, visualize the last place you saw the animal. If you have a compass, take a reading. It can help determine the wounded animal's direction of travel.

- Next, force yourself to wait. Keep quiet, watch, and listen. If not immediately pursued or alarmed by unnatural noises following the shot, animals often bed down nearby when the first effects of the arrow are felt. Under certain conditions, you may see or hear the animal moving off — or falling. Regardless, it's wise to wait between 30 to 60 minutes before taking up the trail. Exceptions are when adverse weather threatens to obliterate the trail, when open country allows you to keep the animal in sight, or when you actually see the animal fall and are positive it's down for keeps.

- After sufficient time has passed, walk quietly to the spot where the animal stood and confirm evidence of a hit. Physically mark this location. Examine your arrow, if found, for evidence of complete penetration (blood streaks from broadhead to nock) and clues to the position of the wound. Greasy, whitish material on the shaft may mean a brisket hit (often non-vital). Greenish-brown matter is evidence of a paunch hit (gut-shot). Smell the shaft for confirmation. Gut shots can be fatal if you allow sufficient time to elapse before taking up the trail. Plan to wait at least four to six hours — or even longer — before trailing paunch-hit game. Bright red blood with bubbles means a lung or artery hit — a very good sign.

- Decide whether you're going to take up the trail alone or get assistance. In the case of dangerous game, it's usually wise to enlist the aid of one or more companions, and where it's legal, carry a firearm just in case. Also, on guided hunts, always listen to your guide's advice and follow his direction. Some guides will instruct you not to follow a blood trail on your own. Do whatever you're told. And when you do have help available, never use more than three or four people on a blood trail. Too many helpers can cause more problems than they solve. Use a large group only as a last resort if the blood trail plays out. Sometimes an organized grid search of the area will lead to locating animals that otherwise might be lost.

- Refrain from rushing. It's quite natural to want to locate your game; however, you should always "make haste slowly," marking the blood trail as you go in just in case you'll need to retrace your steps. Never walk in the path itself; stay to one side of the trail. Don't obliterate sign. If the trail is spotty, take special care to find and mark all blood. A companion comes in handy here, hanging tissue or tying tape to limbs or brush while you carefully continue your search.

- Check leaves and grass for blood, but don't overlook rocks, logs, tree trunks, or bare ground. If blood is scarce, look for scuff marks left by the animal's hooves or pads. Check back along your marked trail from time to time to help get a feel for the animal's line of travel.

- If you lose all blood sign, continue the search by following the general direction the animal was heading. Some bowhunters begin walking in a tight but ever-expanding circle from the last blood sign. Others use companions to fan out and help look for clues. It's wise to conduct orderly searches whenever possible. Random wandering through an area in hopes of stumbling across the animal is always your last resort.

Keep in mind that mortally wounded animals often follow the path of least resistance, avoiding natural obstacles and often angling downhill instead of climbing. Look in and near water. Probe dense thickets. Check brush piles and deadfalls. Think like the animal by putting yourself in his place. Allow your instincts to take over.

If your arrow was well-placed, chances are excellent you'll come across your trophy within the first 100 to 200 yards. But even hard-hit animals possess tremendous stamina, so don't be surprised

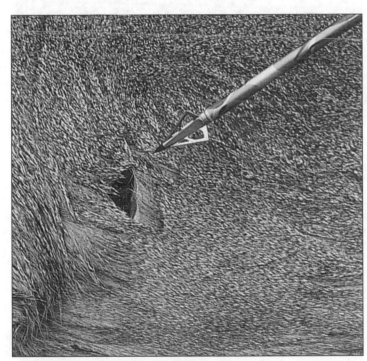

A razor-sharp broadhead and proper shot placement can create massive blood loss and a quick, clean kill.

Here's the perfect ending to any whitetail blood trail. It's the kind of work no bowhunter minds, especially if he has a buddy along to lend a hand.

or discouraged if the trail is longer. And don't let the amount — or lack of — blood fool you. Sometimes, depending where the arrow hit, most bleeding will be internal, so a lack of good blood sign won't mean much. Sure, we all want the kind of blood trail you can follow at a brisk walk, but this is the exception. Stick-to-itiveness is essential for recovering most arrow-hit animals.

Night-trailing is worth mentioning. If game is hit shortly before darkness, you must make a decision whether to follow after a brief waiting period or take up the search at first light the following morning. In some instances — during hot weather, for example — a long wait could result in soured meat and a ruined trophy. And in some areas predators such as bears, coyotes, or other hungry and opportunistic woodland creatures may find your animal overnight. Don't forget about the threat of a nighttime storm obliterating all signs. Still another risk involved is tracking certain dangerous species in the dark.

Really, if your arrow was well placed, there's no reason to postpone your search because of darkness. Blood reflects light well, and Coleman lanterns, carbide lamps, or bright-beamed flashlights can make night-tracking effective. SureFire is one company that even offers a blue filter with their flashlights, since blue illuminates blood during after-dark searches. In most cases at least two people should be present to work out the trail. Generally, the same rules of daytime tracking apply to nighttime searches. *Note: It's always wise to carry a compass or GPS unit after dark since it's easy to get turned around with your attention focused on the ground, not on your surroundings or direction of travel.*

Dried blood appears dark. If you're uncertain that black spot on a leaf or limb is blood or something else, use your fingernail to scrape it off and moisten the flakes to see if they turn red. A drop of hydrogen peroxide will cause dried blood to foam and bubble. A few savvy bowhunters carry a small bottle in their packs for exactly this purpose.

Also, some bowhunters mount string trackers to their bows in hopes of making trailing and recovery easier. Personally, I've never had much use for them, since the line can get tangled and break as the animal runs off. Some bear hunters I know use them because a bruin's body fat can plug the wound and their thick coats soak up what blood does flow. When they work, string trackers can assist you; however, they're not as popular or readily available as they once were. Besides, there's no substitute for well-made shots and well-practiced tracking skills.

Every once in a while someone comes up with an electronic tracking device of one kind or another. I've seen arrows containing a compact unit that will emit electronic signals that can be followed (this assumes you won't get complete penetration or the arrow is pulled out by snagging on brush as the animal flees). I've also seen heat-sensitive units that supposedly will quickly locate downed animals after the shot. Such tackle is expensive and its workability questionable. Remember, too, the Pope and Young Club won't allow the entry of any trophy taken with bows or arrows having an attached electronic device of any kind.

So what's the next step if all of your best efforts fail to locate the animal? Remember, all responsible bowhunters will continue their search until they are certain beyond any reasonable doubt that the animal cannot be recovered. If the blood trail peters out after several hundred yards, chances are good the arrow struck a non-vital area. When the trail is lost and the hunter is convinced the hit was

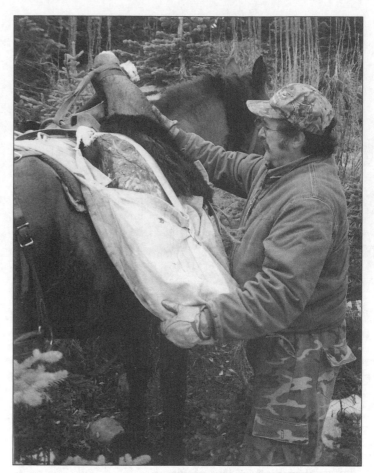

Here are two ways to pack out a bull moose from the Montana back country. Whenever possible, savvy hunters use pack animals to save hours of back-straining effort. Sometimes, however, muscle power and teamwork accomplish the same job.

At times, there's no choice but to pack out meat, antlers and cape on a set of strong shoulders. Sometimes it takes two people to manage a hefty load like this—even if it is a small moose.

Bear hides and meat need prompt attention during warm weather bowhunts. If body heat is retained, the hair can slip and the meat quickly sour. It's best to skin the bruin as quickly as possible, salt the hide thoroughly, and cool the meat if it's to be saved for the freezer.

indeed fatal, he should continue to search the area. Crows, ravens, magpies, jays, and circling vultures may eventually lead to the carcass. The same is true of the buzzing of flies and bees — not to mention the odor of decaying flesh — during warm weather hunts.

Still another option involves the use of dogs, where such practice is legal. I've seen specially trained dogs — from big, flop-eared hounds and labs to tiny but spunky terriers — help recover wounded game when no blood trail was apparent. Some southern and southwestern hunting camps I've visited utilize tracking dogs to aid in recovery efforts. Again, such practice is illegal in some states, so check the game laws.

Remember, too, the Pope and Young Club will not accept any trophies located after the initial search has been abandoned. The moment a hunter gives up his search and resumes hunting, his trophy is ineligible — even if it's later recovered. On the other hand, trophies are accepted where considerable time passes — just so long as the search is not abandoned and the bowhunter does not hunt in the interim. Each case is considered on an individual basis with a ruling made by the records chairman and a committee composed of P&Y measurers.

Dogged determination in tracking and recovering game is always to be commended. I am convinced, however, that bowhunters should resist the temptation to take anything but chest cavity shots at broadside or slightly quartering-away targets. If these animals are standing well within the hunter's effective shooting range, very few big game animals would ever be lost. I've mentioned this in the shot placement section: A double-lung hit will quickly kill any animal. Anytime. Anywhere.

Field-Dressing Game

I'm always amused to hear people mention the "wild taste" or "gamy flavor" of venison and other big game table fare. If properly cared for in the field, the meat of virtually every big game animal can be transformed into mouth-watering meals. While an animal's age, physical condition, diet, and kitchen treatment all contribute to that meat's ultimate taste, it's the bowhunter's responsibility to promptly care for the carcass and any game animal tagged.

An ATV can make transporting a big deer back to camp a snap. It sure beats a long drag, even when there's snow on the ground to make pulling the carcass easier.

Approach every downed animal cautiously, of course. Make certain it's dead before taking hold of its antlers, horns, or head. Move in from behind, staying clear of hind legs should the "dead" animal begin to kick or thrash about. Be especially cautious if the animal is lying in a bunched up position, if its eyes are closed, or if it's capable of holding its head erect. Do not hesitate to use a follow-up arrow to finish any wounded animals. Dead game generally lies sprawled where it falls. The eyes will be open, glazed, and unblinking.

If a tossed rock or limb or a sharp broadhead jab fails to elicit a response, the animal is likely dead. The final test is to touch the animal's open eye with a stick or broadhead. Dead animals don't blink.

So what do you do first? Fill out your game tag, making things legal. Attach it if local law mandates or simply return it to pocket or pack. But don't forget to affix the completed game tag once you've dragged or packed the carcass out of the field. Know your game laws and act accordingly. Next, time and weather conditions permitting, make time for photos. This is where a buddy or good camera comes in handy, although many cameras have a built-in timer and auto-shoot feature.

Take at least one entire roll of film, preferably more. Remember, film is one of the least expensive items of any hunting trip, and good snapshots will make fine mementos of your outdoor adventures. Turn the animal's head slightly with each click of the shutter. Vary your own body position, too. Include your hunting buddy or guide in some of the photos. Resist the temptation to have an arrow protruding from the animal's carcass. If the shaft is still in the body, remove it. Jutting arrows add absolutely nothing to the photo and may turn off non-hunting viewers.

Also, be sure the lolling tongue is not visible; reposition it or simply cut it off before taking any pictures. If possible fold the animal's legs under it (as if it were bedded). Use toilet paper, paper towels, or a wet rag to clean any excess blood from the wound, nostrils, and mouth. Water from your canteen or pack bottle can help do this job. By all means place your bow so it shows in the photo. Urge the photographer to drop down to the same level, get close, and fill the entire frame with animal and hunter. Sometimes it's good to lie on the ground and shoot slightly up at the trophy and proud hunter, especially if the antlers or horns can be skylined. Take at least a few photos using your camera's flash system. Shun harsh sunlight in favor of shady areas. Using a fill-flash to illuminate the hunter and animal helps. A few veteran bowhunters and guides even carry glass taxidermy deer eyes for field photo sessions. Inserting them eliminates that hollow, sunken-eye look or white-eyed stare of dead game so common in flash pictures.

Try to avoid busy backgrounds (this includes the camo clothing you're wearing). Never sit astride an animal or grasp it by its ears. If you smoke, put the cigarette aside rather than having it dangling from your lips. And don't, for heaven's sake, show a celebratory can of beer in the picture (such shots help perpetuate the anti-hunters' myth that most hunters are drunken slobs who enjoy "murdering" wildlife). Never take photos of game posed on pickup tailgates or in automobile trunks, either. Ditto for animals hanging from their necks in sheds and garages. Pose them in natural settings, even if it's against a bush or tree in your backyard. Treat all animals with the proper respect they deserve.

Once the photo session is wrapped up, lay your bow and camera aside and roll up your sleeves. It's time to turn your attention to field-dressing chores. Essentials include a well-honed knife, rope or cord, bone saw or hatchet, and a steel or ceramic rod for touching up dulled blades. Some bowhunters carry paper towels or pre-moistened hand wipes in their packs, along with plastic bags for holding the heart, liver, and kidneys. A few fastidious individuals even carry several pairs of disposable latex rubber gloves to wear during the gutting process. It's your call, depending on how much of a neatnik you are. If the possibility of Chronic Wasting Disease (CWD) or other wildlife illnesses concerns you, by all means wear latex gloves to avoid direct contact with the animal's blood.

Every unrecovered animal is a wasted animal—and a black mark against hunting. You must make every effort to trail and tag every animal you shoot. Anything less is irresponsible.

At certain times when game is taken miles from where you beached the boat and started the day's hunt, there's no choice but to employ shank's mare and a strong back to pack out the meat and cape—often making more than one trip. Montana bowhunter Chuck Williams took this bull in northern Quebec on a hunt with the author.

It's critical that all fat and bits of flesh be removed from bear hides. After the job is complete, the hide should be liberally salted. If no salt is available, fold or roll the hide (hair side out), and freeze it until it can be taken to the taxidermist.

When skinning deer-sized game, it's best to hang the carcass head-down and begin removing the hide from the rear legs to the animal's neck.

Never cut an animal's throat! This is a surefire way to ruin a cape and annoy your taxidermist. Most arrow-hit game generally dies from excessive blood loss. Cutting the throat is wasted effort. In fact, cutting the throat of any dead animal is a total waste of time — despite the claims of some misguided hunters who blindly follow ol' grandpappy's advice — since the heart must be beating if blood is to be pumped out of the throat incision.

The size of some large animals — elk, moose, and bison, for example – makes on-the-spot field-dressing mandatory. Smaller animals such as deer or pronghorn antelope may be easily moved to a better or shady location. In certain cases, as when hunting over bait, near a water hole, or in some feeding area, it's plumb dumb to gut the animal there. Blood smell and viscera may spook or alert approaching game for days to come. It also may attract unwanted predators, which can spoil hunting.

Regardless of where the actual work is done, most hunters begin the field-dressing process with the animal on its back or side, lying slightly downhill, whenever possible. A rope or stout cord may be used to tie the legs apart and help hold the carcass in position, although a hunting buddy can serve the same purpose.

First, if evidence of sex is required by law, leave the udder or testicles alone; otherwise, slice these identifying tissues away and discard them. Next, make a long incision upward from anus to sternum (or completely to the throat just under the lower jaw if the cape is not going to be saved for mounting). Keep the cut shallow along its entire length, taking pains to avoid slicing into the intestines or stomach below the diaphragm. Sliding your index and middle fingers along on either side of the knife's upturned blade (between the skin and entrails) works well to keep the cut shallow, but this usually takes some practice.

Some hunters next will make a deep, circular cut around the anus, as if coring an apple. Others simply split and saw through the pelvic arch, being careful not to puncture the bladder. I prefer the latter, but either way works well.

Next, reach up into the chest cavity and locate the esophagus and trachea. Cut completely through these tubes and then lay your knife aside. Firmly grasp the windpipe and feeding tube, pulling downward to loosen the chest contents. Retrieve the heart if it's to be saved. Then slice the diaphragm muscle free of the ribs. Pull down hard, tugging and cutting as necessary, until the freed entrails roll out between or beside the rear legs. Make sure the rectal tube and any spilled fecal matter is removed. Pellets, urine, and

Once the hide has been removed to the base of the skull, use a knife and bone saw to separate the head from the carcass.

intestinal matter or fluids can cause tainted meat unless promptly cleaned away.

If it's possible to elevate the animal in some cool or shady spot, do so as quickly as possible once the field-dressing chore is finished. Hanging allows pooling blood to drain from the body cavity and air to circulate completely around the carcass. Propping the chest cavity open helps. Remember, body heat will be retained longer wherever the animal is in contact with the ground.

Porous game bags are a wise early-season investment. Such bags and a sprinkling of black pepper will help to discourage ever-present blowflies and bees. Never hang an animal in direct sunlight. Speaking of hanging, I prefer to initially hang my animals in a head-up position to allow proper drainage and to prevent fluids from collecting in the chest cavity. Later, when I'm ready to peel off the hide, I normally swap the animal's body position and skin down from rear legs to neck.

Use a strong nylon rope and don't hang horned and antlered game by the throat if you plan to mount your trophy. Rope marks may later show in the rope-damaged cape. Always tie such animals by their antlers or horns.

With larger game, it may be necessary to quarter the animal at the kill site, and some bowhunters opt to bone out the meat on the spot where the animal fell. They insist it's dumb to pack out bones and everything that isn't edible or destined for the taxidermist. Even so, the hide, cape, horns, and antlers of some big game animals can amount to quite a load for one man — especially if the backpack is aleady crammed with choice backstraps and tenderloins. Don't try to carry too much in one trip. If a companion is nearby, enlist help (packing game quickly tells you who your real buddies are). With larger game, pack animals are a viable option, along with the strong backs and shoulders of willing hunting pals. Paid guides and outfitters normally provide meat care and packing service as part of the hunt package. Find out before your hunt begins and plan accordingly.

In bear country, especially where grizzlies and brown bears live, a gut pile or cooling carcass is an open invitation to a free meal — and potential trouble. In reality, it's generally unwise, and often illegal, to hang game in hunting camps where a bear might be attracted by the tempting food smell. Common sense precautions can

Larger animals such as moose, elk, and this bison, cannot be easily moved and must be skinned on the spot. A dorsal cut along the animal's back works as well as the usual slit from anus to sternum.

avoid possible confrontations between hunters and hungry bruins.

If the animal can be dragged or packed to camp or a waiting vehicle, this process is best accomplished by two or more people. On antlered or horned game, pulling the animals by their headgear is possible and much easier than grasping by the forelegs. Take care to avoid bruising the meat through rough handling, and try not to spoil the potential mount by rubbing bare spots in the hide during the dragging process. Some hunters place a canvas tarp under the animals to protect the hide and make dragging easier.

Some game is small enough for one person to pull or carry; however, never overexert yourself. An excited, out-of-shape bowhunter is a prime candidate for a coronary. And although bowhunting is generally a safe sport, it's smart to tie fluorescent tape or cloth to any animal being carried, especially if the firearms season is open. Also, make sure your completed game tag is not lost between the kill site and camp. Some game wardens can get downright testy over such details.

(Left and Bottom) Savvy hunters like Larry D. Jones often bone out elk and other large game before packing chores begin. Carry game bags and sturdy pack-frames for the meat. Remove all four quarters and then collect the backstraps, tenderloins, ribs, and neck meat. Leaving heavy bones in the woods lightens the packing load.

Once you reach camp or a vehicle, give further consideration to preserving the meat and hide. Wash and clean the meat of all blood, hair, and any woodland debris. Allow the clean meat to cool. If a motor vehicle is being used to transport the animal, be certain that legal requirements are met and all tags properly filled out and in place. In some hunting areas, portions of the animal must be visible for easy identification by wildlife officers. Do whatever is required.

Never tie an animal to the vehicle's hood where motor heat can cause tainting problems. Carry the game on a roof rack or on the trunk. And use a game bag, tarp, or blanket to protect it. Don't skin the carcass before hot, dusty trips to town or camp. If possible, make sure the animal's body heat has dissipated long before the journey begins. Never transport game in a closed trunk or unventilated trailer where air cannot circulate. Thoroughly cooled carcasses or game quarters may be wrapped in tarps, sleeping bags, or other well-insulated material for transportation. On long hauls, dry ice or large coolers containing bags or blocks of ice can help preserve the meat's flavor. Some bowhunters I know construct specially insulated meat boxes for their out-of-state hunts and include them as an important part of their gear.

Once the meat is transported home or to some nearby processing facility, butchering and packaging can take place. Afterwards, you can look ahead to some mouth-watering meals.

Skinning and Caping Game

If your trophy is destined for the taxidermy shop, you need to be aware of certain skinning and caping techniques necessary to ensure the best results for a lifelike mount.

Simply explained, caping refers to skinning the shoulders, neck, and head of any trophy animal. It is accomplished by making a single incision from a point between the shoulders up the back of the neck to a spot just below the antlers or horns. A cut is then made completely around the animal's body behind the shoulders. Then, the shoulders and neck are skinned until the junction of the neck and skull is reached. At this point the hide and head may be freed

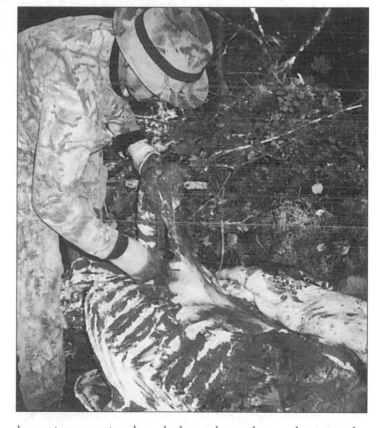

by cutting or sawing through the neck vertebrae and twisting the head and cape loose. Unless you're proficient at skinning out the skull and turning the ears, this job is best left to the taxidermist. Special care must be taken skinning around the animal's ears, eyes, and lips. Salt the cape liberally and roll or fold the hide, hair side out. Store in a cool, shady place, and get the head and cape to a taxidermist as quickly as possible. Spoilage may occur if the temperature climbs above 45 degrees.

Freezing heads and capes is an even better option where large freezers are available. Just remember that the sooner any

Finally, after completing boning chores and salvaging all edible meat, Larry collects the ivory from this Roosevelt bull. (Note that the cape was not saved for mounting, but the antlers were removed to be packed out with the tasty venison.) Prompt field care makes for good meals later.

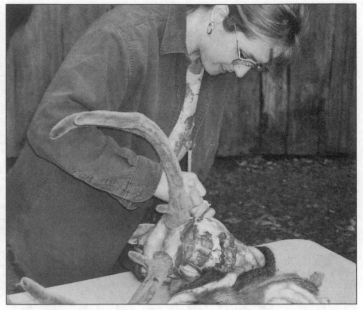

If an animal's cape is to be saved for mounting, its skull must be skinned. Care should be taken when cutting around the ears, eyes, and lips. That's veteran outfitter TinaMarie Schaafsma caping a California blacktail. Once the hide is separated, it's salted or frozen until delivery to a taxidermist.

taxidermist receives your trophy animal for mounting, whether well-salted or frozen, the better the chances for an excellent mount. If possible, speak to your taxidermist before any hunt. Ask for advice and follow instructions for preserving and delivering your trophy in the best possible condition.

If a rug is planned — a common practice with bears and cougars — or if a full-body mount is what you want, the skinning process is longer and somewhat more involved. In these cases an incision is typically made from anus to sternum (on rugs the cut may continue to the animal's throat or lower jaw). Additional cuts are then made down the inside of each leg to a point just above the paw or hoof. The skin is then peeled and cut away from the body until completely free. The tail may be cut loose at its root or split up the underside to facilitate removal of the tailbone. (Note: On long-haired mounts such as bears, it's possible to skin the animal from the back down, making a long dorsal cut and freeing the hide on either side down the entire length the animal's body. I prefer the method described above.)

In warm weather, it's probably best to remove the skull and feet from the hide once skinning is complete. As previously noted, special care is necessary when cutting around the ears, eyes, nostrils, and lips. The same is true for the base of the antlers of horns (where a Y-shaped cut is made from the back-of-the-neck incision to the antler base). Additional care is needed when removing the paw cartilage; hooves are merely removed at the ankle joint. It's always best to cut as close to the skull as possible, but allow the taxidermist to do the final trimming of unnecessary skin. Try to remove as much clinging meat as possible before heavily salting the hide. Be sure to work salt into folds and creases before folding the hide, hair-side out, for storage or transport. Do not store the hide in a plastic garbage bag unless it is bound for the freezer.

If the animal is not going to be mounted, the skinning process often starts with the removal of the animal's front legs at each knee joint. A cut is then made through the tendons behind each hock and the animal is hoisted, head down, by hooks or a gambrel. Then

skin around each hind leg just below the hocks, extending the cut down the inside of each rear leg. Take care not to cut into the meat itself and don't let the hair touch exposed meat. Peel the hide down, pulling and cutting as necessary, until you reach the front legs. Make cuts from the exposed knee joints up the inner leg to the chest. Free the skin from each leg and shoulder. Continue to tug and cut until the skin is hanging over the head with most of the neck exposed. Cut deeply and completely around the neck near the head, then twist or saw to free the head with its attached hide. The animal is now completely skinned.

Once this skinning chore is complete, it's ready to be cut up by a handy do-it-yourself butcher or a knowledgeable meat processor. Strict health laws sometimes make it difficult to locate a processing facility that will accept wild game; however, in certain parts of the country, especially in heavily hunted states and provinces, finding someone to cut and wrap game animals is relatively simple. Anyone initially attempting to process the game himself should refer to a diagram showing correct cuts and use a well-illustrated step-by-step butchering guide.

Some bowhunters insist that venison and other wild game tastes best if it's properly aged before processing. They often let the animals hang from several days to a week or more in 40-degree or slightly lower temps, swearing this step makes the meat yummier. Others process the animals immediately with excellent results. In truth, there's probably no one best way to age or treat game animals bound for your freezer. People have vastly different tastes — and ideas — and only experimentation will determine what's just right for you and your family.

Just remember one undisputed fact: The meat of most any big game species can provide numerous tasty meals for you and yours over a period of several months. It's lean and healthy and naturally chemical-free. No bowhunter should ever miss out on the culinary qualities of the various big game critters he pursues.

Chapter 14
Answers to Common Questions

IT SEEMS LOTS OF FOLKS we meet have lots of questions about bowhunting techniques and tackle. Wherever we go, whether it's some hunting camp or any other place where bowhunters gather, we're asked to provide answers and offer personal opinions on a wide variety of topics. Here's a representative sampling of some of the most common queries we receive each year:

Hunting Bows

I've been hunting with firearms and a crossbow for some time but I want to move to a compound bow. What would you suggest? This would be my first time choosing archery tackle for hunting.

First, visit one or more area archery dealers or pro shops. While simply checking the latest compound bows in a Cabela's or Bass Pro Shops archery catalog can show you what's available, that's no substitute for hands-on examination. You should be able to hold, examine, and possibly shoot prospective bows that grab your interest. Further, a knowledgeable dealer can answer any questions and help you come up with a bowhunting setup that's just right for you.

Remember, selecting archery tackle is extremely personal. Unlike a firearm or crossbow, which might work for a lot of people, a bow must be matched precisely to your build and strength. In particular, draw length and draw weight must fit you perfectly. In addition, personal taste and budgetary limitations typically enter the picture. Listen to your dealer — and experienced bowhunting friends — but in the end choose the bow that fits you and feels just right for you.

Also keep in mind that arrows must be matched to you and your bow. This is where a pro shop dealer can play a vital role. He will help you select arrows spined and cut to your exact draw length and draw weight. The very best bows won't shoot well with mismatched arrows. A good pro dealer can also provide advice on accessories — or necessities — such as sights, shooting gloves, tabs, or mechanical release aids, arm guards, arrow points, and so forth.

Finally, read books and magazine articles on the basics of shooting. If possible, practice with an experienced archer who can help you with form. You might even consider paying for a lesson or two.

In shooting a bow, your body is an integral part of the shooting system, and you must develop good form from the beginning. Bad habits can stick with you for years and destroy your accuracy — and enjoyment. Get started right. With proper practice and the right attitude, you'll be shooting a compound bow quite well in short order. —M. R. James

I shoot a 61-pound compound bow with a 26-inch draw and 24-1/2-inch 2013 aluminum arrows tipped with 85-grain heads. I get 241 fps from this setup. How much kinetic energy am I getting? Will I be able to hunt elk with this bow?

Unfortunately, you didn't describe all of your arrow's components — particularly the insert and fletching type. Both the fletching size and material affect finished arrow weight, because vanes are heavier than feathers, and aluminum inserts are heavier than carbon.

Once you know your arrow's total weight, you can calculate kinetic energy with the following formula: Arrow speed times arrow speed; times arrow weight; divided by 450,240, equals kinetic energy in foot pounds. Example: 241 fps x 241 fps = 58,081 x 390 grains = 22,651,590 divided by 450,240 = 50.310 foot pounds of kinetic energy.

Because there are so many variables in regard to shot placement, I hesitate to estimate a minimum amount of kinetic energy needed to kill an elk. But with proper shot placement your setup should have enough kinetic energy to take elk cleanly. I would, however, suggest that you use fixed-blade broadheads with your current setup.—Dave Holt

Could you recommend a book that deals with tuning compound bows?

Check out *Tuning Your Compound Bow* and *Tuning and Silencing Your Bowhunting Shooting System*, both by Larry Wise. These are two of the best booklets I've seen on the subject. Printed by Target Communications, they're available for $11.95 each from Bowhunter Books (call 1-800-358-6327 to place credit card orders).—M. R. James

I'm a new traditional bowhunter looking for some equipment recommendations. First, would you recommend a recurve or longbow for hunting? Should I get a custom or production bow?

Welcome to traditional archery. I believe a recurve is the best choice for a beginning traditionalist, because learning how to shoot it accurately is fairly straightforward. If you have been shooting a compound bow you'll find the transition comes quickly. The only real difference between the two bows (compound and recurve) is the letoff.

To begin with I might lean toward a production model rather than a custom bow. A custom bow is typically more expensive and is built to your exact specifications. Beginning with a production bow will give you an opportunity to decide what you like — draw weight, bow length, etc. —And you'll have a better idea of how to spend your money after you've shot a bow for a while.— G. Fred Asbell

I'm shopping for a new compound bow, so how does letoff percentage affect bow speed?

All else being equal, a bow with more letoff will shoot its arrow a little slower because slightly less energy is stored in its limbs. Also, bows with low brace height, radical cams, and short axle-to-axle lengths are generally faster, but they are often more difficult to tune and shoot accurately. Basically, speed and accuracy are at opposite ends of the spectrum, so a compromise must be reached.

In many cases I feel too much emphasis is placed on arrow speed and not enough attention is paid to accuracy. Accuracy with broadheads is the bottom line for bowhunters. I often see this fact acknowledged verbally, but then ignored by that same individual through equipment choices.

As for your choice of bows, much depends on personal preference and your shooting style. I would recommend that you choose a bow with a length of 40 inches or more and that you try several different models and brands.—Dave Holt

A fellow bowhunter told me that the lighter the draw weight of your hunting bow, the more damage it will do to an animal since the arrow will not completely penetrate through the body. Is this true?

Your question takes me back to the 1950s and early 1960s. A popular notion at that time was than an arrow which only partially penetrated an animal's chest cavity was preferable to an arrow passing completely through. The idea was that, when the animal ran away, either the motion of his running or the trees and brush striking the protruding arrow shaft as he fled would cause the arrow to flail about and the broadhead would inflict further damage inside the animal.

Today, it is generally accepted that an arrow which passes completely through the animal is preferable. When the arrow completely penetrates the body, more vital organs have been hit, there is no arrow shaft in the animal, and thus nothing impedes the flow of blood from the entrance and exit wounds. This will more than likely mean a much greater loss of blood, a better blood trail (on both sides of the animal), and a quicker, more humane death. Also, when the arrow passes completely through an animal, its flight is often less frantic and of a shorter duration.

Shoot a bow you can draw and shoot comfortably and accurately, keep your broadheads razor-sharp and your arrows flying straight and true, and you'll maximize your effectiveness as a bowhunter.— G. Fred Asbell

During long periods of time when a compound bow is not in use, should the weight be let off? I've always done it, but heard it's not necessary.

Personally, when storing spare compounds for long periods, I usually loosen each bow's limb bolts several turns to be on the safe side. While most modern bows aren't adversely affected by long periods of inactivity, relaxing the tension doesn't hurt. Check the recommendations in your own bow's warranty and service manual.

Actually, there's no reason to let your favorite bow gather dust. Don't overlook indoor leagues, 3-D competition, interactive target shooting, and other "off season" activities that will keep your shooting eye and reflexes sharp year-round. Regardless, if you don't shoot your compound for long periods of time, be sure to avoid any storage area that could expose the bow to extreme heat. This certainly includes leaving any strung bow inside an enclosed vehicle even for a few hours on a hot summer day.—M. R. James

Hunting Arrows and Broadheads

I can shoot tight groups with my field points, but when I change to my broadheads I never hit where I'm aiming. I know it has something to do with my broadhead alignment. How can I fix my broadhead problem, or should I just use mechanical heads?

First, are you shooting helical or straight fletching? Straight fletch may work fine with field points but may fail miserably with bladed hunting heads. Going to slight helical twist (or more severe helical fletching) could solve your problem of inconsistent arrow flight.

Second, are your field points and broadheads the same weight? If not, it could be the heavier broadheads are the basis of your difficulty.

Third, you might experiment with several arrow sizes. Perhaps you need a stiffer spine. A visit to your nearest archery dealer or pro shop could give you the chance to test-shoot different shafts and settle on the one that's best for you and your bow.

Finally, the big advantage to shooting mechanical heads is they generally fly and impact much the same as target points. If you can't correct your problem by changing fletching or arrow size, you may want to give open-on-impact head a try, but be sure to use the very best you can find.—M. R. James

Is it safe to shoot wooden arrows from compound bows?

Contrary to popular belief, wooden arrows can be shot from compounds, but the spine (stiffness) must be correct regardless of the draw weight. Hard-cam compound bows are capable of storing significantly more energy in their bent limbs than recurves, longbows, and round-wheel compound bows of equal draw weight and draw length. Consequently, they require a stiffer spine.

For example, a recurve bow pulled to 30 inches with a 60-pound draw weight may store 58 pounds of energy in its bent limbs. A round-wheel compound set to the same specifications might store 60 pounds of energy, while a hard-cam compound could store over 85 pounds of energy. In addition, recurve and longbow shooters generally have an inch or two shorter draw length, which automatically reduces the amount of stored energy and, therefore, arrow spine requirements.

As you can see, the compound bow would require stiffer shaft than a traditional bow or round-wheel compound of equal draw weight. If you shoot a heavy-draw-weight cam bow or have a draw length

The late, great Fred Bear popularized bowhunting and designed numerous bows, broadheads, and accessories, many of which are still best-sellers after more than half a century.

over 30 inches, you may have a difficult time finding wooden arrows stiff enough to meet your needs.

If you do locate the proper shafts to meet your personal spine and straightness requirements, I see no reason not to shoot wooden arrows from your compound bow. But do be cautious, and check your wooden arrows for damage and cracks after each shot. If a damaged wooden arrow goes unnoticed and is shot from any bow, it could explode and cause serious injury to the archer.—Dave Holt

I'm thinking of switching from a 2-blade, non-vented broadhead to a 3-blade, vented head. Will this fly better? I've had trouble with the 2-blade broadhead

planing — not severely, but enough to make my shot patterns off a little.

Based on my experience, I predict you'll find more consistent arrow flight and better groups with three-blade heads. I distinctly remember the wind-planing and noise problems I enountered with the Pearson Deadhead, for one (and that was a vented two-blade broadhead). The difficulties immediately vanished when I switched to three- and four-blade heads.—M. R. James

For the past three years I have used a 100-grain three-blade broadhead and taken four animals with it. However, I want to try something new. My choices include a 125-grain two-blade head, a 100-grain four-blade, and a 112-grain

three-blade. All of these look like winners, although they have different weights, different numbers of blades, different cutting sizes and capabilities. What are your thoughts?

You should remember several important factors in choosing a broadhead. The most important of these is accuracy, sharpness, and strength. Broadheads must group as well as your field points. As a general rule, large broadheads are more difficult to control and are more prone to accuracy problems. Do not confuse the accuracy question with broadheads and field points having the same point of impact. They are separate issues.

I have noticed that a two-blade head may cut totally with the grain of the meat. When this occurs, it allows the wound to close more readily. A light blood trail and longer recovery distance may result. A three- or four-blade head is more likely to cut across the grain and thus open a larger wound, providing a better blood trail. In addition, my broadhead test project in hide and meat showed that a three-blade broadhead cut 36 percent more tissue than a two-blade of the same width.—Dave Holt

Feathers or vanes? Which fletching do you prefer and why?

I shoot both feathers and vanes. Each has good and bad points. Feathers are lighter and more forgiving, probably a bit faster out of a hunting bow. They also generally offer more control of a broadhead-tipped arrow in flight. Some veteran bowhunters, myself included, give them a slight edge in the accuracy department. On the minus side, they aren't as durable as vanes, they're noisier, and they can be adversely affected by wet weather. Vanes are less expensive, naturally waterproof, and longer lasting.

I prefer feathers, but I often shoot vanes during rainy or snowy weather. Also, on certain hunts where boats are used daily — caribou hunts, for example — I favor vanes since my tackle often gets drenched during long rides across rough water. But I rarely if ever shoot vanes out of my recurve or longbows. As any veteran knows, you can't shoot vanes off a stickbow's shelf. By the way, I always waterproof my feather fletching, but prolonged exposure to moisture will cause the feathers to eventually lay down — and that's not conducive to proper arrow flight and pinpoint accuracy.— M. R. James

Does the direction of helical fletching matter and does it make any difference how the broadhead is aligned in relationship to the fletching?

In a word, no. Time was folks believed a right-handed shooter should use fletching with a right helical twist and vice versa for lefties. Today most experts agree it doesn't make much if any difference. Personally, I prefer arrows fletched with with three five-inch feathers or vanes and a moderate helical twist. This works well in controlling the 125-grain broadheads I normally shoot.

Don't fret over aligning your fletching and broadheads except as a last resort to correct broadhead flight problems. Just make certain that each head is perfectly mounted on a properly spined shaft. Concentrate on making a good release and placing your shaving-sharp

broadhead in the vitals. The result should be a short blood trail and a beaming bowhunter, shot after shot, season after season.—M. R. James

Accessories

I have been bowhunting since 1978 and have never used a stabilizer. I recently read an article on how important stabilizers are. Is a stabilizer really worth it, and are there any drawbacks to installing one on your bow?

A stabilizer on a hunting bow essentially does three things. First, it adds weight and prevents you from torquing the bow and jerking it off target at the instant of release. Second, the added weight keeps the bow "on target" better than a lighter bow (which is why so many tournament shooters use stabilizers). Third, a stabilizer absorbs vibrations, making the bow quieter and more comfortable to shoot.

The drawbacks? The added weight, which is a benefit, can also be a headache (or more correctly, an arm ache) if you lug around a heavy bow all day or all week on a backcountry hunt in rugged terrain. Also, if the stabilizer is too long, it can snag on brush and limbs as you walk or still-hunt.

I use stabilizers on my compounds and favor using a bow quiver, too, because I, for one, like the extra weight and have no problem

Dwight Schuh is one successful bowhunter who understands the value of using good optics. He considers binoculars an important part of his hunting gear — and won't leave home without 'em.

handling it. Some bowhunters hate bow quivers and do better (they say) without one. These same folks may not want to use stabilizers, either. My advice is to try a hunting stabilizer for yourself and see how you like it and how it affects your shooting, negatively or positively; however, just remember to keep it short (no longer than six to 10 inches) and simple. Once you're used to it, you probably won't even know it's there. If for some reason you don't care for it, pitch it. If you've been successful for years without one, chances are it won't make all that much difference.

I've said many times that once a person masters the basics of shooting a bow, bowhunting becomes 90 to 95 percent mental and only five to 10 percent physical. Confidence in your equipment is what matters most. If you think you'll do well, chances are you will, with or without a stabilizer.—M. R. James

I'm going to buy a new release aid before next season in hopes that its totally new feel will help me control my target panic problems. Which release should I start with? Do you have any advice? Keep in mind that I'm a hunter, not a competitive target shooter. I know it will take a little grit and determination, but I'm prepared to put in the effort.

It's a great idea to try as many release aids as possible, but it's difficult for me to pick the one best suited for you. My first choice, however, would be a back-tension release. This style is difficult to master, so be prepared to commit plenty of effort to the learning process. This type of release can do a lot to control target panic. I would also recommend a good coach. I realize how frustrating target panic can be, but it sounds like you have a great attitude. I urge you to keep up the effort and read as much as possible on the subject.—Dave Holt

Do you recommend a shelf rest or an elevated rest for a recurve bow?

I prefer the shelf or rug rest. I am an advocate of simplicity. The simplest, most dependable, least complicated method of getting an arrow from you to the animal is from a shelf or rug rest. Some argue that the elevated rest gives better accuracy. This may be true under controlled conditions — and I am told that elevated rests are best for compound bows since few models are designed for shelf-shooting — but under actual hunting conditions, I'll take the solid dependability of the shelf every time. Be aware, however, that shooting from the shelf requires the use of feather fletching. If you shoot vanes, you'll have to use an elevated rest.— G. Fred Asbell

Does the Pope and Young Club have any restrictions about using certain fiber-optic bowsights?

North America's keepers of bowhunting records have a rule against the use of any electronic device attached to the bow or arrow. This would include battery-powered lighted sights and rangefinders, game-tracking electronic arrows, etc. Tritium sights are acceptable, as are the common non-electronic fiber-optic bowsights.

Speaking of P&Y rules, in late 2003 the club announced that it will begin to accept all eligible big game entries taken with compound bows having more than a 65 percent letoff. Animals taken with the high letoff compounds will be designated with an asterisk in the records. For full information, contact P&Y Headquarters, P. O. Box 548, Chatfield, MN 55923; (507) 867-4144.—M. R. James

I have read Dwight Schuh's book, Bowhunting for Mule Deer, *published in*

1985. I wonder if nearly 20 years later the optics field has changed much and what he uses now or would recommend.

I'm not an optical engineer, so I can't say whether the quality of the glass and resolution have improved greatly. Personally, I doubt that any of us average hunters could notice any difference in sharpness between binoculars made in the 1980s and those made today. But certainly the design has changed. Today's binoculars are more comfortable to hold, and many of today's models can be used comfortably with eyeglasses. Many are fully waterproof, and I suspect they're more durable than some models from the past. So, yes, overall the binoculars of today are probably a little better. But will you necessarily see more game with them? Probably not.

One of my best binoculars is a Bausch & Lomb Zephyr 7x35. I bought this binocular, used, in 1976, so it probably was made in the '60s. An optical engineer testing the Zephyr on a professional lens bench said it was as sharp as they get.

One thing that has changed since I wrote that book is the use of big binoculars in the 15X to 20X range. Today, many serious big game hunters mount these big binoculars on a tripod and sit for hours, scouring the countryside. This method started primarily with Coues deer hunters in Arizona, but now serious big game hunters employ the same approach for mule deer, bighorns, elk, bears, and other species. It's really the ultimate in game spotting. Some of the most popular binoculars for this are the Zeiss 15x60, Swarovski 15x56, Fujinon 15x60, and Docter 15x60. Many other excellent high-power binoculars are available. Just as important as good optics is a good tripod. The binoculars must be rock-solid to be of any value, so a heavy, well-made tripod is essential. Also, most serious hunters fork over big dollars for fluid tripod heads so they can pan smoothly.

What optics do I personally use now? Day in and day out, I go to my Bausch & Lomb 8x42 Elite for general glassing, and a Docter 15x60 on a Slik 444 Sport Tripod with a Jim White custom ball-bearing head for long distance glassing. To conserve on weight, I often carry a Leupold 20x50 spotting scope on backpacking trips instead of the big binocs.—Dwight Schuh

I am looking into getting a portable ground blind. I plan to use it to bowhunt deer and turkeys. I have narrowed my search to Double Bull I.C.E. Blinds and The Magnum Invisiblind. Have you used these blinds?

I've successfully hunted whitetails and gobblers from both models you mention. Each is a quality product. The question you need to answer is how portable you want your ground blind to be. Double Bull blinds are much easier to set up, take down, and move. I use my own Invisiblind more as a permanent ground blind since it takes more effort to disassemble and relocate. The final choice is yours and should be based on your personal needs and desires.— M. R. James

My safety belt, which works like a lineman's climbing belt, is invaluable when I'm hanging stick ladders and stands. But then I have to unhook my climbing aid and rehook it above my stand. This is a tricky maneuver that could be dangerous. Other than using a climbing stand — I hate climbers — do you know of any safety system that would let me stay attached to the tree the whole time?

Absolutely. Any quality safety harness will do exactly that. The Summit safety harness, for example, has two safety components — a climbing belt for use as you're installing steps or climbing sticks, and a safety tether to keep you from falling while you're on stand.

You climb up using the climbing belt. Then, before detaching the climbing belt and climbing onto your stand platform, you attach the safety tether above the stand. Then you unhook the climbing belt. *Voila!* You are protected at all times.

A number of companies make similar safety harnesses with both a climbing belt and safety tether. In this day and age, with all the great safety devices available, bowhunters have no excuse for anything less than 100 percent protection, ground to stand and back to ground.—Dwight Schuh

I'm looking for data on bowstrings — creep, stretch, life span, accessories, etc. Are the same string materials used for compounds and stickbows?

Most industry experts agree that "stretch" means temporary elongation and "creep" means permanent elongation. Years ago 16- and 18-strand Dacron bowstrings were common. Since Dacron creeps initially and stretches with each shot, shooters had to recheck the brace height and nocking point after "breaking in" a new bowstring. Today, however, strings made of Fast Flight or other synthetic materials don't stretch like Dacron and can provide additional arrow speed (up to 10 fps). Modern strings combining Fast Flight and Vectran creep very little. Be aware that some stickbow manufacturers advise against Fast Flight strings that may damage the limbs, while others build their bows specifically for use with Fast Flight strings.

Normal shooting eventually causes wear and tear on bowstrings, causing them to fray with age. Wax your string often and keep an eye open for any broken strands. Carry a spare string (one that's already broken in, if possible) while hunting. (Some hunters also have a portable bow press and Allen wrenches in their packs just in case a bowstring emergency arises in the field.) And some compound models allow strings to be replaced without special tools.

Accessories such as string silencers, brush buttons, nocking points, and peep sights do affect arrow speed slightly. I, for one, don't worry about it because the effect is generally minimal. Concentrate on accuracy and shot placement rather than fretting over arrow speed.—M. R. James

Bowhunting Game

What can you tell me about the so-called "Super Slam" of North American big game animals? How many bowhunters have completed the Slam, and how many species are involved? Also, what other trophy requirements must be met?

At this writing only five bowhunters have taken all 28 species of North American big game recognized by the Pope and Young Club: Chuck Adams of Wyoming, Jimmy Ryan of Alabama, Tom Hoffman of New York, Dr. Jack Frost of Alaska, and Gary Bogner of Michigan. Adams was the first to complete the "Super Slam" back in 1990, while Hoffman was the first to collect all of these animals that qualified for the P&Y records. Several more bowhunters are within a couple of successful hunts of completing their own "Slams" and joining this rather exclusive group.

Since there's no official "Super Slam" organization or formal recognition, there are no steadfast rules or minimum measurements. The 28 animals included in the "Super Slam" are: Alaska brown bear, black bear, grizzly bear, polar bear, bison, barren ground caribou, central barren ground caribou, mountain caribou, Quebec-Labrador caribou, woodland caribou, cougar, Columbian blacktail deer, Sitka blacktail deer, Coues deer, whitetail deer, mule

deer, Roosevelt elk, Yellowstone elk, Rocky Mountain goat, Alaska-Yukon moose, Canada moose, Shiras moose, muskox, pronghorn antelope, bighorn sheep, Dall's sheep, desert bighorn sheep, and Stone's sheep.—M. R. James

I am having trouble getting elk to answer my calls. Since I rarely hear bugles I am mostly cow calling because I do not wish to sound out of place. During the rut, or when it should be — mid-September — I almost never hear bugling. Later on, say in October and early November, there is bugling. Why is this?

It would be helpful to know where you're hunting, at least in which state. Studies in Oregon, where hunting pressure is fierce and where the bull/cow ratio is very low (fewer than 10 bulls/100 cows), have shown that the peak of the rut takes place sometime around the middle of October. That's because spike bulls are doing most of the breeding.

You will also hear bugling later if a cow comes into heat late. Here in Idaho, where the bull/cow ratio is pretty good, I one time heard a bull bugling his guts out on November 3. He was with some cows, and I suspect one of them was in heat.

Let me make one other observation: You say you don't do much bugling because you don't hear much bugling. I think your reasoning is faulty. The very reason for your bugle call is to get the bulls stirred up and bugling. The time you should be bugling most is when you don't hear any bugling. Even in the best elk country, you might go for days without hearing a bull bugle on his own. I've experienced that many times. When that happens, I get on my call, and pretty soon the woods are ringing with the sounds of bulls. How sweet it is. So that's your mission — to make them bugle. That's why you have that call. Use it!—Dwight Schuh

I have a question regarding the effectiveness of my wife's bow setup. Her draw weight is 40 pounds, and her draw length is 26 inches. She shoots Gold Tip 35/55 graphite shafts tipped with Wasp 75-grain heads. This setup produces about 34 foot pounds of kinetic energy. Is this enough energy for black bears out to 15 to 20 yards (such as hunting over bait)? I know that Dave Holt has written that kinetic energy, not broadhead type or arrow weight, is the key to penetration.

Black bears are tough critters and proper shot placement is the key to consistent success. Unless a sharp broadhead penetrates both lungs, a bear can cover a great distance and may not be recovered. That's why broadside or slightly quartering shots are the only shots to consider.

Regarding equipment, there's little question that your wife's setup could put down a bruin if the arrow is properly placed within the kill area. But since you quoted Dave Holt, you should also know that in his classic book, *Balanced Bowhunting*, he states: "If your bow and arrow combination delivers less than 45 foot pounds of kinetic energy, you may want to consider the traditional style broadhead" (with a blade-type point which is generally agreed to have superior penetrating ability).

Regardless, having collected several dozen bruins since 1970, I know that hunters who have the patience and presence of mind to take only perfect, point-blank shots at bears standing 10 to 20 yards away — and then make accurate shots — can consistently kill even the biggest bears with most legal hunting tackle.—M. R. James

I live in southeast Idaho where I hunt on a dry farm that consists of pockets of dense timber and brush surrounded by CRP fields and the occasional alfalfa or

grain field. The trees are not large enough for a stand. How do you pattern mule deer here? How much can I disrupt these pockets of trees (trimming shooting lanes, pathways) without spooking the deer? I have observed deer coming out to the edge of the fields to feed in the evenings. Any suggestions or advice would be appreciated.

You can certainly look for tracks and trails as clues to good sites for blinds, just as whitetail hunters do, but I would suggest you watch from a distance with binoculars in the mornings and evenings. Soon, you will begin to discern movement patterns. Generally, the best way to pattern mule deer is visually.

You could ease a commercial ground blind against the brush to intercept deer coming into the fields. You might also consider pit blinds. If deer are coming out anywhere near brush or rocks that would help conceal a pit (and assuming the landowner doesn't mind your digging pits), this is a great way to go.

Obviously, you have to be careful about banging around in brushy bedding areas. For making new setups during the season, I suggest you stick to the fringes of fields. But, if you hunt this area every year, I suggest you go into those woody areas in the spring or early summer and construct ground blinds near the best trails. Then you can just sneak in during the season and be ready to hunt with no disturbance.—Dwight Schuh

What is the recommended height for hanging a tree stand?

I'm not sure there's any set height for tree stand placement, but 12 to 15 feet is probably a nationwide average. There are many factors to consider, including the tree itself, the terrain, background, surrounding cover, prevailing winds, etc. The higher in a tree you go, the steeper your shooting angle and the more difficult it will be to achieve a deadly double-lung hit. That is one of the main reasons I seldom put my portable stands higher than 15 feet.—Dr. Dave Samuel

If you come upon a tree stand in the woods, is it okay to use it until the owner shows up?

People who use other bowhunters' tree stands without permission are out of line. It marks them as thoughtless, lazy individuals who have no regard for the rights or property of others.

Would these people like to walk out of a store and find some stranger sitting in their car or astride their motorcycle in a public parking lot? Would these people like to go out into their yard and find a stranger using their barbecue grill or picnic table? More importantly would these people want to go to all the effort to scout an area, locate a good spot, hang a stand, trim shooting lanes, and arrive to find a stranger in their stand? Or perhaps worse, how would they like to find a gut pile near or under their tree?

Sure, an argument can be made that some woods are public lands and a few greedy bowhunters sometimes hang numerous stands in an attempt to lock up a large hunting area just for themselves. But the point is, if a particular piece of property (such as a tree stand) belongs to someone else, why would anyone feel that he or she has a right to use it without getting the owner's permission? Common sense — plus the Golden Rule — should apply here.—M. R. James

What is the most effective way to remain scent-free when hunting in the mountains?

During transportation, seal your clothes inside plastic garbage bags or special garment containers specially designed for hunters. In camp, weather permitting, hang them outside to air thoroughly. A Scent-Lok suit can help to hold down odor from your body, and scent-eliminating sprays can reduce odor in your outer clothes. These all help, but in a camp environment, none of them is guaranteed. Your only guarantee is to keep in the wind in your favor. Remember, a puff bottle works well to check the wind.—Dwight Schuh

Are mechanical broadheads effective on most big game animals?

As any broadhead collector will tell you, expandable-blade, open-on-impact heads are nothing new, really. They've been around in one form or another for many decades. Most of the early versions were widely viewed as bowhunting "gimmicks." Horror stories abound about their poor field performance. Bounce-outs, glance-offs, and blades' failing to open upon contact were apparently the rule, not the exception, back then. Fortunately, today's top of the line modern mechanical heads are high-quality products, constructed much better than early models, and designed to perform flawlessly.

I've taken some game with these true-flying broadheads and seen ample evidence of just how devastatingly effective they can be. Regardless, I've witnessed rare failures. That's why I prefer my conventional hunting heads and plan to stick with them for my own bowhunting adventures, especially on hunts for thick-skinned, heavy-haired big game animals.—M. R. James

Game Animals

Why is it that in one part of the country a rack with four points on one side and five points on the other may be called a nine-point while in another part of the country that same rack would be called a four-point. Why don't they call it what it is? A 4x5 buck?

Good question. The standard answer is there are two ways to identify the size of a deer rack. In the east, folks count each and every point on both beams (and call anything they can hang a ring from a "point"). That's where you come up with 8 points, 9 points, 10 points, etc. Out West, some hunters disregard the eyeguards or sticker points and count only the main beam points on one side. For example, a 4x4 mule or blacktail deer with eyeguards is known as a 4-point buck (Western count). It's those parenthetical words that let readers know the buck in question actually has headgear with 8 to 10 total points.

Still other folks, as you suggest, identify the size of the rack by the number of total points on each beam (e.g., a 3x3, 4x5, or whatever). And this practice is more common west of the Mississippi than back east. So what it apparently boils down to is a matter of regional preference. I'd suggest you not worry about trying to change things and just identify the points as you see fit. Most any serious deer hunter will understand exactly what size your buck is.—M. R. James

I'm just 16 but have been around hunting my whole life. My question is about deer genetics. The area my family and I hunt has plenty of bucks, but they're all basically 8-pointers. My dad shot a 157-class whitetail but it was only an 8-point buck with a sticker, making it a true 9-pointer. There were big empty spaces where his G-4s should have been. And this past gun season I took another mature buck, but he was only a 125-inch 9-pointer. I know of only one 10-point buck ever taken in our area. Is this apparent lack of 10-point bucks just a matter of genetics?

Without question, genetics affect antler configuration. Whether the two bucks you cite come from the same genetic background would be sheer speculation, but it is possible. Age also affects antler development, and my guess is that age is a bigger factor than genetics in determing the number of eight-pointers in your area. If genetics is the controlling factor, you can't do much about that. However, if I were shooting 157-inch animals, I sure wouldn't be concerned. Sounds like you have big bucks in your area!—Dr. Dave Samuel

Occasionally, I find a deer track that is wider than normal and may have two dots to the rear of it. What causes this?

The two "dots" to the rear of the track are caused by the dewclaw, which is the small appendage located above and to the rear of each hoof. The reason for its appearance within the track at one time and not another generally has to do with the softness of the ground, the weight of the deer, or whether the deer was running or walking. When snow is on the ground, in a muddy area, or following a rain, the deer's hoof sinks into the earth/snow farther and the dewclaw makes contact and leaves its mark. When the deer is running, the additional force of its body weight causes the track to splay and sink deeper into the forest floor, and the dewclaw will often show at this time. Some deer hunters wrongly believe that only a buck's dewclaws will show in a track. Not so.—G. Fred Asbell

Is a 6x6 bull elk called a "royal" elk, and if so, why? Is there a name for a 7x7 elk?

The sixth point on a bull elk's rack is called the royal point, and that's why some folks refer to 6x6 bulls as royals. The seventh point on an elk's rack is called the imperial point. Likewise, 7x7 bulls are known by hunters as imperial bulls. Hope this helps clarify things.—M. R. James

How long will a deer live if it is hit in one lung? If you just nick the lungs will the deer die as quickly as with a solid lung hit? If you hit the diaphragm without hitting the liver, will this be fatal? Is there a spot between the spine and lungs that will not produce a fatal hit?

A deer hit solidly through both lungs most often drops in less than 15 seconds. Beyond this, it is impossible to make anything but general statements. For this reason, we must all use scalpel-sharp broadheads and strive for perfect shot placement.

A half-inch change in arrow location can make a world of difference. For example, the left lung is slightly smaller and has three lobes. The right lung is slightly larger with five lobes. In addition, the liver is located on the right side. In many cases, much of the bleeding occurs internally, and this makes it difficult to know if a large vein or artery was severed.

Even if you understand animal anatomy and shot angles, the best you can do is make an educated guess about arrow placement until the animal is recovered and a proper autopsy is conducted. If you suspect a marginal hit, wait several hours before tracking the animal, conditions permitting, and then proceed slowly. In the case of a paunch hit, wait at least 8 hours. If the animal was not disturbed after the shot, it will almost always be bedded within 200 yards.

My field autopsies and research with veterinarians indicate that there is no broadhead-sized void between the backbone and top of the lungs. The lungs and chest cavity operate in a vacuum condition; they shrink and expand in unison. In addition, the aorta, the body's primary artery, rises from the heart to a point just under the spine and then continues rearward. Part of the reason for the void

assumption is that the bottom of the spine lies lower in the chest cavity than is commonly believed. A hit just under the spine may strike only a few lung lobes, but with the proper angle and reasonable penetration, such shots should cause both lungs to collapse. A bilateral pneumothorax is fatal.—Dave Holt

I've heard that venison is low in fat and very nutritious. What about other game animals such as caribou?

All wild game meat is low in fat. Though some has the same levels and cholesterol as domestic beef, the low fat content makes it very healthy. In addition, there are certain polyunsaturated fatty acids found only in wild game. It appears that these acids reduce arteriosclerosis, thus making such meat extremely healthy. Nothing generates more pro-hunting attitudes than providing a nutritious, healthy meal that tastes great. Why not hold a wild game dinner for all of your non-hunting neighbors and friends? One suggestion: Properly prepared venison makes fine table fare.—Dr. Dave Samuel

Does the size of the rub indicate the size of the buck that makes it?

Yes and no. Deer hunting veterans generally agree that whopper bucks will rub small trees as well as larger ones. A bowhunter finding rubs on finger-sized saplings cannot really tell whether a forky or his great-granddaddy racked the trees and stripped their bark. But at the same time, when you come across a huge rub on a thigh-thick tree, it's safe to assume no pint-sized buck did the damage. Big rubs are made by mature bucks. Find one or more large, sticky-wet rubs with deep antler gouges and hefty limbs snapped off, and you can bet your favorite broadheads that a mature buck — perhaps a real butt-kicker — is in the area.

Remember, rubs are important for at least three obvious reasons. First, unlike deer droppings and tracks, rubs alone tell hunters that antlered bucks are moving through or hanging around the hunting area. Second, they can mark travel routes, direction of travel, and movement patterns. Third, where clusters of rubs and scrapes appear season after season, many savvy bowhunters know to set up ambush sites. Rub-rich breeding areas are attractive to rutting bucks, and sooner or later the rub-makers are going to appear once again.—M. R. James

Can deer distinguish human urine from other types, and is this a problem when bowhunting?

Unfortunately, the only way to know the truth is to ask the deer, and they can't tell us. However, there is some scientific data that might help. If you eat meat, not only will your body odor be different, your urine will smell more as well. One would think that since deer do not eat meat, their urine and our urine would smell different, at least to a degree. The enzymes in deer that break down the vegetation they eat are the same ones that break down the roughage in humans. Thus, when we eat vegetables, our urine probably smells somewhat similar to deer urine. Maybe it is chemically the same, too. Anyway, some researchers who work with pheromones suggest that our urine, when we eat veggies, is not as much a scent problem as when we eat meat. Having said that, it would seem that for most humans, urine odor would be somewhat of a negative signal to deer. I'd recommend keeping a urine bottle handy and eating lots of greens with your deer steak.—Dr. Dave Samuel

Section II

Expert Strategies

Whitetail Deer

Classification

Native to North America, common whitetail deer (*Odocoileus virginianus*) have existed in the present form since the Pleistocene period, perhaps as long as a million years. Their ancient Cervidae ancestors, however, likely roamed this continent for millions of years during the evolutionary process. Today, the worldwide deer family — some 17 genera in all — ranges across all continents, excluding Antarctica.

Origin and Distribution

It is believed the common ancestor for all deer species — excluding elk, moose, and caribou — originated in Europe. As noted, the deer commonly called whitetails are truly American deer, having evolved from animals that first crossed the Bering land bridge into the rugged terrain of what would become Alaska, gradually spreading south. Modern-day whitetails are found in all of the 48 contiguous states, eight Canadian provinces, and Mexico. From a population low of only 500,000 at the start of the 20th century, whitetail deer have thrived in recent decades and now number between 20 and 30 million. Theirs is a truly remarkable wildlife success story. They reign as the undisputed kings of all North American big game in both numbers and popularity.

Biologists recognize 17 prominent whitetail subspecies, including the following: Florida Key deer, Virginia, northern woodland, Dakota, northwest, Columbian, Coues, Texas, Carmen Mountains, Avery Island, Kansas, Bull's Island, Hunting Island, Hilton Head Island, Blackbeard Island, Florida, and Florida coastal whitetails.

The diminutive Coues deer of Arizona and certain other southwestern regions is the only whitetail recognized as a separate species by both the Pope and Young Club and Boone and Crockett Club.

Identifying Characteristics

The whitetail's antlers and tail make these deer easily distinguishable from their Western cousins, the blacktails and mule deer. Tails are long and full, brown on top but snowy white underneath, quite conspicuous when flared or raised in alarm. Besides this readily identifiable trademark that gives the species its name, a whitetail buck's antlers commonly consist of two main beams with individual unforked tines growing upward from the beam. Most mule deer and blacktails have bifurcated antlers that branch into Y-shaped forks.

Despite regional differences in size and coloration, whitetails typically are grayish-brown animals with white circles around each eye and white bands behind the jet-black nose, beneath the chin, and on the throat. The underbelly of each deer is also snowy white.

The average whitetail buck stands around three feet at the shoulder and weighs about 150 pounds; does run perhaps 20 percent smaller. Northern woodland whitetails are the largest and darkest species, often topping 200 pounds, while the tiny deer of the Florida Keys are the continent's smallest whitetails, seldom weighing more than 80 pounds. Coues deer bucks rarely weigh much over 100 pounds.

Whitetails have preorbital or lachrymal glands in front of each eye that are less conspicuous than those of mule deer or blacktails. These facial glands are used to mark rub trees and bushes with scent. Deer also have interdigital glands between each toe that emit a yellow, waxy substance bearing an individual scent identifying that animal to all others. The metatarsal gland is located in small tufts of hair found between the toes and heels on the outside of each rear leg. The tarsal glands, each about three inches long, are swirls of dark hair located at the hock on the inside of each rear leg. These glands emit a musky odor that attracts the opposite sex during the annual rut.

Whitetails, like other ruminants, have four-chambered stomachs consisting of the rumen, the reticulum, the omasum, and the abomasum. They often feed quickly, filling the storage section and returning to bedding areas where they regurgitate, rechew, and reswallow the food to properly start the digestive process. Whitetails require 10 to 12 pounds of food each day. Adult deer have 32 teeth including eight incisors, 12 premolars, and 12 molars. No deer have upper teeth in the front of the mouth.

Bucks lose their antlers each winter and grow a new velvet-covered set starting each spring. A buck's diet, age, and genetic makeup determine the size and shape of the antlers.

Habitat/Diet

Highly adaptable animals, whitetail deer have the greatest range of any North American game species. They are animals of the bushlands and forest edges, equally at home in virtually any terrain where suitable food, water, and cover exists. Better than any big game species, these deer have learned to coexist with man and continue to expand their range in many parts of this continent.

Whitetails eat most types of available vegetation, although favorites include cultivated crops such as alfalfa, clover, corn, soybeans, and rye, as well as natural foods including red maple, dogwood, sumac, willow, white cedar, pine, and fir. In season, apples and white oak acorns attract the special attention of hungry deer.

Senses

Deer have exceptional olfactory abilities and commonly use their nose as their first line of defense against all predators. Their sense of hearing is well above average. Eyesight is good, and deer are quick to detect motion; however, stationary bowhunters may be overlooked even at close range. Deer vocalize through bleats, blats, and grunts, although they most commonly communicate by stamping their forefeet, flicking their tails, and flashing their snow-white rump hair. Their loud snorts of alarm are all too familiar to most whitetail hunters.

Reproduction

Each doe's estrus period usually begins during November — depending on the part of the country where whitetails live — and lasts for about 30 hours. If not bred during this time, she will come back into heat each 28 days. Rutting bucks constantly scent-check for receptive does and will service as many partners as they can locate during the breeding season. After a gestation period of about 200 days, fawns normally are born in May or June. Does giving birth for the first time usually drop a single fawn weighing four to five pounds; twin births are common thereafter.

Life Expectancy

Bucks reach their prime at about five years of age; however, relatively few live that long, especially in heavily hunted parts of the country. Wild whitetails can live eight to 11 years. One captive animal reportedly lived to be 19.

Venison is lean, nutritious, and highly regarded table fare. Its taste — except for the meat from older bucks killed during or after the rut — is comparable to prime beef, especially if the animal has been properly dressed, cleaned, and cooled in the field. Deer that commonly raid crops planted by farmers and ranchers are especially tasty.

Trophy Bowhunting Records

The best typical whitetail buck ever shot by a bowhunter was arrowed by Mel Johnson in a soybean field just outside Peoria, Illinois, in 1965. Its official Pope and Young score is 204 4/8. The top P&Y non-typical is a Nebraska buck arrowed by Del Austin along the Platte River in 1962. Bowhunting's World Record typical Coues deer scores 130 1/8. It was tagged by Arizona bowhunter Sergio Orozco in 2001. The top non-typical Coues buck, another Arizona deer, scores 124 0/8 and was shot in 1987 by John George Evans.

Chapter 15
Whitetail Deer – Everyman's Deer

WHITETAIL MOVEMENT near my tree stand had steadily slowed as the warm fall sun climbed higher into the surrounding tree branches. I was about to call it a morning and climb down when a slight movement to my right instantly changed my mind. Two deer were walking through a sun-dappled opening across the caliche road, angling my way through the thick Texas brush. I could tell at a glance that both were bucks.

As the lead deer stepped clear, my heart jolted into a staccato drumroll. He wore a thick, whitish rack. And his second point on each beam forked in typical mule deer fashion. There was no mistaking this big whitetail. He was exactly as the ranch manager had described him. I was looking at the *muy grande* deer locals called "The Alberta Buck." Honestly, he looked as if he'd have been more at home in the Bow Zone around Edmonton or Calgary than here in the Lone Star brush country. He was unlike any south Texas buck I'd ever seen.

Gotcha! Even during the rut when bucks let down their guard, does keep a wary eye open for danger. This old gal knows something's wrong—and the trophy buck trailing her is going to follow her when she bounds away. Count on it!

My racing mind shifted gears, speeding to the business at hand, calculating yardage, shot angle, and the buck's body position. I slowly raised my bow, drew, and anchored. About then the big deer paused to nose the ground where a doe had stooped to urinate earlier in the morning. His chest was screened by twigs, and I couldn't shoot. Meanwhile, the second buck continued to pick his way past my stand, likely bound for his daytime bed deep in some nearby thorny jungle. I knew at any instant his *companero* would follow. My bow arm began to tremble. Unless something happened *pronto* I'd have to let off, maybe missing my chance at tagging the unique buck.

Then the heavy-antlered whitetail raised his head and walked forward, stopped, and stood staring after his traveling companion. I finally released. There was an audible *thunk!* as my aluminum arrow caught him behind his muscular shoulder. Instantly I knew that the big deer's traveling days were over.

Four-plus decades spent prowling this continent's whitetail woods has taught me that deer hunting can be an emotional roller coaster ride. One day nothing goes right and you start to wonder if you'll ever get another shot at a big whitetail. But the next day the unexpected happens and some boss buck steps out of the shadows, giving you reason to silently thank the Good Lord for that special moment.

Whitetails are indeed special. Young or old. Rich or poor. It makes no difference to deer what your age or social status. Whitetails have a way of humbling the wealthiest and enriching the poorest among us. They're beautiful, wary, plentiful, adaptable, challenging, and readily available to hunt. Amazingly, they are found in abundance across most of North America. For this reason alone I consider them Everyman's Deer.

Most whitetails are arrowed from tree stands in situations not unlike the one I described at the beginning of this chapter. It's estimated that three-fourths of the whitetail deer arrowed annually are killed by bowhunters shooting down from elevated stands. Shot distances probably average less than 25 yards. True, a few folks hunt them at ground level, and every year some of them take bucks by design or accident. Illinois bowhunter Judy Kovar, for example, shuns trees and hunts exclusively from ground blinds or by still-hunting. She's tagged over half a dozen record book bucks, too. But Judy has some Northern Cheyenne blood flowing through her veins and credits her ancestors for her exceptional patience and hunting skills. Most experts universally agree that hunting from trees is the most effective means of consistently taking these snowy-rumped deer. Getting close to wary whitetails usually takes proper planning — with a bit of luck thrown in.

Most of us don't actually hunt whitetails. We hunt spots that whitetails frequent, hang a stand, climb aboard, and wait for them to appear. Matching stalking skills against the super senses of these animals leaves most bowhunters mumbling to themselves as they watch deer bound gracefully away. Only during the annual breeding season do bucks become downright careless — and vulnerable. Consequently, many whitetail hunters await the rut with eager anticipation. The majority head for the deer woods on opening day and return to their tree stands every chance they get. Thanks to liberal bag limits and months-long seasons almost everywhere, whitetails "rule," as today's teens are fond of saying. And as previously hinted, no other species is found in greater numbers over a wider area of our continent. Is it any wonder then that a poll of serious hunters has found that whitetails are the most popular big game animal on earth?

G. Fred Asbell speaks for countless thousands when he explains his passion for whitetail deer. "My neck starts to swell in late October each year, and my toenails begin looking birdlike about the same time — and I know what has to be done. Sure, I like bowhunting other types of big game. Hell, who can argue with mule deer and elk hunting? But whitetail hunting — it's almost an addiction. If you are truly a dedicated whitetail hunter, you'll have little time for hunting much else. And there is really no reason anyone should feel sorry for you. You've got your hands full. You've got the best."

Whitetail hunting is bowhunting to most North American archers. As I observed in an editorial I wrote for an issue of *Whitetail Bowhunter*, "...while most bowhunters can only dream of distant hunts for elk and bear and moose and the like, there is one big game animal that belongs to us all — whitetail."

Hunting Strategies

Hundreds of books and tens of thousands of magazine articles have offered millions of hopeful readers countless details on whitetails — and surefire ways to effectively bag these plentiful animals. At one weekend seminar session, where deer hunting experts offered educational how-to seminars — complete with booths where the pros sold their books, video, and audio tapes — I overheard one audience member grumble, "I'm learning more about whitetails than I really want or need to know!"

He's right. While an entire industry has blossomed around hunting whitetail deer, and some people make their living telling others how to tag some braggin'-size buck, there are a handful of basic, proven, time-tested methods that consistently put venison in the freezer and antlers on the wall. Among the techniques we'll examine briefly are hunting from tree stands and ground blinds at different times of the season, still-hunting and stalking opportunities, driving or nudging deer, rattling and calling, as well as the use of scents and decoys. Now read on — and learn.

Tree Stands and Ground Blinds

As already noted, the most popular and effective way to hunt whitetails is to take a stand along a well-used trail near some feeding or bedding area. And for most archers — including you and me — that means climbing into an elevated perch. Ground-level blinds — either those made of natural materials or manufactured from camo cloth, stretched over a lightweight frame, and anchored in

Most bowhunters focus attention on the annual rut when big bucks pursue does throughout the day. Many believe this brief period is the best time to collect a trophy whitetail.

This buck responded to rattling "horns." Note the belligerent body posture (ears back, tail tucked, stiff-legged walk) meant to intimidate rival bucks.

Bucks make numerous scrapes preparing for the onset of the annual rut. Some are never visited again; others, like this scrape in a commonly used breeding area, are worth watching.

Rub lines can show a buck's direction of travel. Such sign can indicate a buck's routine travel route.

place — can and do work. I shot a good buck from one last deer season at only 14 yards; however, patiently sitting in wait above a deer's normal line of sight offers several distinct advantages. First, your visibility is greatly improved. Second, movements you make drawing your bow are not as easily noticed. Third, human scent is less of a problem in overhead stands.

Remember, deer know their home territory as well as you know your own home. Even subtle changes are immediately noted. When a blind pops up overnight like some morel mushroom, area whitetails are likely to notice — and perhaps shun the area until they're convinced the structure is harmless. On a season's-long hunt that might not be a problem, but on a short-term hunt, it can be a recipe for failure. Ground blinds of any type should be erected in advance of the hunt and, whenever possible, left in place.

When suspicious or alerted, whitetails commonly stamp a forefoot and flare their tails to warn nearby deer of something's-not-quite-right-here danger. They'll also adopt a stiff-legged walk, moving away from — or sometimes closer to — the object that snagged their attention. Head-bobbing is common, too. If truly boogered, as when a wafting whiff of man-scent reaches them, they'll likely utter an explosive whoosh! and bound away in that all-too-familiar tail-waving departure known to deer hunters everywhere. As if that's not bad enough, deer commonly stop just out of sight and continue to snort, broadcasting the hint of danger to every woodland creature within earshot. It's a commonplace and frustrating experience for all of us at one time or another. It underscores the need for careful concealment and remaining as scent-free as possible whenever we take a stand in the deer woods.

When I use a ground blind — and I've used my share over the years — I try to remain flexible. Natural ambush sites — a blowdown, fenceline brushpile, rocky outcropping, or some shaded hidey hole where I can hunker down and wait comfortably for deer to

appear — can occasionally produce good results. They just might be your only option in brushy places where few if any mature trees allow you to hang a stand. In all natural blinds it's vital that the background breaks up your human shape. The stand should be out of any direct sunlight and the background solid enough not to backlight any slight movements you make. Unless you're able to wait in relative comfort and remain well concealed, fidgeting or raising your bow to shoot may alert nearby game. Any natural blind's foreground should provide an adequate field of vision and at least two cleared shooting lanes.

If I'm inside a manufactured blind, I always try to place it in shadowy woodland nooks and crannies, commonly "brushing in" my blind with limbs and branches. In short, I'll do everything possible to make it blend into its surroundings. Locating these portable structures works well in overgrown fencerows or the weed-choked corners of fields where deer emerge to feed. In areas where baiting is allowed, they're a perfect answer to semi-open areas surrounding feeders. These cloth blinds help contain telltale odors and many come equipped with handy shoot-through window screens. The dark mesh covering shooting windows helps hide movements and usually will not affect arrow flight. (Note: Always test shoot your broadhead-tipped hunting arrows before taking a shot in the field!) Personally, I prefer these portable blinds over any natural structure I've seen or used, but expect to pay several hundred dollars to buy one of your own.

Never overlook the obvious, either. I've hunted farm country deer from barn lofts, sheds, windmills, and even upstairs rooms in deserted farmsteads. Check out old farm equipment — a rusted combine, hay rake, manure spreader, or other abandoned implement falling into ruin among high weeds. Such spots may be easily utilized. Hay bales, carefully arranged (with the landowner's permission of course) are still another option. A friend of mine with a severe leg injury recently took a P&Y whitetail from a hay bale blind located at the edge of a field where deer emerged to feed. So keep your eyes and mind open. Savvy whitetail hunters take advantage of common farm and ranch possibilities.

"I hunt deer, not trees," says Dave Holt, one of the country's most consistently successful whitetail bowhunters. But Dave, through long years of firsthand experience, has the knack of being able to size-up tree stand possibilities at a glance. Not everyone is so blessed.

Selecting just the right tree can pose a real problem for lots of bowhunters, especially those unfamiliar with deer movements in a particular hunting area. Naturally, stands must be hung close to where deer will pass or you're wasting your time and energy. Trees should be large enough to hold your stand and break your outline. Although a few trees offer limbs and crotches where you can sit and wait in relative comfort, most times a portable stand works best. An uncomfortable hunter can't sit still for hours at a time. Perching on a limb or standing in a tree fork hour after hour can become an endurance test. Portable stands can turn most any tree into a comfy ambush site within minutes. Although we've already touched on this subject in the chapter "Tree Stand Savvy," some things bear repeating.

There are dozens upon dozens of well-built tree stands available, and there's one to fill your needs and fit your budget, too. Many are lightweight yet sturdy models that are a breeze to pack and hang. Climbing models and large, semi-permanent elevated platforms with built-in ladders also are available. Whatever your personal choice, be sure to include a safety harness or belt. Unfortunately, each hunting season falls seriously injure — and occasionally kill — some bowhunter not strapped in. Hunters who don't use safety belts or a harness are accidents waiting to happen. Ask yourself, is it worth risking broken bones, paralysis, and even death? And if you think it can't happen to you, you're either naive or in a state of denial.

Permanent stands are viewed with increasing disfavor by hunters and nonhunters alike. Boards and platforms nailed to trees are woodland eyesores and can quickly become unsafe after long exposure to the elements. Heavy nails used in construction may damage or even kill trees, posing hazards long after the stands have rotted

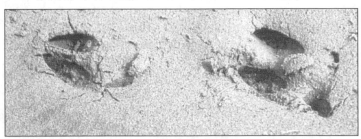

A decoy placed near a tree stand can sometimes pull another buck within bow range. Calling and rattling complements any decoy setup.

away. More than one chainsaw and sawmill's buzzsaw have been ruined by coming in contact with a hidden steel spike left in the tree by some thoughtless hunter. Serious injuries have resulted, too. My best advice: Don't nail boards into trees. If you do, remove 'em!

Ideal early season stand sites are found along well-used trails between bedding and feeding areas, preferably where two or more deer trails merge. Stands hung close to water and mineral licks may work, as will those near seasonal food sources such as clover, acorns, apples, persimmons, and other whitetail taste treats. But be prepared; hunting pressure is likely to cause overnight changes in daily travel and feeding patterns. Whitetails are fast learners. This is especially true of older bucks that become a separate species of savvy deer by their fourth or fifth year. Some become strictly nocturnal feeders. Other simply shun obvious trails and favored feeding areas.

Many beginning bowhunters — and some veterans, too — can't seem to resist hanging their stands along field edges where visibility is good. While seeing distant deer may boost a hunter's morale, most successful whitetail hunters set up away from such openings. They know does and fawns typically appear first. Bucks often hang back, seldom appearing until the final moments of shooting light, if at all. I, for one, much prefer to wait in heavier cover located closer to daytime beds. This just makes more sense if it's antlers you're after. But always approach stands around bedding areas as quietly as possible,

This is the biggest whitetail deer rub the author has ever seen. Rest assured, the buck that tore up this tree was no dink! While big bucks will rub small trees, little bucks don't rub trees like this.

(Above and below) Fresh deer tracks are a surefire sign deer are in the area. Many veteran hunters care only about tracks with the deer still standing in them!

This Invisablind, carefully hidden along a well-used deer trail leading to a feeding area, paid off for author with a nice eight-point buck.

and never hunt there if the wind is wrong. I've learned that both mornings and evenings are good times to hunt such spots, and in recent seasons I've seen increased midday deer movements. Such high noon activity is common during the rut, but in some deer country it seems bucks don't mind moving during daylight hours. Keep that in mind where you hunt. All-day vigils — especially during the chase phase of the annual rut — can pay off, but it takes planning, patience, preparation (both physical and mental), and discipline to endure all-day sits.

Personally, I seldom spend more than three to four hours in my stand. Time tends to dull senses and long periods of inactivity can lead to careless mistakes. Also, I am rarely concerned about seeing lots of deer while on stand. Therefore, I frequently hang my stands in fairly thick cover where deer — especially big-antlered bucks — feel most secure. As I tell people, "I'm only concerned about seeing one deer each day. That's the unwary buck standing broadside only a dozen yards away."

Keep in mind that proper stand placement and patience likely have accounted for the demise of more big bucks than anything else.

Later in the season, when the rut takes off, scrape-watching may pay off — assuming you're watching the right scrape. Don't forget that whitetails tend to use the same general breeding areas season after season, generation after generation. If you can locate such a hot spot — normally marked by antler-slashed trees and numerous freshly pawed scrapes with the telltale overhanging limbs — treasure it. Does and bucks alike frequent these areas. Stands hung downwind near hot scrapes can provide shots at scent-checking bucks. And for my money, one of the very best times to take a rutting whitetail is after a rain. That's when lusty bucks are likely to be on the move at any time of the day or night, freshening scrapes and checking their breeding signposts for evidence of visits by receptive does.

But to be an effective scrape watcher, you should realize that there are several different kinds of scrapes, each made at different times of the season. With the approach of fall, whitetail bucks begin to mark their home territories with scrapes and rubs. Each bears the distinctive scent of its maker. These random scrape sites, common-ly found along field edges and travel corridors — offer proof positive that there are bucks in the area, but these scrapes may never be revisited.

When the rut draws near and the mating urge surges, however, scrapes become serious advertisements that read: "Hot does wanted. Stud services available." First, bucks routinely paw out new scrapes along their random travel routes, creating obvious scrape lines that are checked from time to time during daily wanderings. Finally, as rut activity flares, bucks create primary breeding scrapes in secluded corners of their territory and hang around nearby, waiting for hot does to visit and scent-mark the scrapes by urinating in them. These are the scrapes that deserve the most attention from serious bowhunters.

Honestly, it's the does — not bucks — that determine whether a scrape becomes hot or not. As noted, scrapes are a buck's way of advertising for female companionship. Unless a willing doe responds, the scrape will be abandoned as the buck moves on and repeats the entire process elsewhere. If a doe does show interest, the buck joins her, trailing her puppy-dog fashion until she finally allows him to mount her. Once their ardor cools, each goes separate ways with the buck hotfooting it back to his primary scrape are or creating some new scent post where he waits anxiously for a new lady love to appear.

And don't think that a doe bred by one buck won't accept and submit to another buck. Deer researchers have discovered and reported that it's not all that unusual for twin fawns to be fathered by different bucks. Apparently, neither horny bucks nor hot does are monogamous during their rutting relationships.

This buck/doe breeding cycle continues until the rut peaks, passions subside, and both sexes forget what the excitement was all about. Calm returns to the woodlands and deer resume a routine lifestyle. Any does unbred during this period will come back into heat within a month, prompting a "second rut" which includes a resurgence of breeding activity. Such secondary ruts have neither the length nor the intensity of the initial breeding period.

As already documented, rutting bucks are prone to doing some downright stupid things, yet they're seldom pushovers. The does they're traveling with remain constantly alert and either warn the buck of nearby danger or simply bound away to safety, taking the lust-blinded Romeo with them. Noise and scent must always be kept to a minimum, even when you're perched in a well-placed tree stand. Careless movements or sounds can foul up any opportunity at the moment of truth. Deer can and do look up. Mess up one chance at a big buck, and it's almost guaranteed that you won't get a second chance from that same stand.

Dave Holt believes the best chance to ambush a buck is the first time you're hunting from your stand. Odds for success decrease each day thereafter. I tend to agree, although all bets are off during the frenzy of the rut.

Scents used in moderation can complement any stand or scrape hunter's bag of tricks. My own favorites are the doe-in-estrus scents I've effectively used for decades. When nearing any stand, I typically pause long enough to dribble some of the smelly concoction across the soles of my rubber boots and splash a bit more on each pants cuff. Over the years I've had more than one passing buck veer and follow my trail right to the bottom of my tree. For some deer it's been a one-way trip.

I also commonly dab or splash a bit of doe-in-heat scent here and there on common woodland objects — a rotting stump, fence post, rock, low-growing bush, or whatever — located near my stand. The idea is not so much to attract deer or bring big bucks on a dead run; rather, I simply want any buck moving past me to pause long enough to nose the scent, giving me the chance to slip an arrow through his ribs.

During scrape-watching vigils at the height of the rut, I sometimes place scent-saturated cotton balls in black plastic 35mm film containers and hang or set these open canisters near my stand. Another natural use of scent that I've found works well occurs when creating an artificial or "mock" scrape. Manmade deer scrapes

Deer calls, used alone or to complement rattling sequences, add a touch of realism to any hunting setup. Whitetails are more vocal than many people realize.

— created by clearing an area of leaves and sprinkling the ground with deer scents — can attract whitetail bucks. Some serious hunters go so far as to clip a scent-marked overhanging branch from a real scrape as part of the setup. Other use actual deer urine and tarsal glands from previous kills to add an element of realism. Veterans take pains to avoid leaving any evidence of human scent around the faux scrapes, always wearing latex gloves and rubber boots. Obviously, one big advantage to mock scrapes is the fact they can be located within any ideal ambush site. The same cannot be said of real scrapes pawed by live bucks.

Some hunters rely on food or similar attractor scents to pull deer within arrow range. I've done it myself with mixed success, and I much prefer the sex-based lures. In states and provinces where baiting is allowed, corn, carrots, apples, sugar beets, and similar attractants will pull in deer. Ditto for salt and mineral blocks that farmers and ranchers put out for their livestock. But since baiting is illegal in so many hunting areas, always take care to avoid such places to hang your stand. You could end up paying a hefty fine.

Horn Rattling, Calling, and Decoying

During the pre-rut when whitetail bucks feel the first stirrings of unease and aggression, "horn" rattling — real or manmade — can attract any buck within earshot. Much depends on the time of the season, buck-to-doe ratio, and hunting pressure. But the fact remains bucks respond to the sounds of clashing antlers. They either want to defend their home turf or check out — and possibly steal — any doe hanging around the buck fight.

While some hunters create and suggest imitating noisy rattling battles — complete with banging antlers and the accompanying sounds of a brush-raking and leaf-pawing brawl — I've had excellent success with comparatively low-key rattling that begins with a few grunts followed by grinding and twisting the antlers. Sometimes I also take a tree trunk and thump the ground, much as a rutting buck might. I'll then gradually escalate the staged conflict to simulate more serious fighting. But I'll also include brief lulls in the action and intentionally avoid any banging and loud clacking of antlers. My rattling sessions last no more than a minute and a half, and I'll wrap things up with a few more grunts. If no deer appear, I'll repeat the rattling sequence at 45- to 60-minute intervals throughout my stay in the stand.

Cold windless days seem to work best, although I've had little luck rattling in large bucks during the peak of the rut. Small guys

Commercial deer calls imitate a variety of grunts, blats, bleats and other whitetail sounds. How-to audio tapes and written instruction sheets can help make you sound like a deer in no time.

may show, but it seems the big boys have located willing does and would rather make love than war. Post-rut rattling can be effective, too. As long as there are hormone-charged bucks on the prowl, there's a chance to pull one in. I even carry my rattle bag or rattling antlers with me in the early season, gently sparring the way real deer do once any area's bucks have shed their velvet and begin to establish a pecking order.

Just so you'll know, I've used actual antlers and synthetic "horns" with equal success, but I prefer the real thing because I think the sounds carry better. Commercially produced rattle bags — mesh or cloth bags containing wooden or ceramic dowels — are always part of my gear. They can't be beat for carrying convenience, easily fitting in a pocket or pack. And with some practice, any bowhunter can quickly produce realistic rattling sequences. Whatever your own personal choice, keep in mind the idea is to simulate a struggle between two mature bucks. Visualize the fight in your mind's eye and work to sound as authentic as possible.

Rattling teamwork pays off big at times with the rattler concealed on the ground and a companion in a nearby tree stand. Bucks responding to the sound of the antlers have an uncanny ability to pinpoint the exact source of the sounds. This may give the hidden shooter a perfect opportunity to remain unnoticed while drawing and releasing.

Calling can be combined with rattling sequences or used independently. Whitetails are more vocal than many hunters realize, and simulating the sounds they make adds yet another lethal weapon to any bowhunter's arsenal. Commercially produced deer calls imitate deer vocalizations and are intended to attract the attention of real animals. Under ideal conditions, curious whitetails come to investigate the sounds and walk into a sharp broadhead. Detailed instructional audio and video tapes are readily available and are a good investment for any interested hunter. Check out the magazine ads and archery catalogs.

Although using deer calls — or blatting my using your own vocal chords — does work on occasion, you should understand that calls are not a magic means of luring deer within easy bow range. I'm convinced they should be used in moderation or not at all. Also, keep in mind that any deer that responds is going to be alert, looking for the "bucks" he's heard. Such a scenario is not the best-case situation for a bowhunter. I've had my best success with calls when I've used them to pique a whitetail's curiosity or to allay fears in nervous animals, deer that have heard or glimpsed me but were unable to identify what I was. Also, when used in combination with rattling or decoying, deer calls can work and work well.

More than one boss whitetail has been duped by a deer decoy. Some replicas are quite realistic, employing real antlers and deer tails. Scents can be added to provide a realistic olfactory touch. Both sexes may respond to decoys, but during the rut aggressive bucks are prone to approach quickly, sometimes even attacking the sham buck, which he considers a rival interloper. If nothing else, the deer decoy often keeps a real deer's attention riveted in one place, allowing a nearby hunter to get a good shot before the buck realizes he's been duped.

Be careful handling and transporting decoys. Leaving human scent on the decoy can alert deer; wearing latex gloves can help. And for safety's sake, it's a good idea to drape the fake buck in a blaze orange vest or hang surveyor's tape from the antlers and wrap it around the body.

Learn to look for parts of deer, not the entire animal. Spotting the deer before it sees you is the key. Once a whitetail has you spotted, it's too late.

Stalking and Still-Hunting

Stalking whitetails is one of the most difficult challenges facing any bowhunter. While a handful of people may possess the necessary skills to consistently take bucks in this super-tough fashion, comparatively few whitetails fall to stalking hunters. Candidly, in the thick cover deer favor, your chances of seeing a deer before it sees you — much less getting close enough for a killing shot — are pretty doggone slim. Regardless, certain exceptions do exist and spot-and-stalk techniques can work as effectively on whitetails as on any other big game animal. On the famed King Ranch in southeast Texas, for example, I've arrowed half a dozen record-class bucks by spotting them from a distance and carefully stalking within bow range. However, it should be noted that access to the sprawling ranch is limited and these native deer do not know true hunting pressure. They simply are not as wary as deer found elsewhere.

But on public lands not far from my Montana home, and in certain other whitetail areas scattered across the Rocky Mountain West, it's rarely a problem to spot distant deer and plan stalks that will put you close to bedded or browsing bucks. In rolling or broken country, where grassy coulees and rocky canyons provide cover for open country whitetails, stalking these deer is a routine hunting method. Even in Midwestern and Eastern hardwood forests, whitetails are stalkable under certain conditions. I've done it myself. Ditto for deer bedded in unpicked cornfields. Favorite stalking times are windy or damp days when sounds of my movements are masked by Mother Nature.

Compared to stalking, still-hunting typically is often much more productive. The completely camouflaged bowhunter, moving slowly and quietly through prime deer habitat, is in truth a mobile blind. As you ease into the wind one careful step at a time, pausing often to let your eyes carefully check out the surroundings, you have a 50-50 chance of seeing the deer before it sees you. Sometimes feeding or wandering deer may move close enough for you to release an arrow without moving from your tracks. Other shooting opportunities may arise when you're able to ease closer and remain undetected long enough to make the shot.

It's no puzzle why stalking and still-hunting whitetails is so difficult. These deer typically live in areas where contact with humans is an everyday occurrence. They constantly see, smell, and hear

Police officer Will Jimeno, an avid bowhunter who survived the collapse of the World Trade Center on September 11, collected this P&Y whitetail on a bowhunt with M. R. James in November of 2003.

Illinois bowhunter Judy Kovar has taken over half a dozen record book whitetails. She disdains tree stands and hunts bucks from ground level — with obvious success!

people. Usually they simply melt away into the brush; however, when surprised by humans at close range they'll usually explode into instant flight. The first occasion leaves a bowhunter wondering where all the deer have gone; the second offers the poorest possible bowhunting opportunity, a running shot at an alarmed deer.

Driving/Nudging Deer

Low percentage running shots make deer drives unpopular with many bowhunters. Yet each year groups of hunters divide into "drivers" and "standers" and head for the woods. The standers take up positions along trails or known escape routes. Drives then move through whitetail bedding areas, kicking out animals ahead of them in hopes they'll eventually move past waiting hunters.

Such deer drives will effectively put deer on the move — and therein lies the basic problem. Whitetails bounding headlong through the underbrush are risky bowhunting targets. Chances of wounding and losing animals are great. Also, as one knowledgeable deer hunter noted, "Sure, you can drive deer. You can drive 'em anywhere they want to go."

Yet another problem is the end result of disturbing deer in their bedding areas. While drives may stir things up during midday hours when hunting commonly is slow, they also upset the deer, disrupting normal travel patterns for the balance of the day. Sometimes the pressure will push them from an area. Where deer drives are conducted, lots of pre-hunt practice at moving targets is advised or hunters must resist loosing arrows at nearby moving targets and waiting for a better opportunity.

Typically far more effective than haphazard deer drives are "nudges" involving a handful of people. After one person climbs into a strategically placed ground blind or tree stand, the others ease through cover — still-hunting as they go — hoping that any deer slipping out ahead of one hunter may bump into others when they pass by the stand where hidden partners wait. Such "nudges" work best where hunters have an intimate knowledge of the terrain — especially the escape routes — and how the deer are likely to react to a low key push through their home territory. Teamwork is vital.

Speaking of teamwork, noted whitetail hunters Gene and Barry Wensel used to operate a deer camp along the Milk River in eastern Montana. After many years of bowhunting experience there, the twins took advantage of limited bottomland cover, pushing and antlered bucks past waiting friends and clients. They knew that the open lands flanking the river kept the local whitetails predictable.

No discussion of whitetails can be considered complete without passing reference to the tiny Coues deer of Mexico and some Southwestern states. From my perspective, these pint-sized critters are the toughest deer any bowhunter can try to take, bar none. Simply getting within bow range by still-hunting or spot-and-stalk methods will usually push the abilities of any experienced hunter. I recall one late Arizona bowhunt after the mid-January rut had wound down. On that weeklong trip I couldn't have tagged a Coues buck — or doe, for that matter — with a scoped .270. Every single whitetail I saw was already two canyons away and on a dead run, having heard or spotted me long before I saw snowy rumps disappearing over a distant ridge. G. Fred Asbell returned from his first Coues whitetail hunt muttering to himself about the wary nature of these beautiful little brush-loving deer.

But Dwight Schuh proved that stalking rutting Coues whitetails, although difficult, if far from impossible. Dwight tagged a good buck in January of 1997, though he sums up his entire hunting experience in a one-word sentence, "Tough!" Dwight notes these small, gray deer are hard to find in the first place. Second, they're awfully skittish and doubly difficult to approach. He explained how he scored as follows:

"The serious Arizona whitetail bowhunters I've hunted with start

Dave James, the author's son, tagged this big-bodied buck from a tree stand set back in the timber along a trail leading to a popular feeding area.

Many people believe deer are larger than they actually are. Most whitetails stand no more than 3 feet at the shoulder, and some, like this south Texas buck, weigh about 100 pounds when field-dressed.

off by heading for a high point with 15X binoculars mounted on a solid tripod. They sit and glass as long as it takes — all day, if necessary — until they locate a stalkable buck. Most people simply aren't patient enough to sit that long."

Once a buck is found, the stalk itself begins with one or more spotters remaining behind to guide the shooter close with simple hand signals. Dwight's buck was bedded with some does in a shady cut. When signals told him he'd closed the distance to 50 yards, he stopped and glassed the sidehill below until he finally spotted the buck's antlers. Super slow maneuvering eventually put him within shooting position near a mesquite bush. Drawing his bow, Dwight held and released. The arrow looked good all the way, but...

"I missed," Dwight confesses. "My arrow hit something at the last instant and buried in the ground beside that buck. He boiled out of his bed and ran uphill, stopping to stare back toward the bed and my arrow."

Bad mistake. Dwight, only 25 yards away, eased a second arrow onto the string. His second shot didn't miss. "Sometimes a bit of luck comes in handy when hunting Coues deer," he admits with a smile.

Other consistently successful Coues hunters I've talked with prefer to head afield during the rut, when the normally hard-to-find bucks become both visible and vulnerable. In dry years, water hole setups can produce. But whenever possible, savvy bowhunters prefer to find a tree where they can sit and wait, calling and rattling just as if they were hunting any other whitetails anywhere else in the country. Such tactics work. Arizona bowhunter Dennis Eaton, who once held the world record, took his Pima County Coues buck by rattling him in. A friend and frequent hunting buddy of mine, Wyoming native Jim Van Norman, has tagged several record-class

bucks with point-blank shots by setting up a tree stand over well used travel routes.

Bowhunting whitetails, no matter what technique you choose to use, is undeniably the most popular outdoor pastime for anyone willing to accept the challenge of pursuing big game with the stick,

Stalking whitetails is among the most challenging forms of taking North America's most popular big game animal. At times, a combination of skill and luck results in a perfect opportunity to collect a buck.

Colorado bowhunter Janet George used a recurve bow to drop this big whitetail.

Gary Bogner, one of 5 bowhunters to collect all species of North American big game, shows a Coues' whitetail he arrowed in Arizona.

Dave Holt has tagged numerous record book whitetails over the years. He hangs numerous stands and feels the best chance comes when the stand is first hunted.

string, and feathered shaft. A common sight across much of North America, the modern whitetail offers widespread opportunity for bowhunting success. At the same time, no matter where these deer are pursued, the advantage remains solidly with the deer. No bowhunter I know would have it any other way.

Judging Trophy Whitetails

Most mature whitetail bucks have four or more total points on each antler beam. Trophy-class racks boast long, thick tines, sprouting upward from heavy beams. Inside spreads of one and one-half to two feet are common. As is the case with all antlered game, symmetry is the key to high Pope and Young scores in all but non-typical heads.

Generally, whitetail racks are smaller than those of blacktails and mule deer. Estimating antler size and record book score is often a problem because big deer favor thick cover and seldom give hunters long looks at their headgear. Regardless, big antlers are unmistakable to veteran deer hunters in search of real wall-hangers.

Any antlers that extend past the ear tips or exceed the width of the buck's body are above average. And when the height of the headgear approaches the depth of the deer's body from withers to brisket, the rack quite likely is trophy class.

To qualify for Pope and Young record book entry, typical antlers must score at least 125 inches; the minimum score for non-typical racks is 155.

Coues deer have proportionally smaller racks, the inside spread seldom exceeding 12 inches. However, Sergio Orozco's current P&Y world record buck scores an incredible 130 1/8 inches — a score that shattered the former record and earned that buck the Ishi Award, which is the P&Y's highest award. To qualify for the record book, a Coues deer buck must score at least 65 inches (typical) and 95 inches (non-typical).

To score typical whitetail antlers, add the length of each main beam and all points at least one inch in length. Next, total four circumference measurements starting at the burr. Finally, add the inside spread. After subtracting abnormal points and differences between matching antlers, you have the final score. The exact same steps are followed for non-typical racks except the total length of all abnormal points is added to the deer's final score.

Tagging any record book buck is an outstanding bowhunting achievement; however, most any whitetail deer — whatever its size or sex — is a challenging, worthy big game animal for bowhunters. Some folks feel there is too much emphasis being placed on large antlers and flatly declare that any adult deer, legally taken under the rules of fair chase, is a worthy trophy. Whatever your personal feelings or hunting goals, you should understand that the whitetail is truly "America's deer" — and with good reason. If a vote were taken and only one big game species could be hunted anywhere across North America, the whitetail would be the winner. Hands down!

Blacktail & Mule Deer

Classification

Mule deer (*Odocoileus hemionus*) and two smaller blacktail deer subspecies, the Columbian blacktail (*O. h. columbianus*) and the Sitka blacktail (*O. h. sitkensis*) are closely related animals that will interbreed freely wherever their home ranges overlap. Other generally recognized *Odocoileus hemionus* subspecies include the common Rocky Mountain mule deer, as well as the California, the desert, southern, and peninsula mule deer.

Current Distribution

Columbian blacktail deer range from California northward into British Columbia and Alaska; however, for record-keeping purposes all blacktails in Alaska, its coastal islands, and B.C.'s Queen Charlotte Islands are considered to be Sitka blacktails. Mule deer most commonly are found in the mountains, prairies, and desert lowlands of the western United States.

The ancestors of modern mule deer are believed to have originated in Europe, eventually making their way into Asia and on to North America when the two continents were connected by the land bridge spanning the Bering Strait.

Wanderers, mule deer travel widely and commonly move between summer and winter ranges; in some areas actual migrations occur. Blacktails are homebodies by comparison, often spending each year within a single home range, although changing elevations with the seasons.

Identifying Characteristics

Mule deer are blocky animals, standing just over three feet at the shoulder and measuring about five feet in length. Many muley bucks weigh 200 pounds or more, while does are 15 to 20 percent lighter. Both sexes have large, mule-like ears eight to 10 inches long and six inches wide. Blacktails are smaller versions of the same animal.

Coat coloration varies from reddish-brown in the summer to wintertime gray. Antlers of adult mule deer are bifurcated, commonly forking into Y-shaped points rather than having individual tines sprouting from the main beam. Columbian blacktails typically have smaller, darker racks, and Sitka blacktail bucks often grow racks resembling small whitetail antlers, lacking the forking characteristics of most mule deer headgear. Unlike the whitetail, mule deer and blacktails have a dark, distinctive skull cap extending down between the eyes. Two white throat patches are obvious, and the underbelly and inner legs are likewise snowy white. A mule deer's tail is white, round, and tufted with black; a blacktail's tail is dark on top with a snowy white underside. Pale-colored rump patches complete the general physical description.

Both blacktails and mule deer have small tarsal glands located on the hocks of each rear leg. Metatarsal glands up to five inches long — the largest of any deer species — are located above the rear hoof on the outside of a mule deer's back legs. Blacktail metatarsals measure about three inches. Conspicuous lachrymal glands are located in the front corner of each eye and both species have interdigital glands between the hooves, which secrete an identifying odor.

All these deer have 32 teeth, including eight incisors (the fourth incisor on each side is really a modified canine tooth), 12 premolars, and another dozen molars. No deer have teeth on the upper jaw at the front of the mouth. When feeding, the deer fill their rumen with browse and later regurgitate the food mass during the cud-chewing process.

Unlike the lithe whitetail which runs with long, graceful leaps, a mule deer and blacktail will bound away with a ground-jarring, stiff-legged, pogo stick gait that is deceptively fast. Both species have been clocked at 35 mph. Blacktails also are strong swimmers and have been seen swimming long distances between Alaska's offshore islands.

Habitat/Diet

Deer are opportunistic eaters with various grasses comprising the bulk of their summer diet. But no deer will overlook berries, flowers, fungi, nuts, ferns, cacti, or agricultural crops, where available. Browse is a standard wintertime diet.

Mule deer have adapted to a variety of terrain, from brushy desert lowlands and open prairies to high country forests and the alpine parks above timberline. Available forage and cover are more vital to survival than climate. Where water is scarce, deer will obtain necessary moisture from the plants they ingest.

Blacktails are widely regarded as brush-loving animals of the dense coastal forests; however, these deer can and do thrive in a variety of topography. They are found in the dry, rolling California hills where open country and sweltering temperatures are common. But they're equally at home in the high country of coastal mountains and in marine climates including the wet, thick rain forests of Washington and Oregon. They also inhabit the harshly cold and windswept islands off this continent's northwest coast, proving a remarkable adaptability.

Senses

Mule deer and blacktails have keen eyesight, but like many big game animals they tend to overlook unmoving objects. Their hearing is acute and their sense of smell better still. In the typically dense cover they favor, blacktails rely mainly on their noses and ears to detect danger. Open country deer mainly use their eyes to keep them safe. When alarmed, a deer will often stamp a forefoot, alerting all nearby animals, and/or blow a blast of air through its nostrils. Mule deer frequently bed in shady spots on high points with a good view of the surrounding countryside. Here they rely on their eyes and scent carried to them by rising thermals or prevailing winds to detect approaching danger.

Reproduction

Mule deer commonly mate from late November to early December across much of their range; however, in some areas the annual rut begins in October and runs as late as January. Blacktails typically do their breeding in October and November.

Bucks grow restless and become aggressive with the approach of the rut, leaving their summer bachelor groups or solitary lifestyles to begin the search for receptive does. These deer are polygamous animals, collecting small, loose-knit harems. Buck fights occur, but seldom result in serious injury or death. By the time the bucks drop their antlers each winter, breeding season has ended for another year.

Pregnant does carry their fawns just over 200 days. Does giving birth for the first time usually have single births. Twins are commonly born to older does. Newborn fawns weigh about five pounds and grow quickly. They begin to browse within two weeks but often continue to nurse until fall. It is common for the fawns to remain with their mothers through their first year.

Life Expectancy

Mule deer and blacktails may live 10 to 12 years, although there are some reports of deer living into their late teens or early 20s. Mountain lions exact a heavy toll, averaging a kill each week, and wolves also pull down their share of these deer. Black, grizzly, and brown bears will kill any deer they can, often taking the young, sick, injured, and aged animals. Hunters generally harvest a large number of blacktails and mule deer each year. They enjoy the venison, which is usually delicious, although the field care of the meat, the time of year, and the deer's diet will affect the quality of the venison.

Bowhunting Records

The top Sitka blacktail deer was shot by Charles Hakari on Prince of Wales Island, Alaska, in 1987. This buck has an official Pope and Young score of 116 3/8. The best Columbian blacktail killed by a bowhunter scored 172 2/8 inches. It was shot in 1969 by B. G. Shrutleff during a bowhunt in Marion County, Oregon. The top non-typical blacktail was killed by James Decker in Jackson County, Oregon, in 1988; its official score is 194 4/8. The World Record typical mule deer scores 203 1/8 and was taken by Bill Barcus in Colorado's White River National Forest in 1979. The top non-typical muley scores 274 7/8 and was killed in Morgan County, Colorado, in 1987 by bowhunter Kenneth W. Plank.

Chapter 16
Blacktail & Mule Deer – Western Wanderers

REACHING THE BUSH quietly was easy in the fluffy, sound-muffling September snow that cloaked the Wyoming foothills. Kneeling, I nocked an arrow, then risked a peek. Nothing. If the buck was still bedded in this brushy hideout, he certainly was well hidden. Honestly, I couldn't help but wonder if somehow he'd heard or seen me approach, stood, and melted away. This whole stalking setup seemed too good to be true. Doubts began to eat at me. But I knew that somewhere behind the ridge to my right, Pete was circling high to get above the backcountry bowl where he'd watched the big buck bed earlier in the morning. Once Pete emerged on the skyline, we'd soon know if the deer was still here or long gone.

A sudden ridgetop movement drew my attention. Pete appeared, moving upwind of the brush-choked pocket, intentionally showing himself to any keen-eyed buck bedded below. I gripped my bow's wooden handle and waited. Snow suddenly cascaded from a sagging branch just over 30 yards away. The buck had turned his head, bumping the branch with his tall antlers that abruptly materialized amid the drooping limbs. I could see that he was staring over his shoulder at Pete moving along the pocket's rim.

I was surprisingly calm despite the jolt of adrenaline flooding through me at the sight of big antlers so close. Unless this old muley blew out of his bed, I was going to get a close shot. A distinct game trail followed the slope of the knob to my left, emerging from the brush less than 20 yards away. This was the most likely escape route. I tried to ignore the heavy thudding of my heart and switched my full attention to the big muley.

Slow minutes dragged. Pete plodded along the skyline, but still the buck didn't budge. It was as if he knew he was invisible — and safe. All I could do was watch and wait. But then Pete stooped, rose, and lofted a baseball-sized rock into space. It landed with a snow-muted *thump* on the far side of the pocket. The muley's antlers jerked, but he remained bedded. Another rock sailed into the brush with the same results. But when a third rock rattled into the brush, the buck finally stood and stared upward. I forced myself not to look at the heavy rack but rather to concentrate on the depression just behind his shoulder. Then the buck took two cautious steps,

stopped, and looked back.

Now! The arrow came back smoothly and my string fingers brushed my beard at the corner of my mouth. The buck's head jerked around, ears flared, eyes meeting mine. But my arrow's red

Pete Dube shows the author's Wyoming buck. The two teamed up to stalk the bedded muley, with Pete walking a skyline and holding the deer's attention while M. R. James eased to the brushy pocket and shot the buck when he stood.

Locate prairie creekbottoms and you'll find mule deer nearby. Such waterways are magnets for a variety of wildlife. Well situated ambush sites can pay off with close range shots.

and yellow fletching vanished behind his left shoulder an instant before he lunged away. The huge five-by-four slowed to a walk, already unsteady on his feet, before rounding the knob 50 yards away. I knew he wouldn't go far. And he didn't.

That big Wyoming muley, one of the best bucks I've collected in some 40 years of bowhunting these long-eared Westerners, was taken in typical spot and stalk fashion when opportunity pays off in a single heart-pounding instant after countless hours of shooting practice. If big-antlered bucks turn you on, and if the challenge of spot-and-stalk bowhunting is an open invitation to adventure, the highly visible and adaptable mule deer is just the animal for you.

"The mule deer just might be the best all-around bowhunting animal there is," G. Fred Asbell states flatly, knowing full well his words will rankle the emotions of serious whitetail hunters everywhere.

"The facts are that despite slowly declining numbers, muleys are still available for bowhunting in good numbers across their home range. Additionally, they have what many consider to be one of the most spectacular antler formations of any deer, and the true trophy-class bucks may be more prevalent in muleys than any other deer species. That combines to create one mighty fine bowhunter's animal. Another thing about a mule deer buck is that you can make hunting him about as tough or easy as you want.

"Young mule deer aren't as wild and unapproachable as their whitetail cousins at the same age, and they're ideal for the beginning bowhunter. A young forkhorn, all decked out in his first set of masculine headgear, can be about as naive and curious as they come. But as mule deer grow older, predation by man and beast — and long, hard Western winters — turn the survivors into tough, wary animals. By the time the buck has reached maturity, you have an animal that is as difficult to take with bow and arrow as the biggest whitetail — and in my mind, probably more difficult.

"The bowhunter can set his own standards," Fred concludes. "He can shoot a younger animal, if he desires, and he'll likely have

opportunities to do exactly that. Or he can hold out for one of the big, heavy-horned monsters. For the beginner or the trophy hunter, mule deer hunting is hard to beat."

Like Fred, many veteran bowhunters believe taking a huge, trophy-class muley buck is the toughest bowhunting challenge there is.

The author arrowed this P&Y-class blacktail during an early August bowhunt along the northern California coast.

Water holes like this prairie seep attract all sorts of game. This small mule deer group stopped by the author's antelope blind one September morning.

The record books tend to bear this out. Check the Boone and Crockett listings of the all-time best mule deer bucks and compare them with bucks entered in the Pope and Young records. All of the bow-killed mule deer ever taken that score 200 inches and above (typical) number a mere half dozen animals. But the B&C records show over 235 200-inch bucks with about one-third of those wall-hangers coming from Colorado! Such statistics underscore the widespead belief that there are easier ways to collect a monster muley than to head afield toting a bow and arrow. Just don't try selling that idea to any serious bowhunter to whom challenge is a way of life.

Offsetting the difficulty normally involved in tagging a giant mule deer is the breathtaking country these deer inhabit. These are visible, big country deer, whether found feeding above timberline amid majestic mountain peaks, bedded in wooded foothill pockets, or lining out single file across rugged badland settings. Simply walking these wild, remote lands during late summer archery seasons, bow in hand, is a great way to begin any deer season. Bagging one of these Western wanderers, whatever its antler size, is a bonus — and tasty icing on any bowhunter's cake.

Hunting Techniques

Despite having a reputation for being less wily than whitetails, mule deer are not pushovers. As Fred Asbell says, "I don't know who started the rumor that mule deer are dumb. One thing for sure, whoever he was, he wasn't trophy hunting with a bow and arrow — not in my neck of the Colorado woods, anyway. The mule deer I hunt are the most spectacular, unpredictable, aggravating animals I know. I've found them anything but dumb."

Regardless, locating muleys by sight is relatively easy. Therefore, still-hunting and stalking are the two most popular and effective bowhunting methods. In the high country, a favorite spot-and-stalk technique is to walk the ridges — staying off the skyline, of course — and easing downslope early in the day. Rising thermals will carry your scent up and away from deer feeding or bedded below you. Additionally, the high ground offers many excellent glassing positions from which you can locate animals moving below your vantage point.

Always take things slow and easy. That's excellent advice for any still-hunter, and it's especially true for a bowhunter moving through prime deer habitat. Walk a little, look a lot. Unless you spot the deer before he sees you, you'll never get close enough to release an

Like most game animals, mule deer are quick to pick up motion, but tend to overlook camouflaged bowhunters, even at close range.

arrow. And keep in mind that where you spot one muley, chances are good that others are standing or bedded nearby. Mule deer are gregarious animals. More than one careful stalk has been spoiled when other unnoticed deer spooked just as the hunter was close to getting a shot at the buck he was stalking. Never assume any mule deer is alone.

Look for parts of deer, not the entire animal. Horizontal shapes among the vertical tree trunks are invariably worth closer examination. Use your binoculars to determine whether that's a bedded buck or just a dead bush or simply a moss-covered log or stump. Is that reddish-brown patch in the quakies a deer or just a dead bush? And that flicker of movement there in the oak brush...is it a jay or a deer's ear? Finally, how about that forked branch jutting above the sage? Could it be an antler instead of a dead limb?

Once you spot a nearby buck, your still-hunt becomes a stalk as you try to ease close enough to release a well-aimed arrow. Although mule deer are not especially difficult to stalk, neither are they blind nor deaf. They have good noses, too. Keep tabs on wind direction. All adult bucks and does are quick to zero in on any suspicious movement or sound. If you can see a buck's eyes, he can see you, even if he's not looking directly looking your way. Move only when his head is down or his face is screened by brush or behind a tree. Take pains to avoid breaking twigs underfoot. Rustling leaves or limbs scraping on clothing can spoil any stalker's plans.

It's often very frustrating to stalk browsing deer because they easily move through the brush, nibbling as they walk, while a bowhunter has to take one careful, quiet step at a time — and remain unseen and unheard, often by more than one set of eyes and ears. Regardless, hungry deer concentrate on filling their bellies and can be successfully stalked by patient, persistent hunters who take care not to alert them.

If wind direction and terrain permits, sometimes it's best to try

Mule deer can live on treeless prairies that, at first glance, would seem devoid of wildlife. Check out dry washes and coulees where deer commonly bed during the day.

Noted Alabama bowhunter Dr. Warren Strickland shows one of his record-class mule deer bucks taken during an open country stalk. Deer of this caliber are tough to come by.

to determine a deer's direction of travel and circle ahead. It's risky to let a deer out of your sight when making a stalk, since it can change directions or bed down before you reach your ambush site; however, sometimes things will go exactly as planned and the buck will feed past within easy bow range.

In open country typical of the prairie and desert lowlands, a stalking bowhunter must keep the same rules in mind. Take advantage of rolling terrain, walking slowly along dry washes and coulees, taking the time to glass brushy clumps that provide tempting shady spots where deer may bed. Some of this vast country may seem far too open and barren to support jack rabbits, much less big-racked bucks. But first appearances can be deceiving. Walk the land and you'll often find shallow draws and cuts, even on the undulating prairie. And if there's sufficient food and water nearby, it's likely that deer aren't far away.

Keep an eye out for prime bedding spots. Check the base of cliffs

and rocky overhangs where deer have natural protection at their backs and a good view of the countryside unfolding before them. But don't overlook grassy swales and shaded cutbanks, either. Remember that open country mule deer often paw out beds on the uphill side of solitary trees and brushes sprouting from rocky ridges. Again, here's where a good pair of binoculars comes in handy, enabling you to check potential hiding spots from a safe distance. Bedded deer are ideal for stalking, although their eyes, ears, or noses are in constant use even when relaxed deer are chewing their cuds. Some smart hunters start each day by sitting on some high point, just below the skyline, glassing for distant deer. When animals are sighted, no real attempt is made to close the distance until the deer bed down for the day. Only then, conditions permitting, is an approach attempted.

Special attention must always be paid to the area surrounding bedded deer. Once your stalk begins and you've changed positions, things immediately look different. Also, since stalking hunters must remain out of sight until they're within arrow range, it's critical to know exactly where the buck is bedded. Always try to pick out a single easily recognizable landmark — a particular rock, tree, or bush — near the bed. Then carefully close the distance. At times the tops of a buck's antlers may be visible. So much the better.

Once on the Wyoming prairie I spotted serveral bucks bedding in the shade of a dry wash just over a mile away. After circling and keeping the wind in my face, I eventually spotted tine tips jutting out of a shallow ravine just ahead. I eventually closed to within spittin' distance of that four-by-four buck. He was less than five yards away when he finally rose from his dusty bed to change positions. He never knew I was near until my arrow zipped through his chest and buried itself in the prairie soil. That particular midday stalk took several hours. But there's seldom any hurry, really. Unless spooked, the bedded deer likely will stay put — as long as they're shaded from direct sunlight — until evening approaches and they rise and begin to feed.

While stalking is normally a solitary effort, double-teaming bedded bucks can be a deadly effective technique, as proved in my anecdote at the start of this chapter. And my pal Dwight Schuh tells how the buddy system — and a set of prearranged signals — works to a stalking hunter's advantage.

"My friend Larry Jones and I have worked out fairly detailed

M.R. James took this Pope and Young muley during a Wyoming bowhunt. The buck was sighted in the sage and ambushed in a patch of timber along a nearby ridge.

hand signals. When we've located a buck we want, one of us stays at the spotting position while the other stalks. The spotter has the deer in sight all the time, and he can guide the stalker right in. If he points one way or the other, that tells the stalker the buck is that direction. If he waves his hand in a circle over his head, that means the buck has gotten up to feed. If he bends over and touches his toes, the buck has moved downhill. Arms held in a big circle means everything is okay, keep going. If the spotter pretends he's shooting a bow, that means the stalker had better nock an arrow and get ready because something is about to happen. If the spotter waves his arms violently, it means the buck has spooked and the stalk is off."

Frightened mule deer typically leap from their beds and bounce away in high gear. This is especially true of bigger bucks. A few deer may simply stand and stare — giving you ample time for a shot — but don't count on it. Generally, it's best to shoot while the animal is still bedded or when he eventually stands of his own accord. If you're above and behind the bedded deer, you may be able to drive the arrow down into the buck's chest, much as you would from a tree stand. If he's on the same level, take care to avoid the heavy shoulders and hams which shield the vitals. Place your shot accordingly or wait for a better shooting opportunity. On a recent Wyoming hunt, I shot at a quartering buck standing half hidden below a ridgeline. He was less than 20 yards away, but my arrow hit a rock and deflected harmlessly into space — surprising me as well as that lucky buck. I'd intentionally held low to ensure a solid mid-body hit but overcompensated. Even decades of experience can't guarantee success.

On occasion I've successfully hunted mule deer from tree stands. This is good news for some whitetail hunters who are more comfortable waiting in elevated perches than moving slowly along the ground in hopes of getting a shot. In fact, the same tree stand tac-

tics that work so well on whitetails can be equally effective on muleys, especially if the stands are hung near water holes, mineral licks, salt blocks left for livestock (if legal), or other deer magnets. Trail-watching can pay off at times; however, mule deer wander widely across their range and may be here today and miles away tomorrow. This makes normal stand hunting tough unless the ambush site overlooks well-tracked trails leading to popular feeding areas. In some dry mule deer country where browse is hard to come by, irrigated ranch crops such as alfalfa and certain grains regularly lure deer down from the surrounding hills each evening. These green oases have been the undoing of more than one hungry crop-raiding muley.

Does, fawns, and yearlings typically are the first to visit the fields, but patient hunters can be rewarded with a shot at a buck moving past just before dark. Haystacks and windmill platforms are two other possibilities when searching for possible ambush sites. Remember, too, since hungry deer commonly feed throughout the nighttime hours and do not leave the fields until dawn, your morning stands must be located far enough away from the field that you won't spook the animals either getting to or entering your stand.

Ground blinds — natural or manmade — are equally effective where good trails pass close by. Deadfalls, rockpiles, and brushy clumps can be converted into convenient hiding spots. Some bowhunters dig shallow pits and use limbs, brush, vegetation, rocks, and the like to create a well concealed blind. Others drape camo

Marv Clyncke often hunts near or above timberline in his native Colorado. He's one of Colorado's best known and most successful bowhunters.

netting between boulders or bushes and simply settle back in the shadows to wait. A few employ specially manufactured blinds, often helping them blend in by breaking up their shape with brush, limbs, and other natural materials. Deer are quick to notice unusual objects along familiar travel routes. Whenever possible, erect or construct ground-level blinds in advance of your actual hunt. This gives game the chance to get accustomed to the structures before you actually hunt from them.

The ideal ground blind has adequate cover behind the hunter to break up his silhouette and hide movements. Also, there should be enough cover in front to shield a hunter from view. Clear at least two shooting lanes in natural blinds, and cut two or more shooting windows into cloth blinds. Always locate your ground blind to take advantage of the prevailing winds.

Stands are most effective when used patiently and intelligently. Location is the key, of course, and this requires a knowledge of surrounding terrain and game travel patterns. Some guides use tree stands placed at time-tested sites to position their clients within arrow range of bucks. There's no disputing the fact this type of hunting can and does work well. But for many mule deer hunters, myself included, stalking bucks is more exciting than simply sitting and waiting for some deer to saunter past. So we take an active rather than passive role in pursuing muleys. Regardless, you should always use the hunting method that works best for you.

Be aware that mule deer are quick learners. If hunted from trees, they soon learn to look up to detect danger, just as whitetails do. And they seemingly are always alert to potential trouble approaching from eye level. Little wonder. Cougars commonly roam across much of the mule deer's home range, averaging one or more kills per week. Careless mule deer simply don't last long. And when hunting pressure grows intense, a muley can quickly become as goosey as any whitetail. This is especially true of larger, older bucks.

In areas where stands are located in shelterbelts, along creek bottoms or in natural saddles between high ridges, and in rimrock country, driving deer can result in close-range shots. But this technique works best if the deer are not spooked but merely nudged from their beds. The idea is to make them move out slowly ahead of the drivers, not crash away pell-mell through trees and brush. Running deer are always risky targets for bowhunters, and frightened deer, adrenaline pumping, are always harder to put down with either a bow or rifle. Yet deer walking slowly past hunters stationed along escape routes may present an excellent shot. I've hunted with some guides who offer spot-and-stalk or stand hunting sites early and late in the day when deer are up and feeding. The midday hours are then spent conducting organized drives or pushes through bedding areas. This can work, but it presents several obvious problems. Many "organized" drives dissolve into chaos, resulting in alarmed muleys bouncing off in every direction, heading for quieter surroundings. Also, mule deer do not tolerate human pressure well. Repeatedly bother them in bedding areas and they just might leave the country.

Weather changes affect mule deer movements. When they sense an approaching storm, deer may be on their feet and feeding at any time of day, taking cover only after the storm hits. A light mist or gentle rain doesn't seem to bother them; however, storms with heavy downpours will quickly send them into hiding. Heavy snows commonly push deer from higher elevations into sheltered canyons where browse is readily available. Sometimes veteran bowhunters eagerly await the late season hunts when huge ridgerunners are driven to lower elevations by the advancing snow line.

White-clad bowhunters, dressed in warm winter camo, can enjoy good success still-hunting deer late seasons, especially when the snow is wet or powdery underfoot. Crusty, icy conditions make wintertime stalking an exercise in frustration. Rarely will even the best bowhunters get close enough to release an arrow. Regardless, where mule deer compete with livestock for scanty winter forage, good ambush sites are haystacks and cottonwoods overlooking trails and feeding areas.

During the pre-rut and rut, some bowhunters who live in mule deer country report success at rattling or calling bucks in. They use horn-rattling and grunting routines similar to those that work for whitetails. But many mule deer seasons begin and end prior to the annual rut. This fact precludes routine calling methods. Ditto for the use of doe-in-heat or other sex scents that work near scrapes

Dave Holt has collected his share of mule deer with the hunting bow. He gives the species high marks for providing bowhunting excitement to thousands of deer hunters.

Sitka blacktails are smallish animals of coastal ranges and certain islands off Alaska and Canada. Dave Holt arrowed this buck on an early-season bowhunt in Alaska.

Mule deer are gregarious animals of Western North America. Spot one and it's likely there are others nearby.

pawed by rutting bucks. The nomadic nature of mule deer makes scrape-watching a chancy undertaking at best, even when the hunting season coincides with the fall rut.

Some bowhunters insist that attractor scents will lure mule deer, piquing their curiosity if not tantalizing their taste buds. Others focus on the use of masking scents that help camouflage human odors. Hunters head for the hills hoping to intercept moving deer, not pull deer to them.

Because of the open terrain these long-eared deer inhabit, some bowhunters wrongly believe it is necessary to take long distance, arrow-lobbing shots. However, most Pope and Young record book bucks have been shot by stalking bowhunters at distances of less than 40 yards. Prepare accordingly and always resist the urge to release arrows at deer standing beyond your effective shooting range. Getting close and taking close-range bowhunting shots at mule deer are practices commonly shared by successful hunters. Long range kills are the exception.

Mule deer are solid, blocky animals. Well-placed arrows through the chest will stop even the biggest muley bucks; however, marginal to poor hits often result in a long, difficult tracking job.

Blacktails — both the Columbian variety and the Sitka deer of our continent's northern reaches — are smaller versions of the mule deer. Brush-loving animals, they can be successfully hunted by stalking, but there are other options for the savvy bowhunter.

Recently, on an August bowhunt in the coastal mountains of northern California, hunting buddy Tom Nelson and I each shot record book bucks from treestands located along travel routes near feeding areas. These deer may be found and hunted anywhere from high peaks to sidehill thickets and lowland jungles. More difficult to approach than Sitkas, they can be arrowed by patient still-hunters who employ routine slow-and-easy stalking methods. But, as Tom and I proved, good bucks can be taken from tree stands that are strategically hung near trails, near clearcuts, or natural openings where the animals come to feed. They may be routinely duped by realistic rattling and calling efforts during the fall rut.

Sitkas are the least hunted, least pressured of all North American deer, often spending their summers in open high country along the Alaskan coast, moving lower into dense cover as fall approaches. Still-hunting Sitkas is somewhat easier than for other species, but calling works well starting in the early fall and continuing through the rut. Liberal bag limits and healthy populations combine to make the Sitka blacktail an especially appealing bowhunter trophy — a true sleeper species.

Whether looking for a special trophy, stocking your freezer with tasty venison, or simply seeking a challenging yet readily available big game animal, don't overlook mule deer or blacktails. These deer are tailor-made for bowhunters.

G. Fred Asbell calls big mule deer bucks the toughest of all North American big game trophies to bowhunt.

Dwight Schuh rattled-in this Oregon blacktail in November and brought him down with a 30-yard shot. It was a foggy, rainy day—which describes most November days in western Oregon. The official P&Y score of this buck is 108 0/8.

George Shurtleff poses with his world record Columbian blacktail buck, the biggest ever tagged by a bowhunter. Its official Pope and Young score is 172 2/8.

Judging Trophy Mule and Blacktail Deer

Adult mule deer bucks commonly have four to five points on each antler, including the brow tines (although missing eyeguards are not uncommon). True trophy-class animals have wide, tall, thick-beamed racks that may span 24 to 36 inches and more

For years one standard of mule deer excellence has been a "30-inch buck." This reference to antler width is somewhat misleading as a trophy standard, since many record book bucks have lesser spreads. In fact, in measuring trophy antlers only the inside spread is included in the total score. A quick check of the Pope and Young Club's Fifth Edition record book finds only five muley bucks with inside spreads of 30-plus inches listed near the top of the typical category. While spread is impressive, it's symmetry, antler mass, tine length, and total points that are most important in determining a buck's score and record book standing. In fact, unusually wide racks may be penalized in the scoring process since deductions are made if the inside spread of the main beams exceeds the antler length.

Small-bodied muleys with average racks may fool the novice, especially if the hunter has spent lots of time around whitetails. True trophy racks will immediately grab anyone's attention. Long-tined and thick-beamed, they often jut well past the deer's body by one-third to one-half. Mule deer and Columbian blacktails with abnormal points may be entered in the non-typical category. The Pope and Young Club also accepts velvet entries for all deer species. There is no separate non-typical category for Sitka blacktails.

Columbian blacktails have proportionally smaller bodies and more delicate features than mule deer. Their antlers seldom "jump out" at the hunter like those of their larger cousin. Many big blacktail bucks have perfectly balanced, thick-beamed dark racks that approach or exceed the ear tips. By way of comparison, B. G. Shurtleff's world record Columbian blacktail has seven points on each beam and an inside spread of 20 4/8 inches. Meanwhile, the long-standing World Record muley, killed by Bill Barcus, is another seven-by-seven buck that has an inside spread of just over 30 inches.

Sitka bucks wear the smallest antlers of all. Their racks often lack forks and resemble whitetail antlers. They rarely have an inside spread exceeding 18 inches. In fact, the current World Record sitka has a spread credit of slightly more than 13 inches.

To qualify for the P&Y records, a mule deer must have typical antlers scoring at least 145 inches, or non-typical antlers measuring a minimum of 170 inches. Columbia blacktails must have a minimum of 90 inches (typical) and 125 (non-typical). Sitka blacktails need to tally at least 75 inches to qualify for the record book.

Scores of both mule deer and blacktails are determined by adding the inside spread of the main beams, the length of each beam, each point, and four circumference measurements. Any differences are then subtracted.

No matter how you choose to pursue muleys or blacktails, on your own or with help from a pro guide, these deer are worth consideration by any serious bowhunter. They're widespread through western North America, relatively economical to hunt, and challenging enough to satisfy the demands of most any string-puller.

Black Bear

Classification

The black bear *(Ursus americanus)* is the smallest and most abundant of the North American bears. Unlike its larger, more belligerent and more powerful cousins — the Alaskan brown bear, the grizzly, and the polar bear — the furtive and largely nocturnal black bear is amazingly adaptable, quite capable of coexisting with man wherever adequate food and cover are available.

Origin and Distribution

Ancestors of the North American black bear first appeared on this continent perhaps half a million years ago, arriving from Asia via the Bering land bridge. In time these bruins found the mountains and forests of what would become Alaska and Canada to their liking. Roaming to the east and south, black bears eventually reached the Atlantic coast and Gulf of Mexico. Regardless, today's largest populations of bears are found across Canada, while Alaska remains the single most populous black bear state. Huntable numbers are found in approximately half of the lower 48 states. Bears live in terrain that varies from boggy, brush-choked swamplands to rocky, high country ridges and basins; however, northern North America's mixed and conifer forests remain a favorite haunt. It has been estimated that between 300,000 and 400,000 black bears exist in modern day North America.

Identifying Characteristics

Despite the name, black bears are found in various color shades ranging from jet black to light blond. Throughout much of the Rocky Mountain West, the animals commonly have brownish coats and often are referred to as "cinnamon" bears. The so-called glacier bear *(U. a. emmonsii)* of southeast Alaska has a bluish-gray coat, and the white coated Kermode bear *(U. a. kermodei)* of British Columbia is yet another subspecies of black bear.

Variations in pelage coloration notwithstanding, all black bears have a straight facial profile and lack the prominent shoulder hump characteristic of browns and grizzlies. Eyes are small, the ears well-rounded. Blacks have five toes on each paw, each tipped with a curved and non-retractable claw. These claws are much shorter than those of browns and grizzlies, and they seldom appear in pad marks unless the ground is muddy or snow-covered. Of all the bears, blacks are the only bruin species likely to climb trees after reaching adulthood.

Adult black bears possess 42 teeth, including four long, sharply pointed canines, 12 incisors, 16 premolars, and 10 molars. They communicate by growling, roaring, grunting, huffing, snorting, and — when angry or alarmed — popping their teeth. Sometimes sows with cubs can be heard making a throaty *glunking* sound.

Long, lustrous body hair often makes black bears appear larger than they are. Average size blacks weigh 150 pounds and up. Large bears weigh upwards of 300 pounds, but some 600-pounders have been taken, and the largest black bear on record topped 800 pounds. Sows generally are up to one-third smaller than boars. Adult black bears stand between 24 and 36 inches at the shoulder and are four to six feet long.

Amazingly quick and agile for such large animals, black bears can cover the ground at impressive speeds of up to 30 mph. These powerful animals rarely pose a serious threat to humans except when wounded or surprised at close range; however, occasional unprovoked attacks have resulted in maulings and human deaths. Protective sows in the company of their young cubs are an obvious danger and always should be given a wide berth.

Diet/Habitat

Hungry black bears, simply put, will eat almost anything. Seeming ever-starving, these omnivorous animals will graze on grasses and sedges; they lap up adult insects and their grubs; they gobble fruit and vegetables and berries; they devour garbage and carrion, rodents and fish, eggs, crops, nuts, bark, honey, and — as previously indicated — just about anything edible. Feeding opportunists, the non-selective bears accept food wherever they find it, a fact which has not gone unnoticed by hunters who attract bruins by placing tempting baits at strategic locations, where they wait for the hungry bears to turn up in search of a free meal.

As noted, woodlands, swamplands, and high country terrain all suit black bears, so long as there is available food and cover. They can and do adapt to the presence of man and sometimes live in the shadows of city skylines and suburban homes, even in heavily populated states like New Jersey. Elusive nocturnal wanderers, wild bruins roam a home area of five to a dozen or more square miles in their seemingly endless quest to fill their stomachs. Unlike their clownish, panhandling ursine counterparts seen in some state and national parks, free-ranging black bears generally are shy, retiring animals that will try to avoid contact with man.

Senses

A bear's sense of smell is legendary. Bruins can easily follow the windborne scent of food for a mile or more, and they also use their noses to detect nearby or approaching danger. Their large ears, biggest of the North American bear family, quickly pick up unnatural noises. A bear's eyes are quite small by comparison to its bulk. Many hunters believe eyesight is only fair to poor; however, bruins likely can see better than many people think.

Reproduction

Black bears typically breed during the months of June and July. Solitary boars seek out sows in heat during this period and remain with them until breeding is completed. A large boar will breed every willing sow he encounters; sows usually will not breed before their third year of life. The fertilized eggs do not begin immediate development. Rather, they remain detached from the uterine wall until fall. Gestation averages five to eight months and the cubs — usually twins or triplets — are born in late January or early February while the sow is denned. Cubs will weigh four to five pounds by winter's end and commonly remain with their mother for a full year or longer, sometimes denning together the following winter. Separation generally occurs during the next breeding season.

Life Expectancy

Black bears commonly live until their mid-teens, with some surviving into their twenties. Exact aging is possible by wildlife professionals who extract a tooth and determine the animal's age by counting growth layers of enamel.

Black bear roasts can be quite good if the meat was handled properly in the field and later prepared by a knowledgeable cook. Coarse and dark, bear meat always should be well cooked to avoid the possibility of trichinosis. Serving undercooked bear meat is an open invitation to parasitic invasion of the digestive tract. The resultant fever, muscle pain, and intestinal distress will be enough to make any sufferer swear off bear meat for life.

Bowhunting Records

Robert J. Shuttleworth killed the Pope and Young world record black bear in Mendocino County, California, in 1993. The giant bruin's skull scores 23 3/16 inches.

Chapter 17
Black Bear – Woodland Wraiths

IT WAS EARLY SEPTEMBER of 1993. California bowhunter Bob Shuttleworth was bear hunting in Mendocino County, hunkered in a brushy bowl surrounded by rolling hills of manzanita, oaks, and pine trees. Raising a varmint call to his lips, Bob shattered the morning stillness with the quavering cries of a dying jackrabbit.

Moments later a black bear moved down the slope behind him. Two more bruins suddenly appeared only 50 yards in front of Bob. And when the larger bear padded within 20 yards of his hiding spot, Bob slowly raised his compound bow, eased it to full draw, and sent an arrow through the huge bruin's chest. The massive animal roared, spun twice, and crashed away into the dense underbrush, running mere seconds before dying on its feet and collapsing.

Although Bob Shuttleworth didn't know it at the time, he had just authored a page of bowhunting history. That giant California black bear turned out to be the largest of its species ever arrowed. Its skull officially scored an incredible 23 3/16 inches, larger than many grizzly bears in the Pope and Young records.

"It's quite an achievement," Bob says in retrospect. "Amazing really."

Perhaps even more amazing is over a decade after Bob's arrow dropped the giant black bear, it continues to hold the top spot in the P&Y listings. Next to whitetail deer, more black bears are entered and accepted than any other big game species. At the end of 2002, there were 5,625 bruins listed in the bowhunting record book. This fact underscores the popularity of bear hunting — and the exceptional quality of Bob Shuttleworth's bruin.

G. Fred Asbell calls the black bear "one fine big game animal" and "one of the smartest, wariest animals on four legs." Those exact sentiments are share by thousands of North American bowhunters who have experienced the addictive excitement of pursuing and tagging this popular animal.

"I think the black bear was made to order for the bowhunter," Fred explains. "Few long-range shooting possibilities here. Most black bears are taken by bowhunters inside 25 yards. And at 25 yards

Bears are plantigrades, like humans, and walk on the entire soles of their feet. Unlike grizzlies and brown bears, claw marks seldom show in tracks except in mud or snow.

M. R. James and Dwight Schuh tagged these two record book bruins on a bowhunt over bait in northern Saskatchewan. Black bears actually come in a variety of colors. Dwight's boar was a golden brown; the author's was a more typical raven-coated boar with a white chest patch.

a big black bear is an awesome creature. He can and does attack on occasion, and is quick enough to catch a horse from a standing start. Even though attacks are rare, it's hard to convince yourself you are completely safe there in the rapidly approaching darkness, even if your stand is 15 feet in the air. And this bit of danger, combined with the fact that the black bear can appear out of nowhere without a sound, can hear like a bat, and probably has the best nose in the woods, makes for a tough, unforgettable hunt and a memorable outdoor experience."

Fred's words hit the bull's-eye for me and other bear hunting veterans. They perfectly explain the appeal of hunting these woodland wraiths with the stick and string. That element of danger, however slight, is what sets bear hunting apart from other routine bowhunting pursuits. Even after over 30 years of hunting big black bears across much of Canada and more than a dozen states, I readily admit I still experience a twinge of unease when some brute of a bruin fixes me with that baleful ursine stare — especially if I'm on the ground and the bear is standing a few short yards away.

Take it from me: there's something unsettling about simply walking through the inky blackness in bear country after a day's hunt, knowing these big creatures are nearby, listening to your footfalls, smelling your scent. That knowledge can make the faintest off-trail rustlings seem sinister. And if you want a real heart-stopping thrill, flush a grouse from underfoot sometime when your thoughts are focused on black bears. Then you'll know exactly what bear country excitement is.

In truth, your likelihood of being attacked and mauled by a black bear is remote. While I know several bowhunters who carry the scars of such rare woodland assaults, your chances of injury are much greater driving home from work in rush hour traffic than entering the bear woods. Only twice in over three decades have I been menaced by growling, teeth-popping, hair-bristling bruins primed for attack. And each bully quickly succumbed to a well-placed broadhead. One of these animals had an infected leg, which likely accounted for his testy disposition. The other was a true wilderness animal that likely had never faced a man and therefore had no reason for fear. Personally, I'm convinced that anyone who maintains a healthy dose of respect for black bears — and who uses appropriate caution and common sense while hunting — will never face any real danger.

Ironically, during my closest enounters with blackies, I have been carrying a camera, not a hunting bow. Once, in Colorado, I was nearly run down in an oak brush jungle by a large bear that was spooked by a buddy and was simply heading for safety. He tore past me close enough to touch (honestly, that thought never entered my mind) and vanished in seconds. Regardless, that brief look at the business end of a charging bruin is forever branded into my mind. It's one view I hope to never see again, especially if the next onrushing bear is coming for me, not simply hightailing it down a game trail that I happened to be standing in.

Another encounter involved a Wyoming bear that decided to check out the interior of the camp's tent just after daybreak one summer day. Shouts and a well-aimed frying pan sent him on his way with me in close pursuit, clad only in my longjohns. Huffing and growling, that young blackie stalked around the campsite while I snapped photos of the posturing yearling. Twice he slapped the ground, popped his teeth, and bluff-charged. Finally, out of film and out of patience with his juvenile foolishness, I ran directly at him, yelling and flailing my arms. The last time we saw of him he was a black blur among the pines, heading north toward Montana.

Finally, during videotaping sessions in far northern Saskatchewan, I've sat in ground blinds with one or more bears standing less than 10 yards away. On occasion some bruin has bluff-charged after checking me out. That's why I've learned to operate the camera with one hand. The other? It's holding a can of bear spray with my finger on the trigger.

Remember, most black bears are shy, secretive animals that go out of their way to avoid you. Most you'll see will be afraid or per-

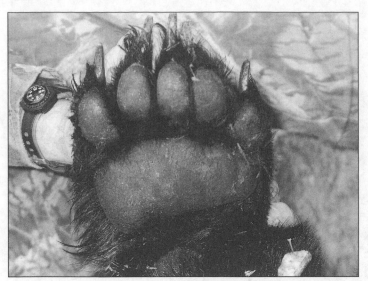

Some hunters believe a bear's size can be determined by its tracks or pads. Standard wisdom calls for measuring the width of a front paw and adding one inch. For example, a bear track spanning 5-inches would be left by a 6-foot bruin.

haps curious. Even the rare grouchy bruin seldom poses a serious threat. Of course, a sow with cubs-of-the-year is another matter entirely. Give these bears plenty of room — and then some. Always! Sows are super-protective mothers and are fearless when facing a big boar bear — or a man.

Knowledgeable game biologists consistently rate black bears near the top when it comes to ranking intelligent, elusive game animals. Their testimony helps to explain the challenge any bowhunter faces when trying to take a bruin. But despite the difficulties involved, black bears remain a widely sought and highly prized bowhunting trophy. They are, in fact, North America's favorite bear.

Hunting Strategies

There are four routinely effective methods that bowhunters use to take black bears. These techniques involve baiting, pursuing with hounds, still-hunting and stalking, and calling. Of the four, calling bears is the least used and understood. Undoubtedly it's the most exciting and definitely not for the faint of heart. But as bowhunter Bob Shuttleworth capably demonstrated in this chapter's opening paragraph, it certainly produces positive results, especially in prime bear country.

Calling

Simply explained, calling bears is an attempt to lure hungry bears to the hunter by mimicking the sounds of injured animals or birds. It's exactly the same principle used by varmint hunters to shoot critters that simply can't pass up the chance for an easy meal. In fact, the use of calling as a bear hunting strategy likely resulted from bruins lumbering close to surprised callers who'd expected to see a coyote or bobcat respond to their agonized cries. Reports of face-to-face encounters between bear and caller eventually led some adventuresome souls to intentionally set out to call bruins. While some bowhunters may not relish the thought of being stalked by a big bear with a growling belly and food on his mind, others thrive on the accompanying adrenaline rush.

Actually, there are two major disadvantages to calling bears within arrow range. First, approaching bears already are on red alert,

their acute senses finely tuned to locating the easy meal. It's difficult to try to draw a bow, aim, and release an arrow at close range without being detected. This is especially true if you're eye level with the bruin. Second, any head-on or front-quartering shot is not a good bowhunting shot; chances of a wounded, unrecovered animal are simply too great for the average hunter to risk. Faced with an approaching bruin, you should wait, hoping the bear will turn and stand broadside. This offers you the ideal opportunity for making a good shot and quick, clean kill.

Yet another disadvantage may be found within the bowhunter's mind. If you have a gnawing concern (no pun intended) about being a hungry bear's center of attention, you could lose focus. Shooting a hunting bow under pressure-packed field situations calls for total concentration and self-discipline. A worried hunter makes mistakes. Shots may be rushed. Accuracy suffers. So if you're fretting about that big bruin padding your way and eventually stopping a few yards short of standing in your lap, you won't be able to concentrate on putting your arrow where it belongs.

Here's a suggestion. Two-man calling teams — with one caller and one shooter taking turns — can double up on bears with excellent results. Bruins have a uncanny knack of being able to pinpoint the exact spot of the distress cries. With a caller hidden on the ground and a buddy waiting in a downwind tree stand, chances are the bear will be totally focused on the calling and not give the elevated stand so much as a second glance. Also, such a setup eliminates the problem presented by a frontal or front-quartering shot.

Commercial game calls that produce the cries of small game and birds in misery can attract a hungry bear at any time of the year. Deer calls which imitate lost fawn bleats or distress cries work best in the spring. Ditto for calls which mimic elk or moose calves. Try bear calling sometime. It works.

Still-Hunting and Stalking

Still-hunting and stalking bears is without a doubt the most difficult and challenging bowhunting method — but it can be done. While locating a stalkable bruin is seldom easy, slipping quietly within point-blank range is doubly difficult. Regardless, a combination of skill and patience — with a dash of luck thrown in — sometimes rewards the persistent hunter.

Here in Montana, where it's illegal to bait bears or chase them with hounds, one favorite spring bowhunting method is to ease quietly along gated logging roads. Succulent grasses sown by timber companies as part of the reclamation process often lures bears into the open and provides good spot-and-stalk opportunities.

In fact, to locate bears anywhere you choose to hunt, think food. Seemingly always hungry, black bears forage constantly when on the move. And while much of their range consists of dense woodlands and brushy jungles, they often move into open terrain if it contains a tempting food source. Lush grasses and tender greens pull them onto open hillsides during the spring. Ripe berries are another strong bear magnet, in season, as are salmon runs when the shallow waters of wild backcountry rivers and streams come alive with spawning fish.

Feeding bruins have their attention so fully focused on filling their bellies that they may be approached by a careful stalker who keeps tabs on the wind and avoids unnatural noises. Along remote streams, the sound of rushing water and splashing fish will help cover the sound of your approach.

Dwight Schuh took this black bear on Prince of Wales Island, Alaska, while using the spot-and-stalk method.

G. Fred Asbell poses with a black bear arrowed during a spot-and-stalk Canada bowhunt.

Don't neglect kill sites, either. Bears may be lured to the offal left by hunters who've tagged a moose, caribou, elk, deer — and even other bruins. A stand strategically located near a ripening gut pile just might provide you with a big game bonus if a hungry bruin waddles up to dine on scraps left over from your field dressing chores.

Some savvy bowhunters never pass up the chance to stake out gut piles. If the weather is warm, a few even take steps to make the kill site easier to locate. They'll drape a green hide over the offal for a day or two and let the sun speed up the ripening process. When things start to get good and smelly, they simply peel off the hide and allow wind currents to carry the tempting odor far and wide. Few hungry bears can resist the urge to follow their noses to the odoriferous food source.

Consequently, it's a good idea to invest in the purchase of a bear tag, even if other big game species are your primary target. Besides the possibility of maintaining a kill site vigil, there's always the chance you'll encounter a bruin as you still-hunt other game (as have several elk and caribou hunters I know). Every year some fortunate bowhunters take black bears while hunting other game, simply by being in the right place at the right time.

Chasing

Where legal, chasing bears with hounds is a far more effective means of filling your bear tag than calling or stalking/still-hunting. In reality, however, it's much more difficult and physically challenging than most people might imagine. It's generally the most expensive form of bear hunting, too, usually requiring the services of a professional guide who owns a pack of specially trained hounds.

As with all hunting sports where tracking dogs are used, the thrill is found in the long chase itself, in watching and listening to the dogs work out the bear's trail, and eventually bay up or tree the bruin. The kill itself is often anticlimatic. Yet to be successful, a pack

of durable, gutsy hounds must trail, jump, and eventually hold an angry bear at bay until the hunters arrive. In the remote and rugged woodland terrain comprising much black bear country, every bear/hound race has the potential of soon becoming a cross-country endurance run. More often than not, the bear will refuse to tree or stand and fight. Such chases leave the bruin, dogs, and hunters all tired but wiser for their efforts.

Perhaps the most popular way to find a bear to run involves early morning drives along old logging roads and forest trails in 4WD vehicles that have keen-nosed strike dogs chained to special platforms atop the trucks. When bear tracks are seen or scented along the roadway, the dogs usually go crazy, yowling and struggling to leap down. The hunters quickly pile out to check the tracks, which offer clues to the animal's size and direction of travel. If the tracks are fresh and the trailing conditions right, the strike dogs are unchained to unravel the scent trail. Other hounds are turned loose as the chase heats up and unfolds, until the bear is bayed or eventually escapes. Meanwhile, hunters must try to keep up with sounds of the chase by following the dogs on foot or by driving along outlying backroads. They pause from time to time to listen for distant baying. In vast roadless areas, especially in the Rocky Mountain West, horses frequently replace motor vehicles.

Regardless, more often than not, Lady Luck turns her back on the hunters. As the day heats up, scent trails typically disappear, especially where the bruin has crossed open country. Unless the dogs manage to catch and jump the bear early in the chase, they may find

Dave Holt stands about 6 feet tall and weighs about 200 pounds. That will give you an idea of the size of the bear he arrowed on a Canadian bowhunt.

ily outdistancing the trailing dogs. Such long-legged "running bears" may cover dozens of miles across rugged terrain, even swimming lakes or rivers, to elude pursuers.

I remember one daylong chase in Michigan's Upper Peninsula that covered more than 25 miles and ended with that bear still on the move. Another Colorado chase, which started just after dawn, ended 12 hours and as many miles later. I finally arrowed that bruin — a large 20-incher — but only after he'd led me, the guides, and the hounds through every mountain hellhole and rocky, brushy canyon in that corner of the country. I was so exhausted that I worried about having the strength to draw my bow. Such long, energy-draining chases make me wish that vocal critics who claim bear hunting with hounds is "easy" could have been tagging along.

While there is no argument that shooting a treed bear is not especially difficult, following a yapping hound pack to the tree is the true challenge facing the hunters. It often takes physical and mental toughness to get the job done — and those who succeed generally feel they've earned the killing shot. The other option is passing up the shot, calling off the hounds, and leaving the treed bear to run again another day.

Bears bayed on the ground in brushy deadfalls or amid jumbled boulders are an entirely different matter. They're fighting mad, ringed by barking, darting hounds that nip at them, and seldom offer a stationary target. The adrenaline coursing through such bayed bruins makes them tougher to kill, too. Hound owners abhor such

themselves with no spoor to follow as the day wears on. Even when scent lingers and a hot chase continues, it's common for the hounds to move out of earshot, leaving hunters with no sporting way to keep tabs on the race.

Although many houndsmen equip valuable dogs with electronic tracking collars, the rules of fair chase prevent turning these devices on during any actual pursuit. Radio signals may be followed to the collared dogs only after the day's chase is over and the wandering hounds are being recovered by their owners. Any trophy bear located and arrowed after following radio signals is ineligible for record book entry.

Other typical problems faced by hound hunters include inexperienced dogs that forget about the bear trail when they jump a deer, elk, or coyote, and take off in yammering pursuit. Also, some older and chase-wise bruins — the biggest bears, usually — simply refuse to tree or bay, regardless of the dogs' best efforts. These so-called "walking bears" will remain almost constantly on the move, alternately walking and running, occasionally turning to briefly swat at the persistent hounds. They can maintain such a pace throughout the day, rarely allowing the hunters to move close enough for a fleeting glimpse, much less a killing shot. Finally, some younger bears will simply light out cross-country at the first sounds of pursuit, eas-

Jan Perry is a little lady, but but she finds her bow to be a great equalizer when facing a big black bear such as this record book candidate she shot in California.

situations and worry about a missed shot — or pass-through arrow — striking a valuable dog. And even if the shot is true, a few excited hounds can get careless around wounded bruins and end up getting batted senseless, claw-raked, or bitten by the dying bear. This is one reason most houndsmen insist on catching and chaining their dogs before any arrow is released at a bayed or treed bear.

Bayed bears have been known to charge approaching hunters on sight, so always use caution when working into good position for the killing shot. Occasionally, the mere sight and sound of an enraged bruin — roaring, teeth popping, neck and back hair bristling — immediately reminds some bowhunters that they have pressing appointments elsewhere.

Sometimes black bears cultivate a taste for domestic livestock, raiding farms and ranches to prey on sheep, cattle, hogs, and even poultry. Such rogue bruins quickly become the bane of farmers and ranch owners who generally welcome houndsmen and point out recent kills as ideal starting points for bear/hound chases. The same may be said of grain fields, garbage piles, baits, or any area that has attracted the attention of hungry bears.

The author arrowed this big Oregon bruin after it was treed by a pack of specially trained hounds. Its thick coat was a rich chestnut brown.

Baiting

Baiting black bears, where legal, is the most popular and effective means of collecting a trophy bruin. In fact, about seven out of every 10 record book bears were arrowed by bowhunters sitting near carefully placed baits.

There's more to baiting bears than simply heading into the woods and dumping pails of garbage or pastries. The best baits are created by careful planning and hard work. While topo maps can help locate possible baiting sites, firsthand exploration is necessary to determine exactly where to hang a stand and establish a food source. Ideally, you should situate the bait within or close to heavy cover. Bears are wary animals and may venture into the open only after dark. The best baiting spots are in remote and rugged mountain canyons near streams or other water sources; low-lying areas adjacent to bogs or swamps; and along natural travel corridors or in feeding areas.

Many bait hunters, especially guides with paying clients, will establish several baits over a widespread area before the season

opens. They tote meat scraps, pastries, fish, and other tasty goodies to the baits where they're left for bears to find. Some use strong attractor scents such as vanilla, anise oil, peppermint, and cooking oils or grease to tempt wandering bruins. Beaver carcasses obtained from trappers are another favorite lure. Of course, all bears have a special fondness for sweets and junk food. Honey, peanut butter, cookies, fruits, nuts, popcorn, and even candy and marshmallows will immediately attract any bruin's interest. Some veterans place such tidbits near their stands where a feeding bear might pause to offer them a perfect shot.

Once bears begin feeding at the bait, hunters regularly replenish the food supply in order to keep the bears coming back for more free meals. Now is when the real work normally begins. It takes considerable faith to pack load after heavy load of bait to remote sites only to have it quickly vanish, often disappearing overnight. This is where closed containers such as 55-gallon fuel drums come in handy. Chained or wired to convenient trees, they are used to store the bait supply. Holes cut in the sides of each metal drum allow bears to scoop out goodies but keeps the bruins from completely destroying the bait source. Other hunters place heavy logs or rocks over pits where bait is dumped. Some hunters use timing devices along

Hunting over bait gives hunters a good chance to check out the size and condition of the bruins that stop by for a free meal.

(Above and below) When a hungry bruin eventually approaches the bait, a patient hunter in an elevated stand often has time to closely study the bear moving below him. Shots at small bruins or sows with cubs are passed up in hopes Mr. Big will eventually lumber in to feed. Bears often know bowhunters are present. They'll often check out a tree stand setup before moving in to feed — or leaving.

Where legal, baiting hungry bears is an effective means of collecting a trophy bruin. Patience is mandatory, since hunters must sit and wait quietly in tree stands near bait sites, hoping the bears will appear before darkness falls.

well-tracked travel routes to determine when the bait-raiders normally appear.

The idea of covered bait pits and barrels is to force a bear to linger near the bait while eating, not rush in, grab a mouthful of goodies, and vanish into the underbrush to feed. If a bruin has to move logs or rocks — or paw food scraps from a container — waiting bowhunters usually have ample time to study the bear and make a well-aimed shot, providing it's the animal he wants. Also, logs cut in five- or six-foot lengths can help a hunter judge the size of the bear at a glance. Ditto for a bait drum standing on its end. If a bear is nearly as tall as the drum — or even taller— when standing on all fours, he's a definite shooter.

Keeping a bear returning to the bait — having him establish a regular feeding routine — is one key to baiting success. If the bear makes numerous visits and always finds goodies that appeal to his taste buds, his normal wariness might vanish. In time, a hunter waiting in a downwind stand may get a close shot at the bait-raider. Of course, as with all forms of hunting, there are no guarantees. Even the most active baits can abruptly go dead. Bears can and do change their feeding habits for reasons known only to them. Some simply

move on. In other cases too much man-smell around the bait can scare off the bear or turn him into strictly a nocturnal feeder. These possibilities always make bear baiting totally unpredictable.

Patience is a bait hunter's biggest asset. And in the bug-infested woods typical of most northern bear country, sitting and waiting can be a true endurance test. Droning, biting blackflies, midges, skeeters, and no-see-ums can make life miserable for the unprepared bowhunter. Taped cuffs and sleeves, headnets, gloves, and plenty of

Colorado bowhunter Bill Krenz tagged this whopper during an Alberta bowhunt with the author.

This Saskatchewan bruin is the largest taken by M. R. James in over 30 years of bowhunting across North America. Its skull taped over 21 inches.

potent bug juice — preferably 100 percent DEET — are always a good idea.

When you see a bear approaching, keep calm and remain absolutely still. I'm convinced that most bruins already know you're there. Some may stroll directly to the base of your tree, sniffing your tracks or tree steps, and stare up at you. Others may stand on their hind legs for a better look. A few might even begin to climb the tree itself, a rare practice that can be downright unnerving to the novice who mistakes curiosity for aggressiveness. Each approach is slightly different, and you never know exactly what to expect from the unpredictable bruins. Generally speaking, taking things slow and easy is best. And don't move whenever a bear is looking your way.

You should always wait for a broadside or slightly quartering away shot, and normally it's best to wait until the bear is at the bait, feeding, and visibly relaxed. Bears are tough animals but will quickly succumb to a sharp broadhead through the vitals. Conversely, poorly hit bruins have amazing endurance and can cover great distances in short periods of time. Where it's legal, guides and hunters may use tracking dogs to trail and recover wounded bears.

Arrow-hit bruins usually leave skimpy to marginal blood trails.

(Bottom) Doug Walker of California tagged his P&Y 21-incher while stalking in Alberta's Peace River back-country.

(Right) Reaching remote areas by boat or float plane puts bowhunters in country where huge, unpressured bruins live out their long lives.

Bears often crash blindly away from the bait after the arrow strikes. They may noisily plow through the underbrush but rarely travel far if the broadhead penetrates both lungs. If you listen, you may hear the bruin go down and thrash about mere seconds after the shot. Mortally wounded bruins sometimes emit eerie death roars or moans. This is a sure sign the shot was well placed and your bruin is down for keeps.

Blood trailing a wounded bear can be a spooky experience. Often the shot is taken shortly before dark. This means searching for the bear in thick cover by lantern light, or waiting until dawn the following day (if weather conditions permit). But bears left unrecovered overnight are subject to cannibalization by other bruins or smaller woodland scavengers. Also, during spells of warm weather, special steps should be taken to immediately locate the carcass. Bear hides and meat are notorious for retaining body heat and demand prompt attention to prevent spoilage and hair slippage. Each season hundreds of prime bear pelts are ruined due to inattention or improper treatment.

Regardless, appropriate caution and common sense must be employed during any attempt to follow a wounded bear. Unless you are certain the bear is dead near the bait site, it's wise to give the bruin ample time to succumb to its wound. Where it's legal, some guides carry shotguns loaded with buckshot — just in case there's a close range encounter with an angry bear. Once the animal is spotted, make sure it's dead before venturing too close. More than one "dead bear" has come back to life when the trackers approached. No trophy is worth getting mauled. Don't hesitate to administer a coup de grace, if necessary.

Bear hunting over baits normally begins in the late afternoon with the vigil lasting until dark. I've had surprising success both with both morning and midday hunts, as well as all-day marathon sits. My all-time best bruin — scoring over 21 inches — was arrowed in the middle of one Saskatchewan morning; another 20-inch boar that I arrowed in the same area the following June was killed in the middle of the afternoon.

Their body fat and thick coats often prevent massive external blood loss. Fat plugs entrance and exit wounds, stemming blood flow. Long hair quickly absorbs what blood does escape, and hunters shooting down from tree stands must get a low exit wound if there is to be any trail at all. Bows with ample kinetic energy to achieve total penetration are musts for any conscientious bowhunter.

Because blood trailing can be a problem, a few guides and hunters insist on using string trackers. These devices mount on the bow and contain spools of thin line attached to the hunting arrow. After the shot, the line plays out, leaving a trail the bowhunter can follow to claim his prize without concern over a poor or non-existent blood trail.

Typically, many guides use the morning and midday hours replenishing baits, relaxing, fishing, and possibly hunting other species in season. Whatever time you head to the bait to start your day's bear hunt, I suggest that you move in as quietly as possible. At times a bear is already feeding at the bait or bedded nearby. Dave Holt once tagged a record book Alberta bear that his guide spotted as they arrived for an evening hunt.

Regardless of such success, some baiters like to approach noisily, rattling the bait pails, talking loudly, or tromping through the brush. They believe bears grow used to such commotions and quickly learn that the human activity equates to fresh food. I've seen stands near lakes or rivers where bears approach the bait when they hear the boat's motor coming or leaving. You just never know when a hungry bruin is going to stroll in for dinner. Rob Nye, a veteran Saskatchewan bear guide I've hunted with several times, has had aggressive bears meet his boat and not allow him ashore. Other times he's confronted bears while carrying buckets to the bait site, bluff charging him in a hurry to get at the goodies he's carrying. And more than one overzealous bruin has met his undoing when a hunter has climbed into his stand just after his guide or hunting partner freshened the bait and walked away.

Again, baiting is mostly a waiting game and comfort is essential whether you're sitting in a tree stand or situated in a ground level blind. Some sort of padded seat and bow holder are good ideas. A safety harness is mandatory for hunters in elevated stands. Also, you should practice shooting while seated to avoid unnecessary movements that could spook an approaching bear. I know some bowhunters who prefer to stand, bow in hand with arrow nocked, during the final hour of legal shooting light when bears are likely to appear.

Soft, quiet camo clothing is critical since most shots are taken at very close range. I often wear a bug-proof jacket and headnet over my normal hunting attire. Quiet tackle is another must. Avoid noisy arrow rests, cable guards, and compound bows with creaking cams or wheels. Stands should be rock-solid and not shift or squeak underfoot. Carpeting on the stand's floor is another good idea, as is wearing rubber boots to reduce human scent left in walking to and from the stand. Some hunters complete their preparations with an application of scent-killing spray. This may be a plus when hunting pressured bruins; however, most of the backcountry bears will know you're there. They simply don't care because they're at the top of the woodland food chain.

Whatever hunting technique you use to bowhunt the unpredictable black bear, you'll quickly come to recognize the animal's innate cunning, extraordinary senses, remarkable intelligence, and amazing adaptability. These factors combine to create a highly appealing, immensely challenging adversary.

Judging Trophy Black Bears

Skull size is the sole determining factor for entry in the Pope and Young bowhunting records. The cleaned skull's length plus width, taped to the nearest one-sixteenth of an inch, are added to determine the official score. To qualify for the record book, a black bear skull must measure at least 18 inches.

Since it's nearly impossible to accurately estimate the size of a live bear's skull, a bowhunter seeking a P&Y trophy must try to take the largest animal possible and hope the skull size exceeds the qualifying minimum. Clues may be offered in pumpkin-headed bears

with ears that appear short. Also, look for the blunt snout and forehead crease common in larger, older bears. Of course, "trophy animal" is a subjective term. Many bears fairly taken are true trophies, regardless of their size. Pelts with long, glossy hair — whatever their coloration — are highly prized, even when the bears do not qualify for the record book.

But when a really big bear is your goal, where do you hunt? As noted at the beginning of the chapter, California is one state known for large bruins — and I'm not talking about the UCLA linemen. Given his choice, Dr. Dave Samuel, who has hunted and tagged giant bears for several decades, says his big bear studies point him in a northerly direction.

"The far North is where to head if you want to find big bruins," Dave insists. "Alaska, Ontario, Manitoba, Saskatchewan, and Alberta are all big bear areas." I tend to agree. While other provinces and states may be home to outsized bears — states like Pennsylvania, for instance — few areas have the sheer numbers of quality animals that are found in the northland woods. Licenses are readily available, as are numerous black bear hunting camps. But wherever you decide to hunt black bears, alone or by employing the services of a qualified guide, you'll likely find them a fascinating, challenging quarry. Black bears, in fact, deserve any serious bowhunter's consideration — and profound respect.

Big black bears are...well, simply big. The hide of this Alberta giant dwarfs the hunter, Dr. Dave Samuel, and his guide who each stand about six feet tall.

Classification

Unarguably the largest and most dangerous of North American big game, the Alaskan brown bear *(Ursus arctos middendorffi)* and the grizzly bear *(Ursus arctos horribilis)* are recognized as separate species although mammalogists generally agree they are one and the same animal. Bear experts admit they are unable to tell the animals apart and classify both under the Latin name, *Ursus arctos.* Their all-white cousin, the polar bear *(Ursus thalarctos maritimus)* is the true King of the North, reigning as undisputed ruler of the frigid waters and frozen wastelands at the top of the world.

Current Distribution

Brown bears are animals of Alaska's coastal range and certain islands near the mainland. Grizzlies, once widespread through much of western North America, are now found mostly from inland Alaska across northern Canada to the Hudson Bay. Notably, British Columbia and western Alberta have healthy numbers of the hump-shouldered bruins; however, in the lower United States only Wyoming and Montana have growing numbers of the big bruins, most living in or near Yellowstone and Glacier National Parks. The great white bears are found along the arctic coastal areas of Alaska, Canada, Russia, Greenland, and Scandinavia.

Identifying Characteristics

Alaskan brown bears are huge, formidable animals that may weigh as much as 1,500 pounds. On all fours the bears stand perhaps four and one-half feet at the shoulder and may reach nine or more feet in length. Most big males weigh between 800 and 1,200 pounds with females averaging between 500 and 800 pounds. Standing erect, some brown bear boars tower over eight feet. Grizzlies are proportionally smaller animals, standing three and one-half feet at the shoulder and weighing up to 800 pounds or so. These bears average six to seven feet in length for males, less for females.

Polar bears are huge, long-necked, pear-shaped animals with thick, whitish-yellow pelage that blends well in a world of ice and snow. Eyes, nose, lips, and claws are black. Adult boars stand four feet at the shoulder and are about eight feet in length. Males average nearly 1,000 pounds while females typically are smaller and lighter. There are reports of some polar bears weighing in excess of a ton.

Both browns and grizzlies have dished-in facial profiles and obvious shoulder humps. Each comes in various colors from dark brown to blond. Hair is long and thick, and grizzlies commonly have conspicuous silver-tipped guard hairs. Tails are stubby, shorter than the five wickedly curved claws found on each forefoot; these often are three to four inches long. Claws on the bears' hind feet are considerably shorter.

Polar bears have sloping heads that appear smallish. Like the brown and grizzly, these long-legged bears are plantigrades, walking on the entire soles of their feet; however, a polar bear's footpads are covered with short, insulating hair that provides traction as these animals walk or run across the ice. There are five toes on each foot and curving claws are sharp but relatively short. They walk with a distinctive shuffling gait and are amazingly quick and agile for such large animals. Powerful swimmers, polar bears have been sighted at sea more than 100 miles from the nearest landfall. They also have been clocked running across snowfields at speeds of 30 mph.

Adult brown, grizzly, and polar bears have 42 teeth including four prominent, curved canine teeth, 12 incisors, 16 premolars, and 10 molars. Naturally aggressive by nature, all these giant bears possess awesome power and surprising speed, making them a potentially dangerous adversary for anyone they encounter — including bowhunters.

Habitat/Diet

Seals are a polar bear's main source of food, although like other members of the ursine clan, these bears are feeding opportunists and take full advantage of whatever food is available, be it a beached whale or a dead walrus. These sea-going bears also catch fish, birds, and arctic rodents such as mice and lemmings. They roam hundreds of miles across the icy northlands, occasionally riding drifting ice floes in their search for ways to satisfy a constant hunger.

The omnivorous browns and grizzlies also take advantage of whatever suste-

nance is available. At times the bears graze like cattle, digging up edible roots and tubers or stripping certain trees for their bark. Rodents, insects, birds and their eggs are gobbled eagerly. Carrion is never overlooked and live animals — especially the old, injured, weak, and the young — are killed and devoured. Nuts and berries, in season, are favorites, and annual fish runs attract many brows and grizzlies to streams and rivers.

Modern day grizzlies are elusive animals of remote mountain regions and untracked wilderness areas. Their affinity for privacy is well-documented, although the great bears seemingly adapt to varied sparsely unpopulated terrain as long as ample food and cover are available. Unlike their inland cousins, Alaskan brown bears prowl the coastlines and tributaries where fish are plentiful and provide a stable source of food, accounting for size differences between the species. Neither variety of grizzly migrates, but the animals do range for miles across their home territory.

Senses

These bears' sense of smell — like that of the black bear — is fabled. It is used constantly to find new sources of food and scent — and to avoid hunters. Smallish ears do an excellent job sorting and identifying surrounding sounds. Eyesight is the weakest sense of these giant bears, widely regarded as poor by many hunters.

Reproduction

June and July are primary breeding months for browns and grizzlies. The wandering, solitary boars seek out receptive sows and stay with them until mating is completed. Sows typically do not breed until their fourth year and then only every second or third year thereafter. Gestation varies from seven to eight months, thanks to delayed implantation of fertilized eggs. Cubs are born in January or early February while sows are in their winter dens. Two to three tiny newborns are common and cubs are covered with short hair — brown for Alaskan browns and gray for grizzlies. Fed on a diet of rich milk, the newborns grow quickly and readily follow their mother from their north-facing den in April or May. They continue to nurse for several months, supplementing their diet with meat provided by their mother. These family groups often den together the first winter.

Although scientific information about the breeding habits of wild polar bears is scanty, available data indicate the females come into estrus during a three-month period between March and May. Solitary males seek out mates, breed, and then return to their wandering ways.

Gestation periods are about 240 days with most cubs born in December and January while sows are holed up in snug crevices created by shifting ice. Most polar bears den briefly during the most severe winter weather; however, males seldom stay inactive for very long periods. Conversely, females may remain denned with their newborn cubs for several months. Twin births are common. Newborns are about 10 inches long, blind, and helpless. Sows breed only every other year and usually are three to four years old before giving birth for the first time.

Life Expectancy

Brown and grizzly bears frequently live 15 to 20 years in the wild. Some bruins, reared in captivity, have lived into their 30s. Captured polar bears have lived into their 30s and 40s in zoos. It is believed that wild, healthy bears may live into their third decade.

Meat from these huge bruins is seldom eaten except by natives who make use of any available food source. Bear meat should never be undercooked.

Bowhunting Records

Two Alaskan brown bears share the world record title with identical scores of 28 7/16 inches. One was arrowed by Dr. John "Jack" Frost on Unimak, Island in 1985; Monty Browning shot the other at Ursus Bay, Alaska, in 1995. Two grizzlies also share the world record for that species. Derril Lamb killed his giant grizzly near Moose Lake, British Columbia, in 1987, and a decade later Jim Boyer tagged his top trophy along Gathto Creek, B.C. Each bear tapes 25 13/16.

Finally, two polar bears share the P&Y title with scores of 26 6/16 inches. One was arrowed by Richard McIntyre off Cape Lisburne, Alaska, in 1958; the other was killed by Edwin DeYoung in 2002 on a hunt near Hanley Bay, Nunavut (NWT).

Chapter 18
Brown, Grizzly, & Polar Bears – Big Trouble

MONTANA ELK HUNTER Doug Thielmann remembers the charging bear's beautiful pelage. Its coat was dense and dark brown with an adult silvertip's usual white-tipped guard hairs. The fur was rippling in the late afternoon sunlight as the big sow quickly closed the distance between them. Doug also vividly recalls the bruin's humped shoulder, the rounded ears, and the tiny eyes locked on his. There was no mistaking the onrushing sow's deadly intent. She's going to kill me, Doug thought.

Moments earlier the bowhunter had emerged from a tangle of thick timber high in the Gallatin National Forest west of Yellowstone Park. As he stepped onto a grassy bench, he was dressed in camo and carrying a recurve bow. But Doug also packed a holstered .44 Smith & Wesson magnum pistol. It's legal for Montana archery hunters to carry firearms while hunting game in big bear country, and many Big Sky bowhunters routinely pack pistols or bear repellent — or both.

Doug had barely stepped from the trees when he saw a movement in the high grass maybe 60 yards away. A sow and her two yearling cubs — each youngster weighing probably 150 pounds apiece — were moving past. None had seen Doug who instantly began backing away, retreating toward the trees behind him.

"I'd made it maybe 10 feet when I heard the big sow start woofing," Doug says, "and I saw her stand erect, tossing her head. Then she looked my way."

The grizzly had caught the bowhunter's scent. It obviously didn't like what it smelled. "She dropped back on all fours and bounced toward me, smacking her pads on the ground and popping her teeth. Then she beelined straight toward me in a rush."

Pistol in hand, Doug frantically yelled and waved his arms. At 20 yards the sow broke off the menacing bluff charge, abruptly turned away, and lumbered back toward her twin cubs. Doug's mind was racing. He quickly looked around for a tree to climb, wondering if he should move or stand his ground. And when he looked back toward the bears, he could no longer see the animals. Relieved, Doug briefly believed Lady Luck had smiled on him — but then he witnessed a blood-chilling sight that forever is burned into his mind. The 300-pound sow was coming again. On a dead run. Straight for him.

Instinctively, Doug raised his pistol and fired at the bruin's broad head when the animal was mere feet from him. The sow collapsed 10 feet away, a bullet hole in the center of the skull just above her eyes. The shaken hunter stumbled to one side and fired an unnecessary insurance round into the bear's thick neck. But there was no time to be relieved. When Doug glanced up, the two yearling grizzlies were running his way. Again Doug started shouting and waving his arms. The young bears stopped at 20 yards, growling and popping their teeth. Doug started backing away, anxious to leave the area, but the angry yearlings followed, growling and huffing. The bears actually trailed Doug about 300 yards before he finally lost sight of them. Doug instantly hurried back to camp, and early the next day rode a horse to trailhead to report the incident to federal wildlife authorities. Officers who investigated the kill site ruled the shooting justifiable.

The sow, it turned out, was no stranger to area fish and game officials. Her ear tags and lip tattoo told a troublesome story of previous captures and relocations after getting into repeated trouble with people. As this incident indicates, occasionally the unpredictable

This Alaskan brown bear was fishing the shallows for salmon when something or someone caught its attention. He may turn and run — or head straight for the intruder at a dead run.

A brown bear or grizzly ranks among the biggest and most dangerous big game animals on earth. Sows with cubs are especially protective — and testy. You should always give them a wide berth and pray you don't stumble into a group like this at close range.

travel costs, and taxidermy expense, if successful. At the high end, a polar bear hunt is often priced around $25,000. Brown bear hunts typically fall between these two extremes. Most bear hunts will last at least 10 days.

Bowhunts for these bears mandate the use of guides armed with large caliber rifles — just in case. A hurried shot resulting in a bad hit can quickly turn into a nightmare situation. Although a sharp broadhead through both lungs will kill the biggest bear than ever lived, no hunter or guide relishes the thought of blood trailing a wounded bruin into some alder jungle where visibility is measured in mere feet.

Likely the best and safest way to bowhunt grizzlies is to hang a tree stand along some salmon stream or near the gutpile of a fresh moose or caribou kill. When baiting was legal, several record book silvertips from British Columbia were taken by bowhunters — including Fred Asbell — shooting from elevated stands. In certain areas, the same tree stand tactic works effectively for brownies, too.

If tree stand hunting is not possible or practical, this leaves still-hunting and stalking as likely choices. Dwight Schuh arrowed his grizzly in this spot-and-stalk fashion several years ago. Easing close to a big bear is seldom easy. A bruin's nose is second to none in the animal kingdom, and their ears can quickly pick up the unnatural sounds a stalker might make. Regardless, if a bear is busy feeding on ripe berries or digging for rodents, you just might slip within range if you're patient and luck is on your side.

During the annual salmon runs, browns and grizzlies frequently can be found prowling the shorelines of streams and rivers, gorging themselves on the protein-rich fish they catch or find dead along the banks. This is no undertaking for sissies. Usually, visibility is limited by dense stands of willows or alders. You must pick your way through the brushy jungles along bear trails littered with the remains of fish and fresh droppings. Coming face to face with a bruin or surprising a feeding bear at close range are distinct possibilities. For this reason, some bowhunters opt to don hip boots or waders and ease into the water, moving slowly upstream through the sandy shallows, eyes sweeping the shore for any hint of movement, ears straining to hear a sudden splashing around the next bend. It's an exciting, pulse-pounding way to hunt the giant bears.

Another reliable way to locate brown bears is to find their winter dens, dark holes often dug on north-facing slopes near dense brush or alder thickets. Fresh dens usually have a fan of dirt below its entrance. Stalking the nearby hillsides surrounding dens can pay off at times. The bears emerge lethargic after months of inactivity and a close-range approach is possible. It's wise to approach any bear from uphill, if possible. Alarmed and wounded bruins often run downhill and head for nearby cover. Keep in mind that brown bears typically are most active from late afternoon until nightfall, but don't neglect the morning hours, either.

In coastal regions, keep an eye peeled for beached carrion. A dead seal, walrus, or whale will draw scavengers, including hungry

big bears can spell big trouble for hunters.

As someone who lives and routinely hunts in grizzly country, I know the concerns — and dangers — of encountering or surprising grizzlies. In truth, there is something about merely glimpsing one of these great bears at a distance that still kindles a cold fire in most any hunter's soul. Part of it is an innate fear that dates back to the dawn of time when our skin-clad ancestors killed these hulking giants with flint-tipped shafts — or died in a savage rush amid roars, slashing claws, and crushing jaws. But part of it is the grudging respect — and admiration — the modern day hunter feels for a fearless rival that not only has survived countless centuries but still reigns as undisputed monarch — the supreme predator — ruling those few remaining wild places still largely untouched by man.

Decades have passed since I stepped out of a spike camp tent overlooking some unnamed Alaskan stream and found grizzly tracks in the damp sand just below camp. But I can still recall the tension conveyed by the sight of big pad and claw marks etched there in the creekside sand, of knowing that the bear had passed close by during the dark night, curious but unafraid, knowing that as I slept only a flimsy strip of weathered canvas had separated us. Throughout the balance of that long, late summer day spent stalking barren ground caribou bulls, I couldn't help but cast suspicious glances at each patch of dwarf willow large enough to hide a bruin. The gnawing knowledge that he was there, somewhere close by, was unsettling. But any hunter who does not fear these huge bears, or at least greatly respect them, is a fool.

The fact is these bears can kill you. This compelling reality makes sharing the field with them — much less bowhunting them — a deadly serious, exciting undertaking. They are, to me, this continent's ultimate hunting challenge.

Hunting Strategies

First, hunting the big bears is both costly and time-consuming. Expect to pay a minimum of $5,000 to $7,500 (and perhaps a trophy fee) for a grizzly hunt — not to mention the license fees,

In Montana and certain other states it's legal to carry a firearm while bowhunting in big bear country. A large-caliber pistol and bear spray offer elk and deer hunters some sense of security, just in case.

bears, which are ever-opportunistic feeders. Locate a natural blind downwind and settle back. You may eventually end up with a good shot. Dr. Jack Frost of Anchorage reportedly arrowed his world record brownie in 1985 in this exact fashion as it fed nearby on an odoriferous whale carcass.

On Kodiak Island, where bowhunting Sitka blacktails is popular, the big bears have learned that following the windborne scent of fresh blood or meat is a shortcut to easy pickings. More than one hunter has had his trophy buck snatched by a hungry bruin. And few are willing to argue over ownership rights. Other hunters have reported bears responding to deer grunts they've uttered in hopes of attracting rutting bucks. And some rifle hunters swear that the big bears are attracted to the sound of gunfire, obviously equating the sound of a rifle with fresh meat — and an easy meal. These are not comforting thoughts to any bowhunter packing meat back to camp through dense brush along trails frequented by hulking bruins. More and more bow and arrow deer hunters pack heavy firepower of their own and employ the buddy system when field dressing and packing meat. One hunter always remains armed and alert while the other tends to the meat.

Even where it's legal to carry a firearm while bowhunting, I never fail to tote along a canister of pepper spray. While a well-placed bullet may drop a bear in its tracks, a wounding shot may only escalate an already dangerous situation. Blast a fogging faceful of powerful bear repellent into a bear's eyes and tender nose and he's going to get the idea there are easier ways to mooch a meal of tasty venison. Besides, such sprays carried in a handy belt holster are a good insurance policy in any face-to-face meeting with a crotchety bruin.

Once in Wyoming, just outside Yellowstone, I killed a mountain goat and packed the hide, horns, two quarters, and the backstraps

to trailhead over five miles of rugged, rocky terrain. By the time I returned for the final load, a grizzly already had staked a claim to the balance of the carcass, and I nearly blundered into a bad situation. But one glimpse of the silvertip was all I needed. I immediately backed off, comforted by the can of bear spray I snatched and held at the ready. Although I've never had to use it, just having the spray handy always provides peace of mind.

Both browns and grizzly bears may be hunted in either the spring or fall, depending on the hunting unit and license availability. Licenses can be pricey and hard to come by. Your outfitter can provide advice and the necessary assistance you'll need. A long winter can keep the bears denned later than normal, spoiling your hunting plans. Hunting in gale-force wind and rain is usually a waste of time, too. And try to avoid booking hunts during the time of a full moon. Bruins tend to be less active during the daylight hours then.

Some early spring hunts involve snow machines that aid in covering large chunks of ground in searching for the highly mobile interior bruins. In the fall, I've drifted Alaskan rivers looking for bears feeding along the banks. In coastal regions, fishing boats may be used as an offshore base of operations with a dinghy employed to ferry a guide and hunter to land when a bruin is sighted feeding on the open slopes or along the shore.

One advantage to spring bear hunts is gradually improving weather and prime pelts. In the fall, a multiple-species hunt is a distinct possibility. As a bonus, you're almost sure to be treated to an autumnal display of brilliant color that quickly transforms the remote valleys and high basins into a breathtaking mountain landscape you'll never forget.

Polar bears are typically hunted in the late winter or early spring between March and May. The most common and effective hunting method is Eskimo-style from outpost camps, with sled dogs or snow machines, crossing the frozen wastelands at the top of the world.

On a typical hunt the bowhunter and Inuit guide set out across the ice. When fresh tracks are found, they are followed until the bear is spotted. At this point the dogs are turned loose to chase and bay the bear. The hunter and his armed guide, back-up rifle at the ready, quickly move in for a close range killing shot.

Polar bears, like their brown and grizzly cousins, are quick, agile, and powerful animals, always potentially dangerous. Each year a

Montanan Dyrk Eddie arrowed this polar bear near the Arctic Circle. Such bowhunting adventures are costly — not for the faint of heart.

few of these great white bears stalk and confront native hunters. Some are shot in self-defense. On occasion hunters have been mauled or killed during these deadly showdowns.

Fred Bear, the legendary bowhunter who pursued polar bears on three separate occasions, fully understood the danger of facing these bears. On the first two hunts in 1960 and 1962, he arrowed polar bears which promptly turned, charged, and were killed by his rifle-toting guides. One of these wounded bears was dropped at less than 30 feet!

Finally, in April near the mouth of Alaska's Colville River, some 150 miles east of Point Barrow, Fred began his third and final quest for Nanook. No dogs were used on this hunt. Rather, seal carcasses were dragged across the ice, laying scent trails for bears to follow. Also, pots of blubber were kept bubbling around the clock in hopes of attracting hungry bruins. At last, in early May after 20 days afield, Fred's chance came when a big polar bear was sighted crossing the ice pack. One arrow at 50 yards stopped the bear and ended Bear's quest for what he called "a handsome trophy."

A mere handful of bowhunters — likely no more than two dozen bowmen — have successfully hunted polar bears. This fact should not be surprising. The hunt cost is steep, the weather conditions rugged if not downright brutal, and the quarry is potentially dangerous. Regardless, thanks to stringent game management practices and limited annual harvest, the polar bear is now found roaming the Arctic in good and growing numbers. And a ban which once prohibited the importation of polar bear hides and skulls into the U.S. has been lifted. These big bears are waiting to challenge any hunter with the resources, toughness, and desire to venture into the far away frozen northlands in search of a unique bowhunting trophy.

Brown, grizzly, and polar bears are big, muscular animals with heavy coats. Accurate arrow placement with a bow capable of generating sufficient foot-pounds of penetrating energy is mandatory. And never hesitate to add one or more follow-up shots, even after a mortal hit. These bears and their stamina should never be taken lightly.

The necessary close-range encounters between bowhunter and bruin inevitably raise the nagging questions of actual risk and

danger. In truth, some veteran guides and outfitters refuse to book bowhunters. They know that arrows kill by creating massive hemorrhage and that even a mortally wounded bear is capable of attacking and mauling — and killing — both hunter and guide. Others know a well-placed arrow is lethal and readily accept the heady challenge of helping any serious client work to within 30 yards or less in order to deliver a killing shaft to a big bear.

Bowhunting these huge animals is a deadly serious business. Chances are if you combine caution and common sense, you'll never be in any profound danger. Personally, I feel far more comfortable walking through the heart of bear country at night than strolling down most any darkened big city street.

Judging Trophy Bruins

As with black bears, skull size measured to the nearest 1/16 of an inch is the sole determining factor in judging trophy class brown, grizzly, and polar bears. Estimating the score of a live bear's skull measurement is chancy, at best. Naturally, the weight and size of the bear are good yardsticks and may help a trophy hunter evaluate the bruin. The color and condition of the animal's coat are yet another consideration. Huge hides with long, glossy hair — free of any rubbed spots — are prized by most bear hunters, regardless of the animal's official record book score.

A few hunters and guides place considerable emphasis on how many feet the hide "squares." If you hear someone say the shot a brown bear that squared 10 feet, for instance, you'll know he's talking about measuring the hide lengthwise from nose to tail, adding the spread between the front paws, and then dividing by two. That's just one more standard of excellence and comparison that some bear hunters use.

Most any adult bear will appear large to an excited bowhunter. But truly big bears have massive bodies and appear to lumber ponderously as they walk. Their heads may actually seem small by comparison to their bulk. Older animals generally have the largest skulls; however, some big bears have relatively small heads due to such factors as genetics and diet. Older brown and grizzly bears commonly have a darker coat; older polar bears may appear yellowish in color.

Some bear guides swear that tracks are reliable clues to body size. They claim if you measure the width of the front pad mark, add one inch, and covert that total to feet, you'll have the approximate size of the squared hide.

Bears are heavier in the fall months, adding body weight to nourish them through their winter sleep. Females commonly have narrower skulls than males. Look for animals with wide, massive-looking heads. Also, keep in mind that brown and grizzly bears have obvious shoulder humps and walk with a heavy, rolling gait. Big males are usually found alone except during the breeding season.

To qualify for the Pope and Young listings, a brown and polar bear skull must score at least 20 inches when its length and width are totaled. The minimum score for grizzly skull is 19 inches.

As you can tell, there are many factors — not just skull size — that can be used to determine a trophy-class bear. Without doubt, any brown, grizzly, or polar bear taken with the bow and arrow is an exceptional trophy. Big bears are fascinating, challenging big game animals worthy of any serious bowhunter's consideration and respect.

Pronghorn Antelope

Classification

Although not really members of the worldwide antelope family, pronghorns *(Antilocapra americana)* are commonly known as antelope. The truth is, this graceful, fleet-footed species is unique to the North American continent; today's pronghorns are the sole survivors of a family scientifically known as *antilocaprines*. Ancestral fossils dating back 20 million years have been unearthed and identified.

Current Distribution

Today's upwards of half a million pronghorns range across much of America's western prairielands. Wyoming is home to the largest numbers of these animals with Montana, South Dakota, and Colorado other top pronghorn states. In prehistoric times vast pronghorn herds ranged over some two million square miles of the continent — from the Midwest to what would become Oregon and California, and south from the Canadian prairies into Old Mexico. Millions of pronghorns were reported living west of the Mississippi during the 1800s — as many as 40 to 60 million animals — but advancing civilization resulted in a wanton, widespread slaughter that left as few as 12,000 to 15,000 animals by the 1920s. Fortunately, strict game laws, scientific studies, and restocking programs have brought the pronghorns back from the brink of extinction.

Identifying Characteristics

Handsome and agile, pronghorns are reddish-tan and white animals. Bucks have black facial masks and distinctive black cheek patches. Both sexes may have horns; however, the horns of does are tiny by comparison, rarely reaching ear length, and lacking prongs. The bucks' headgear is much more impressive. Mature, trophy class bucks often have heavy horns measuring from 12 up to 18 or more inches in length.

Like deer, pronghorns shed their headgear annually. Actually, by November of each year most pronghorns have lost their black outer horn-sheaths. A permanent inner core — unbranched and bone-like — remains affixed to the skull. Growth of the new horns, each with distinctive, forward-pointing prongs on the bucks, usually takes four to five months.

Pronghorns have snowy white rumps and communicate by flaring their heliographic-like rump patches, especially when alarmed. Their short, sharp alarm snort is similar to that of deer except higher pitched. Body hair is coarse and bristly. Tracks are similar to those of the deer that share the same range; however, pronghorns have no dewclaws. Droppings also are quite similar to deer scat.

Built for speed, pronghorns can accelerate quickly and skim across the prairie at speeds upwards of 50 miles per hour. They undoubtedly are the fastest animal on the North American continent and their large lungs and oversized heart make them capable of running at high speeds for extended periods. Gaping mouths and lolling tongues are typical of running pronghorns.

Although capable of jumping fences easily, pronghorns rarely make the attempt. More commonly they swerve and follow the fenceline, struggle through the strands of barbed wire, or stoop and deftly slide under the fence, often creating shallow depressions or "antelope slides" at popular crossing points.

Habitat/Diet

Most generally seen in the open, windswept spaces of western prairies and high plains, pronghorns also are found at higher elevations and have been observed wandering in brushy foothill terrain at the fringes of mountainside timberlands.

Once falsely accused of competing with domestic livestock for vital range grasses, pronghorns in fact prefer to browse on forbs and brushy shrubs, especially sage. They have an acquired taste for alfalfa and will raid ranchland crops; however, they rarely pose any serious threat to ranchers or their animals. It is also a fact that pronghorns have relatively small stomachs (the capacity is about half that of a domestic sheep, for example). Cud-chewers, these animals are capable of ingesting some plants that are poisonous to livestock. Besides sagebrush, favorite foods include bitterbrush, thistle, juniper, prickly pear, rabbitbrush, and saltbrush.

Well adapted to arid terrain, pronghorns can exist on relatively little water. Regardless, where stock tanks, impoundments, seeps, creeks, springs, and other water sources are available, regular visits by thirsty animals can be anticipated. This is especially true during the hot summer months when animals may visit water holes several times a day. In areas of heavy hunting pressure, bucks are capable of going several days without drinking, although they often slip in to water under the cover of darkness. During times of a full moon, pronghorns may water at any time of the day or night.

Reproduction

Bucks begin gathering harems by late August. During the rut itself in late September and early October, dominant bucks service their does after fighting off rivals for breeding rights. Posing or posturing is common during the rut and fights are often simple pushing and shoving matches. Battles do grow violent on occasion, resulting in injury and even death. Sparring bucks typically lower their heads, lock horns noisily, and struggle for an advantage. On rare occasions the hooked horns become hopelessly locked together, spelling almost certain doom for both combatants.

Biologists estimate that the dominant buck in each herd will do much of the breeding — perhaps 90 percent — with most copulation taking place at night when the harem is less likely to be on the move. As is true with all ungulates, the act of coitus itself lasts only a matter of seconds.

Fawns weighing about five pounds each are dropped during May and June, some eight to nine months following the rut. Does pregnant for the first time generally have one fawn; twin births are common among older does. Unspotted and virtually odorless at birth, the fawns gain strength rapidly, soon standing to nurse or trailing their mother on wobbly legs. Within a few days the newborns can easily outrun a man and healthy animals quickly develop the ability to outdistance four-legged predators.

Senses

Undoubtedly, a pronghorn's large eyes are its key to survival. Stories of just how well these animals can see border on the mythical. In truth, next to mountain goats and sheep, no North American game animal has better vision. Pronghorns can detect and focus on moving objects several miles away. And thanks to their oversize, protruding eyes, the animals have a wide field of vision. This makes slipping within arrow range — even from behind — seldom easy. Additionally, pronghorns possess excellent noses and above average hearing.

Life Expectancy

Pronghorns are considered to be short-lived animals, reaching full maturity quickly but rarely living past eight or nine years of age. Coyotes and other predators exact a heavy toll on the fawns in some areas, and adult animals, weakened by long winters or trapped in deep snows, may become easy prey as well. Despite the predation losses and severe winter die-offs, which can decimate some entire herds, pronghorns face a bright future.

Pronghorn antelope provide good table fare, although their meat has a distinct odor and flavor not found in other venison. Since most bowhunting occurs in the late summer months, prompt attention to the care of meat is vital. Recovering, dressing, and cooling the animals as quickly as possible are the key to good meals later on.

Bowhunting Records

The top Pope and Young pronghorn was arrowed in Yavapai County, Arizona, in August of 1995. Marvin Zieser's buck scored 91-4/8 inches.

Chapter 19
Pronghorn Antelope — Prairie Speedsters

AN ETERNAL PRAIRIE WIND rattled the locked blades of the windmill rising over the small pool glimmering in the morning sunlight a dozen yards in front of my old wooden blind. The handsome buck I was watching had appeared shortly after daybreak, circling downwind and instantly catching a whiff of man-scent. Spinning, he ran a short distance and turned to stare back my way. Thirsty but uneasy, he continued to pace nearby.

Moments later a lone fawn walked past my shooting window and drank not 10 yards away. I'd missed seeing the youngster approach and grumbled at my carelessness. If it had been a big buck, I'd have been caught completely unprepared. Of course, I knew that no mature buck — or doe, for that matter — would parade in to drink without first scent-checking a water hole for danger. Adult animals

seem to realize four-legged predators — and bowhunters — can be lurking near any source of life-sustaining water. Even that little fawn would soon wise up, or pay dearly for his carelessness.

Over the next hour and a half several pronghorn groups approached but stopped short when they caught some telltale trace of danger on the breeze. A few youngsters and thirsty does nervously eased in, drank quickly, and then raced away. Mostly the wary animals simply circled the windmill site, always stopping downwind when they smelled me. That big buck I'd seen earlier eventually joined a band containing seven does and their leggy fawns. Half a dozen times the herd started in to drink but always turned and sped away before getting within arrow range.

And it wasn't as if I hadn't showered and thoroughly misted my

Pronghorn antelope are handsome animals of the open prairies, where stalking presents a real challenge to bowhunters. These small, wary speedsters depend mainly on their amazing eyesight to warn of approaching danger.

During the annual rut it's possible to lure bucks within bow range by using a decoy of a small buck. That sometimes brings a jealous rival on the run to chase away the competitor.

prairie dust. By the time I scrambled through the door at the rear of my blind to keep the wounded buck in sight, he already was staggering. Seconds later he collapsed. He hadn't traveled 50 yards before going down for keeps.

That 2003 action took place on Frank Moore's famed Spearhead Ranch north of Douglas, Wyoming. It was my very latest pronghorn quest and my September success was typical of hunts I've enjoyed over a long career that began in 1971 with an antelope bowhunt on the northwestern Nebraska plains. Back then Indiana huntin' buddy Jack Reinhart and I had spent a mostly frustrating week stalking mule deer and pronghorns. While we tagged a couple of muleys, we totally blanked on antelope. The lone shot I got was at least 40 yards and that sharp-eyed buck had me spotted before I'd even raised my bow. It goes without saying he was long gone before me arrow sliced through the empty prairie air where he'd been standing. Humbled, I returned home with a newfound respect for these beautiful, graceful, and elfin animals.

At the time I knew there had to be a better way to get within good arrow range. All I had to do was find it. And a year or two later I arrowed my first thirsty pronghorn from ambush, hunkered hidden in a sagebrush blind near a Wyoming water hole. The distance of my shot? A mere seven yards! Instantly I knew then I'd uncovered the key to unlocking consistent pronghorn hunting success.

lightweight camo with scent-eliminating spray before leaving camp. Although such sprays help, I also know nothing can completely mask the telling man-smell. Anyone who breathes is emitting scent.

I briefly considered calling it quits, but decided to stick it out. The morning already was heating up. Everywhere I looked I could see distant pronghorns moving across the Wyoming prairie. If it weren't for that doggone wind....

Suddenly an idea hit me. Unzipping my daypack, I fished out a clean camo t-shirt and pair of spare socks. I also retrieved the paper napkins from my lunch cooler, along with a roll of toilet paper. Next, I quickly began plugging every crack and seam where I could feel air entering the old antelope blind. Maybe I couldn't eliminate all evidence of my presence, but perhaps I could contain things a bit within the sun-bleached wooden structure. Minutes later, I admired my handiwork and sat back to see what would happen next.

Admittedly, sit-and-watch bowhunting for pronghorn antelope involves much more watching than hunting. Like bear hunters who sit on a stand near some active bait, pronghorn hunters who sit in blinds near water holes let the animals eventually come to them. It's an extremely effective means of tagging these wary, keen-eyed creatures. The reason is obvious. Water is universally scarce throughout most antelope habitat. To survive, pronghorns must know each reliable water source within their home range. On hot summer days they often travel several miles to slake their thirst. Daily visits to water are common. A patient bowhunter on a dawn-to-dark vigil can sometimes get a point-blank shot simply by concealing himself near some small water source.

Over the next hour or more several thirsty does and fawns moved in and drank their fill. Still the big buck hung back. But when his little herd finally approached, he trailed them. Obviously, my improvised cloth and paper caulking job had eliminated much of my airborne scent. And when he stopped to watch the does and youngsters drink just in front of my sight window, I slowly drew, aimed, and released. My arrow disappeared behind his shoulder just below the line where tan and white hair merged. Instantly pronghorns exploded from the water hole in a shower of mud, water, and

Trophy class bucks like this one have long, curving horns with distinctive prongs.

Most pronghorns tagged by bowhunters are shot from blinds near water holes where the animals come to drink. This is the setup the author used while hunting the Spearhead Ranch in 2003.

Here's a blind's eye view of a buck and doe cautiously circling downwind to check for danger. M. R. James later shot this buck after plugging cracks in the old blind to help contain telltale scent.

Hunting Strategies

Although stand-hunting for antelope is obviously the most effective bowhunting method there is, bar none, several other techniques offer the resourceful bowhunter a realistic chance at filling a tag. Stalking these so-called "prairie goats" is possible, although I remain convinced it's one of bowhunting's toughest challenges, requiring time, patience, and more than a smidgen of luck. Decoying and calling rutting bucks work well at times and are hard to beat for pulse-thumping excitement. Ditto for duping a wary yet curious buck by "flagging." Finally, under certain conditions, driving or "nudging" antelope along fencelines or through narrow prairie bottlenecks may result in a close-range shot.

Regardless, according to the latest Pope and Young Club records, about half of the big bucks taken each year are killed from ground blinds near water; another 25 percent — give or take — fall to spot-and-stalk bowhunters. Surprisingly, despite the open lands they inhabit, most antelope are killed at normal bowhunting yardages of between 10 and 40 yards.

Hacking a pit blind out of the sun-baked prairie earth is hard, sweaty work. Yet, many successful bowhunters — and savvy guides — gladly risk blisters and heat strokes during the pre-season in order to reap the later benefits of point-blank shooting opportunities. After carving out such blinds near water sources where area wildlife routinely comes to drink, hunters ring the pits with sage or some other natural shrub. Next they create one or two handy shooting holes to cover any nearby watering spot and approach route. The final step is simply sitting patiently and waiting for a thirsty buck to wander in. Lightweight portable camo cloth blinds and permanent structures — such as those used season after season by me and other Spearhead Ranch bowhunters — are other good options.

It's always wise to construct or erect such blinds in advance of the season's opening day — or your planned hunt. Pronghorns, deer, and other game immediately will notice the new structure and typically need time to get used to its presence. They may become instantly skittish when changes are apparent around a favorite drinking spot. Tracks or glassing should quickly tell you where the animals water. Ideally, any water source is small enough to be covered by a single ambush site. Nothing is more frustrating than to be perfectly hidden but have all the animals come in to drink well out of your effective shooting range. In such instances, two blinds might be called for. Some dual setups allow hunting buddies to effectively stake out the same watering location and share each day's action and excitement.

Blinds always should have a dark interior. Pronghorns easily detect movement, especially at close ranges. Obviously you will need to be able to draw your bow and get off a shot without being spotted. Burlap backing or camo material can be hung in place to eliminate backlighting problems created by some see-through blinds. Also, a roof or covering of some sort always helps, not only to shade the blind's interior but to provide relief from the merciless summer sun. Just be sure there is sufficient clearance to raise and draw your bow. I once had a novice pronghorn guide construct an elaborate blind for me, only to discover belatedly that he hadn't left enough headroom necessary for raising and drawing my bow.

Adequate room within any blind not only provides uncramped comfort for the bowhunter and his equipment, but also helps when

Dave James collected this nice buck on a Wyoming hunt with his father several years ago.

Michigan bowhunter Beth Nelson shot this record book buck at the Spearhead Ranch north of Douglas, Wyoming.

the time comes to make the killing shot. Many successful antelope hunters pull their bows unseen behind cover and only after reaching full draw do they lean slowly into the blind's shooting window, pick up their target, and release a well-aimed arrow. Camouflaged tackle — not to mention camo face paint or headnet, combined with a gloved or camouflaged bow hand — can help a bowhunter remain unseen while making the shot.

The best time to release an arrow is when an animal has lowered its head and begun to drink. Be patient. Pronghorns often hurry to the water's edge and then stand staring about for signs of danger. They often lower their heads as if to drink, then jerk erect as if hoping to detect some telltale clue of a nearby predator. When satisfied all's well, the nervous animals rapidly drink their fill — usually within a matter of seconds — before quickly departing the area. At times cautious bucks will hang back, watching as does and fawns approach and drink, before they move in to take their turn.

When a buck's muzzle is in the water, or lowered to feed, he's relaxed and briefly focused on drinking or eating. This is when he's most vulnerable to a killing shot. Colorado bowhunter Judd Cooney, who once held the bowhunting world record for pronghorn antelope, suggests not releasing an arrow until you can see the animal swallowing or hear him slurping up the water. Shooting at

skittish animals approaching or leaving a water hole is unwise. Antelope possess lightning reflexes and their arrow-dodging ability is well known. At best such chancy shots at moving targets results in a clean miss; at worse, a shot wounds the animal.

Portable blinds with shoot-through netting are ideal, but they need to be firmly pegged in place. Otherwise, stiff prairie winds can turn these lightweight structures into camo tumbleweeds, or at least cause the fabric to rustle or slap noisily. Finally, leaving these cloth and plastic enclosures in areas where livestock waters is asking for trouble, unless you think you can shoot from a trampled, flattened blind.

Other stand possibilities worth consideration include the haybale blind and the windmill "tree stand." I know several bowhunters who've tagged feeding bucks in alfalfa fields from ambush sites. They simply constructed a makeshift haybale blind that hid them from view. Another variation is hiding atop some haystack near where antelope come to feed. Ground blinds situated near "slides," where pronghorns routinely belly under fences, creating well-worn depressions in the prairie soil, or along fences near pasture gates leading to feeding areas, may produce shots for the patient hunter.

At the opposite end of the sit-and-wait spectrum, I know some savvy antelope hunters who swear that pronghorns completely ignore silhouetted bowhunters standing in plain sight — providing the hunters choose to wait in ambush on elevated windmill platforms. The theory is that since antelope don't expect danger from above, they will walk directly under a bowhunter standing or seated in full view on an elevated platform. Although I've never tried this method myself, I have hunted pronghorns from tree stands along prairie creekbottoms on a couple of occasions. Based on those limited experiences, I wouldn't hesitate to give windmill perches a try. None of the pronghorns passing under my trees ever gave me so much as a suspicious upward glance. Obviously any hunter perched atop a windmill or haystack should be prepared to spend long hours exposed to the boiling sun. This means having plenty of water and wearing sunscreen or some appropriate skin-protective clothing. Also, it goes without saying that you must obtain the landowner's

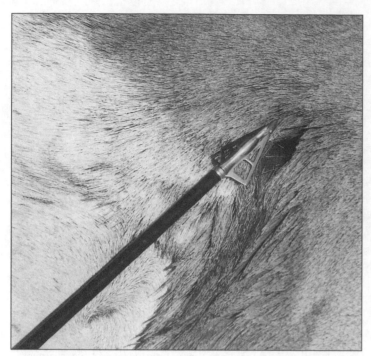

Pronghorns have a "built-in" aiming point where the reddish tan merges with the white of a broadside animal. This buck didn't travel 40 yards after the Rocky Mountain head sliced through both lungs.

Dave Holt has collected a host of record book pronghorns over the years. He knows firsthand how deadly water hole hunting can be in the dry prairies antelope call home.

permission before rearranging haybales or climbing a windmill in hopes of getting close to some unsuspecting pronghorn. Ditto for digging pit blinds.

Much has been made of an antelope's reluctance to jump fences. While I've watched bucks clear ranchland fences with ease, more often than not they'll drop down and belly beneath the strands of barbed wire so common to western pastures. Often they'll follow fencelines — at times walking or running parallel to these fences for miles — and this can assist in the successful driving of antelope toward hunters waiting in improvised blinds or strategic hiding spots. The downside of pushing pronghorns toward hidden hunters is that most shots will be taken at moving targets and poorly hit antelope can be difficult to recover.

Among the best pronghorn blinds I've ever seen and used are the permanent blinds created by Frank Moore on the Spearhead ranch. Frank, who specializes in offering bowhunts for trophy class antelope, learned the value of proper concealment from the late Don Schram, a veteran Illinois bowhunter who decades ago advised Frank how to set up point-blank shots for his clients. After some trial and error testing, Frank came up with completely enclosed triangular structures constructed of wood (the same style of blind I used on the hunt mentioned at the start of this chapter). Half of these structures are above the ground and half below. A single shooting window faces the water hole and the hunter sits comfortably on a padded seat with his back to the point of the triangle. Small eyeholes on either side of the blind allow good visibility to the left and right; the adjustable shooting window gives excellent coverage of the water hole and surrounding terrain. These blinds are painted white and reflect the broiling prairie sun. Interiors are completely dark and surprisingly comfortable, even on the hottest September days.

In recent years Frank — himself a successful bowhunter — has begun gradually replacing these slowly deteriorating structures. He

now favors eight- and 10-feet diameter cast iron culverts that are stood on end and half-buried near watering sites. Peep holes, a shooting window, and hinged door are cut into the metal with torches. Mounds of dirt are then piled on a flat top welded in place. These round and spacious all-metal blinds are amazingly cool — and effective.

Spearhead Ranch hunters, like clients on many guided hunts across antelope country, are dropped off before daylight and often spend the entire day waiting and watching. Lunch, chilled water or juices, adequate reading material, a cushion, and urine bottle — even a plastic bag for fecal waste — make each daylong vigil pass quickly in relative comfort. Frank and his guides make several routine checks from distant glassing points throughout the long summer day. Any hunter who shoots an animal is asked to hang a highly visible red pennant on the side of the blind. This signal brings immediate help to recover and load the pronghorn for a trip to the walk-in cooler back at ranch headquarters. Since prime pronghorn hunting near water always takes place in hot weather, prompt attention to field dressing duties and cooling the carcass are necessary in order to prevent spoilage of the meat and the trophy's cape.

Speaking of spoilage, an antelope's horns — like those of mountain sheep and goats — will eventually begin to smell unless the outer horn sheath is separated from its bony core and the fleshy membrane inside is completely removed. Many taxidermists routinely remove the horns by submerging the antelope's skull and horn base in boiling water until the horn can be pulled or twisted

Arizona is home to some of the biggest pronghorns in the West, including the current P&Y World Record. Dyrk Eddie of Montana shot this P&Y-class "prairie goat" during Arizona's 2003 season.

free. Usually the process takes only a matter of minutes. Then once the inner membrane is cut away, a preserving paste or fiberglass putty is placed inside the hollow horn. The horns are then fitted back onto the bony core where the drying agent cements them to the skull plate. This procedure prevents ultimate horn shrinkage and spoilage.

The outer sheath of a pronghorn's horns is composed of hardened, hairlike material, which if improperly treated or ignored, can shrink amazingly fast. To illustrate just how fast shrinkage can occur, I'll cite the example of two bowhunters who took nearly identical huge-horned antelope on the same day. Both bucks green-scored exactly 82 7/8 P&Y inches. One buck was quickly taken to a taxidermist for horn treatment; the other set of trophy horns was left to dry by natural means. After the required 60-day drying period had elapsed and the bucks were officially taped for record book entry, the treated horns taped an even 82 inches, a loss of less than an inch. But the other buck's horns had shrunk to 80 6/8 inches! Let this serve as a word to the wise antelope hunter.

Incidentally, the Pope and Young Club generally accepts the scoring of horned animals that have been treated by taxidermists, so long as the treatment does nothing to enhance the score. In 2003, P&Y changed its pronghorn scoring form to ask if the sheaths have been reattached to the cores by the use of such fillers or adhesives. If so, the horns' base circumference measurement cannot exceed the second taping point. This precludes the possibility of inflated base circumference scores caused by any preserving bonding agents. Even pronghorns with split or broken skulls may be measured so long as it's clear that the horns' final score is not affected by the damaged skull.

As previously noted, stalking feeding or bedded pronghorns is challenging but quite possible. And take it from me, arrowing an

antelope by the spot-and-stalk method is an immensely satisfying experience no matter the size of the buck you manage to bring down. Broken or rolling terrain helps. Coulees and arroyos can keep you out of sight while you slip close. And since you can expect to spend much of your time bellying close or crawling on hands and knees — often across rocky ground, through sage, and around cactus clumps — durable clothing is a good idea. Some stalkers I know even wear knee and elbow pads.

Since rattlesnakes share much of the prime pronghorn habitat, it's wise to always keep an eye peeled. Coming face to face with a big diamondback while crawling through the sagebrush can spoil any stalker's day. And since the snakes may seek refuge from the day's heat in shady areas, always carefully check out your blind before climbing inside. This is especially good advice if you can't begin your hunt until the day has started to heat up.

On the same subject, it's usually best to have a buddy drive you to your blind if antelope are visible in the area. Vehicles don't seem to alarm the animals the way a man on foot will. Ranch vehicles may be a common sight to the pronghorns; however, a person walking across the prairie invariably attracts much more attention — and suspicion. Remember, too, antelope can't count. When you walk to your blind, have a buddy walk along. After you're inside and set up to begin your hunt, have him walk away. Watching animals will focus on him and promptly forget about you. Once he's walked or driven out of sight, things soon should be back to normal.

Once in northwestern Colorado, my son Dave and I drove back to a remote water hole at midday. We chased a herd of thirsty pronghorns away as we approached the blind. But less than an hour after Dave had driven away, leaving me comfortably settled for the afternoon hunt, I shot a buck at 15 yards when the same herd returned to drink.

Once again, hot weather is the ideal time to ambush a thirsty pronghorn, but sudden rain showers and unexpected cool spells can spoil things for sit-and-wait hunters. Readily available water sources mean the animals don't have to make daily visits to drinking sites. And in cool weather the pronghorns can go without water for much longer stretches of time. In these cases about all you can do is hope some animals will come to your water hole out of habit — or you'll have to try some other hunting technique.

During the rut, decoying works well if you can convince a jealous herd buck that some nearby lady-stealing rival poses a threat. Although the practice of decoying dates back to prehistoric Native American hunters, South Dakota bowhunter Mel Dutton is generally credited with popularizing this particular action-packed brand of pronghorn hunting. Along the way Dutton developed a full-size, lifelike plastic antelope decoy and he proved it lured bucks into bow range. Big bucks!

Mel's principle is quite simple, really. After locating a distant pronghorn bank, the hunter keeps out of sight and carefully makes his way to a nearby ridgetop or other high point, staying downwind from the antelope. There he raises the decoy — patterned after a medium-sized buck that must seem to be an impudent young whippersnapper to any pronghorn old-timer — so the antelope can see it. One of three things is likely to happen next: the decoy will be seen but ignored; the herd buck will quickly gather up his harem and herd them away; or the buck will make a beeline straight for the upstart rival, hell-bent on delivering a severe butt-kicking in defense of his does. It's in the latter case that things can get down-

The author's son, Dave James, has collected several potential record-book bucks during his own bowhunting career.

Any legal antelope can be considered a trophy if taken within the rules of fair chase. Pronghorns rank as one of bowhunting's most popular–and frustrating–trophies.

right interesting for the bowhunter crouched waiting behind the pronghorn decoy.

Dutton, for one, suggests painting your face black. When you raise up behind the decoy to take your shot, the blackened face confuses the antelope into mistaking you for yet another black-faced buck, perhaps causing him to hesitate just long enough for you take the shot at a stationary target. Dutton also urges that you come to full draw before rising up to shoot, then aim and release in one smooth motion. Fooled pronghorns don't often hang around once they realize they've been duped.

Although Mel says he prefers early mornings, decoying can work at any time of the day and provide fast-paced action throughout the annual rut. Some bowhunters combine decoying with aggressive grunting to provoke possessive herd bucks.

Still another variation of the decoying technique is to appeal to the animals' natural curiosity by "flagging" — waving a hat, handkerchief, or bandana above some hiding spot. This technique works better for rifle hunters than bowmen since any approaching buck is fully alert and wired for immediately departure. Besides, even bucks attracted to the flagging ruse rarely approach within good arrow range. And even if they do, trying to pop up, draw your bow, and get off a shot is doomed to almost certain failure.

Proper pre-season practice for pronghorn hunters should include plenty of shots taken from a crouching, kneeling, or sitting position. Such shots are common whether you're stalking or hunting from ambush. If you're planning to hunt from a ground blind, get used to shooting through small openings in the brush. And if a windmill platform or tree stand ever figures into your plans to ambush a pronghorn, practice shooting downward at sharp angles. Antelope are small targets and pinpoint accuracy is critical. Don't let their size fool you, either. Pronghorns are tough critters.

Never sit back after the shot and wait 30 minutes to an hour before taking up the blood trail, either. Keep your buck in sight. Always! Following tiny drops of blood across the sun-baked prairie is no easy task. It's far, far better to maintain visual contact on the open plains. Even a mortally hit buck that drops within a minute or two can cover amazing distances. And if he falls somewhere out of sight on the sage-dotted prairie, you might not locate him for some time — time that can spoil the meat on any hot weather bowhunt. Finally, if possible, don't leave your trophy unrecovered overnight. Coyotes have a fondness for antelope venison and can quickly gobble up much of any unattended carcass they happen across.

Bowhunters who live in or near antelope country can easily scout and plan relatively inexpensive do-it-yourself pronghorn

Older bucks have impressive headgear. Long, thick, ivory-tipped horns with jutting prongs are the signs of a mature animal—and a record-book candidate.

Arizona bowhunter Marvin Zieser poses with the Pope and Young world record pronghorn, shot at a water hole in August of 1995.

hunts. Topo maps will save time in getting to know any hunting area, but nothing substitutes for scouting the terrain firsthand, looking for and locating the animals and noting where they feed and drink. The biggest problem with planning public land hunts is hunting pressure. It's downright discouraging to have carefully planned stalks spoiled by slobs in off-road vehicles trying to run down any antelope they see. And there's nothing more disappointing than to work long, hot hours constructing a blind at some remote water hole only to find a claim jumper in your pit on opening morning — or another blind constructed nearby. Unfortunately, problems such as these are becoming increasingly common in many public hunting areas.

This fact accounts for the growing popularity of hunting private lands behind locked gates. More and more modern-day antelope hunters are seeking permission to bowhunt private ranches, even if it means leasing the land for the duration of the season or perhaps paying the landowner a daily trespass fee. Still another option — especially for out-of-state bowhunters with limited time — is booking a hunt with an experienced pronghorn guide or outfitter. Such hunts aren't cheap, although the cost depends on the services provided. Private land hunts may range from deluxe, fully-guided outings to non-guided drop camp arrangements in good antelope country. The price tag can vary greatly, some costing several thousand dollars. Check out the display and classified ads in the where-to-go sections of *Bowhunter* and other outdoor magazines. Fish and game departments can provide lists of licensed guides, as well as full details about season dates, license costs, and application procedures, along with current hunting regulations. A telephone call to a local Chamber of Commerce or sporting goods store can lead to contacts with landowners willing to accommodate antelope hunters. But checking out possibilities and planning such hunts always takes time, if done correctly. Allow yourself a year or more preparation time for your antelope hunt,

whether you go with a guide or make the trip on your own.

Pronghorns represent a worthy bowhunting challenge — and make a great trophy. Just ask any bowhunter who's spent seasons afield pursuing these handsome prairie speedsters.

Judging Trophy Pronghorns

The present minimum score for entry in the Pope and Young record books is 67 inches. Immensely popular with bowhunters, pronghorns rank only behind whitetails and black bears in the total number of record book entries. Starting the 2003 archery season, more than 5,000 pronghorns were listed in the P&Y records.

Bucks with thick, long-pronged 12- to 13-inch horns may qualify for the book. Headgear this size is not uncommon. But, in truth, antelope horns often appear larger than they really are, due mainly to the diminutive size of the animals themselves. Even average-sized bucks may have horns with well-developed prongs extending above the ears. But trophy-class bucks typically wear long, heavy horns with good mass and huge, forward-sweeping "cutters," as hunters commonly call the bucks' prongs.

If you want to arrow a trophy buck, look for horns as long or longer than the buck's face, keeping in mind that an antelope's ears are about six inches high. The tall, massive horns, and jutting prongs of exceptional trophies will appear almost unreal — somehow artificial looking — compared to normal bucks. When you see a genuine trophy, more often than not you'll immediately realize you're looking at a truly special animal. And it's a good bet you are.

Pronghorns are measured by adding the length of each horn and each prong, as well as four circumference measurements taken starting at the base and extending upward toward the horn tip at the first, second, and third quarters. Time was when an unusually wide inside spread resulted in a scoring deduction if that spread exceeded the longest horn. That spread penalty has since been eliminated.

Elk

Classification

Second only to moose as the largest North American deer, elk probably originated in Asia and first made their way to this continent about a million years ago by crossing the trans-Bering land bridge. Today the Pope and Young Club recognizes two of six identified subspecies of wapiti — the Rocky Mountain or Yellowstone elk *(Cervus elaphus nelsoni)* and the Roosevelt or Olympic elk *(Cervus elaphus roosevelti)*. The other four North American subspecies include the Manitoban, Eastern, Tule, and Merriam elk.

Current Distribution

Roosevelt elk inhabit western Washington and Oregon, northwestern California, and — thanks to transplanting efforts — Alaska's Afognak and Raspberry Islands. Although once found roaming across much of North America's plains and forestlands, modern Rocky Mountain elk are restricted mostly to the Western foothills and mountains from Canada south to Arizona and New Mexico. Colorado has more elk than any state or province. Transplanted herds have been successfully re-established in numerous other states where elk once roamed, including certain states east of the Mississippi — Michigan and Pennsylvania, for example — where limited hunting possibilities now exist. The nationwide elk population early in the 21st century is estimated upwards of one million animals.

Identifying Characteristics

Larger and darker than other members of the elk family, Roosevelt elk bulls commonly grow shorter, thicker antlers than their Rocky Mountain counterparts. A mature bull may stand five feet at the shoulder and top 1,000 pounds, although the live weight of adult Roosevelt bulls begins at about 700 pounds; adult cows may weigh up to 600 pounds. Rocky Mountain bull elk average 600 to 800 pounds; cows are about 25 percent lighter. Mature bulls stand 58 inches at the shoulder and have a body length of eight to 10 feet.

Elk are brownish-gray herd animals with whitish-yellow rump patches, dark undersides, and black legs. Necks and heads are chestnut-brown. Cows typically are lighter in color than bulls. All elk have obvious lachrymal glands or tear ducts on the inside corner of each eye. Small metatarsal glands are found on the outside of the rear legs.

Ruminants, elk are largely nocturnal and feed mainly on grasses and sedges. They fill their paunches before retiring to secure daytime bedding areas where they chew their cuds and await the next feeding foray. Of all members of the deer family, only elk have two extra teeth in their upper jaw. These rudimentary canine teeth, known as "elk ivory," give these animals a total of 34 teeth instead of the usual 32: two canines, eight incisors, 12 premolars, and 12 molars.

Elk are more vocal than other antlered game. Cows and calves usually communicate with bird-like chirps, mews, coughs, and barks. Bulls are fairly quiet except during the rut when the mountainsides ring with their shrill, whistling bugles and throaty grunts. Roosevelt bulls typically bugle less than Rocky Mountain elk.

Strong swimmers and agile leapers, elk can run short distances at speeds in excess of 30 mph. If alarmed, these animals can trot for miles at a ground-covering gait, which puts considerable distance between the elk and any pursuer. When pressured, bulls may become more nocturnal, seldom bugling during daytime and often completely vacating an area.

Habitat/Diet

Roosevelt elk are found in the hilly and mountainous regions of the Pacific northwest. Their coastal home range is usually wet and thick, a combination of deep forests, cedar swamps, and alder-choked river bottoms. Logging roads and clearcut areas with new growth vegetation attract elk, but movement in these open areas takes place only early and late in the day. Since deep, high country snow doesn't threaten the Roosevelts the way it can imperil their Rocky Mountain cousins, Roosevelt elk are not known to migrate.

Yellowstone elk often pass the summer months in the high country, resting and feeding in alpine meadows until the fall and winter snows force them into lower valleys. Grasses comprise 80 percent or more of an elk's diet with browse — conifers and deciduous growth including willows, alders, and quaking aspen — rounding out their preferred table fare. Elk living near farms and ranches may ravage cultivated crops and raid stores of winter hay intended for livestock. Once known as animals of the plains, some elk still make their home in open, broken country. Today's transplanted animals are as much at home in hardwood forests as the brushy jungles along river drainages. Salt and mineral licks will attract the big animals wherever they are found.

Senses

Elk possess an exceptional sense of smell and use their noses as a first line of defense to warn of approaching danger. Their acute hearing also plays a major survival role. While elk are quick to detect movement, unmoving hunters are frequently overlooked even at close range.

Reproduction

Bull elk are the male chauvinists of the animal world. After spending solitary spring and summer months alone or in small bachelor groups — growing fat and a new set of impressive antlers — with the first stirrings of rut in late August or early September the bulls set about joining or gathering herds of cows and calves. Actual breeding often begins by mid-September and lasts for several weeks, usually winding down in October. Bulls collect as many cows as they can and jealously guard their harems, servicing cows as they come into season and keeping busy driving off rival bulls. Challenging bugles are commonly heard during this period and some serious battles for breeding rights do occur.

Calves are born between eight and nine months later. Cows and their newborns rejoin the herd within a week or so. Single births are the norm although twin births are not rare. Reddish calves are white-spotted and weigh about 20 to 30 pounds at birth. They begin to feed on grasses within the first month and usually are weaned by the time the annual breeding cycle begins again.

Life Expectancy

Elk often live into their mid-teens and some reach their third decade of life. Considered excellent table fare, elk venison is highly prized by hunters.

Bowhunting Records

The top Yellowstone elk (typical) was arrowed in Rosebud County, Montana, in 2000 by noted bowhunter Chuck Adams. That seven-by-seven bull scores an official 409 2/8. The best non-typical Yellowstone elk was killed by Steven Mullin in Idaho during a Shoshone County back in 1981; its score is 420 5/8. The all-time best Roosevelt bull was killed in Tilamook County, Oregon, in 1985 by bowhunters Dale Baumgartner and Ken Sisco. Its official score is 367 3/8 inches.

Chapter 20
Elk –
Epitome of Wildness

IT WAS MIDDAY in the Wyoming wilderness when the big herd bull answered our fluting bugles. He was at least two timbered drainages away, likely bedded with his cows, and answered our challenge more out of reflex than anger or concern. But he let us know he was there. And that was enough. So it began.

Tim and I step off the high ridge, slip-sliding down the cliff face in ankle-deep loose dirt and stones. We rock-hop a rushing stream and claw our way up into the timber, hurrying along a tracked game trail until the ground falls away to our left. We again plunge downward, digging in our heels and riding small scree avalanches into the next basin. And then we fight our way upward again, sweat stinging our eyes, lungs aflame, until we reach the bench and stop, gasping, to look and listen.

I move ahead a dozen paces and kneel beside a deadfall. Tim bugles behind me. The bull answers just ahead. I pull an arrow free and snap it on the string. Tim bugles again, but when the bull answers he is moving away.

I jam the arrow back into the quiver even as I clamber to my feet. Another footrace. Sprinting among the pines, dodging low-hanging branches, and hurdling blowdowns. Down and across a sunny, boulder-strewn chute. Up into the cool trees beyond. Finding another deadfall hiding spot even as Tim bugles again.

This time the bull's scream is close. Indignant at being pursued, he is just ahead. Defiant. Angry. By the time I nock my arrow, I can hear brush breaking uphill to my left. Dark legs appear, moving. A heavy, ivory-tipped rack floats toward me, somehow disembodied.

Early morning bugling from mountain high ridges can elicit challenging responses from bulls in the timber below.

186

M. R. James shows one of his best bulls. This Colorado elk was arrowed on a spot-and-stalk hunt. Cow calls pulled him within 30 yards of the author.

Fresh rubs are a sure sign the rut is starting to heat up. As the bulls grow more aggressive, they may respond to either cow calls or bugles.

Some hunters prefer cow calling, especially in hunting areas where the bulls are being pressured by bugling bowhunters. Seductive sweet talk can lure elk close.

He is 30 yards away and closing.

God, I think, awestruck, *the size, the beauty of him!*

Still he moves toward me, head-on, as noiseless now as a tan shadow. Drifting downslope, passing behind a pine at 20 yards, he doesn't see me come to full draw, hear my thudding heart, sense me near. He only knows the rival bull is close by, a threat to his cows waiting in the timber above. On he stalks. Closer. Closer.

Turn, I pray, *please turn!*

And at last, as if by my will alone, he does turn. Over my bow hand I watch the bull ghosting past, broadside, huge yet silent, striding, until my arrow's red and yellow fletching appears against his side, tight behind the shoulder, just where I'd willed it to fly.

You always remember your first face-to-face encounter with a red-hot rutting bull. It makes you forget about all those magazine cover bulls you've ever seen. Your elk is real! He is dry branches splintering just beyond the ridgecrest; he is a flash of tan and chestnut amid dark firs and white-trunked aspen; he is an unmistakable sour-sweet smell on the mountain thermals.

Watch him stride closer. Intent but wary. Purposeful. Determined. Suddenly he faces you, all sweptback antlers, raised head, bloodshot eyes, and slobbery, gaping mouth. His deafening, guttural scream seems to shake the very ground. Spurts of urine soak dark underbelly hair beneath heaving flanks. There is no mistaking his in-your-face "Here-I-am!" challenge. He is primed for a showdown battle. He is ready.

Are you?

Few bowhunting experiences call for more emotional self-control. Bull elk are the true Jekyll and Hyde of the animal kingdom — one moment docile, the next belligerent and threatening. And always awesome, especially at close range bowhunting yardages.

I know. Memories of that big six-by-six wilderness bull are forever branded in my brain. And whether you take your own bull through such a contentious confrontation or silently by well-planned or opportunistic ambush, you soon will come to realize why so many serious bowhunters regard large-antlered elk as exclusive, elegant big game animals.

Here's some prime Colorado elk country. The quakies, canyons, and dark timber surrounding open feeding areas provide the bedding cover herds need.

Modern elk are intelligent, adaptable animals. Pressure them too much and the bulls grow call-shy, making them doubly difficult to locate, much less tempt within arrow range. Like savvy trophy-class bucks, they become even more reclusive, more nocturnal. They'll mostly stick to impenetrable black timber jungles, leaving their day beds only after the curtain of darkness drops across the land. Still, they are there, leaving behind their tracks and droppings and antler-slashed trees as mute evidence of their unseen presence. And for most elk addicts, such sign alone is enough to lure hunters into the field to partake in one of the most frustrating yet satisfying, exacting yet exciting bowhunting challenges available anywhere on this continent.

Dwight Schuh perfectly sums up the appeal of elk hunting with the following words:

"Does any serious big game hunter not dream of hunting elk? Deer are more numerous than elk, moose are bigger, sheep are more glamorous, bear more mysterious, yet something about elk turns most hunters on and captures their dreams and imaginations. Maybe it's that they're big, brawny, brawling animals that wake a sense of wildness in hunters; that they live in pristine country, America's last frontiers; that they grow huge trophy racks, that they yield mountains of meat. Or that they bugle."

Anyone who has heard their haunting cries echoing from forested canyons and felt the primordial restlessness triggered by that singular, soul-stirring call of true wildness, already understands the undeniable appeal of elk hunting. For all others, discovery awaits.

Hunting Strategies

Each season hundreds of elk are routinely arrowed from ambush. Many more are tagged by patient still-hunters and stalkers. Despite such successes employing these time-tested bowhunting techniques, there is no question that the most exciting elk hunting involves bugling or cow-calling rutting bulls to within point-blank distances of waiting hunters.

Montana bowman Dyrk Eddie shot this Roosevelt bull on an Oregon hunt with Larry D. Jones. Calls drew the elk within 25 yards.

Dwight Schuh, who authored the classic bowhunting book Bugling for Elk, *shows proof positive his techniques work. He tagged this bull in Colorado, home to more elk than any other state.*

Chuck Adams arrowed his Pope and Young Club world record Montana bull in September of 2000. It also won the P&Y Ishi Award as the outstanding animal taken during the 1999-2000 recording period.

Unfortunately for any hopeful bowhunter wanting to experience this ultimate calling thrill, a word of caution is in order. Modern-day bulls are wising up. A couple of decades ago, before the glut of well-manufactured diaphragm calls and grunt tubes — along with their full complement of instructional calling tapes and videos — Colorado bowhunter Marv Clyncke and a handful of other serious elk hunters were tooting on homemade calls created from plastic pipes and duping bulls with their manmade sounds. A few hunters even used their own vocal chords to imitate bugling bulls — and a handful still do. But now it seems every elk hunter who heads for the hills packs along a variety of elk calls created for every possible occasion.

Not surprisingly, when the September hills suddenly come alive with elk music — not to mention man-smell — even the most naive bull can soon figure out that something's not quite right. Throw in a near-miss or two as arrows whisper out of the shadows where some vocal "elk" was supposed to be and surprised bulls grow naturally suspicious — and much more cautious.

This doesn't mean bugling won't work. It's just more difficult than it used to be. But properly employed, bugling still provides plenty of hot, nerve-jangling action.

"My experience has shown that the most effective use of the bugle is for locating bulls," says G. Fred Asbell. "One thing I'm fairly sure of is that the success of bugling is dependent on a lot of factors including heavy hunting pressure, the time of year, time of day, the weather, how much natural calling is going on, and how good you are at bugling, to name a few."

As already mentioned, pressured bulls are typically call-shy. But in lightly hunted remote areas, bulls usually are much more talkative and responsive. Common sense dictates how much — or how little — to use your elk bugle.

"When in doubt," Fred advises, "don't bugle. Also, if the elk are already bugling, I keep quiet. I've gone complete seasons without taking my bugle out."

Each time you do call, one of several things will happen. Most often your ringing challenge will be greeted by a mocking woodland silence. But this doesn't mean your call went unheard — or ignored. Some bulls approach silently, simply curious or perhaps looking for companionship. These often are young or sub-trophy bulls who want to check things out before making their presence known. This is especially true if they've been run off by the sharp tines of a grouchy herdmaster with no tolerance for interlopers. Other bulls, for reasons known only to themselves, go about their daily elk business seemingly oblivious to any calling, real or artificial. Still others eagerly bugle back before the echo of your own call bounces back from across the canyon.

When a bull answers, it can be a reflexive or meaningful response. Herd bulls may answer once, then gather up their cows and promptly put distance between themselves and any challenger. Some bulls bugle almost constantly as they move their harems away, as if warning all listeners to steer clear. At times, when surprised or threatened by close-range bugling, they turn to fight. Such occasions may offer you a perfect chance to slip an arrow into the bull's vitals, as was the case with my Wyoming bull mentioned at the start of this chapter.

Keep in mind, bugling not only locates bulls, it sometimes attracts bulls. And when elk respond, you always must be prepared to act and act quickly. Sometimes this means simply ducking behind the nearest blowdown and nocking an arrow; in other instances it means striking out on a cross-country chase as Tim Doud and I did.

Many successful elk hunters often run headlong toward a bugling bull, making no effort to be quiet. Their idea is to get close as quickly as possible before bugling, thus startling the herd bull with a jarring challenge and making him believe a rival is moving in to steal

Dave Holt is one of Colorado's most successful elk hunters. He's collected an impressive number of record-class bulls over the years.

Veteran Tennessee bowhunter Kathy Butt proves elk huntin' isn't only for the guys. She's arrowed several elk, including this 6x5 New Mexico bull.

his cows. Since elk on the move are noisy animals themselves, there is little reason for stealth until the final stages of your approach. Clattering rocks and snapping branches are common elk country sounds. Just avoid talking aloud to a buddy, banging your bow against some boulder, or dropping an aluminum arrow onto rocky ground. Such unnatural woodland sounds will alert every animal within earshot. Also, never forget that while you can fool an elk's eyes and ears, you'll never fool his nose. Always keep the wind in your face or quartering toward you. Otherwise you're just wasting your time and energy. Nothing, absolutely nothing, spooks an elk faster than a snootful of human odor. While masking scents can help, you're doomed to failure if you put your entire faith in them and ignore wind direction.

Perhaps the best time to try bugling is shortly after sunrise, preferably on cool, quiet days. Elk commonly move less when it's hot, preferring to take things easy in some shady spot, often in heavy timber on north-facing slopes. Their thick, insulating hides must make them miserable on hot, sunny days. Don't expect them to exert themselves needlessly just because you're tooting on a bugle, no matter how realistic the sound. Also, windy days put animals on edge, and wind hampers calling since the sounds of your bugle — and any response — will not carry as far as on calm, crisp days. Calling from canyon rims or high ridges is an ideal starting point.

Plan on covering lots of ground during the early morning hours. Stay off the skyline and keep an eye on open mountain parks. Even if the bulls aren't vocal, distant animals may be seen foraging on succulent grasses as they head back to their daytime beds. Bugle from time to time as you walk from spot to spot. Wait and listen. If there's no response, move on and try again. When hunting with a buddy, it's a good idea to keep some distance between you because in rough terrain you may not hear one answering bugle that comes back loud and clear to your buddy listening only a short distance away.

Arizona bowhunter William Wright tagged his one-time world record Yellowstone elk in 1992. The giant bull scored 404 Pope and Young inches.

· Speaking of hunting buddies, teamwork can pay off big time when it comes to bugling up a rutting bull. Since elk have an uncanny knack for pinpointing the exact location of a call and walking to that exact spot, it's a definite advantage to have a bull's attention focused on a bugler while a buddy crouching out ahead of the caller does the shooting. And since some wary bulls tend to hang up just out of bow range, shooters positioned 40 to 50 yards ahead just may end up getting a killing shot. Also, such a setup allows the caller to break branches or rake trees between bugles. Such tactics sometimes are all it takes to drive a hung up bull berserk, luring him even closer. Taking turns calling and setting up for the shot is an excellent two-man tactic for arrowing responsive rutting bulls.

While many bowhunters head back to camp during the midday hours, or at least take things easy, snacking and napping, others persistently walk and call throughout the day, trying to evoke a response from some nearby bull. But when the weather is unusually hot, such tactics likely will cause you to only work up a sweat with nothing to show for the effort. However, it's possible to prod a bull to action during the middle of the day and I know several good elk hunters who walk and call all day long. The choice is yours.

Evenings can be an excellent time to prod a rutting bull into a face-to-face confrontation. Rested and primed for another long night of carousing, bulls often grow vocal and aggressive as the sun dips behind the surrounding peaks. The last hour or so of daylight is ideal for bugling. The main drawbacks with evening hunts are twofold. First, it's common to run out of legal shooting time before luring the bull within arrow range. Second, tracking and recovering arrow-hit bulls is harder in the dark. Another problem during the early season is that untended venison spoils quickly. Unless you're able to promptly locate the carcass and take care of the meat, it's going to sour and you'll miss out on some great meals.

When the elk fall silent and your best calling efforts fail, consider taking a more aggressive approach. Oregon bowhunter Larry D.

Jones, one of the nation's most successful game callers and a frequent hunting buddy of mine, once advised me to try to make bulls respond. He has proved that you can sometimes goad them into action by going into a bugling frenzy. "String bugles together," Larry urges. "Scream. Shriek. Bray. Grunt. Try all the tricks in your calling repertoire." He's seen it work at times when nothing else will. I've watched him in action and know Larry has enough experience under his belt — and enough big antlers on his walls — to give serious elk hunters no reason to doubt him. You may want to keep this in mind as a last ditch bugling possibility.

Here's one final bit of advice about bugling. Although there are any number of excellent commercial calls which can transform most any bugler's best efforts into realistic elk music, remember that a variety is not only the spice of life, but it's best when it comes to bugling rutting bulls. Some callers simply repeat the same bugle time after time, again and again, ad nauseam. These same people often complain that they can't seem to get a bull to come those final few yards necessary to get a good shot. They don't seem to realize that no real bull sounds exactly the same each time he bugles. Neither should you.

For big game hunters used to sitting and waiting in a ground blind or tree stand, still-hunting elk is difficult but far from impossible. Fred Asbell calls it "the most productive method" for two reasons. "First, elk are often here today and someplace else tomorrow — particularly during the rut. I feel that if I'm out there moving with them, my chances are greater. Second, elk are large, highly visible animals when they are moving about. A reasonably sharp-eyed bowhunter can generally spot elk before they spot him." Of course, getting close is the stalker's challenge.

While it's unlikely you'll ever stumble upon an alert herd bull bedded down in thick mountainside brush, and remain undetected long enough to draw and arrow and make a killing shot, you just might get a shooting opportunity simply by moving slowly and quietly through prime elk habitat — as long as the wind doesn't betray you. Take your time. Move your eyes more than your feet. Should you happen to spot a bull browsing nearby, it's definitely possible to stalk close enough if you don't get in a hurry. Even better, try to determine the feeding bull's general direction of travel, then circle ahead and let him come to you. Just remember that where you see one elk it's likely others are nearby. And keep constant tabs on the breeze. Always!

It's quite common to combine still-hunting with bugling and/or cow-calling. Some bowhunters routinely pause to bugle, hoping to prompt a response. Others simply chirp and mew as they walk, listening and watching as they ease through the timber. Cow calls can be especially effective putting nearby animals at ease. Break a limb underfoot. Cow call. Kick a rock loose. Cow call. Such sounds are natural. Use 'em.

Once in New Mexico, guide Mike Ray and I were edging down a well-tracked game trail with the wind in our faces. We suddenly bounced a five-point bull from his sidehill bed. Mike instantly dropped to one knee and cow-called as I quickly nocked an arrow. That bull stopped, turned, and began angling uphill toward us. I eventually missed a 35-yard shot when my arrow clipped an unseen twig, but Mike's reassuring calls had completely relaxed that alarmed bull. I've seen the same results on other occasions. If you spook an animal but it doesn't know for sure what you are, try a cow-call or two. It just might help you fill your elk tag.

This giant non-typical bull was shot by Montana bowhunter Terry Crooks and stands as the state record with an official Pope and Young score of 409 0/8.

Impressive. That one word pretty well sums up the headgear worn by trophy-class elk like this New Mexico bull.

One cow-calling technique involves aggressive cow calls. Some hunters swear that receptive cows can be vocally demanding during the breeding season. Rutting bulls are quickly attracted to these persistently whining, chirping, mewing cows even when more conventional calling methods fail. This cow-calling procedure is not unlike the overly aggressive bugling that Larry D. Jones recommends for rutting bulls. Noted game callers Wayne Carlton and Jerry Peterson, both veteran elk hunters, endorse this special "hot cow" calling method. Calls and instructional tapes are readily available for anyone wanting to give this unusual technique a try. And for those wanting to stick to more conventional cow calling methods, take a look at such foolproof calling devices as the Estrus Squeeze Me cow call from Hunter's Specialties or the Primos Hoochie Mama.

Good quality optics are a must for the serious still-hunter and should be a regular part your own field gear. Any compact, lightweight binoculars will do so long as they provide a bright, clear field of vision. Use them to glass high country parks and open hillsides where elk feed early and late in the day. Check out the shady areas surrounding openings and use binoculars to study that suspicious patch of distant tan or that whitish tree branch along the ridgetop that looks exactly like an elk antler. Always look for parts of animals, not the entire elk. Good binoculars certainly save a lot of needless steps and answer a lot of puzzling questions. Just remember that any time you can see the animal's head, the animal can see any careless movements you might make. I'm convinced that elk have better eyesight than many hunters believe.

Some consistently successful elk hunting veterans swear that backpack bowhunting is one of the best ways to take a big bull. These individuals simply fill their packs with enough grub and gear for several days, then head into the backcountry. Once elk are sighted, the patient hunters dog them at a distance, waiting for an ideal opportunity to close in. Each night they make a cold, quiet camp wherever they happen to be, resuming their dogged pursuit at first light. By shadowing the elk, they're ready to take advantage of any stalking or ambush situation that might arise. It's not for everybody, but it's a technique that works for certain woods-wise bowhunters. Another variation of the backpack bowhunt employs the use of horses or llamas — not just shank's mare — to get into remote elk country. And no one will ever argue that pack animals aren't especially handy once your elk is down.

At the opposite end of the spectrum, tree stands and ground blinds situated along game trails or overlooking mineral licks and wallows can sometimes pay off for the patient bowhunter. Ditto for water holes in dry country such as Arizona's arid terrain. Every year many elk — including some monster bulls — are tagged by stationary bowhunters who opt to try the ol' reliable sit-and-wait bowhunting method. Speaking personally, stalking big bulls is so doggone exciting — and challenging — that I use a stand only as a last resort. But if you lack the stamina, stalking skills, or confidence to hunt elk with both feet on the ground, by all means take up some likely ambush position and settle back to wait for elk to wander by. It happens.

Naturally, bugling and cow-calling, cow-in-heat scents, and even decoys can be part of any ambush hunter's bag of tricks. A handful of elk hunters even swear horn-rattling can work at times to sucker a rutting bull close enough for a killing shot. Nudging elk is yet another option where stands are strategically positioned near escape routes; however, quick shots at running game are risky and should be avoided under normal circumstances.

Oops! No chance for a shot here with part of that pine tree covering the bull's vitals. Besides, he's got you pegged and is about to head for a less congested corner of the woods.

Elk are large, durable animals that can be tough to stop whether hit by a bullet or broadhead. Most frontal shots are sheer folly and any arrows that hit the muscular shoulder area rarely penetrate much past the sharp broadhead. More than one trophy bull has been thusly "vaccinated" — and educated — by such misplaced broadheads early in their lives. Such shots do little damage and wise up bulls in a hurry. Always wait for a broadside shot at a stationary target, aiming for the ribs at a mid-body point behind the shoulder. For the best results, always hold out for the lethal double-lung hit.

Big bulls can take an arrow through the vitals without flinching, although they'll commonly crash away in a blind, brush-busting run. Some savvy bowhunters quickly bugle or cow-call following each shot in an attempt to stop the bull, whether or not the arrow flies true. This trick works at times and can save long tracking jobs — or provide the chance for a follow-up shot. Regardless, always listen carefully if the bull does run out of sight. It's not all that uncommon to hear a mortally wounded bull eventually crash to earth.

As previously noted, elk meat spoils unbelievably fast in hot weather. Thick hides hold in body heat, especially where the carcass is in contact with the ground. Prompt field dressing, skinning, and cooling are necessary if you expect the meat to be prime table fare. Porous game bags placed over each quarter and wrapped around choice cuts will help keep the meat clean and discourage those ever-present early season bees and blowflies. No matter how you look at it, handling a downed elk is hard work. One veteran Colorado guide I know summed it up nicely when he said, "Compared to packing out a big bull, finding and shooting him is a piece of cake!"

Judging Trophy Elk

Monarchs are the largest of all trophy bulls, carrying eight points on each side of their huge racks. Imperial bulls sport seven points to a side while royals have six tines jutting from each antler beam. But no matter what the bull's total number of points or record book score, any mature bull elk legally taken under fair chase rules is a true bowhunting trophy.

To qualify for the P&Y records, a Rocky Mountain elk's antlers must score at least 260 total inches (typical) or 335 inches (non-typical). Included in the final score for typical antlers is the inside spread of the main beams, the length of each main beam and each point, plus four circumference measurements. Any unusual non-typical points are deducted from the total score unless the bull is being measured for the non-typical category. In that case, all abnormal points are added to the other routine measurements. The minimum score for entering a Roosevelt elk in the listings is 225 inches.

Record book bulls generally carry antlers that are four to five feet or more in length with good mass and at least six points to a side. Some big five by five racks have sufficient length and mass to meet Pope and Young Club minimums; however, such bulls are the exception.

"Judging the size of a bull can be difficult in heavy timber," G. Fred Asbell warns. "Often you'll not get the kind of look you'd like to have. Look for mass and look for the 'Y' on the rear of the antlers — often a fifth and sixth point."

Another way to size up a potential trophy is to look at the bull's first two tines. If they extend well out toward the nose and curl up, this is likely an exceptional animal. Remember, too, thick, ivory-tipped antler tines all along the beams are clues that you're looking at a keeper.

Under normal hunting circumstances, you often will have only a moment or two to size up the quality of the bull standing before you. Experience helps, of course, but trust your instincts. A big-antlered bull looks...well, big! And if you have the impression you're looking at a good bull, take the shot. On a recent trophy hunt in Colorado I passed up a good six-by-six bull because he just didn't look big enough. There was little doubt he'd make the record book, but my gut instinct told me not to raise my bow. Not long after passing the shot, I glimpsed and arrowed a bigger bull in thick timber when I sensed he was something special. Indeed he was, officially scoring 342 4/8 Pope and Young points. Again, learn to trust your judgment.

Moose

Classification

The Pope and Young Club recognizes three separate species of North American moose: the Alaska-Yukon moose *(Alces alces gigas)*; the Canada moose *(Alces alces americana and andersoni)*; and the Shiras or Wyoming moose *(Alces alces shirasi)*. These animals, easily the continent's largest deer, are descendants of Siberian moose that traveled across the land bridge to North America more than one million years ago.

Current Distribution

Moose presently range from Alaska across much of Canada and several northern states; however, the Shiras moose is an animal of the Rocky Mountains. Moose hunted in Idaho, Montana, Utah, Washington, Colorado, and Wyoming are all identified as Shiras moose. The moose of other contiguous states and most Canadian provinces are considered by bowhunters to be Canada moose. Moose of Alaska, the Northwest Territories, and the Yukon are all considered to be Alaska-Yukon moose.

Identifying Characteristics

Moose are dark brown animals whose glossy pelage of short, coarse hair may appear black. Their lower legs, eye circles, inner ears, and nostrils are gray-white. Thick-chested and powerful, moose have a stiff neck mane, prominent shoulder humps, and a tapering long-legged body that ends in a stubby tail. Long-faced with a distinctive Roman nose, moose have a floppy "bell" or pendant of loose skin hanging from the chin. Mature bulls grow large, palmated antlers that may span six feet or more and weigh nearly 100 pounds.

Shiras or Wyoming moose, the smallest members of the Alces clan, may stand six feet at the shoulder and weigh up to half a ton. Mature Alaska-Yukon bulls typically stand a foot taller and weigh hundreds of pounds more. Some northland giants weighing 1,800 pounds have been documented. The average size of Canada moose falls somewhere in between the two.

Moose run with a distinctive ground-covering gait and have been clocked at speeds of 45 miles per hour. They also are very strong swimmers. Although not especially vocal animals, they do utter a variety of sounds not unlike domestic cattle. Perhaps the most common sounds are the coughing grunts made by both cows and bulls. During the rut these deep, raspy calls are used to attract mates.

Habitat/Diet

Moose are browsing animals, favoring the new growth from bushes and trees such as fir, birch, aspen, and willows. Moose also seek various sedges and water plants, including water lilies and pondweeds. Food availability dictates the size of any moose's home territory. In times of plenty, moose usually stay within a limited range, perhaps no more than one square mile. The search for browse may prompt a move into new areas, but moose do not usually range far or migrate, per se. During their annual rut, bulls often roam widely in search of willing cows. And in Alaska and mountain terrain, moose may spend summers in higher elevations and return to the lowland thickets and swamps in fall or winter months when snow shrouds the high country.

Senses

All moose have relatively poor eyesight but an exceptional sense of smell, complemented by acute hearing. Like many animals, they tend to overlook stationary hunters, even at very close range; however, a suspicious noise or telltale scent is enough to send them crashing away in a brush-busting flight to safety.

Reproduction

Breeding season often covers a period of several weeks starting in September or October. Rutting bulls are especially aggressive and short-tempered. They have been known to attack man, beast, and even inanimate objects — like motor vehicles — with a blind fury that underscores the need for caution around such large and powerful beasts. Fights for breeding rights are common and sometimes savage, occasionally ending in death.

Cows have a gestation period of between 240 and 250 days. Most calves are born in May or June and weigh about 25 pounds at birth. Cows are extremely protective mothers and may attack any intruder — including man. Calves often remain with their mothers during the first full year of life. Predators, including bears and wolves, take a high toll of young moose.

Life Expectancy

Moose mature fully within the first six years of life, although they continue to grow in size and weight. Cows are generally bred by their third year; young bulls are capable of breeding but often are denied by older bulls. Moose commonly live into their teens and some into their twenties.

Bowhunting Records

The all-time best Shiras moose was killed in Sheridan County, Wyoming, by bowhunter Richard E. Jones in 1987; its official Pope and Young score is 185 6/8. Charles Roy tagged the World Record Canada moose near Cap-Chat, Quebec, in October of 1988; his big bull scores 222 1/8 inches. Dr. Michael L. Cusack tagged the top Alaska-Yukon moose near Bear Creek Alaska, in 1973; the huge bull scores 248 0/8 inches.

Chapter 21

Moose – The Continent's Largest Deer

BELIEVE ME, AT THREE SHORT YARDS a red-eyed rutting moose is an imposing sight. Fortunately, as the bull pushed through the drooping tree branches of the rain-wet fir where I crouched waiting, his full attention was on the young bull he'd been chasing, not me. It wasn't until I quickly drew my bow and focused on a swirl of dark hair just behind his massive shoulder that the surreal apparition towering over me noticed the slight motion and stopped short. But he'd barely swung his broken-antlered head my way when my broadhead-tipped arrow disappeared through his thick chest. The surprised bull jumped sideways, stood a moment as if pondering what had just occurred, then turned and slowly strode back the way he'd come. He didn't make it 35 yards.

"Unforgettable" is one word that springs to mind whenever I recall my point-blank 2002 encounter with that northwestern Montana bull. Even though I'd arrowed my first Shiras bull a decade earlier (with a 40-yard killing shot), and even though I'd later collected P&Y Canada and Alaska-Yukon bulls (with well-placed arrows released at more reasonable ranges of between 15 and 20 yards), no previous moose encounter had been as exciting — or memorable. Of course, in all honesty I have to admit that "unforgettable" applies to most up-close bowhunting encounters with the largest of all North American deer.

Massive, palmated antlers — combined with the impressive bulk of any mature bull — makes a moose one of the most awe-inspiring critters any modern day bowhunter can opt to pursue. And don't let their butt-ugly features and ungainly physical appearance throw you. There's something truly stately and unique about these majestic northland giants. Perhaps that's why the French Canadian woodsmen called them *l'original*. To me it's an appropriate title, an excellent word choice.

Some people wrongly believe these big hombres to be seriously lacking in the brainpower department. Personally, I've never found moose to be as downright dumb as some folks claim, except maybe during the peak of the rut when bulls go ga-ga with the need to breed. Moose are different, yes. They're indifferent, too. But dense, no. Tipping over a browsing bull with a big bore rifle may not present much of a stalking challenge. But try fooling the ears and nose of that same feeding bull by stalking close enough to deliver a well-aimed arrow. That's the kind of one-on-one experience likely to give any disbeliever a newfound respect for these big animals.

As mentioned, rutting bulls behave unpredictably. They've been known to mistake the sounds of someone chopping firewood for rival bulls fighting. And with their less than keen eyesight, bull moose have made improper amorous advances toward domestic livestock, from pack horses to mules to dairy cattle. Getting within near-touching distance of distracted rutting bulls may be duck soup. It can be somewhat foolhardy, too.

Early one mid-September morning, while the guides were busy packing panniers and saddling horses for our long ride from a wilderness elk camp back to trailhead, I snatched up my camera when I heard a lovesick bull grunting in the willows below camp. We'd seen moose almost daily during this week-long Wyoming bowhunt, and I thought it would be neat to get some eleventh hour wildlife photos. Hurrying to the willow-lined creek, I moaned like a hot cow in the throes of estrus. Almost immediately limbs cracked as the bull headed my way. Seconds later a paddlehorn pushed through the screen of willows and stepped into the clearing no more than 30 yards from me. It wasn't until he fixed me with a randy stare — and I could see his neck mane bristling like the quills on the back of an angry porcupine — did it dawn on me that messing around with Mother Nature is sometimes stupid. Stories of bulls flying into a rutting rage and attacking everything from pickup trucks to freight engines came to me in an adrenaline-laced rush.

Though this was a "small" bull with diminutive velvet-covered antlers, he still stood nearly six feet at the withers. And one glance at those long, spindly legs convinced me that even with a headstart I'd be no match for him in a dash for the nearest trees growing half a football field away. All at once taking moose photos was the last thing on my mind.

Exactly how long we stared at each other is anyone's guess. After what seemed to be a lifetime or two, he grunted, turned, and retreated into the willows. I walked weak-kneed back to camp, vowing not

Calling moose during the rut is exciting—and it works! Alex Gouthro of Thunder Bay, Ontario, Canada, is an expert caller and guide who has duped many bulls with his realistic cow talk. A birch-bark call amplifies the manmade moans that imitate a receptive cow moose, carrying the sounds far across the lake's surface.

Walking in the shallows between calls simulates the splashing of a walking cow and adds realism to the calling sounds.

Water poured from the call sounds like a cow urinating in the lake. It's another realistic touch to any calling setup designed to attract rutting bulls.

to repeat such a dumb stunt — at least not unless I was armed with something more appropriate than a 35mm Minolta. I'm just glad he decided I wasn't really his type.

Another time, while manning a video camera on an Alaskan moose hunt with ol' pal Larry D. Jones, I nearly got run down by a giant bull that crashed past me after one of Larry's arrows buried itself in his vitals. The replay of that encounter always elicits gasps and excited comments from television and video viewers. That experience — and the face-to-face staredown with the Wyoming paddlehorn — almost made me swear off wildlife photography and videography. I feel much more comfortable holding my favorite hunting bow than any camera ever made.

Rutting bulls — reeking of urine and red-eyed with lust — are eccentric, unpredictable, cantankerous creatures. But if the thought of easing close to a hulking animal wearing headgear wider than some men are tall doesn't give you pause, the rut is prime time to venture into the wilds and collect a trophy bull — along with

enough memories to last any hunter's lifetime, or at least until your next moose hunting adventure.

Hunting Strategies

Each year some bowhunters successfully still-hunt, stalk, and call moose to within point-blank arrow range. Still other patient bowmen tag bulls from strategically placed tree stands and ground blinds. And a handful actually arrow their moose from drifting canoe and rubber rafts. The point of mentioning such a variety of hunting techniques is to point out one obvious fact here at the very beginning: There's more than one good way to take a trophy bull.

Still another apparent truth regarding "trophy" moose was made by famed archer Howard Hill, who collected his very first bow and arrow moose in 1925. In his book, *Hunting the Hard Way*, Hill recounted his adventures pursuing Canada moose in the Fraser River country of British Columbia. Toward the very end of his hunt, he stalked and shot a "little fat bull" that ran a few yards and toppled over after the broadhead penetrated both lungs. "The one small bull was the only moose that was taken by our party," Hill said, "but it was a great trip. After all, hunting is just that, hunting, and the size of the bag taken is never the first consideration with a true lover of the outdoors." Amen.

Hunting early and late in the day is best no matter which hunting method you may choose. Moose tend to be on the move at daybreak, bed down in thick cover during the midday hours, and then reappear shortly before dusk. During the rut, this daily pattern changes and bulls may be seen on the move throughout daylight hours.

Although some people tend to think of moose as animals of the lowlands, especially the thick, boggy country bordering remote streams, rivers, and lakes, savvy hunters don't overlook likely high country terrain. In parts of Alaska, Canada, and Rocky Mountain states, for example, big bulls often are found hanging out at or near timberline in what some hunters might glance at and dismiss as sheep country. In fact, many large-racked moose will spend the entire summer and early fall near lush highland meadows and grassy plateaus, where constant mountain winds help the animals find relief from hordes of tormenting insects. They move lower when the deepening snows drive them from their alpine homes.

Still-Hunting and Stand Hunting

Bowhunting these high-country monarchs is difficult during the pre-rut. Trying to still-hunt their thick bedding cover or stalk feeding bulls across open alpine pastures is usually futile. I've tried and know just how tough getting close can be. More times than not you'll end up spooking your bull or getting only a brief shooting opportunity, usually at longer ranges than should be seriously considered. Your best bet for success is to spend time glassing early and

late in the day, then setting up an ambush point between the bull's feeding and bedding area and intercepting him as he comes or goes about his daily business. Given a choice, I'd opt to try for him later on. Calling a rutting bull close is one of moose hunting's biggest thrills. And even later in the year, after the passion of the rut wanes and snow clogs the mountain valleys, moose typically are much easier to locate and stalk in their lowland feeding and bedding areas.

I first learned the value of moose hunting patience while prowling Wyoming's Tetons during an early September archery-only season. Each long day started and ended in the saddle. Countless wilderness miles were covered afoot and on horseback. But over the week of hard summertime hunting for a trophy-class bull, I ended up with only two iffy shooting opportunities. But later, during a post-rut November bowhunt, my chance for a big Shiras bull finally came one snowy, frigid afternoon.

A dark shape ghosted past from right to left. I twisted around, peering through the gently falling snow for an opening in the mountainside brush, trying to judge the bull's bobbing rack. The moose was only 35 yards away and broadside.

I don't really remember bring my 70-pound bow to full draw. I do remember concentrating on the hollow behind the bull's muscular shoulder. And then the aluminum arrow was streaking away. There was a sickening *click* as the shaft clipped an unseen twig and deflected to the left. *Thunk!* The bull lunged forward a dozen steps and stopped in a willow jungle. I snapped another arrow onto the string without taking my eyes off the bull. I knew I'd hit him — but where? I came to full draw again and waited for him to step clear.

Downhill, the big bull was swinging his head, checking his surroundings. Fully alert, he showed absolutely no effects of my first arrow. I focused on his ribcage but dared not risk a shot until he was clear of the willows. And then he was on the move again, quartering away at about 40 yards. I swung with him and released just as he stepped into the clearing.

The arrow's fluorescent green nock and brilliant red/yellow

(Above and below) Bush planes can easily ferry hunters and their gear into the heart of prime moose country, saving days of overland travel through dense timberlands. Law prohibits hunting during the same day flights are made.

fletching made following the flight of my arrow easy — and this time no unnoticed branch altered its course. It plunked solidly into the big animal at midbody, angling down and forward. The moose bulldozed through the deep snow in a brush-flattening rush, angling away downslope. Seconds later all was once again quiet on the mountainside except for the whispering snowflakes and thudding of my heart.

That Wyoming bull's four-foot rack sported 20 points and landed solidly in the Pope and Young Club listings. And while such recognition is nice, more satisfying was the memory of the stalk and the stick-to-it-iveness that resulted in a fine bowhunting trophy.

Stalking bowhunters must always watch the wind direction and where they place their boots. As already noted, moose have above average hearing — and one whiff of man-smell will end any stalk in a heartbeat. The key is to take your time, ease ahead one quiet step at a time, move ever so slowly downwind until the

The author shot this record book Alberta bull on a fly-in hunt. The big moose fell less than 75 yards from the lakeshore.

Watercraft is the normal mode of transportation for hunters and guides around lakes and waterways.

unsuspecting bull looms dead ahead. This is no easy trick in thick brush or in the mucky, boot-sucking terrain so common in prime moose habitat.

But if stalking is not your bag, or if you're reluctant to head off into the vast wilds where moose are commonly found, stand hunting can bring about similar results. In certain spots — near well-tracked stream crossings, over wallows, mineral licks, or at the intersection of clearly defined game trails — waiting can pay off for the patient bowhunter. It's a natural for the experienced whitetail hunter who is used to spending long, stationary hours in a tree stand or ground blind.

Float or Fly-In Strategies

More adventuresome souls should check out the package deals provided by some Alaskan and Canadian outfitters who offer float trip hunts through the heart of prime moose country. Inflatable rafts or other watercraft, boats, or canoes simply drift silently with the current while hunters keep a wary eye peeled for moose feeding among streamside willows or in the shallow waters near shore. If the rut is underway, floating hunters often stop and cow-call from gravel bars or sandy stretches of beach, hoping to lure nearby bulls from dense cover.

In Alaska, I've watched moose simply stand and stare dumbly at an approaching raft until we were well within bow range. In other instances they've splashed away at the first glimpse of our drifting inflatables. Regardless of their reaction, you should keep in mind that curiosity sometimes kills moose as well as cats. Always be prepared. The only no-no in drift hunting is shooting a swimming bull, an unethical if not outright illegal practice.

Hunting lakes can be deadly effective, too. Boats are an efficient, silent method of covering prime moose country. Steer clear of long shoreside stretches of thick timber; moose prefer willow and alder patches near grassy flats. They also like sun-drenched marshy areas along feeder streams where aquatic vegetation grows in abundance. Always check out lake inlets and outlets, too. And on warm late summer days don't forget that bulls sometimes can be seen cooling themselves in the lake shallows.

On one Ontario fly-in bowhunt with Alex Gouthro, one of the province's top moose guides and callers, I watched Alex pull bulls great distances across open water with his lakeside calling techniques. His normal calling routine goes something like this:

After beaching the boat and allowing things to quiet down, Alex first slogs through the sandy shallows in his hip boots, high-stepping to imitate the sounds made by a moose walking in water. He then utters a series of mournful cow calls, using a handmade birchbark megaphone to project the sounds. As a coup de grace, he scoops up lake water in his birch call and allows it to trickle slowly out, simulating a cow or rival bull urinating in the lake. Adding extra enticements, Alex will back into the brush and break limbs, scraping tree trunks with a scapula or boat paddle — creating noise not unlike a real bull polishing his antlers. I watched as one riled up bull emerged from the treeline on the opposite shore, paced briefly, then plunged into the water and swam directly to where Alex had set up. Seeing is definitely believing!

Lakes and rivers can be good, highly efficient glassing points, too. Bulls bedded or feeding on nearby ridges sometime may be spotted from below. The glint of sunlight on large antlers or the black hulk of the animals themselves can give them away even from a mile or more. Once the surrounding landmarks are noted, the boat is beached and the stalk begins. Since uphill stalks through heavy cover are generally a waste of time, the ideal stalk involves circling around the ridge or hillside, climbing high, and coming out above the moose, then working slowly and quietly downslope. It's perhaps the toughest way to bowhunt moose — but it can work!

Fly-in drop camp moose hunts offer yet another possibility, despite the fact some unethical guides and hunters have abused airplane use in finding and shooting trophy bulls. In truth, legal aircraft scouting by responsible, ethical hunters is one of the best ways to locate big-racked bulls and check out their home territory. Hiring a bush pilot to ferry you and a hunting buddy into the back country can be a worthwhile investment of time and money. The problem that faces most fly-in hunters is not locating one or more stalkable bulls; the problem is handling hundreds of pounds of moose meat once the bull is down.

Dr. Dave Samuel stalked and shot this P&Y Shiras bull during a Utah moose hunt in 2002.

Only when you walk up to a dead bull can you truly appreciate the size of these woodland giants. Actually, field-dressing and packing out any moose is at best a two-man job, unless the hunter happens to dress in blue, wear a cape, and has a big red "S" emblazoned on his chest. And when it comes to getting the meat from the kill site back to camp or to some shoreside pick-up point, you'll quickly realize that you're facing dozens of backbreaking pack treks. Often through thick brush. Over uneven terrain.

This is where pack horses or mules are worth their weight in solid gold broadheads. In some hunting camps, especially in the Rocky Mountain states where Shiras bulls are hunted, livestock — even pickup trucks — may be used with little fuss, muss, or bother. In the case of that Montana bull mentioned in this chapter's opening paragraphs, a single telephone call arranged for an area outfitter to meet me at trailhead with two pack horses. That call — and the packing fee — saved me and my hunting companions a day or more of backbreaking labor, plus the risk of meat spoilage.

I've always been lucky. Another bull I arrowed dropped in the trail less than 100 yards from where my horse was tied. An Alberta bull went down 50 yards from a lakeshore. An Alaskan giant dropped 100 uphill yards from a river. Such good fortune makes packing meat a relative snap. But more often than not Lady Luck won't smile on you and you'll quickly discover — as have so many moose hunters before you — that shooting a bull is the easy part. This is especially true if the weather happens to be warm, and prompt skinning and cooling is absolutely essential in order to salvage the tasty moose venison.

Savvy fly-in hunters should make arrangements with their pilots to check on them from time to time throughout the hunt. A pre-set signal, such as draping a rain slicker over a bush or tent, denotes the need to land and ferry meat back to civilization. Such attention to detail can spell the difference between good table fare and a pile of soured, inedible, and maggoty meat. Only greenhorn moose hunters ever head into the back country without knowing in advance exactly how they'll transport the antlers, cape, and meat — quickly and efficiently — after the bull is on the ground.

Speaking of meat, bears and other predators may pose a problem

M. R. James tagged this Wyoming bull on a November bowhunt in the Teton Mountains.

to any successful moose hunter. Gut piles, cached meat, or the carcass itself may quickly attract hungry bruins. Some hunters will hang a shirt, jacket, or other clothing item nearby, relying on the garment's man-scent to keep hungry creatures at bay. Others urinate or spray bear repellent around the meat stash. Such preventative measures can help; however, prudent hunters always exercise caution each time they approach a kill site. No moose ever lived that is worth a bowhunter being mauled — or worse — by a possessive bear.

Despite their bulk, even the biggest bulls quickly succumb to a well-placed arrow and sharp broadhead. As with any big game animal, the primary aiming point should always be the heart-lung area located immediately behind the front shoulder. Shots at running moose — unless they are already wounded — are foolish.

Blood trailing any wounded bull calls for appropriate caution. Hard-hit animals often bed down when the first effects of an arrow

Dave Holt stalked and shot this Shiras bull in north central Wyoming during a September bowhunt.

are felt; however, any wounded bull capable of holding its head erect should never be approached recklessly. Don't hesitate to release one or more follow-up arrows from a prudent but effective shooting distance to keep the bedded animal anchored.

Regardless of your chosen moose hunting method and the outcome of that adventure, it's a safe bet to predict that a single moose hunt will not slake your thirst for this singular kind of bowhunting excitement. The mere sight of a grunting Roman-nosed bull striding ever closer — his hackles raised below brush-polished antlers that seemingly float toward you like some terrible specter — is one sight you'll never forget. Guaranteed!

Judging Trophy Moose

Giant moose, no matter which of the three recognized species, have an exceptional antler spread complemented by heavy beams, huge palms, and numerous points. Unlike the scoring of all other antlered game, only with moose is the greatest spread measurement included in the official score.

In addition to the spread, the number of normal points, the width of the palms, length of the palms (including brow points), and one circumference measurement of each beam base are added together. Once any differences in symmetry are subtracted, you'll arrive at a final score.

To qualify for the Pope and Young listings, Alaska-Yukon bulls must have a minimum score of 170; Canada moose must score at least 135; and Shiras moose must score a minimum of 125.

Whatever species of moose you may choose to hunt, there's no doubt about it when a true trophy-class bull steps out of the willows and turns his massive rack in your direction. But any bowhunter who frets about the size of any bull's antlers — and whether or not it will make the record book — is too wrapped up in numbers. Any big-antlered moose is worthy of your complete respect, no matter its official score. And certainly any moose taken by a bowhunter is a trophy animal.

Montana bowman Scott Koelzer has shot several P&Y bulls in British Columbia.

Caribou

Classification

The Pope and Young Club currently recognizes five species of caribou. These include mountain caribou *(Rangifer tarandus mountanus)*, barren ground and central barren ground caribou *(R. tarandus granti)*, woodland caribou *(R. tarandus caboti)*, and Quebec/Labrador caribou *(R. tarandus caribou)* from the two eastern Canadian provinces identifying this species.

Current Distribution

Mountain caribou range through western Canada's mountainous terrain above and below timberline. Barren ground caribou are found from Alaska across northern Canada's tundra and prairies, while central barren ground caribou are found east of the MacKenzie River in parts of the Northwest Territories and Alberta. Woodland caribou are inhabitants of Newfoundland and its surrounding areas, while Quebec/Labrador caribou are found within those provincial boundaries. A few caribou live in northern states, although bowhunters must travel to Canada or Alaska to hunt these high-antlered animals whose ancestors crossed the Bering land bridge from Asia about one million years ago. In Europe and Asia these same animals are called reindeer.

Identifying Characteristics

Gregarious animals, both male and female caribou grow antlers; however, bulls' headgear is generally much larger than the spindly racks worn by does. Big caribou bulls may weigh as much as 600 pounds, stand four to five feet at the shoulder, and exceed seven feet in length. Average bulls and cows are smaller in size and weight. The barren ground and mountain caribou usually are larger than their relatives.

Coloration varies with mountain caribou regarded as the darkest of their race. Body color is often a rich brown, although many caribou are gray-brown. Neck capes range from a startling white to dirty gray. White hair typically grows around the muzzle, inside the stubby ears, on the rump patch, underbelly, and above each hoof.

The antlers of caribou are the largest in proportion to body size of any species, some beams reaching five feet in length. Antlers are bifurcated, palmated, and sport numerous tines. Bez points sweep forward over the face above the brow tines, which may be palmated vertically into one or two "shovels" (most commonly a spike and a single "shovel" compose the brow tine configuration). Woodland caribou have the smallest antlers of the five recognized trophy categories.

Splayed hooves are round and concave, ideal for tundra travel. Ankle bones click audibly as the animals walk. Nomadic and migratory, caribou wander widely across their range, almost constantly searching for available food. They can run short distances of speeds topping 30 mph; however, alarmed caribou quickly fall into a ground-covering gait easily maintained for lengthy periods of time.

Habitat/Diet

Ruminants, caribou are herd animals with a preference for lichens or reindeer moss, although certain grasses, plants, and shrubs — including dwarf willow and birch — are a part of their daily diet, where available. They fill their paunches as they feed on the move. Later, during cud-chewing rest periods, they regurgitate the food for rechewing and reswallowing. Adult animals have six incisors, 12 premolars, and 12 molars for a total of 32 teeth. Like other members of the deer family, they have no teeth in the front of the upper jaw.

Caribou herds are found from heavily forested timberlands to treeless tundra expanses, from above timberline to stunted, brushy hillsides of sub-arctic prairieland. Powerful swimmers, they easily cross lakes and rivers during their wanderings and are well insulated against the bitter cold of northern winters.

Reproduction

Breeding season occurs in October as bulls begin to collect harems and battle rivals for dominance. Fights may be violent and death sometimes occurs when the combatants' antlers lock or one bull is able to puncture an opponent's body with a sharp tine. Generally, however, these fights are aggressive pushing and shoving bouts which end when one bull tires and flees. Calves are born during May and June. The brown-coated, unspotted newborns weigh between 10 and 20 pounds and are able to follow their mothers within a few hours of their birth.

Senses

Caribou rely mainly on their eyes and nose to detect danger. On the open tundra they will detect moving objects and often circle downwind in an effort to identify by scent what their eyes have seen. Stationary objects are generally overlooked. Their hearing is adequate but the least important of the self-preservation senses.

Life Expectancy

Caribou often live 10 to 12 years in the wild; efforts to raise caribou in zoos have met with little success.

Caribou meat is tasty, a fact attested to by thousands of north country natives who depend on caribou as their primary source of red meat. As with any game animal bowhunted during warm weather months, however, prompt attention and adequate field care are necessary to prevent spoilage and waste. And do not be surprised if your caribou bloats immediately after death. Intestinal gases cause the bloating; greenish stomach matter often flows from the mouth and nostrils.

Bowhunting Records

The best-ever mountain caribou was killed in the MacKenzie mountains of the Northwest Territories by bowhunter Chuck Adams in 1995; its score is 413 6/8. The number one barren ground caribou was arrowed near Lake Clark, Alaska, in 1984, by Dennis Burdick; its score is 448 6/8. The best central barren ground bull scores 420 6/8 and was shot by Al Kuntz near Hungry Lake in the Northwest Territories in 1994. Bowhunter Carol Ann Mauch killed the World Record Quebec/Labrador caribou in 1984 on a Tunulik River hunt; her bull scores 434 0/8. Dempsey Cape's 1966 Victoria River, Newfoundland, bull continues to top the woodland caribou category with a score of 345 2/8 inches.

Chapter 22
Caribou — Northland Nomads

MY HEART LEAPT as if jolted by an electric cattle prod. Just when I'd almost given up ever getting a shot, the huge woodland caribou I'd been stalking turned and walked directly toward me.

Seventy yards. Sixty. Fifty. Forty.

The monstrous stag loomed closer. I simply waited, crouched in the alders, holding my breath and grasping my bow with a white-knuckled death grip. This was easily the biggest woodland 'bou I'd ever seen, dwarfing his two traveling companions — each a record book bull that most bowhunters would be happy to tag. Minutes earlier I'd blown a chance at this stag-of-a-lifetime when I'd tried to draw with one of his buddies feeding less than 10 yards away. My slow, cautious movements instantly spooked the nearest stag and all three alarmed animals pounded off in different directions.

When the giant had finally stopped on the Newfoundland skyline maybe 90 yards away, I figured it was all over. But after standing and staring my way for several minutes, seemingly puzzled over what had boogered his comrades, he turned and started back my way. The other two stags were somewhere behind me. He seemed anxious to rejoin them.

Thirty yards. Twenty-five. Twenty.

Then the great stag stepped into a narrow shooting lane within the alders. I raised and drew my bow in one practiced movement. He caught the motion and turned to his left, striding toward the thick brush. But he was under 20 yards and I was already locked on him, holding low on his massive chest. Then my arrow's red and yellow fletching flashed to and through the sweet spot behind the stag's heavy shoulder. Instantly I knew I'd just collected the trophy

Caribou are powerful swimmers. Lakes and rivers present no barrier for migrating herds. While it's unethical to shoot swimming animals, bowhunters often set up ambushes at natural crossings.

M. R. James arrowed this giant woodland caribou stag during a Newfoundland bowhunt several years ago. It's the bull described in the opening paragraphs and continues to rank near the top of the P&Y records.

of any bowhunter's lifetime.

Feast or famine. Fun or frustration. These words pretty well sum up caribou hunting. These nomadic northland animals, although often quite visible and stalkable, can drive a bowhunter nuts. Make a good stalk and you can end up with a gimme shot, as I did with my giant woodland 'bou back in '99. At that time he ranked fourth all-time in the Pope and Young records. Schedule your hunt right and you just might find a great trophy and on certain days find yourself surrounded by hundreds — perhaps thousands — of caribou. Hit it wrong by a day or two, and you can spend a full week or more staring at empty tundra.

Another perfect example comes to mind. Back in 1990 G. Fred Asbell and I traveled to northern Quebec to chase caribou and celebrate turning 50 (we were both born in southern Illinois in 1940 and grew up less than a two-hour's drive apart). We arrived by float plane and found the riverside camp teeming with migrating animals. It was an awesome, unforgettable sight. The next day Fred and I each shot bulls near a river crossing where all we had to do was set up in the willows and settle down to wait. None of the other bowhunters in camp bothered to shoot bulls that first morning. With so many animals around, "Why hurry?" was their understand-

able attitude. But by the end of that first evening the migration flow had slowed to a mere trickle. And by the following day only a straggler or two could be seen on the nearby hillsides. Abruptly, hunting had gone from a duck soup feast to a caribou hunter's ration of bread and water. Although we eventually filled our second tags with record book bulls (mine fell on the final day of a five-mile inland hike from our boat), it wasn't easy.

Caribou hunting, in truth, is seldom easy. People who strike it rich during the usual September migrations often return home with the wrong idea. A few even incorrectly state that caribou are stupid animals. But more often than not, these folks simply haven't actually hunted caribou; they've shot caribou.

Sometimes shooting a huge bull can be downright simple. All you really have to do is hunker down in the willows near a well-used river crossing, as Fred and I did. When the swimming bulls emerge from the water and pause briefly to shake themselves off there on the rocky shoreline, you release a well-aimed shaft. Voila! Instant success. Well, that's not caribou hunting; that's caribou shooting and there's a big difference. Ask anyone who's spent long hours, perhaps days, duck-walking and belly-crawling over rocks and slogging across soggy tundra just to get closer to some distant big-racked bull. Or better yet, try it for yourself and make up your own mind.

Regarding their intelligence — or lack thereof — my ol' pal Asbell astutely commented, "I've heard them called stupid, but I don't agree with that. I don't think that can be said of any animal that survives in the Arctic, where big growly things with huge teeth and hungry bellies prowl. Caribou are simply on a different wave length, as they say. They are quite different from whitetail deer, which is, I guess, the bowhunter's most common frame of reference. And they just don't always do things quite like other animals do things, but that does not make them stupid or easy."

To my way of thinking, all species of caribou are tailor-made for bowhunters. They're truly magnificent big game animals, beautiful and plentiful, yet totally mobile and unpredictable. Moderately skittish yet eminently stalkable, caribou are a worthy test for the still-hunter, since getting within 30 yards or so on the open tundra is challenging — but far from impossible. They can be hunted solo or with a knowledgeable guide. And unlike bowhunts for sheep, goats, or the great bears of much of Canada and Alaska, the price tag of a caribou hunt is usually much more affordable for the average hunter.

Even so-so bulls will likely appear big to any bowhunter used to looking through his sight window at whitetails or mule deer. Dave Holt, who has personally collected more trophy-class horns and antlers than many hunters will see during their lifetime, calls judging caribou "more difficult than judging pronghorns." He confessed that after his first caribou hunt, he'd been fooled by the racks of the animals he shot; they were good bulls but hardly great caribou trophies. "Although I took my time and looked over dozens of animals before releasing an arrow, I should have waited and been more selective," Dave admitted. "After I filled my tags, I saw some huge bulls that made my trophies look small."

Caribou antlers, to me, are among the most breathtaking trophies available anywhere. Their length and spread are commonly measured in feet, not inches. And believe me, it takes discipline and self-control not to become all weak-kneed and trembly by the mere sight of an approaching white-maned bull. Those long, upswept antlers sprouting like tree branches against the north country sky are awesome. It was G. Fred Asbell who summed up the caribou quite nicely with these insightful words.

"I consider caribou the most spectacular animal I've hunted with bow and arrow. With his towering, heavily palmated antlers and his snowy-white campe, the caribou — more than any other animal on the face of the earth — can honestly be called spectacularly beautiful. You might even want to call him majestic. I've seen giant-antlered caribou bulls silhouetted in the evening sunset on glacier-topped mountains that made me positive God had purposely given them such a magnificent crown and put them up there, on a throne high above the rest of the world, and intended them to be king of the Arctic tundra."

Hunting Strategies

Glassing and stalking big-antlered bulls are the basic elements of most any successful caribou bowhunting adventure.

The late Dr. C. Randall Byers, former records chairman of both the Pope and Young and Boone and Crockett Clubs, shot this huge mountain 'bou on a bowhunt with G. Fred Asbell.

Remember, these animals are wanderers — here today and usually someplace else tomorrow. Locating them is your first challenge, and a good way to do this is to find some ridge or other high point, settle back with your binoculars and start scanning the distant hills. But don't spend too long in one spot. Caribou will be on the move, and you should move, too. A change of perspective — even involving relatively short distances — can open up new vistas unseen from a single glassing point. Mornings and evenings are ideal times to locate feeding 'bou, but it's also possible to glimpse grazing or bedded, cud-chewing bulls at any time throughout the long daylight hours. Once the animals are spotted, it's time to figure out how to close the distance. Just beware of sharp-eyed cows; these old matriarchs commonly are the self-appointed guardians of caribou herds.

Another effective, popular way to find animals is to travel the rivers and lakes by boat, always scanning the shoreline and surrounding hills for visible game. A few weak-willed "hunters" have yielded to temptation and shot swimming bulls. Also, some lazy "guides" use power boats to haze swimming caribou to where their clients are waiting hidden on the shore. But both unsporting practices are unethical, if not downright illegal, and all bulls taken in such unscrupulous fashion are ineligible for entry in the Pope and Young Club records. Rightfully so! However, boats properly used to ferry bowhunters to and from hunting areas — or to cover large chunks of remote northlands real estate in search of stalkable bulls — can be a godsend in any caribou camp with nearby waterways. Scouting by air on the way to camp is yet another effective method of finding good bulls.

Three of the most viable options are fly-in, horseback, and float-trip hunts. In once case you'll pay a charter fee to be dropped off by bush plane in the heart of prime caribou country; in the other you'll drift-hunt along a river meandering through likely caribou habitat, or ride horses into the mountain foothills in search of nomadic bulls. Regardless, all these options typically involve the spot-and-stalk hunting technique so common to most successful caribou hunting, including Newfoundland hunts for woodland

G. Fred Asbell stalked and arrowed this big mountain caribou bull during a September hunt.

Stalking bedded caribou on the open tundra can be difficult, but patience pays. Use all available cover to get within good arrow range.

Because caribou live in such remote country, hunters generally travel in float planes to reach distant hunting camps. Beavers and Otters are the planes of choice for most caribou outfitters.

stags. These island animals are the smallest antlered of the five recognized caribou species and do not really migrate, especially in the vast numbers common to other species. Finding, stalking, and arrowing stags moving across the muskeg is likewise a matter of glassing and stalking — with a pinch of skill and patience thrown into the mix.

Yet another possibility involves driving — or nudging — caribou. I know of several instances where bowhunters have waited until companions worked into position and then pushed bulls past the hidden hunters. This seems to work best where possible escape routes pass through natural bottlenecks in the undulating tundra terrain. Two of my hunting buddies — Montana bowmen Chuck Williams and Mike Wheeler — saw this nudging ploy work to perfection in the Territories. Setting up on the point of a rocky island where alarmed bulls often fled before swimming to safety on the mainland, Chuck and Mike waited while their guide circled inland and let a small band of bachelor bulls see him approaching. Moments later Mike downed a fleeing record book candidate at only 10 yards. And although I've taken part in 'bou drives as both a driver and shooter, I enjoy stalking caribou too much to devote much time to this particular hazing technique.

Stalking and Ambushing

My initial spot-and-stalk caribou took place over two decades ago in early August just south of Prudhoe Bay, Alaska. At that particular time of year it never really gets dark, although a kind of twilight settles over the land in the early morning hours when the summer sun slides briefly behind some far mountains. At such times it's possible to glass for caribou 24 hours per day, and the hunting opportunities are limited only by your physical endurance. I soon learned it's easy to wear yourself out chasing after distant bulls. Long hikes over the springy, uneven tundra while wearing ankle-fit hip boots and a backpack — filled with the day's grub and foul weather gear — can sap the strength of most any bowhunter. I quickly discovered that hunting smart, not continually, is the key.

Keep in mind, too, that early each hunting season the swarming clouds of ever-present insects can drive caribou to high, windy ridges where they seek relief from their biting, droning tormentors. Mountain snow patches can be a magnet, too, drawing concentrations of animals seeking comfort from both pesky bugs and summer heat. And don't overlook nearby alpine meadows and bowls. Caribou commonly feed and bed in and near such spots, especially where lush grasses and sedges abound. Look for bulls on high, open points where they have a clear view of the surrounding terrain.

The endless hordes of summer insects, at times, can drive caribou — or the unprepared bowhunter — to the brink of madness. I've watched tormented bulls suddenly tear off across the tundra, running pell-mell perhaps a mile or more, only to spin and come dashing back, then stick their heads smack in a clump of dwarf willow seeking to protect their eyes and nostrils from the swarming bug clouds. They sometimes will stand head down, stamping their feet, seemingly oblivious to everything except finding temporary relief from the infernal winged pests. Obviously, such head-in-the-bush situations can work to any nearby stalker's advantage, if the bowhunter can move close enough to take the shot before the bull launches into another bug-crazed dash. On one Alaskan bowhunt, I watched my Alabama hunting buddy Merrill Jones stalk and arrow a good bull in exactly that fashion. Another time I dropped a bull that I'd stalked and all but given up on after he bolted and tore off in a vain attempt to escape the swarming bugs surrounding him in dark, undulating clouds. He high-stepped it a good half mile before wheeling back my way, slowing to a head-down walk just as he passed within 20 yards of where I huddled next to a moss-covered boulder. Like most bowhunters, I normally hate the bothersome tundra bugs — but at certain times they can be a valuable ally and become almost bearable.

Stalking bedded bulls is difficult but not impossible, especially in rolling or broken country. Caribou are sound sleepers, and it's possible to quietly walk up on a lone bull that has dozed off; however, where several animals have bedded down together, chances are not all of the caribou will be asleep at the same time. Slipping close without being spotted by one or more sets of watchful eyes is a true stalking challenge. Where possible, remaining completely out of sight — and keeping only the tops of the bedded animals' antlers in view during your approach — is best.

As previously mentioned, sit-and-wait hunting techniques will work during the migration when thousands of restless animals are on the move. Also, constructing a blind or hiding among boulders or in brush near natural funnels — or even overlooking a natural mineral lick — can pay off big-time for the patient bowhunter.

Regardless of how you choose to hunt, always watch the wind. Whether stalking or waiting in ambush, you'll be in big trouble if you disregard any swirling breeze that might carry your telltale scent toward nearby bulls. In heavily hunted areas, the caribou will most likely bolt and gallop away at the first whiff of man-danger. And even if they've not been pressured, suspicious, scent-alerted animals commonly circle you at a distance, well out of good bow range, using their eyes and ears to confirm your presence. Some veteran caribou hunters insist that these alarmed animals can secrete a warning scent from their hoof glands, a scent that will spook other any other animals passing that spot. While I have not personally seen this happen with caribou, I have witnessed the delayed reaction warning system work while deer hunting, and I have no reason to believe that it doesn't happen.

Speaking of the wind, I personally favor windy days for stalking caribou. Not only does the wind help keep the bugs teeming around eyes and ears to a mere zillion per cubic inch of air space, but the rustling willow or birch leaves, or the sound of the wind itself sweeping across the open tundra, will mask any inevitable noises you'll make as you slip within arrow range.

After the Shot

Arrow-hit caribou are not especially tough to put down, although they tend to run until they drop. Also, in the case of a marginal hit, they may cover quite a distance before finally folding or bedding. In open country hunting situations, keeping a wounded animal in sight is not uncommonly difficult. One exception is in boggy, wooded areas such as those found in Newfoundland or in the alder thickets and willow jungles of Alaska and certain parts of Canada. Blood trailing across wet, swampy terrain is always difficult. Whenever possible, it's best to keep any arrowed bull in sight until he goes down for keeps or until a follow-up arrow can be delivered. And in this wild land shared by hungry wolves and bears, leaving game animals or meat caches unattended overnight is asking for trouble.

In early season hunts — when the tasty caribou venison is prime — special care should be given to both antlers and meat to prevent spoilage. It's a good idea to pack along lightweight game bags to store unboned quarters and choice cuts. Skinning and cooling always should take place as quickly as possible during warm weather hunts. Also, the velvet should be stripped from the antlers or the antler preserved through injections of formaldehyde or some other preservative. Otherwise you'll end up with a smelly rack that no one, including your favorite taxidermist, is going to want to get near, much less touch.

Because of their size, caribou are too much for a lone hunter to pack out whole. Quartering the carcass or boning out the meat before backpacking the venison to camp are common options. If pack horses or power boats are handy, the chore is not especially difficult for two men to handle. And I've seen some hardy Indian guides deftly skin a bull, bone all of the edible meat, wrap it in the

Dwight Schuh stalked and shot this central barren ground caribou bull during a late summer hunt in the Northwest Territories.

caribou hide, and pack everything out in a single trip, leaving the hunter to carry the antlers and cape — a necessary task that any successful bowhunter welcomes.

Big racks may pose a problem on certain fly-in trips where air cargo space is at a premium. Splitting the skull of a trophy bull makes for easy transport; however, it immediately makes the animal ineligible for entry in the record books. Paying for excess baggage is an option although this can be costly, especially if the airline charges by the square inch rather than by the pound. Savvy hunters check out such details well in advance of booking their air travel. Outfitters and guides — along with airline personnel — can aid in planning and arranging details for shipping antlers and meat or getting the trophy rack and cape to an area taxidermist.

Keep in Mind

Trying to catch up to moving caribou is usually an exercise in frustration. Feeding animals can easily outdistance a stalking bowhunter. Your best bet is to determine their general direction of travel and work around to intercept them as they pass by. Since caribou often feed into the wind, be careful to avoid being scented while working into an ambush position.

If a herd approaches your hiding spot, don't get impatient. Big bulls may be bringing up the rear. Waiting and watching sometimes can pay off with a shot at a true trophy animal. More than one antsy caribou hunter has shot a big bull only to have a big-racked monster stroll into view seconds later. And one additional plus is the fact that bulls moving in a herd are not as alert as when they're alone or in small groups.

Mobility can be the key to any successful caribou hunt. One stretch of tundra can be completely devoid of animals while just over the mountain thousands of 'bou could be filing past. Unless a hunter can move quickly from one locale to another — either by shank's mare, horseback, boat, or aircraft — chances of tagging a trophy bull are somewhat limited. Always make plans accordingly.

Finally, the annual caribou migration is a large-scale, long-

(Left) Dr. Dave Schrody traveled from Iowa to Newfoundland to tag this giant woodland stag. He was hunting the same area where the author shot his own huge 'bou.

(Below) Dave James took his first caribou by glassing the feeding bull from a ridge and then stalking across a valley until within 25 yards. His Indian guide, Leon, watched the stalk and obviously approves of the result.

distance trek that sends tens of thousands of fidgety animals moving along ancient trails used by countless generations of caribou. But timing your hunt to coincide with this restless surge is chancy at best. One or two days, much less a week or two, can make the difference between hunting feast or famine. There are numerous early hunting areas in both Canada and Alaska that contain good populations of huntable animals. Given a choice between gambling on locating migrating bulls or stalking them across their summer range, I'll opt for the latter option almost every time.

Judging Trophy Caribou

Complicated. That one word pretty well sums up evaluating and scoring trophy-class bulls. It's easy for first-time caribou hunters — and even some veterans — to misjudge trophy racks. Additionally, more measurements are required with caribou than in scoring any other North American big game animal.

So exactly what does it take for a bull to make the record book? Look for mature racks that consist of four outstanding features: brow points having long, many-pointed, vertical palms or "shovels"; similar-appearing bez points (pronounced "bay" points) located just above the brow's shovels; long, rear-projecting spikes (commonly called "back-scratchers") near the middle of each antler beam; and thickly palmated beam tips with numerous long points jutting skyward.

Noteworthy is the fact that there is no such thing as an abnormal point on any caribou antler. Further, any projection at least one-half inch in length (providing it's longer than it is wide) is deemed a measurable point. In all other antlered species, scoreable points must be at least one inch in length.

All five recognized caribou species are scored in identical fashion. The greatest tip-to-tip spreads are recorded, but this supplementary data doesn't figure in the final score. The rack's inside spread, number of points, length of each beam, brow point, bez point, and rear point are tallied along with the width of each brow palm and top palm. Also, the length of the two longest top points and four circumference measurements also are recorded. Finally, all these credits are totaled — and differences in symmetry subtracted — to determine a bull's final score. Whew! Although caribou racks aren't really as difficult to score as it may seem, the process is lengthy and more time consuming than taping and scoring any other antlered species.

For entry into the Pope and Young records, Quebec/Labrador and barren ground caribou must score at least 325 inches. Central barren ground and mountain caribou must score at least 300. The minimum for woodland caribou is 220 inches.

Cougar

Classification

North America's largest, unspotted, long-tailed cat goes by a wide variety of names. Scientifically known as *Felis concolor* (meaning cat of one color), the furtive animal is more commonly called cougar or mountain lion. Across the continent he's also known as puma, painter, panther, and catamount — plus numerous other imaginative, idiomatic labels, depending on the region and the people identifying the tawny feline.

Current Distribution

Once common throughout North, Central, and South America, cougars now range primarily across the wild, rugged high country of the American West. Cougars also are found in southern Alaska, western Canada, and Mexico. Some big cats continue to prowl certain swamplands, foothills, and forested tracts across scattered parts of the U.S., but huntable numbers are largely restricted to Western mountains.

Identifying Characteristics

Graceful and secretive, cougars are uniformly light brown although seasonal and regional color variations may be found, ranging from gray to russet. Rarely a melanistic (black) specimen is confirmed. Body fur is commonly an inch long and surprisingly soft. Cougar heads are rounded and often appear small compared to body size. Faces usually are marked with dark foreheads, noses, and muzzles, while the front of the muzzles and underparts typically are grayish white. Ears are untufted, rounded, and apparent. White whiskers, yellow eyes, and dark tail tips complete the physical description.

Adult lions commonly weigh between 125 and 175 pounds, stand about two feet high at the shoulder, and are seven to nine feet in length from nose to tail tip. Some legitimate 200-pound cougars have been tagged; however, such trophies are the exception. Females are perhaps one-third smaller than toms.

Agile and strong, cougars are effective killing machines. Each forefoot is equipped with five curving, retractable claws; there are four claws on each hind foot. Powerful jaws contain 30 teeth — 12 incisors, four canines, 10 premolars, and four molars. Streamlined for speed, cougars are startlingly quick over short distance chases after fleeing prey, reaching speeds of perhaps 35 miles per hour. As a lion runs, the loose-appearing skin flap of the belly sways from side to side but does not detract from the sleek, muscular appearance of the big cats.

Habitat/Diet

Cougars are equally at home in the thin air of a Western rimrock canyon or the stifling humidity of a Southern swampland; and from the dark, coniferous Northland forests to the brushy, rock-strewn draws of a Southwestern desert. Adaptable opportunists, the big cats may in fact exist in any terrain where deer — their favorite prey — and smaller animals provide sufficient food.

Lions typically have large home ranges and may cover 10 to 20 miles during a single night's hunt. Toms and females sometimes roam 50 circuitous miles or more during their constant search for fresh meat; females with kittens typically have a much more restricted home hunting territory.

Venison is the staple of life for cougars, and an adult tom commonly kills one or more deer each week. Smaller prey includes ground squirrels, rabbits and hares, porcupines, various birds, and in the Southwest, peccaries. Cougars also may develop a taste for livestock, killing horses, cattle, sheep, pigs, and poultry, much to the chagrin of farmers and ranchers.

A cougar may eat seven to eight pounds during a single feeding. Blood, the entrails, the liver, and the lungs and heart are choice pieces and often are devoured first. Kills made in the open sometimes are dragged to nearby hiding places. In such cases, the strength of the big cats is awesomely apparent. Following its initial feeding binge, a cougar often covers the carcass with sticks, grass, leaves, and small rocks, returning until the meal is gone or spoils. Where game is plentiful, a lion may never return to his food cache.

Senses

Nocturnal and solitary by nature, cougars rely on their eyes and ears to detect prey or the presence of danger. Their scenting ability is above average but rarely used in hunting. Lions commonly sight and stalk their prey in typical feline fashion, bellying close, and then attacking in a rush. Despite folklore legends, cougars seldom if ever spring onto their victims from overhanging limbs or boulders.

Reproduction

Female cougars may come into heat at any time of the year and may be sought out by any of the polygamous males who cross their trail. A female lion will be receptive to breeding for a period of about nine days. Males will remain with receptive females throughout their period of heat, copulating as frequently as their amorous advances are accepted. In some cases males fight for breeding privileges, but rarely are these battles violent.

Kittens are born approximately three months later. A typical litter consists of two or three spotted newborns weighing one-half to one pound each. The kittens' eyes open during the first two weeks of life. Nursing continues for four to six months, although the youngsters are given bits of meat by the time they are a month old. Trailing and imitating their mother, kittens are hunting on their own by six months of age. These family groups generally remain together for a year or more. Female cougars seldom breed before their second or third year.

Life Expectancy

Although some cougars may live until their late teens or early twenties, many do not live past seven or eight years of age. Cougar hunters agree the only truly effective way to bag a trophy is to use a pack of specially trained tracking hounds. Surprising to many is the fact that cougar meat makes excellent table fare. It is said that American's mountain men and trappers of the 1800s frequently would opt to eat lion over venison, when given a choice.

Bowhunting Records

The biggest mountain lion ever tagged by a bowhunter was killed in January of 1993 by Dr. Scott M. Moore in Park County, Wyoming. The giant cat scores 16 1/16 inches. The previous world record mark, shared by one Washington State and two Idaho cougars, was 15 11/16.

Chapter 23
Cougar —
King of American Cats

WHEN MONTANA ELK hunter Barry Wensel heard a twig snap in the shadowy brush just ahead, he quickly stepped off the old logging road. Easing an arrow from his bow quiver, Wensel fitted it to the string. Camouflaged head to toe, he stood scanning the opening, waiting for a bull to respond to his realistic mews and cow chirps. But it was a big mountain lion, not an antlered elk, that materialized not 25 yards away.

"At first I was in awe," Barry recalls, "just getting to see one of the big predators up close. But then the instant we made eye contact, I realized the lion was looking for what he thought was an elk. I yelled 'Hey!' but the cat locked in on me, laid its ears back, and started my way, coming slowly at first but gaining momentum. I honestly don't remember shooting, but the cat spun and ran back the way he came. It was about this time I sat down in the road and got real nervous."

The veteran bowhunter promptly reported the confrontation to an area game warden, and returned to the scene with the warden early the next day. The lion, an adult tom weighing 160 pounds, was found dead 40 yards away with Wensel's arrow buried lengthwise in its chest. There was no doubt the cat had been facing the bowhunter when the arrow struck its sternal notch and penetrated the chest. Evidence revealed the cat was 38 feet away — just over 12 yards — when the arrow was released. The warden officially listed the confrontation as an "attack" on his departmental incident report form.

"I'm convinced the lion didn't recognize me as a man and thought I was an elk," Barry confides. "I consider a camo face mask one of the most important pieces of my hunting gear, but I won't wear one anymore when I'm calling elk. Looking back, I thank God it wasn't some kid or inexperienced bowhunter standing there when the lion stepped out."

Word of such nerve-jangling encounters always gives rise to one inevitable question, "Just how dangerous are cougars?" Certainly, any animal capable of using fang and claw to dispatch a big-antlered buck or bull elk could make short work of any man or woman it happened to encounter. The undeniable fact is mountain lions have attacked and killed humans, as recently as 2004. Regardless, I remain convinced that it is the hunting lion — not lion hunting — that man has cause to fear.

Once found across much of North America, cougars now live mostly in the Western United States. Their populations are healthy and growing to the point human/lion confrontations are becoming increasingly frequent.

212

often tracks in freshly fallen snow, a scratch pile in the forest duff, or a partially covered, partly eaten kill are the only evidence cougars are in the area. With confirmed sightings relatively rare, actual attacks are almost nonexistent.

Of course, a growing cougar population throughout the Rocky Mountain states means that more chance encounters between lions and hunters like Barry Wensel are bound to occur. Regardless, the only way to effectively hunt and harvest mountain lions is by following after a pack of keen-nosed hounds that have been specially trained to scent-track the big cats. As with any form of hunting involving hounds, the challenge is to stay within earshot as the bawling dogs work to unravel the cat's trail, jump the lion, and eventually bring the winded cougar to bay. It's often a long, physically grueling undertaking.

About a decade ago Guy Shanks and I cut a fresh lion track in the December snow. Guy is a retired Montana game warden, part-time guide, and serious bowhunter who was training a promising pup by teaming it with an experienced cat hound. I was tagging along, a cougar license in my pocket and a bow in one gloved hand, just in case. We could see where the cougar had crossed a public road onto private ranchland, obviously heading across the valley toward timbered high country rising in the distance. By the time we located the ranch owner and obtained permission to cross his property and turn out the two hounds, it was late morning. Some seven long hours later, just before daylight faded into a brittle, star-flecked night — with two mountain drainages and at least half a dozen leg-weary miles behind us — I finally arrowed the track-maker. People who believe hunting with hounds is easy should have been along on that particular high country hike.

Unfortunately, the unethical use of electronic tracking collars, 4WD vehicles, CB radios, and snow machines by a handful of lazy, unprincipled hunters more interested in a kill than fair chase hunting, has given all hound hunting a bad name in some critics' minds. But following lions and hounds on foot, watching the milling dogs work out an hours' old track, listening to their excited cries echoing off rocky canyon walls, is the essence of cougar hunting. Once the cat has treed or is bayed within a pile of snow-capped boulders, the kill itself is often anticlimatic.

Hunting Techniques

A hometown acquaintance of mine once remarked, "I'd sure like to get a mountain lion with my bow, but I sure as heck ain't going to use dogs to do it." Stunned, all I could think of to mutter was, "Good luck."

Such naive comments display an incredible amount of optimism — or total ignorance of lion hunting.

The fact of the matter is over the years a mere handful of bowhunters have managed to tag a lion without the use of hounds. These were mostly chance encounters — much like the Barry Wensel incident — where someone stalking or stand hunting for deer or elk just happened to come across one of the big predators. Or vice versa. And although it's possible to use a predator call to lure a mountain lion within good arrow range, all of the bowhunters who have pulled off that particular feat would likely fit around your dining room table — with a chair or two to spare.

A few other lucky souls have reported the opportunity to shoot a cougar unaided, but lacked the proper license. For some, lion season wasn't open at the time. I can recall one such case in a

Montana elk hunter Barry Wensel was cow-calling bulls when this big tom responded to his calls. The menacing cougar was arrowed at 12 yards as it closed in on the camouflaged bowhunter it may have mistaken for an elk. The shooting was ruled "self defense" by a local game warden.

Cougars certainly deserve our respect, and any lion hunter who takes these big cats lightly is a fool. But most cougars have an irrational fear of dogs. And since most often one or more yowling hounds will be between the cat and hunter, there is little cause for worry. Even when a cat "jumps tree" and bails out of its high perch toward hounds or hunter, its primary interest is escape, not attack.

It was the late Willis Butolph, a one-time government hunter and veteran Utah cougar guide who killed or captured over 1,000 lions during his lifetime, who pretty well summed up the danger of lion hunting. On our first hunt together he told me, " Those lions could come down out of their tree, chew up the dogs, and take on hunters, too. They just don't know it. We'd all better pray to heaven they never find out. I for one ain't about to tell 'em!"

Overall, most bowhunters who happen to see lions catch nothing more than a fleeting glimpse of the reclusive felines. Commonly, most up-close encounters are by design with a pack of yammering hounds holding the treed cougar at bay until a well-shot arrow ends the excitement. Many people can and do live their entire lives in prime lion country without ever seeing one of the big cats. In my own big game hunting career, now spanning more than four decades, I've only seen three cougars when not lion hunting. Most

These big cats have an unfounded fear of hounds. When pressured by dogs, they commonly climb a tree rather than fight. Even a lone hound may hold a cat at bay until the hunters arrive.

Although a few lions have been killed by bowhunters without the aid of trained lion dogs, the most effective way to hunt these elusive predators is with hounds. Once a fresh track is found, the dogs are turned loose to follow and tree or bay the lion.

Sangre de Cristo bear camp where an excited bowhunter told me of watching a lion emerge from a rocky hillside and pad past his Colorado bear bait. And I know of one Wyoming bowhunter who has followed a fresh set of cougar tracks until he caught up with and killed the cat. He's done it at least twice. On occasion, I've even taken up a stand near a fresh lion kill, waiting and hoping the hungry cat would return. But considering the nocturnal nature of these stealthy cats, most such hopeful tactics are doomed to failure. Bowhunters who rely on unconventional hunting methods — or pure dumb luck — to add a lion mount or rug to their trophy collection are going to wind up disappointed more often than not.

In truth, the term "lion hunting" is a misnomer. Hunters and their guides look for lion sign, not the animals themselves, then turn out the dogs to do the work of trailing and treeing the cougar. Most often these chases will end in failure when the scent trail simply plays out or the cat somehow eludes its pursuers in the wild, rugged country these predators call home.

Lion hunting is often a time-consuming and costly undertaking. Booking the services of a good guide and his pack of trained lion hounds is not inexpensive. Add the cost of air fare, license fee, and incidentals, and it's easy to rack up expenses amounting to thousands of dollars. And that's even before you arrive in hunting camp. If a trophy fee is added after a kill is made, you've got more money due. And then there's the taxidermy bill. It all adds up. Fast.

Essentially, there are two methods of booking a lion hunt. The first is to select an open date on your guide's hunt calendar and pray that the weather conditions will be favorable when the time rolls around to start looking for lion tracks. The second is arranging an "on call" hunt where you agree to arrive within 24 hours or so after your guide calls to report a good tracking snow or the fact he's already cut the tracks of a big cougar and is ready to start your hunt.

Savvy bowhunters will spend plenty of time preparing themselves both mentally and physically for any lion hunt. Proper conditioning is vital due to the typical high country terrain where cats live. Warm, waterproof clothing and footwear are a must since most cat hunting occurs during the winter months when deep snow and numbing cold can quickly drain the energy of any ill-prepared bowhunter. Patience and a positive attitude are likewise essential because fickle weather changes can spoil any hunt almost overnight. Sudden storms can bury the high country, obliterating all sign and making hunting impossible until the weather breaks. Unexpected warm spells can work against lion hunters, too, melting tracking snow and bringing off-road travel to a soggy standstill. Even dry ground, warm weather lion hunts in certain southwestern locales can be tough on hunters, horses, and hounds alike. The warming earth quickly dispels scent and by late morning the day's heat can sap the strength — and determination — of most any man or animal. Such are the challenges of pursuing mountain lions.

The author arrowed this record book tom not far from his Montana home in early December. The all-day chase ended at dusk a dozen miles from where the cat's tracks were found.

with the yowl of a distant dog, racing for the high rimrocks where trailing hounds and hunters will have a hard time keeping up. One trick agile cats use is climbing higher and higher, walking narrow ledges and leaping from rock to rock along the cliff faces before eventually topping out. Pursuing hounds, less nimble than the felines, will try to follow but may become "ledged" on the cliff's rocky wall, unable to follow and sometimes unable to find their way down without human assistance.

Even leather-lunged, steel-legged guides can rarely manage to keep up with their dogs during a lion chase. Just staying within earshot is challenge enough. Consequently, few hunters — expecially those from flatland locales, who are not used to the rigors of hurried high country hikes — can expect to take an active part in the pursuit. It's common for one or more assistant guides to quickly follow the chase by horseback or snow machine, if possible, while the guide and his client take their time and follow along at a less hurried pace.

Veteran Alaskan bowhunter Bill Shuster, who finally arrowed his lion after several days of battling waist-deep snow as he followed hounds up and down steep canyons, summed up the feelings of many first-time cat hunters with these words: "Anyone who says cougar hunting isn't sporting just doesn't have a clue as to what it can be like. Of all the hunting I have done, cat hunting is the most exhausting — and sometimes the most dangerous — not necessarily because of the cat but because of the terrain they live and travel in. The cliffs the cats scale and walk can make a mountain goat spooky."

Where it's legal, some guides communicate by two-way radios as the chase unfolds. This fact has raised questions about the hunting ethics of using communication devices and whether they violate rules of fair chase. Critics claim the use of radios is unfair; proponents point to the vastness of lion country and the possibility of losing valuable dogs, some valued at thousands of dollars each. Every lion hunter must decide how he or she feels about pursuing and taking a trophy in this manner. However, the decision should be made before the hunt is booked. Additionally, the subject should be thoroughly discussed with the guide who owns the lion hounds. During a hunt is no time to be debating hunting ethics or arguing about the finer points of fair chase hunting.

Along these same lines, all lion hunters should clearly understand that one or more of the valuable hounds likely will be equipped with radio tracking collars. This is to assist the guide in locating his dogs after the hunt, not to keep tabs on the distant hounds once they're out of earshot. Recognizing the potential for widespread abuse of certain electronic tracking and communication

A typical day's hunt will begin in the early morning blackness, ideally after a fresh overnight snow has fallen, slowly cruising backroads in search of sign. The sweeping headlights of your guide's 4WD reveal the tracks of all nocturnal wanderers that happened to cross the remote roadway. Mostly you'll see deer tracks — perhaps elk or moose along with a smattering of coyote prints — but what you're looking for are the unmistakable pug marks left by a large cat. Once found, they can give clues as to the animal's size and direction of travel. The excitement level of the hounds is one good indication of the trail's freshness. If it's determined there is indeed a good "running track," all that's left is to wait for first light to release the dogs and listen to the music of the chase. All the while you'll know that sometime you'll have to follow the hounds — or seek to intercept them at some point in the chase — and most often that means wading snow and heading one direction — up!

When no tracks are located, a knowledgeable guide often takes one or more leashed strike dogs and checks favorite lion crossings where natural saddles between mountain drainages funnel game movements from one valley to another. Meanwhile, he'll keep an eye peeled for any congregation of scavenger birds — jays, ravens, and magpies — that might mark a lion kill. Fresh kill sites are perhaps the best spot to start any chase since the lion still may be close by, resting with a full belly after gorging itself with several pounds of fresh venison.

Some keen-nosed strike dogs can detect lion tracks that are more than a day old. Such scent trails are iffy propositions and seldom end in a treed lion. Some guides I know refuse to let their dogs run a track that's over 24 hours old and prefer spoor that's less than 12 hours old. Again, fresh kills are ideal starting points. And if the hounds can jump the cat nearby, the chase most likely will be a short one. On the other hand, older hunt-wise cougars may be off devices, the Pope and Young Club amended its Fair Chase affidavit in 1985 to read: "The term 'Fair Chase' shall not include...use of electronics for attracting, locating, or pursuing game, or guiding the hunter to such game." According to Club officials, the change was made to eliminate the use of modern electronic calls, walkie-talkies, and game-locating tracking devices. The amendment was not made to abolish radio collars that may help locate and recover high-priced hunting hounds. Regardless, every bowhunter and guide should clearly understand that if these electronic devices are used between the time when the dogs are released and when the hunt ends with the quarry bayed, the trophy will be ineligible for entry in the P&Y records. Only after a kill has been made may these electronic devices be used to locate and recover any dogs that turned up missing during the chase.

Judging the size and sex of a treed cougar is difficult, but poses no problem for veteran lion hunters and guides. All cats may look large to a novice.

Any houndsman can listen to the sounds of his dogs and tell whether they're working out a cold trail, following a smoking hot track, or have the lion in sight. And once their chopping barks indicate the cat has been treed or bayed up, it's time to get to the scene as quickly as possible. Once at the tree, a bowhunter generally has adequate time to look for a suitable opening and prepare for a perfect shot. Ringed by frenzied, yammering hounds, the lion typically stares down disdainfully at the dogs, growling occasionally, and accepting its fate with a stoic, cat-like apathy.

A good guide can quickly evaluate the treed cougar's size and determine its sex, passing this information along to the hunter. If a decision is reached to pass up the shot and go off in search of another larger lion, the dogs are leashed and dragged away from the tree. If the hunter decides to shoot the cougar, the guide and his assistants catch and tie the hounds nearby to avoid possible injury battling with a wounded cat.

A sharp broadhead though the lion's chest will quickly kill the largest cougar alive. Often the cat is dead by the time it drops from the tree. Even if it bails from its perch after the shot, it seldom goes far if the arrow was well-placed. If necessary, a follow-up shot can quickly dispatch a dying lion. The key, however, is taking the time necessary to get into perfect shooting position and place a keen broadhead directly through the vitals.

After the cat is dead, the guide commonly makes certain no protruding broadhead poses a risk to his hounds, and then releases his dogs to bite and shake the carcass. It's their reward for a job well done (and, by the way, don't fret about the dogs doing permanent damage to the pelt). After the hounds have worried the carcass sufficiently, it's time to leash them again, snap photos, and start the skinning chores. Often the dogs are fed bites of fresh lion meat as a bonus; however, bowhunters should claim the bulk for their own use. Lion meat is tasty and should be saved for proper processing.

Problem lions — those cats that have developed a taste for livestock or whose presence poses a real threat to humans — are

Fresh lion tracks in the snow are the answer to a bowhunter's prayers. But chases are often long and frequently end with the cat escaping. Finding a fresh cougar kill is a great starting point to begin any hunt.

another consideration. Often these cats are killed or captured and relocated by game department personnel, government trappers, or predator control experts; however, at times these cougars may be taken by clients of guides who work with local or state game officials and ranch owners. My first cougar, a big tom I arrowed in 1970, had killed over $3,000 worth of livestock on one Utah ranch during raids spanning several seasons. Another Wyoming cougar I hunted unsuccessfully in the 1980s killed sheep at will and to my knowledge died of old age, well fed to the end on mutton claimed during regular lowland forays. And while mountain lions usually

Colorado bowhunter Nathan Andersohn used a longbow to tag this big tom. Cats like this commonly kill one or more deer each week.

kill for food, occasionally one kills for bloodthirsty sport, slaughtering stock and leaving the animals where they fell. One documented case credits a single cougar with killing 192 sheep during a single bloody attack. Hunts for such rogue cats may occur at any time of the year and provide a truly different kind of lion hunting experience.

Speaking of different experiences, so-called "canned hunts" are the bane of every hard-working lion guide and law abiding sportsman alive. These "hunts" involve a captive cougar that has been trapped or perhaps even purchased from a zoo, game farm, or some private source. After the client is called and arrives to begin his cougar hunt, the unscrupulous guide or an accomplice releases the lion into a tree where the hounds hold it at bay until the unsuspecting hunter arrives and kills it. Ironically, the hunter may return home praising his "guide" and his hounds who were able to locate and tree a cougar so quickly. Meanwhile, the lion guide laughs all the way to the nearest bank, having pocketed perhaps double what he shelled out to buy the cat — all for a few hours' work.

A few unethical guides have been known to locate and tree a cat before calling the hunter, holding the lion at bay until the client can arrive within a day or two. Such "hunts" are mere executions and are commonly shunned by all responsible sportsmen. Cougars are outstanding game animals deserving a much better fate.

Normally, lions are hard to locate and harder yet to take, two factors which undoubtedly account for the singular appeal of hunting these great cats. True, a fair chase hunt may be brief, thanks to good luck and good timing; however, most bowhunters in search of a lion trophy can most often count on lots of riding and walking, looking and listening before they finally draw an arrow. In most successful hunts for cougars, the guide earns his fee and the client earns his lion.

Judging Trophy Cougars

Difficult. That one word pretty well sums up field judging the Pope and Young potential of any cougar. A final score is based solely on the combined measurements of a fleshed out skull after a minimum drying period of of 60 days. To arrive at a total, calipers are generally used to determine the skull's precise length and width to within 1/16th of an inch. Any lion skull measuring 13 8/16 inches or more is eligible for record book entry, providing all fair chase rules have been observed.

Since most any mountain lion will look large to a novice cat hunter, the judgment of an experienced guide may come in handy in helping to reach a final decision whether to shoot or pass. Complicating the matter is the fact that even large lions have heads that may appear small in comparison to their bodies. Bowhunters with their hearts set on a trophy-class lion need to carefully assess the animal before releasing an arrow, although most healthy adult toms will surpass the P&Y minimum.

As an example of the difficulty in accurately field judging lions, I know one lion hunter who almost passed up a treed cat because initially he believed it was a small cougar. He eventually arrowed the lion — and was glad he did. The cat's skull easily exceeded 15 inches, qualifying for both the Pope and Young and Boone and Crockett record books!

Honestly, most bowhunters consider the mountain lion to be a once-in-a-lifetime trophy. Consequently, they should regard any adult cougar legally taken under the rules of fair chase as a true trophy animal, despite its official score and eventual ranking in the records. Any record book recognition the mountain lion may receive is merely a bonus to what likely will be an unforgettable bowhunting experience.

Bighorn & Thinhorn Sheep

Classification

North America's four species of wild sheep are descendants of Asian sheep which first crossed the Bering land bridge half a million hears ago, venturing into the rugged country that eventually would become Alaska. Two species, the Rocky Mountain bighorn *(Ovis canadensis)* and the desert bighorn *(Ovis canadensis nelsoni)*, are found today in certain Western states, Mexico, and Canada. Two species of thinhorn sheep — the pure white Dall's sheep *(Ovis dalli dalli)* and its subspecies the Stone's sheep *(Ovis dalli stonei)* — live in the remote and rugged northland mountains of Canada and Alaska.

Current Distribution

Before the coming of the white man, it is believed as many as two million bighorns could be found throughout western North America. Forced south from Alaska by advancing Ice Age glaciers, sheep followed the Rocky Mountains into new ranges where they apparently thrived, thanks to good feed and a favorable climate. This expanded sheep range once extended from the northern Rockies south into Old Mexico, westward to California and eastward into the Dakotas, Nebraska, and Texas; however, advancing civilization spelled doom for most bighorns. Fortunately, recent bighorn restocking programs have reintroduced transplanted sheep to much of their original range and augmented the scattered bands of surviving bighorns. Today bighorn sheep are found from British Columbia south to Mexico, with most living the Rocky Mountain regions of Canada and the American West. California, Mexico, Nevada, and Arizona harbor the most desert bighorns.

Because of the remoteness of their home range in the rugged mountains of the far north, the hardy thinhorn sheep have not been subjected to the amount of human disturbance and hunting pressure faced by bighorns. Consequently, their modern day numbers easily exceed the total population of Rocky Mountain and desert bighorns. Dall's sheep are found across much of Alaska, the Yukon, and the Northwest Territories. Northern British Columbia is the home of most Stone's sheep.

Identifying Characteristics

Dall's sheep typically are all-white animals while Stone's most often are a blue-gray to charcoal in color. Regardless, many color phases exist with subtle color differences found throughout the thinhorn's northern range. Interbreeding occurs where Dall's and Stone's sheep share the same mountains. Bighorns are sturdy, grayish-brown animals with conspicuous yellow-white rump patches, light-colored stomachs, whitish muzzles, and dark, stubby tails. Typically the sun-bleached pelage of desert sheep is paler than that of their mountain-dwelling cousins.

Dall's sheep have thinner horns than those of bighorns. Their headgear flares outward and does not obstruct peripheral vision. Horns are light yellow and sport obvious growth rings by which a ram's age may be determined. Ewes of all sheep species have horns, but there is no chance of mistaking their short spikes for the spiraling headgear worn by mature rams. The amber horns of any Stone's sheep are typically heavier than those of his snowy-white cousins. Broomed (i.e., chipped or frayed) horns are uncommon among thinhorns, but horns with broken tips are normal among bighorns. Dark brown in color, the headgear of mature bighorn rams is composed of heavy, curling horns that can block the sheeps' peripheral vision.

Dall's and Stone's rams stand about three feet high at the shoulder and generally are lighter in body weight than bighorns, averaging less than 200 pounds. Length is between five and six feet. Stone's sheep are slightly larger animals than Dall's. Ewes of both species average one-fourth less in size and weight. Mountain bighorn sheep are muscular, chunky animals that may weigh up to 300 pounds. The lighter-bodied desert sheep usually weigh between 150 and 200 pounds. Rams stand about three and one-half feet at the the shoulders and average between five and six feet in length. As with thinhorns, ewes run about 25 percent smaller.

Gregarious and clannish animals, sheep often band together in groups segregated by sex. Except during the breeding season, rams prefer the company of other males. Bands of ewes, their offspring, and immature rams are common. Sure-footed and agile in rugged terrain, sheep have hooves with hard outer edges and spongy centers which help in gripping rocks.

Habitat/Diet

Diurnal animals, sheep rarely feed at night; most grazing activity occurs early and late in the day. By mid-morning the sheep usually retire to daytime beds — with a good view of the surrounding terrain — where they rest and contentedly chew their cuds.

At home amid desolate crags and windswept bluffs, mountain sheep usually spend summer months at higher elevations; winter snow typically forces sheep into lowlands where cover and forage are found. South-facing slopes are favored. Desert bighorns are very much at home among buffs and rocky outcroppings in hot, arid wastelands.

Like deer, goats, and pronghorns, sheep are ruminants and have no teeth in the front of their upper jaw. Cud-chewing animals, sheep have 32 teeth including eight incisors, 12 premolars, and 12 molars. Favorite summer foods include most mountain grasses and sedges, although sheep will feed on browse such as willows, sage, and various bushes, especially during the winter months. Desert bighorns will feed on cacti as well as other plants common to arid regions. All sheep are attracted to mineral licks.

Senses

All sheep have exceptional eyesight and approaching a flock of bedded or feeding rams is a challenge to test the skills of any stalker. These animals can observe a moving hunter at great distances, but frequently overlook a nearby stalker who remains unmoving until the ram has looked away. Sheep also possess well-developed senses of hearing and smell.

Reproduction

Thinhorn rutting activity generally begins in October when rams leave their bachelor groups and join flocks of ewes and younger sheep. Rams often engage in shoving matches for breeding rights and sometimes square off in those skull-jarring battles common to bighorns, so well documented by outdoor photographers and moviemakers. May is birthing month for most thinhorns. Ewes leave the flock and drop lambs in secluded, inaccessible spots. Newborn lambs weight six to eight pounds and stand about a foot high. Dall's lambs are sparkling white and Stone's lambs are progressively darker.

Bighorn sheep breeding usually occurs in November with lambs dropped by May or June. Single births are common with newborns weighing eight to 10 pounds. Ewes and their gangly, dark gray lambs typically rejoin the flock within a week.

Life Expectancy

Dall's, Stone's, and bighorn sheep often live into the middle teens. Trophy rams reach their prime in about a dozen years. Disease, falls, and predators claim some sheep each year. Bighorns are especially susceptible to certain diseases and are intolerant of domestic livestock and human disturbance. While far from abundant, modern bighorns face a hopeful future thanks to the efforts of sportsmen and game departments who realize the mountains would not be the same without these graceful, intelligent animals. The remoteness of the thinhorns' northland range keeps hunting pressure to a minimum and both species exist today in good numbers.

The mutton of all wild sheep is quite good, especially if properly handled and prepared. It is regarded by many hunters as much tastier than the meat of domesticated sheep.

Best Bowhunting Trophies

Gene Moore tagged the top bow-killed bighorn in 1983 while hunting in El Paso County, Colorado; his ram tapes 191 3/8. George Harms shot his world record desert bighorn on Tiburon Island, Mexico, in 2000; the big ram tapes 178 2/8. Tony Russ killed the world record Dall's sheep in Alaska's Chugach Mountains in 1988; his ram scores 171 0/8. The best Stone's sheep ever tagged by a bowhunter scores 174 2/8 inches and was killed by Stanley Walchuck, Jr., along the Telsa River in British Columbia in August of 1992.

Chapter 24
Bighorn & Thinhorn Sheep — Mountain Monarchs

THE SUMMER RAIN had stopped by the time I knelt in a rocky game trail to nock an arrow. A cool crosswind, as bracing and clear as some high mountain stream, swept down from the bald knobs looming to the west. It stirred the trailside clumps of glimmering grass and puckerbrush, masking any careless sounds I might make. Thankfully, this same gusting breeze also carried my man-smell of wet wool and drying sweat into the deep canyon to my left, well away from the five unseen bighorn rams bedded somewhere below me.

Suddenly a rock clattered off to my right in the heavy brush, and I realized the sidehill wind bore an unmistakable smell of sheep. My heart began to drum as I peered down into the leafy tangle below. Close. So close. Another stone shifted, grating, this time downhill

to my left. *Were they up and moving? Where were they? Where?*

Then the late morning sun broke through a gap in the roiling gray clouds, washing the mountain in a brilliant, warming light. I squinted in the sudden glare, trying to breathe deeply to calm jangled nerves. And then I saw a moving shadow in the brush to my right. A lone ram was crossing into an opening less than 25 yards down the game trail. Sucking in a lungful of the thin mountain air, I raised my bow.

The white-muzzled sheep paused just as he stepped into the clear, looking up at me uncertainly just as my forefinger nestled into its whiskered anchor point at the corner of my mouth. Instantly a small part of my mind registered every distinct detail: the dark ram's blocky shape, his thick neck, the heavy, close-curled horns with

Quality optics — both spotting scopes and binoculars — are musts for serious sheep hunters. They can save lots of time and boot leather, helping bowhunters locate stalkable rams and judge their horns before starting their approach.

Vertical sheep country requires physical and mental stamina. That's bowhunter Bob Ehle scaling a rocky outcropping. Bob is one of a handful of bowmen to take all four species of North American wild sheep.

This thinhorn ram already has spotted M. R. James moving into shooting position from below. The eyesight of sheep is legendary — and this was as close as the author got.

Veteran bowhunter Marv Clyncke (left) congratulates M. R. James on taking his Colorado bighorn in the Buffalo Peaks hunting area. Marv watched the stalk and shot which the author described at the beginning of this chapter.

their broomed tips highlighted by the summer sunshine...and then my arrow flashed decisively away.

At the time of this memorable shot, it was August of 1996, and I had just stalked and arrowed my first mountain sheep, a Colorado bighorn from the Buffalo Peaks area south of Leadville. Hunting with two friends, I'd managed successfully to slip close to a small band of three-quarter curl rams that we'd located the previous

evening. They'd been feeding along a mountainside when we glassed them and planned the stalk. After a high country rain storm pushed them to cover and they bedded in a brushy thicket, I made my move. Certainly, the elements of luck, skill, and opportunity all played an important role in that sheep hunt, just as these same factors are keys to any bowhunting triumph. However, a word of caution is in order.

Before you venture into the high mountains in search of a trophy ram, you must accept the fact that your shooting opportunities will be rare. If and when Lady Luck finally smiles, you'd better be mentally prepared to succeed, because perhaps no other North American big game animal can evoke so much euphoria — or more gut-wrenching disppointment — in the space of a single heartbeat.

The reason should be obvious. Mountain sheep are distinctive game animals: beautiful, normally wary and aristocratic creatures. Additionally, the hidden basins and hanging valleys where most sheep are found include some of the most spectacular alpine scenery found anywhere. Unlike slow-witted mountain goats, sheep are far more intelligent and usually more challenging to approach within good bow range. And although goats typically favor much tougher terrain, just getting to where sheep live often involves lung-searing, leg-cramping climbs. To then fool their eyes, ears, and noses is as daunting a stalking challenge as any high country bowhunter is likely to face. Consequently, to enter their domain and emerge with a sheep — any legal sheep, ram or ewe — is a heady, soul-lifting tonic. Conversely, to come tantalizingly close and then fail can crush the spirit of the unprepared. Such is the allure of sheep hunting.

Dwight Schuh perfectly sums up a successful bowhunter's feelings at the end of a long, grueling hunt with the following words:

"I picked out the closest ram and guessed him at 25 yards. 'Don't worry about the others,' I kept thinking. 'Just aim carefully.' When

G. Fred Asbell arrowed his bighorn ram in 1977 during a spot-and-stalk hunt in the same Buffalo Peaks area where the author took his ram two decades later.

I released, it looked like a little puff of wind rippled the hair on his chest. When he took off, I knew I had him. The other rams ran around the hill with mine lagging behind. He finally lay down in the rocks. The others stopped and watched him. He got up once and then slid down the hill head first. I'd done the seemingly impossible. I looked at the ram in disbelief. Then I cried a little."

Any sheep hunter who takes all four species of wild sheep — bighorn, desert bighorn, Dall's, and Stone's sheep — is credited with a ram hunting "grand slam." This term is credited to the late Grancel Fitz, an outdoor writer, sportsman, and avid trophy hunter who in 1938 headed the committee that originated the initial Boone and Crockett Club scoring system. Thanks largely to his efforts, the official scoring system still in general use — and the system after which the modern-day Pope and Young Club scoring system is based — was established in 1949.

Over the subsequent years, hundreds of well-heeled riflemen have succeeded in taking a sheep hunter's slam. But it wasn't until October 30, 1985, that Dr. John "Jack" Frost of Anchorage, Alaska, became the first bowhunter to join this select group. Ironically, that same year bowhunters Tom Hoffman of Albany, New York, and Paul Schafer of Kalispell, Montana, completed their own grand slams. Hoffman, an admitted sheep hunting addict, has since completed a second slam and gone on to harvest mountain sheep in all corners of the world. However, as these words are written at the beginning of the 21st century, nearly two decades after the first bow

and arrow grand slam of sheep hunting made bowhunting history, the total number of bowbenders who have taken all four sheep species still numbers in the teens.

It was the late Jack O'Connor, at one time perhaps this country's best-known outdoor writer and sheep hunter, who called wild sheep "the most fascinating and prestigious trophy animal in the world." While some may not agree with such strong bias, those of us who have bowhunted the great rams certainly can understand the basis of O'Connor's enthusiasm.

Hunting Strategies

Bowhunting bighorns and thinhorns generally involves packing in and camping out, followed by hours of meticulous glassing with quality optics. Letting your eyes do most of the walking while sheep hunting is savvy strategy. Once sheep are spotted, the climb — and the hunt itself — begins. Typically, finding sheep is the easy part; getting to them is the next challenge.

The final obstacle faced by bow and arrow sheep hunters is getting close enough to release a well-aimed arrow. A 1979 Colorado sheep hunt described by G. Fred Asbell underscores that difficulty. At the time Fred walked along an open mountain ridge, he'd already spent seven long and frustrating sheep seasons searching for rams and trying to get close.

"That day I'd only gone a short distance when the backs of two sheep came into view perhaps 60 to 100 yards below me. They had

Stalking close to these bedded rams would present a problem to any bowhunter. The open terrain above timberline is prime sheep habitat.

Some sheep hunters use horses instead of shank's mare to get into the alpine country where sheep are found. This allows them to camp near the hunting area without making a daily climb or horseback ride.

their heads down, feeding, and I dropped to the ground instinctively. There was absolutely no cover between us. It was pure luck that both animals had their heads down when I spotted them. I could only think of one thing to do. Lying on my back, I placed my bow with an arrow on the string across my thighs. I then lay back with my head flat on the ground and began inching slowly down the mountain feet first. I figured if I could get close enough to the animals, I could sit up, make a decision, and shoot — if I decided to.

"I'm not sure how long it took, but it seemed like a long time before I saw the very top of a set of sheep horns appear above the grass. As I rose slowly to a sitting position, both rams were looking at me. They were three-quarter curls.

"I wasn't aware of actually saying to myself, 'Do it.' But from my sitting position I came to full draw with the bow canted parallel to the ground and shot the biggest of the two through the chest."

Persistence, patience, and physical stamina are sheep hunting prerequisites. Without strong lungs and legs, sheep hunters are severely handicapped (as if choosing the bow and arrow weren't enough of a challenge!). In no other bowhunting/stalking activity — except perhaps climbing after mountain goats — is pre-hunt conditioning so critical. As Fred's and my own bighorn hunts demonstrate, getting above sheep and moving down into shooting position is an ideal stalking technique. Like goats, sheep tend to watch the slopes below them more than the mountainside above.

Nonetheless, they are quick to detect movement no matter its origin. It's a good idea to stay off the skylines and out of sight until you're well within arrow range.

After getting your doctor's blessing to begin a period of strenuous exercise, push yourself during pre-hunt conditioning. You may suffer at the time but you'll be thankful later. High country hikes — or climbing and running stadium stairs — are good for building endurance and toning muscles. Wear the same footwear and backpack you'll be wearing on your hunt. But don't overdo it once you arrive in sheep country. Overexertion in the thin air of cloud-scraping peaks, some reaching 14,000 feet, is both foolish and dangerous. My own physician summed it up with this terse reminder during a pre-hunt exam: "Don't push yourself beyond the limits of common sense. Sheep country can kill the foolish and unprepared hunter."

Equally important to conditioning are the optics you choose, binoculars for short-range glassing and spotting scopes for long-distance viewing and trophy evaluation. Binocs in the 8x40 range — with a tripod to keep things rock steady — are the choice of many veteran sheep hunters; variable spotting scopes of 15- to 45-power or 15- to 60-power are good choices but you'll also need a tripod mount for proper stabilization. Waterproof optics are always a good idea in sheep country; fogged glass is worthless. Whatever your personal choice, never skimp on optics since you'll spend long hours each day glassing for sheep. Poor optics can cause eye strain, headaches, blurry vision, and lot of needless frustration.

Because sheep are early risers, early day glassing can pay off. They often feed for an hour or two soon after first light before retiring to daytime beds. Midday browsing is also common, and the late evening is another good time to spot sheep on the open slopes. While mornings are undoubtedly best for locating and stalking rams, locating sheep in the waning hours is always good since it provides a likely starting point for the following day's hunt. As previously noted, finding sheep is generally the easy part. The rub arises in getting from where you first spotted them to where they actually are. That usually takes lots of time, more often more than you might imagine. It's a good idea to be prepared to spend one or more nights on the mountain rather than run out of daylight and go

Montana bowhunter Dyrk Eddie tagged this giant Stone's ram on a British Columbia hunt with the author. It missed being the new World Record by a fraction of an inch. The sheep arrowed by M. R. James was ineligible for the Pope and Young records after a young guide shot the mortally wounded ram in the hip with his rifle, believing it was going to escape.

stumbling around the high country in the dark, trying to get back to camp.

Whenever possible and practical, pre-season scouting trips are a good idea. These excursions not only help in locating bands of legal rams but also familiarize you with the hunting area, as well as assist in your physical conditioning. Packing along a topographic map during scouting trips and the hunt itself is smart, too. Topo maps can assist in planning any stalking route once sheep are found.

Camouflage clothing that matches the terrain is a good investment. Add camo face paint or gloves and a headnet. It's smart to cover your moving parts, namely the hands and face. Savvy hunters dress in layers and stash a good set of raingear in their packs. Pack along plenty of water, too. The threat of dehydration is a very real hazard to any ill-prepared sheep hunter.

While most sheep hunting involves stalking, ambush possibilities do exist. I know of a few bowhunters who have staked out mineral licks where rams routinely visit. Others have set up along escape routes and had one or more buddies nudge sheep past in what is the equivalent to a slow-motion deer drive. Still others will try to determine where feeding sheep are heading and get ahead of them, hiding among the boulders or brush and hoping a ram will move within arrow range. While occasionally successful, such methods rely more on luck and the whims of the sheep than individual hunting skill. Personally, I'd much rather stalk a trophy ram than sit somewhere and wait for him to stroll by. Some hunting requires the passive sit-and-wait technique; sheep hunting is not such an undertaking.

When suddenly confronted by a bowhunter, individual sheep react differently. Some will scramble away like scalded cats while others may simply stand and stare and the intruder. A few animals — usually those that have been pressured by other hunters — may instantly run or climb a mile or more before slowing to a walk. Some sprint only a short distance and resume grazing or bed down, seeming to forget what boogered them. Smart hunters understand these different reactions and respond accordingly, remaining persistent regardless of how the sheep may react. It's worth repeating: patience and perseverance are keys to bowhunting success.

I do know a couple of successful bowhunters who have invested considerable time watching sheep in their hunting area. They made no attempt to hide and reported the sheep gradually grew used to their presence. In each case the bowmen were rewarded by close shots at true trophy rams. Whatever works!

Remember, all species of sheep may be successfully hunted by the spot-and-stalk method. And while do-it-yourself hunts are possible, many successful sheep hunters employ the services of a qualified, experienced guide. In some sheep hunting areas, the use of guides is required by law. Combine the cost of hiring a veteran guide with getting to the remote country that sheep call home, and you may better understand why sheep hunts are among the most expensive of all bowhunting endeavors. Even a relatively inexpensive guided hunt is likely to cost thousands of dollars, even tens of thousands! Don't pass out when asked to shell out between $12,000 and $20,000 for some guided sheep hunts — plus travel and license expenses! And keep in mind that guided desert bighorn hunts can cost over $50,000.

Whenever possible, make certain your guide is experienced with bowhunters, bowhunting tackle, and how a sharp broadhead works. Once in British Columbia, I arrowed a fine trophy class Stone's ram as he quartered away below me on an open mountainside. My arrow hit in front of the sheep's hip, angled forward, and emerged mid-body on the opposite side, a bit far back but undoubtedly a fatal

Noted Montana bowhunter and bowyer Paul Schafer shows a Big Sky bighorn he arrowed. Paul, who was one of the first bowmen to complete the Grand Slam of sheep hunting, was later killed in a tragic skiing accident.

hit. The ram dashed less than 100 yards and stood in a rocky chute, looking back at me. I ducked low and started circling to work close enough for a follow-up shot. Suddenly a rifle shot rang out and the big ram dropped with a shattered hip. My worried guide had shot the big ram. And although I ran over and killed that wounded sheep with a final arrow through its chest, the bullet hole made it ineligible for P&Y record book entry. While I certainly understand any guide's concern over the possibility that a client's wounded animal might escape, I have no doubts we'd have recovered that ram in that open, rocky bowl where I shot him. I'd like to believe both my young guide and I each learned a significant lesson that late summer day.

Incidentally, more than one veteran sheep hunter has told me of the additional pressure placed on them by the thought of blowing a shot and returning home empty handed after paying thousands of dollars for the chance to hunt these magnificent creatures. (The Stone sheep hunt mentioned in the previous paragraph cost about $12,000, and such hunts are even pricier today.) My advice: if you are on a tight budget and fret over spending your hard-earned cash on a very iffy venture, try drawing a license in an area where a do-it-yourself hunt is possible — or turn to other game species for your hunting challenges. You can always go sheep hunting after winning the lottery.

Sheep are hardy animals that can cover considerable ground even when mortally wounded, although they lack the life-clinging tenacity commonly found in mountain goats. And although they spend much of their time in upland pastures and grassy basins, they often immediately head for nearby rough country refuges when threatened or wounded. Regardless, a well-placed shaft through the chest will quickly stop any ram. G. Fred Asbell's experience with a Dall sheep during an Alaskan bowhunt perfectly demonstrates the deadly effectiveness of a sharp, well-placed broadhead. It was during a long, frustrating, foul-weather sheep hunt with Tony Russ — holder of the Pope and Young Club's world record Dall's sheep — that Fred's chance finally came when the guide and hunter stumbled across a good ram feeding high along a rushing glacial stream. Fred's first arrow flew just low, micro-inches beneath the sheep's chest.

"I ducked back down," Fred recalls, "thinking he'd run or look around before he bolted. But he never raised his head. Tony looked back at me, and I drew and shot a second arrow. We both watched transfixed as the arrow sped again across the open space. This time it was a tad higher. Perfect!

"The ram didn't move for several seconds and then his hind legs quivered just a bit and he lay forward — and then rolled over and fell the 100 or so feet down into the creek."

In sharing this story of his grueling Alaskan sheep adventure, Fred concluded his comments with a candid admission that likely summarizes the experiences — and feelings — of many sheep hunters. "I haven't made this hunt sound like fun, and I guess it really wasn't. But it was a great hunt, and I learned an awful lot — some of it about me. I felt humbled, very vulnerable, and particularly clean when I finally left Alaska. Alaska and sheep hunting can be quite a test sometimes."

The same might be said of any sheep hunt, anywhere.

Trophy Recognition

The desert and Rocky Mountain bighorn sheep commonly have massive, tightly curled horns. Broomed or broken tips are normal, as are missing chips or chunks of horn material, caused when rutting rams savagely butt heads during breeding battles. The headgear of so-called thinhorns, Dall's and Stone's sheep, is lighter and tends to flare away from the face. Brooming is rarer than with bighorn sheep.

True trophy bighorns are older animals, thick-necked monarchs with horns featuring massive bases and heavy, thick curves that dip below the jaw and curl up past the bridge of the nose. Trophy thinhorns have long, upswept horns with heavy bases and unbroomed tips. To measure any sheep for record book consideration, the length of each horn and four circumference measurements — from horn base to the third quarter — are added. Supplementary data includes the greatest spread and tip-to-tip spread, although these numbers are not figured in the official score.

Minimum scores for Pope and Young entry are as follows: Rocky Mountain bighorn sheep and desert bighorn sheep, 140 inches; Dall's and Stone's sheep, 120. Incidentally, both the names Dall and Stone should always be capitalized. Dall's sheep were named after the biologist, W. H . Dall. A Montana sheep hunter named Andrew Stone — not the rocky terrain where these animals are found — is the namesake of Stone's sheep.

Any adult sheep, regardless of its sex or the size of its horns, should be considered a trophy by the bowhunter who tags it. Relatively few archers will ever claim a sheep during their hunting career, much less tag a record book ram.

Mountain Goat

Classification

The Rocky Mountain goat *(Oreamnos americanus)* is an American original. Not really a goat, this unique animal is thought to be a modern-day descendant of ancient European and Asian antelope families. Distant relatives include the Siberian goral, the Chinese serow, and European chamois. The mountain goat of today has evolved slowly over the centuries to fit its home terrain of high cliffs and windswept pinnacles. The forebears of the mountain goat first arrived in North America between 500,000 and 600,000 years ago when a land bridge spanned the Bering Strait.

Current Distribution

The original range of the mountain goat was limited to prehistoric Alaska's steep slopes; however, over the years the white-coated animals moved into suitable habitat in the Northwest Territories, the Yukon, British Columbia, and Alberta, gradually traveling southward into the western United States. Today, Washington boasts the largest goat population within the contiguous 48 states, with good numbers also found in Montana and Idaho. Transplants have established populations in Oregon, Wyoming, Colorado, Utah, and South Dakota.

Identifying Characteristics

The hair of a mountain goat is long and snowy white, frequently tinged with yellow in older animals. It is lanolin-rich and waxy to the touch. Eyes, nose, hooves, and horns are jet black. Both sexes have shoulder humps, beards, and horns. Billies stand three feet or slightly more at the shoulder and are five to six feet in length; nannies are somewhat smaller. Big, fully mature billies may weigh as much as 300 pounds.

Horns have a digger-like appearance and curve slightly backward. They are permanent, growing throughout the goat's lifetime; growth rings are apparent and may be used to accurately determine the age of each animal. A billy's horns may reach 12 inches although most are at least an inch or two shorter; the slender horns of nannies rarely exceed nine inches.

Goats are awkward-appearing but extremely sure-footed animals. Hooves are squarish with convex hoof pads that form spongy cushions that grip rocks and provide excellent traction. Like other ruminants, goats have four-chambered stomachs and must chew their cuds following feeding sessions in order to start the digestive process. Goats have no teeth in the top front of their mouth, although adult animals have a full complement of 32 teeth — eight incisors, 12 premolars, and 12 molars.

Habitat/Diet

Goats prefer high, broken, and rugged mountain terrain. They commonly are found on the vertical slopes above timberline, although some venture down into timbered valleys on occasion and sometimes take up residence at lower altitudes. Shifts between summer and winter ranges are often noted. Oddly, mountain goats and wild sheep rarely share the same high country peaks.

Diurnal by nature, goats unhurriedly feed during daylight hours and seemingly favor hardy high country grasses, mosses, and lichens. Dwarf willow is a favorite browse plant. Other alpine shrubs and forbs compose the balance of a goat's diet.

Senses

Eyesight is the mountain goat's first line of defense; however, like many keen-eyed animals, goats tend to key in on movement and sometimes overlook stationary objects, even when in plain view. Hearing is good but clattering rocks are not uncommon in the high peaks and seldom cause alarm. Goats have good olfactory capabilities and easily scent danger borne on the mountain air's eddying currents.

Reproduction

Mountain goats breed during November and December. Solitary billies seek out the companionship of one or more nannies, staying with the females until they become receptive to breeding advances. Fights between males are rare. The goats' curving, dagger-like horns are formidable defensive weapons.

Females do not breed until age two and one-half. Their gestation period is approximately six months in length and kids are born in May and June. Nannies commonly have single births, however, twins are not rare, especially in areas of good habitat. Kids weigh six to seven pounds at birth and stand about 12 to 13 inches at the shoulder. The newborns are able to follow their mother within a matter of hours, but the nannies and kids usually do not rejoin the family groups for several days.

Life Expectancy

Goats have few natural enemies and frequently live into their teens. Predators such as cougars, eagles, and bears may claim some goats. On occasion a fall or avalanche proves fatal.

Hunters generally agree that goat meat, although edible, is not quality table fare and cannot compare with other game species.

Bowhunting Records

Lyle Willmarth shot the world record mountain goat in Park County, Colorado, in 1988. The billy scored 52 4/8 inches.

Chapter 25
Mountain Goat — Peakmasters

I STILL DON'T KNOW where that mountain goat came from. One moment I was carefully picking my way down through a jumble of granite boulders; the next instant I sensed someone — or something — watching me. Turning my head slightly, I saw a creamy-white goat standing on a ledge just above and behind me. Snowy body hair riffling in the cool September wind, its head was cocked with an almost quizzical expression on its elongated face. Perhaps the hump-shouldered creature was wondering exactly what

I was doing there so high on this remote Wyoming mountain — a mind-gnawing thought that had come to me more than once during this particular late summer morning climb.

At the time I spotted the goat, I'd been slowly descending along a series of dizzying, windswept cliffs. Without hesitating, I stepped down onto a flat-topped rock and paused, pulling an arrow free and nocking it. Taking a deep breath of the rarefied mountain air, I twisted at the waist and raised my bow. The goat hadn't moved. I nestled my string fingers into their anchor point at the right corner of my mouth, held briefly, and released. My arrow blurred upward, disappearing low into the goat's chest and exiting mid-back behind the hump. As he belatedly spun away, I could see the red stain already spreading. He would not go far, I knew. And he didn't.

Mountain goats are perhaps the easiest — yet most difficult — big game animal any bowhunter can decide to pursue. Seemingly slow-witted and phlegmatic, these sure-footed beasts live among the rocky precipices and craggy spires where modern man seldom ventures. In truth, it is their remote and rugged high country habitat, not an innate wariness or the elusive nature of these animals, that makes goat hunting a true challenge for the bowhunter.

Frankly, tagging a mountain goat is relatively simple matter for most riflemen. A British Columbia guide I hunted with bragged to me that

Mountain goats truly live near the top of the world. It took the author a day and a half to climb from the valley floor to reach prime goat country.

Goat hunting means climbing. Goats are right at home among the dizzying cliffs and rocky spires where few animals — and fewer men — dare to venture. Theirs is a hard, unforgiving, and dangerous land. Hunters need to be in good physical shape and take care to avoid falls that could result in injury — or death.

Goats commonly feed in high alpine parks and meadows near rugged country where they can find solitude and safety.

none of his goat hunting clients had ever spent more than a single day afield before dropping a trophy-class billy. Another crusty Wyoming outfitter summed his own feelings about goat hunting with this cryptic assessment: "Goats are easy. It's getting the license that's the hard part."

Such skeptical sentiment among certain sportsmen is nothing new, really. During the late 1800s, the eminent author and scientist Dr. George Bird Grinnell, Editor and Publisher of *Forest and Stream*, once the nation's leading hunting magazine, summed up his feelings about goat hunting with these blunt words:

"The goat is an animal far less wary than the sheep. His watch is concentrated upon approaches from below. All the hunter has to do is to get above him, to make at once for the summit of the ridge which he proposes to hunt, and the unsuspecting creature will never give you a thought. Upon my word, it is inexcusable to kill him, except for a specimen in a collection; he is so handsome, so harmless, and so stupid!"

Dr. Grinnel, a rifle hunter, based his harsh judgment on his personal hunting experiences for Rocky Mountain goats over a century ago. During the subsequent decades, others have discovered goat hunting's truths for themselves, ultimately making up their own minds about its undeniable appeal and personal challenges.

Whatever a mountain goat's IQ, I personally believe these animals deserve the attention, admiration, and respect of any adventuresome bowhunter. In the first place, goats are hardy, handsome animals that rank alongside the Creator's finest sculpturing. The timeless beauty and virtually untouched wildness of their home range, combined with the spiritual euphoria any visit there evokes, is well worth the lung-burning, leg-cramping effort of an exhausting climb. Second, getting within good bow range is a far different matter than reaching out and touching a black-horned billy across some yawning canyon simply by aligning your crosshairs and squeezing the rifle's trigger. For my money, there are few undertakings in bowhunting that are more physically challenging — or more personally satisfying.

Stated simply, goats and the mountains they call home are indeed special. And while pursuit of these peakmasters certainly is not for everyone, those prepared individuals who have tested their mettle on a high altitude hunt generally agree that the experience borders on the spiritual; it rejuvenates the soul. For some, it is an endurance test that must be repeated. Dwight Schuh expressed the sentiments of many bow and arrow goat hunters. He said that when he first applied for a goat tag, his aim simply had been to collect a billy and call it quits.

"But somewhere along the line," he confessed, "all that changed. When you've scaled the fearsome peaks and fought the snow and the vertical jungles and lived with the great white goats...you just can't put it behind you, shed it like a coat and go on, check it off as done, and forget it, mission accomplished.

"As long as mountains rise into the clouds and the great white

Goat hair snagged on low-growing shrubs, along with numerous goat beds and piles of scat, are indicators that you're in prime goat country.

demands good physical conditioning and stamina, it's hunting the rugged high country above timberline.

Frankly, unless continually harassed in heavily hunted areas, goats do not expect danger to approach from above. They often spend long hours among towering pinnacles serenely surveying the world unfolding below without so much as an upward glance. When suddenly confronted with a threat from above, they sometimes are slow to react, if my own stalking experiences are any indicator. More than once I have crept down and had surprised mountain goats below simply stand and stare up at me with a look of puzzlement on their horse-shaped faces. It's almost as if they wonder not what the strange camouflaged shape is, but rather how I got so close, unseen and unheard.

In the rough and broken terrain goats call home, it's quite easy to stay out of sight of the animals. This is both a stalker's blessing and curse. If the goats can't see you, you can't see them either. And take it from me, it's a gut-wrenching disappointment to spend long, laborious hours clawing your way up to where you last saw Mr. Billy only to find the mountainside mockingly empty. This is where the buddy system — with one bowhunter making the stalk while a companion hunkers down behind a spotting scope and keeps tabs on the goat from some distant vantage point — saves a lot of time and frustration. A set of prearranged hand signals can let the stalker know exactly where the unseen goat is and whether he's still bedded, feeding, or on the move. This way the bowhunter can concentrate on staying hidden and closing the distance until he's ready to take the shot. In some instances after the stalker is in shooting position, the distant spotter shows himself intentionally in an attempt to distract and hold the goat's attention until his partner can release a well-aimed arrow.

goats stand like statues, looking, always looking, I'll be a goat hunter. Let's face it. Goat hunting isn't a goal. It's a condition of the heart."

Hunting Strategies

Most often it's a waste of time to try to stalk close to a goat from below. Circling wide and slowly approaching a feeding or bedded billy from above — or from either side on the same level — is arguably the best means for a bowhunter to eventually ease within good arrow range. Of course, getting to the same level or above a mountain goat you've spotted from below generally means hiking and climbing — and then climbing some more! Throw in a handful of unexpected uphill finger-clinging detours around sheer rock cliffs, across treacherous avalanche chutes, or through brush-busting pockets clogged with boot-grabbing undergrowth, and the approach that once appeared so simple from a distance fast becomes a grueling test of human endurance best combined with mule-stubborn determination and gritty patience. If any single endeavor in bowhunting

The author eyes a British Columbia billy feeding on an open sidehill. While goats have excellent eyesight, they sometimes seem unconcerned about people in plain view — unless approached directly.

A bearded snow-white billy with black, dagger-like horns makes an *exceptional trophy. Few of these animals come easily to bowhunters, a fact that makes any eventual success so very sweet. Goat hunting is among the most physically demanding of all North American hunting.*

When it comes to getting within shooting distance of goats, the seemingly ever-present mountain winds can be a stalking bowhunter's best friend and worst enemy. True, eddying currents of air can carry your scent to the goats and betray your presence; however, that same wind can mask the occasional scuffing of lugged boot soles on granite, the muted crunch of shale underfoot, and other careless or unavoidable sounds a stalking hunter makes. The fact is, the intermittent clatter of shifting or falling rocks, at times accompanied by cascading snowmelt, is quite common in goat country. It rarely draws a sidelong glance from the nearby billies, nannies, or their kids. But let these same animals get a single whiff of you and the stalk is immediately over. They'll be gone with the wind in less time that it takes to say "Billy Goat Gruff is outta here!"

One additional word of caution about avoiding detection: Goats may overlook unmoving objects, even at point-blank distances, but they are quick to detect movement, either up close or at long distances. Trying to pop up from behind a boulder and to draw and release an arrow at a nearby animal is often doomed to failure.

Surprised goats usually run first and wonder what spooked them later. And don't be tempted to hurriedly follow escaping goats along narrow ledges and across cliff faces. It's sheer folly.

Locating goats during the late summer and early fall seasons is seldom difficult, so long as a hunter's equipment includes the mandatory optics, namely good binoculars and a variable power spotting scope. Their snowy white coats cause them to stand out amid the gray rocks and green alpine saddles, even from a distance of several miles. Personally, despite the one major disadvantage that matters only to hunters in search of a majestic trophy – less impressive coat quality – I prefer early season goat hunting. For one thing the high country weather is generally mild, even downright pleasant, pesky insects notwithstanding. And, as already mentioned, goats are much easier to spot before the first snows blanket the tall peaks. As for the biggest disadvantage mentioned above, the bearded, pantalooned goats are not yet wearing their luxurious winter coats. Early season mounts frankly are not as impressive those taken later in the year.

Late season goats usually are found at lower attitudes, although the bad weather and deep snows that have pushed them from the higher peaks are not ideal for bowhunting. Sunny days will find the goats moving up across higher, snow-free slopes; however, late fall and early winter storms may force the animals lower again. Daily

Dave Holt shot his billy late in the season when snow and cold added to the normal difficulty of finding and getting close to these high mountain dwellers.

Bowhunter Tom Hoffman arrowed this big billy one of his many high country adventures. Note the horns' thick bases and the prime winter coat. Billies such as this one make exceptional life-size mounts.

movement of goat groups and individual animals is more erratic and unpredictable during the late seasons.

Whatever the time of year, goats do not normally move at night, typically rising early and feeding until midday. They then bed down on high vantage points to contentedly chew their cuds, rest, and take in the alpine scenery. As afternoon shadows lengthen, they will rise again and resume feeding until nightfall when they bed for the night. Hard rain or heavy snows will disrupt their daily feeding routine and normal movement pattern between bedding and feeding areas.

Besides attempting solo stalks and using the buddy system, goat hunters have several other options that have proved effective on occasion. The first method involves setting up along a known escape route. Once in the Canadian Rockies I took up such a vantage point and watched as my guide topped a ridge near a big, yellow-haired billy. The goat immediately rose from its bed and moved in my direction, dropping out of view while still over 100 yards away. Moments later I heard rocks clattering nearby and seconds later a goat stepped into view just below me. I was at full draw before I noticed it was not the old billy but a young nanny that stopped perfectly broadside at a dozen yards, gaping at me. I let off and watched her finally scramble away down the trail. The billy never showed. He apparently had bailed out and taken another path to safety. But my point is this sort of goat "push" or "drive" can work at times. In fact, native hunters of centuries past effectively employed this same bowhunting technique.

Yet another ambush method is to take up a position near a natural salt or mineral lick. Such spots attract goats and other mountain wildlife, and a well-concealed bowhunter just might fill a goat

tag by playing the waiting game. Speaking personally, the challenge of spot-and-stalk goat hunting is far more appealing and exciting.

Finally, the ultimate thrill of goat hunting may well be the unique method employed successfully by G. Fred Asbell and a handful of other hunters — namely, letting the goats see you but acting totally disinterested while working closer. Some years ago Fred filled a Colorado goat tag this way, taking the lead from bowhunter/photographer Dennis Bader, who often gets good up-close photos of mountain sheep and goats by staying in the open, moving slowly and indirectly toward the animals in a non-threatening matter.

After spotting four distant goats while on a scouting trip with Bader and a mutual friend, Steve Fausel, Fred left his two companions behind and skeptically stepped from behind the final bit of cover while still some 600 to 700 yards away. "With nothing to lose, I stood up and began to move toward the goats, which got up from their beds and stood staring my way," Fred recalls. "After walking about 20 yards, I got down on my hands and knees like some sort of grazing animal, stayed put for a few minutes, then stood and moved slowly forward along a trail that would take me closer to the goats."

Some two unhurried hours later — after a continuous series of moving forward a little and pretending to graze a little, never hurrying or making eye contact with the animals — Fred saw that two of the goats had moved away up the mountain. Incredibly, the other two goats had bedded down again and Fred was within 35 yards of one billy.

"I was flabbergasted," Fred admits. "He wasn't even watching me anymore. It came to me then that this thing was going to work after all — and suddenly my heart was clanging in my throat. I carefully

Dwight Schuh got this billy goat in western Montana in mid-October with a 35-yard shot.

fitted an arrow to the string of my longbow and abruptly everything turned deadly serious."

Crawling, Fred inched within 12 yards before gripping his bow and slowly standing, sure the billy was going to flee out of his bed like a scalded dog. But the billy simply eyed Fred and nonchalantly rose to its feet. "As my bow came up and the arrow came back," Fred says, "my mind leaped ahead to just how you go about getting a goat off the mountain without a packframe."

Keep In Mind

Goat hunters have two basic choices: guided and do-it-yourself hunts. While fully guided hunts are pricey, often costing thousands of dollars plus license and transportation fees, drawing a goat license in most states is an extremely iffy proposition. So if your heart is set on trying for a trophy billy, booking a goat hunting in Alaska or Canada is the best way to go.

Goats are not really gregarious animals. In fact, big billies are loners by nature, although small bachelor bands may hang together through part of the year. Whenever possible, try to locate and stalk a single goat rather than many. The more watchful eyes you have to avoid, the greater your chances of making a critical blunder during the final stages of your stalk.

Patience, a bowhunting virtue, is absolutely indispensable when it comes to goat hunting. Impatience, pushing things instead of waiting, likely has spoiled more stalks than anything except the vagaries of mountain wind. Take your time planning and carrying out any stalk. And always carefully note key landmarks near the goat — a patch of snow, a specific boulder, a mountain cataract,

gully, or whatever — before beginning your climb. Things will look different as you move closer, and you can't afford confusion about where the animal was bedded or feeding when you began your stalk. Again, "easy does it" is excellent advice for most any stalking situation. Mountain goats are hardy animals that cling tenaciously to life. They can be extremely tough to put down unless the bullet or arrow is well placed. Avoid all running shots unless the animal is already wounded. Whenever possible, wait for a broadside shot at a stationary target. And never hesitate to quickly follow up any initial hit with a second arrow to anchor the animal.

Goat country is mostly vertical. A dead or dying goat may drop into some gaping chasm or cartwheel hundreds of feet down the mountain (as a Montana billy once did on one of my wilderness hunts) before coming to rest. Never let momentary excitement or enthusiasm cloud your good judgment. Remember the sobering fact that more than one goat hunter has tumbled to his death while attempting to follow a wounded animal or recover a fallen trophy. Think safety, always.

Mountain terrain can be unforgiving. Prepare yourself mentally and physically for a splendid, trouble-free experience, not a wretched hunt that will haunt your memory for years to come. If hunting alone, leave word of your exact hunting area and timetable with friends or family. Consider packing a cellular or satellite phone for emergencies. Better yet, share the high country experience with a companion who has a can-do attitude and will help you with everything from planning and executing the stalk to packing out a portion of the meat or the cape. And always take pains to avoid slips and falls when coming off the mountain under a heavy pack of goat meat and hide. A broken ankle, leg — or worse — can spoil an otherwise perfect hunting adventure.

Judging Trophy Goats

It's extremely difficult for most hunters to distinguish billies from nannies. Generally, an older billy's coat has a yellowish cast (although in some hunting areas the pelt of mature nannies may be yellow, too). Most often, however, a large, solitary animal will be a billy, especially if its coat has that telltale yellowish cast. Watching a distant animal urinate is yet another clue to its sex. Nannies commonly squat to relieve themselves; billies simply lower their backs a bit.

Horns, although similar in appearance, may help the careful observer identify gender. Nannies have slender horns that taper gradually to a distinct curve at each tip; the tapering horns of billies are thicker at the base and curve nearer the middle. Remember, average horns measure eight to nine inches and anything above this norm almost certainly makes that goat a record book candidate.

Horn length is directly related to the animal's age. Look for thick-based horns that are over twice the length of the animal's ears or at least three-fourths the length of the goat's face. To qualify for the Pope and Young listings, a Rocky Mountain goat's horns must have a total score of 40 or more inches (horn length and four circumference measurements).

To me, goats are a unique bowhunting trophy. Spotting, stalking, and taking either sex with the stick and string is a noteworthy achievement. These alpine animals represent more than a high country challenge; they embody freedom and survival and the very essence of wildness, elements that are all too rare in our modern day world.

Bison & Musk-Ox

Classification

Commonly known as the American buffalo, the ponderous hump-shouldered beasts are unrelated to the true buffalo of Asia and Africa. Bison *(Bison bison)* are thought to be descendants of ancient Asian cattle that found their way from Siberia to Alaska via the trans-Bering land bridge perhaps one million years ago.

The musk-ox *(Ovibos moschatus)* is an unusual animal whose Latin name labels it a strong-smelling sheep-ox. In truth, musk-oxen are members of the cattle family and rutting bulls do have a distinctive musky odor; however, these inhabitants of the remote northlands are a one-of-a-kind big game trophy having little in common with sheep except the ability to grow a soft fiber — called *qiviut* by Eskimos — which can be woven into warm, cold-battling clothing.

Current Distribution

Bison once roamed across much of North America in vast herds estimated to number over 50 million animals. But by the 1890s, settlers, market hunters, and the military had killed all but a few hundred head. Today thousands of bison roam established refuges and private lands. Only a few free-ranging herds may be found on the continent, with the Henry Mountains of Utah, the Wrangell Mountains of Alaska, northern Arizona, and certain areas of Alberta, British Columbia, and the Northwest Territories having limited hunting opportunities for wild American buffalo.

Greenland harbors the largest herds of musk-oxen found today, although good numbers of the animals range throughout the Canadian-Arctic and parts of Alaska. Once hunted to the brink of extinction by native North American hunters and explorers, musk-oxen have been successfully reintroduced throughout much of their original range and appear to be thriving.

Identifying Characteristics

Both male and female bison are bearded animals with short, curved horns that they never shed. Coloration varies from brown to black. The head, neck, shoulder hump, and front legs are covered with long, shaggy hair while hair on the flanks and rump is quite short. The tail is short and usually tufted. Bulls are massive animals, sometimes standing six feet high at the hump and having a nose-to-tail measurement of 10 to 12 feet. Many bulls weigh nearly a ton. Cows are usually smaller, seldom weighing 100 pounds.

Musk-oxen are sturdy, hump-shouldered, and sweep-horned animals with long, flowing guard hair over their thick undercoating. Adult bulls stand up to five feet at the shoulder and may typically weigh in excess of 600 pounds; body length may approach eight feet. Cows are considerably smaller. Coloration is dark brown to black, complemented by sun-bleached guard hair. The area above each hoof is white.

Both bison and musk-oxen have four toes, counting the dewclaws, on each foot. Adult animals of each species have 32 teeth including eight incisors, 12 premolars, and 12 molars. Ruminants, they store food collected in the rumen, the first section of their four-chambered stomachs, and later regurgitate and rechew the food during periods of cud-chewing relaxation.

Habitat/Diet

Bison are grazing animals and prefer prairie grasses. Although commonly thought of as creatures of open ranges and grasslands, they also are found in woodlands and brushy areas along waterways. Water is essential to the big animals' existence although they may go for days without drinking. Exceptionally hardy animals, bison are capable of withstanding periods of blistering prairie heat and the numbing cold of winter. Like many animals, their greatest periods of activity occur early and late in the daylight hours. The balance of each day is spent resting, chewing cuds, and wallowing. Dust and mud baths help to deter attacks by bothersome insects that often pursue bison in droning, undulating clouds.

Musk-oxen inhabit harsh, remote lands of constant summertime light and continual darkness each winter. They graze on various subarctic grasses and browse on dwarf willows, birches, and woody shrubs. Periods of feeding activity are followed by periods of rest and cud-chewing.

Senses

Gregarious by nature, bison are considered slow-witted but unpredictable. They rely mainly on their noses to warn of imminent danger. Hearing is considered good but vision is poor, especially when it comes to distinguishing stationary or slow-moving predators.

The musk-oxen depend largely on their eyesight to warn of approaching danger on the open terrain where herds frequent. Their sense of smell is good and they use their olfactory abilities to locate food buried beneath the snow.

Reproduction

Summertime is the breeding period for bison with most rutting activity occurring during July and August. Bulls gather harems of one to several dozen cows and often battle rivals for breeding rights. Fights between mature bulls are bellowing, head-butting, ground-shaking sessions that may obscure the combatants in clouds of prairie dust. The bulls are extremely possessive and dangerous during the rut. Cows come into heat and are fertile for about 24 hours. If not impregnated, they come into estrus 28 days later. Single calves are usually dropped in May of the following year; twins are the exception, although not especially rare. Humps and horns begin to develop on calves within the first few months following birth. Bison are considered mature animals by the age of five, though growth continues for some time. Cows are capable of breeding by the second or third year and generally calve each year of their long lives.

Rutting battles between musk-ox herd bulls and challengers are common during the breeding season. Rivals clash head-on, seeking to knock their opponents to the ground. Horns are used to hook and gore with sometimes fatal results. Harems are gathered and fiercely protected by the dominant bulls. Cows usually come into heat in late August and remain in estrus for just over 24 hours. Bulls repeatedly breed receptive cows and gestation takes place just over eight months, with most births coming in May. Cows seldom give birth to more than one calf at a time; newborns weigh about 30 pounds and are black in color. They are able to follow their mother within a few hours of birth and can keep up with the herd within a few days. Calves often suckle for up to a year, but are able to feed on vegetation less than a week after birth. If threatened by humans, wolves, or bears, musk-oxen often move to high ground and form a defensive circle with calves inside surrounded by the adult animals.

Life Expectancy

Bison often live into their mid-20s and some animals have lived beyond 40 years of age. Predators claim an occasional calf or weakened animal; however, bison have few enemies and usually live long, sedentary lives. Musk-oxen may live up to 25 years, although the rigors of life in a harsh northern environment claim weaker animals with regularity.

Bison meat is considered equal to or better than beef. The meat from musk-oxen is likewise good, although darker and drier than that of cattle.

Bowhunting Records

Bowhunter Duane "Corky" Richardson killed the current World Record bison in Coconino County, Arizona, in March of 2002. His giant bull has an official Pope and Young score of 129 6/8 inches. Colorado bowhunter Bob Black traveled to the Northwest Territories in 1996 to take the best-ever musk-ox bull on a hunt near Kugluktuk (Coppermine). His trophy bull scores 127 2/8.

Chapter 26
Bison & Musk-Ox — Prehistoric Survivors

"THE MAMMOTH BISON was only 20 yards away, standing broadside in a riverbank willow jungle. But he may as well have been 200. There simply was no way to thread an arrow through the maze of tangled limbs and dry, frost-curled leaves.

"This scarred and aged mountain bison was what the local Indians call a gypsy bull. A nomadic loner. A true survivor. Of seasonal battles for rutting supremacy. Of prowling wolf packs. Of menacing grizzly bears. Of bitter wintertime temperatures with drifting snows and ground-crusting ice that seasonally smother the life-sustaining grasses. As tough and unforgiving as the rugged British Columbia wildlands he had ranged a full decade or two, this particular bull had no real reason to fear much of anything. Or anyone.

"Calling these huge beasts impressive is appropriate, yet somehow sadly inadequate. Take it from me, when you're crouching in the shadow of a giant bison at under 20 yards, a gypsy bull is a truly awesome sight."

These are the words I used to introduce readers to my latest bison hunting adventure, which took place near Pink Mountain, B.C., in October of 2001. Thanks to lots of patience and more than a little bit of luck — I finally managed to arrow that giant gypsy bull.

My very first bison "hunt" occurred some two decades earlier. Actually, I was culling a bull from a privately owned bison herd and little actual hunting was involved. Once the big bull was spotted, I simply slipped across the high-fenced pasture and closed in for the shot. There never was any real doubt about my stalk's outcome, only the uncertainty about what to expect when my arrow struck home. This "bowhunt" is typical of how many modern bison are killed by archers. You pay your money and you take your choice.

But in the early '90s, I got my first taste of what it's like to bowhunt wild, free-ranging bison when I headed for a remote chunk of Utah real estate in the shadows of the Henry Mountains. And what a difference! Not only were these bison difficult to find amid the juniper and cedar jungles, but they were as tough to approach as any elk I've hunted. Some of the bison I spooked during blown stalks ran for miles before slowing to a ground-eating walk — and even then they just kept going and going. The bull I eventually

killed was in a small herd that caught my scent and bolted on my hunt's first day when I was still crawling closer some 50 to 60 yards away. I killed him on the hunt's final morning — more than 15 miles from where I'd first stalked him. Talk about goosey game animals!

It is impossible for most modern bowhunters to visualize a rolling prairie blackened as far as the eye can see with great hump-backed beasts, snorting and bellowing as they move beneath undulating clouds of powdery dust that their hooves raise in passing. It is equally difficult for all but a handful of modern day hunters to actually participate in a one-on-one stalk for these great beasts. Options are limited to small herds of animals found on certain private ranches or quest for the few free-ranging bison today only in remote corners of Alaska, Utah, Arizona, and Canada. Incidentally, the Pope and Young Club record-keepers accept bison entries only from the free-ranging herds listed above where the state or province recognizes bison as wildlife and requires a big game hunting license or tag to hunt them. No ranch-raised animals or bison from state-owned parks are eligible.

The primary challenge in hunting these huge, unpredictable creatures is found in first locating and then stalking close enough to make a killing shot. For rifle hunters, obtaining one of the coveted bison licenses, sometimes a once-in-a-lifetime permit, or saving pennies to cover the price of the license and hunt, is often more difficult than downing a trophy bull. For bowhunters, it's much tougher, but most good archers with time, talent, and cash can add this unique trophy to their collection.

A comparatively uncommon North American trophy waiting to challenge any modern day bowhunter is the musk-ox. These blocky, hardy Arctic animals are found in desolate wastelands known as the "Land of Little Sticks" by Indian hunters and the "barren grounds" by white sportsmen. Musk-oxen also are found on certain windswept islands of the far north.

In recent years the musk-ox has become increasingly popular among serious bowhunters. Typically hunted during the late winter and early spring months (it was -20 degrees when I arrowed my

Bison are herd animals, often quite visible but difficult to approach within good bow range. Many trophy-class bulls are loners, except during the breeding season. Stalking these wild, free-ranging bison is a true bowhunting challenge.

The author stalked and arrowed this lone "Gypsy Bull" on a British Columbia hunt. This record book bison weighed nearly a ton.

Northwest Territories bull) or in the late summer (Dwight Schuh tagged his Victoria Island musk-ox in August with daytime temperatures averaging in the 60s), these shaggy animals generally pose a twofold challenge. First, getting to where musk-oxen live is no simple matter, usually involving long-distance travel by airplane and long, bone-jarring rides on snow machines or ATVs. Second, the harsh weather and sub-zero cold typically encountered on winter/spring hunts are less than ideal for bowhunting any big game species. Regardless, the undeniable appeal of participating in this one-of-a-kind bowhunting experience appears irresistible to certain adventuresome souls.

Healthy, growing herds and more outfitters specializing in musk-ox hunts spell a bright future for bowhunting opportunities for anyone seeking this unusual animal. And lest any hunter worry abouut the quality of available trophies, the Pope and Young Club reported that during the 1995-1996 recording period at least five musk-ox scored higher than the then-existing world record. My own trophy bull taped a mere inch off bowhunting's all-time number one bull. Seems the good ol' days of musk-ox hunting are now!

Hunting Techniques

It was the legendary archer Howard Hill who set out to kill a buffalo bull, Indian style. Dressed in buckskin and deer hide moccasins, riding bareback astride a leggy pinto, and using only a hackamore to guide the galloping pony, Hill rode alongside a fleeing bull and drove an arrow through the animal's lungs. Within seconds, before Hill could draw and release a second well-placed shaft from his trusty longbow, the running bull cartwheeled in a cloud of dust and slid to a stop on the Wyoming prairie, stone dead.

Few others have the talent — or gritty courage — to try to take a bison in this manner. Without question, spot-and-stalk hunting is the most common method of bison hunting. In open country these huge animals are among the most visible North American big game species a bowhunter can pursue. If the terrain is unsuitable for stalking, staking out well-used trails or wallows, or waiting in ambush are yet other possibilities; however, bison typically roam over large areas and waiting in one spot for animals to appear can be chancy if not a total waste of time.

Private ranches are the modern hunter's most convenient source of a trophy-sized bull. Although the ranch-raised animals rarely offer the hunting challenge of a free-ranging bull, any bison mount is impressive hanging on the wall, and the animals' meat is generally excellent. And any bowhunter who simply wants the experience of taking a trophy bull — or perhaps seeks to recapture the romance of an age when Indian hunters sought out these same ponderous beasts armed only with their hand-crafted bows and arrows — can book dates and pay the asking price for the opportunity to kill a buffalo. Expect to pay thousands for the privilege.

If you want a strictly fair chase bison hunt, set aside considerable time in addition to a goodly sum of money. Obtaining a special permit will be the biggest challenge. For example, Utah typically allows one non-resident bison per year for its Henry Mountain herd and accepts sealed bids for a second license. These are once-in-a-lifetime permits and cost between $1000 to more than five to six times that amount at the time I hunted there. Frankly, your chances of getting a Utah permit are not all that good. Bison licenses in Arizona and Alaska are not abundant, either. Ditto for Canada. And keep in mind the Pope and Young Club won't accept bison trophies that do not come from free-ranging herds.

Hunting partners Bob DeLaney and Dyrk Eddie also took P&Y trophy bulls on their hunt with M. R. James near Pink Mountain, B.C.

Based on my own buffalo hunting experiences, I've found that free-roaming bison tend to be brush-loving animals. They may stick to or hang out near thick cover along river or creek bottoms, sometimes taking cover in available heavy timber or brushy jungles if hunting pressure disturbs them and disrupts their routine. For the hunter, finding high vantage points and spending time glassing distant terrain can save a lot of boot leather and pinpoint stalkable animals. Glassing is a great way to begin any day's buffalo hunt.

Ranch-raised animals typically are more visible and much less wary, having seen men and motor vehicles perhaps daily throughout their long lives. Wild bison are a different breed. While it's fairly easy to fool their eyes, even in open terrain — provided you take your time and move slowly at all times — you won't fool their noses. Let a cow or bull catch a snootful of nearby man-scent and

likely the whole herd will vacate the premises in a ground-shaking exodus that leaves you staring at only tracks with dust hanging in the prairie air.

The size and unpredictible nature of these beasts can be unnerving when you finally close in for a killing shot. Although bison appear slow-witted and docile, they are surprisingly quick and nimble for such huge animals. Precise arrow placement is mandatory since wounded bulls possess extraordinary endurance and are potentially dangerous, especially if they should decide to vent their anger on the nearest source of their sudden discomfort. I'll admit that more than once I've nervously eyed the surrounding terrain when stalking big bulls and wondering just what would happen if an angry bull headed my way after the shot. Even a mortally wounded animal could easily stomp and gore any hunter into a largely unrecognizable blob of prairie dust before giving up its ghost. That's not an especially comforting thought to have while crawling across the treeless prairie where plains bison are commonly found. It's also one reason some guides insist on backing up their bowhunting clients with a large caliber rifle.

One other possible danger lies in the herd itself. Except for the occasional monarch — like my gypsy bull — that seems to prefer a solitary existence except during the breeding season, bison travel in herds. Often where you find one buffalo, you'll find others nearby. And once an arrow or bullet hits and the scent of blood is in the air, you never know just how the herd will react. They may show total indifference, completely ignoring their wounded or fallen companion. But at times they have been known to become enraged, even attacking and goring the dying or dead animal. No hunter wants to get in the way of an angry bison — or a herd that decides to leave the area in a big hurry. In either case a hunter will come out second best every time.

Although not even distantly related to the North American bison in any scientific sense, musk-oxen closely parallel the bison in several ways. These gregarious herd animals commonly live in open terrain where spot-and-stalk hunting techniques are the most effective hunting method. Known as *Omingmak* to native hunters, a

The author tagged this huge musk ox bull that ranked near the top of the Pope and Young listings.

word meaning "animal with skin like a beard," they rely more on their eyes than their noses to alert them to approaching danger. These are large, shaggy beasts that, like bison, make an unusual, desirable, once-in-a-lifetime big game trophy for anyone wanting to experience a unique, challenging hunt.

Commonly, musk-ox hunting involves flying to some remote Eskimo village or hunting camp where dog sleds, snowmobiles, or ATVs ferry hunters and guides on teeth-rattling rides across the vast tundra. Once a distant herd or lone animal is spotted, the hunter approaches on foot. At times it's possible to move in on feeding or bedded bulls. More often than not, it's impossible to remain undetected in the open terrain. Often as you try to slip close enough for a killing shot, the alerted animals usually run like heck or turn to face the approaching threat. Pursuing a running herd is generally futile, and it's not fair chase to use motorized vehicles to chase after musk-oxen. But once a musk-oxen bull decides to make a stand and confront his pursuer, it's generally a matter of time before the big bull offers a broadside shot. Regardless of the situation, care always should be taken when moving close and setting up for the shot.

The reason? Musk-oxen have been known to charge and injure hunters. My own outfitter, Fred Webb, made it clear to me before my trip that my Inuit guide would not hesitate to use his rifle to stop any charging bull. And I'll admit I began to worry when I finally closed within 40 yards of two good bulls. Each animal faced me, pawed the frozen tundra, rubbed his face on a foreleg, and seemed to be warning me, "That's close enough, buddy!" Although it turned out these bulls were bluffing, my nervous native guide kept his rifle ready, repeatedly cautioning me, "No closer! Shoot now!" In the end I opted not to risk a front-quartering shot in the bitter cold, biting crosswind. When my shooting opportunity finally came, I had remained out of sight just below a ridgeline and crept within 25 yards of the broadside bull I killed with a single arrow to his chest.

Stalking challenges and the possible dangers involved with

point-blank encounters aside, most musk-ox bowhunters return home safely with both a unique trophy and fond memories. Veteran bowbender Len Cardinale of New Jersey spoke for many with these words about his own musk-ox hunt:

"To me these cold weather creatures are the symbol of toughness and endurance. They survive under conditions that would defeat most species, and are unknown to most hunters except for the Eskimo tribesmen and occasional sportsmen who seek them for their horns, hides, and delicious meat. The memories I took from the Arctic will stay with me always. I would not trade my experience there with those people, in that environment, hunting the shaggy one, for anything! It was fulfilling and rewarding — an adventure I feel grateful to have experienced."

Adventure, indeed! Bulky cold weather clothing and the sub-zero temps — combined with unpredictable animals and the heady excitement of the moment — made my own hunt unforgettable. The same can be true for any 21st century bowhunter. All that's important at the moment of truth is to remember to take your time and pick an exact spot on a broadside, stationary animal — then deliver a well-placed arrow. That's critical to quick, clean kills. Even the biggest bull will pile up in a hurry after a sharp broadhead slices through his vitals.

One other bit of good shooting advice is to hold slightly lower than the imaginary mid-body line. A shoulder hump can create an illusion of chest cavity depth that causes high hits — and potential trouble. All marginal hits should be immediately followed by a second arrow. Both musk-oxen and bison are tough animals, deserving the full respect of any ardent bowhunter.

Hunting the shaggy beasts of North America's prairies and mountains — and the Arctic wastelands — is frequently time-consuming and physically demanding, and it's almost always costly for non-residents. Any hunt's price tag — hunt fee, license cost, transportation, and taxidermy bill — adds up in a hurry. Expect to pay many thousands of dollars.

Trophy Recognition

Both sexes of bison and musk-oxen have horns, although seldom will any cow's lighter, thinner headgear qualify for the Pope and Young records.

Five measurements are taken to score bison horns — horn length and four circumference measurements. Spread measurements (inside and greatest spreads) are supplementary data and not included in the official score. The minimum score for record book consideration is 100.

The horns of musk-ox are unlike that of any other North American horned game. Their base is composed of an enlarged solid mass known as "boss." It's a casque of horn, similar to that found on the heavy, sweeping horns of Africa's Cape buffalo. The horns are separate but grow closely together with heavy hair often sprouting from the gap. The seven measurements necessary for musk-ox include two supplemental spread measurements (greatest spread and tip-to-tip spread), horn length, width of boss, and three horn circumference measurements. To qualify for the P&Y listings, a musk-ox's horns must score a total of 90 inches.

These big animals make impressive trophies, whether or not they are listed in the Pope and Young records. To me, each species represents a singular bowhunting experience and any adult animal fairly taken is worthy of a place of honor in any bowhunter's wildlife room.

Tiny Targets

Chapter 27
Tiny Targets —
Small Game & Varmints

ALTHOUGH BIG GAME slakes an annual thirst, stalking and shooting at small game and varmints often primes the pump. Keeping your shooting skills sharp in the off-season — or during lulls between your big game bowhunting adventures — is always a good idea. And while slinging arrows at foam or paper targets can be beneficial, even fun, there's really no better substitute for big game than bowhunting something. Anything! It's certainly not kids' stuff to hunt smaller critters. It's smart practice, and it's great sport, too!

No handbook covering the expert strategies and techniques of modern-day bowhunting would be complete without a brief look at half a dozen or so of bowhunting's most popular tiny targets. Following, in no particular order of importance, are facts and how-to-hunt tips on smaller game that can add enjoyment — and hunting excitement — to your days afield.

Javelina and Feral Hogs

If ever any small game animal was made for bowhunters wanting to hone their stalking skills, it's the collared peccary — or javelina — of the American Southwest. Small, grayish, and pig-like in appearance, javelina inhabit the dry brushlands of Texas, Arizona, and both New and Old Mexico. Gregarious animals, they commonly travel in groups that provide some protection from predators, the old safety-in-numbers principle.

Individual animals usually stand under 24 inches at the shoulder and measure less than 36 inches from snout to rump. Each is equipped with sharp, two-inch tusks that give them an undeserved reputation for fierceness. When spooked, they often flare their salt-and-pepper manes to appear larger than they actually are. More often than not frightened javelina will noisily scamper off to safety, grunting, squealing, and clacking their teeth. If cornered or wounded, however, these quick and agile animals are capable of putting up a fierce fight. Regardless, I believe that most tales of hunters being charged by javelina are told by people who just happened to be standing where a scared peccary chanced to run. A stalk and shot I made in south Texas one October is a perfect example of such a "charge."

After spotting several javelina feeding along in the high grass just ahead, I made a quick stalk and nailed the biggest animal in the group. He squealed and the rest of the small band exploded like a covey of quail. The mortally wounded boar spun in a circle and then headed directly my way. He tore past me, practically brushing the leg of my camo pants, and collapsed 15 yards away. Only after my heart stopped pounding did I realize I was standing smack dab in the middle of a game trail, a natural escape path. Had that javelina been charging me, he certainly could have taken a chunk out of my leg before going down for keeps.

Peccaries usually are up and about feeding early in the morning, but they often hole up in shady areas during the heat of the day. Javelina often root holes in sandy soil and plop themselves down in the shade until evening, when they rise and resume feeding. Mesquite thickets and shallow caves are utilized as well. Omnivorous, brush-loving animals, they mostly eat vegetation — with prickly pear a special favorite — but few javelina ever pass up a meal of insects, rodents, reptiles, birds, or their eggs. Hunters checking for signs of feeding activity look for freshly chewed prickly pear pads and signs of rooting in the hardpacked earth where the animals dig for tubers and tender plant roots. Bedding areas are marked by lots of tracks, scat, and shallow depressions in the soil.

Javelina have excellent hearing and an even better sense of smell. Their eyesight is poor to average, but they quickly pick up suspicious movement, especially at bowhunting yardages. To successfully stalk them, you must work into the wind and move quietly until close enough for the shot — and moving silently over rocky ground or through dense undergrowth can be a real challenge. Frankly, I rarely worry about being seen much beyond 50 yards or so, but I try to ease ahead only when the animals' heads are down. In open terrain such as treeless grasslands, I take special pains to avoid being seen when closing in for the shot. You need to keep low and stay off the skyline. All it takes is for one animal to spot you and snort to send the entire herd scurrying away. Any careless movement or noise at close range will end any stalk, *muy pronto*.

Perhaps the best way to locate javelina is to glass from high

M. R. James believes javelina are tailor-made for bowhunters wanting a spot-and-stalk challenge. He's tested his stalking skills on these "pigs" throughout the American Southwest.

Feral hogs are ideal for off-season hunting challenges. Anthony Guidry was 12 when he made his first successful California bowhunt with proud grandmom Jan Perry acting as guide. Both javelina and hogs are tasty table fare.

points overlooking feeding areas or *senderos*, open lanes or roadways winding through dense brushlands. Good optics are a must. Once distant animals are spotted, it's smart to hurry over and move in slowly as you get near the spot where the animals were last seen. Once the stalk begins, use your ears as well as your eyes to locate feeding pigs. On numerous Arizona stalks, I've heard the animals well before I saw them. Also, keep in mind that peccaries dislike cold, windy days. So don't expect to find them feeding on open hillsides then; check out ravines or dry washes when they seek refuge from chilly winds.

Besides the common spot-and-stalk method used to take most javelina, calling the animals — using a predator call to create the high-pitched squeals of an injured javelina — will sometimes work quite well. Such calling can create instant excitement when a herd of frantic, squealing peccaries responds on a dead run to check out the source of the sounds. Successful callers caution that once calling begins, the cries should continue until the javelina arrive. If you stop calling, the animals typically stop coming. Calling is something to try when a stalk is out of the question — or when you simply want to spice up your hunt with instant excitement.

Javelina are tough little animals, but they quickly succumb to a sharp broadhead through the vitals. Their kill area is fairly small and care should be taken to pick an exact spot on the ribcage. It's easy to misjudge distance in open country, and these animals aren't very big. But since javelina aren't especially hard to stalk, shots taken at 20 yards or less are common. Always try to keep arrow-hit animals in sight as long as possible, and carefully mark the spot where they were last seen. Blood trailing is no different than for other game, except wounded javelina often dive back into thick, thorny brush that makes following a nightmare.

Again, javelina are ideal for bowhunters and a unique trophy in

their own right. Regardless, in the winter months it's possible for deer hunters to include one or two stalks for javelina as part of any day's adventure. They aren't bad eating, either, and make a distinctive mount in any bowhunter's trophy collection. When skinning a javelina, however, take special care not to touch the dorsal scent gland. The odiferous musk this back gland secretes is unpleasant to smell and easily transferred from fingers to the meat if you are careless.

A larger, far-more-dangerous distant cousin of the javelina is the free-ranging feral hog, whose ancestors originated in Asia and Europe and were first imported to North America in the 1800s. Bowhunting wild boars is not for the faint-of-heart, although some hunting preserves offer "wild boar" hunts behind game-proof fences where kills are guaranteed. Take it from me, this put-and-take, pay-for-what-you-kill experience is not the same thing as stalking large, free-ranging hogs one-on-one in dense swamplands, coastal marshes, brush-country thickets, and rugged canyons where actual feralhogs roam unfettered.

Wild hogs typically are lean, muscular animals with faces only another pig could love. Long, curving tusks that are readily visible give these animals a somewhat sinister air. Body hair is sparse, stiff, bristly. Size and coloration of these animals vary greatly depending on diet and genetics. Some large hogs easily top 300 pounds and stand 36 inches at the shoulder, with an overall body length of five feet or more. I know one Texas hog arrowed near Victoria that topped 500 pounds and was nearly seven feet long, but hogs that size are true exceptions. On a recent south Texas hunt, I arrowed a 200-pound red-coated boar that locals claimed was large for that particular area.

Wild hogs, like javelina, are gregarious and often can be found in herds ranging for a handful to dozens of animals. They, too, are

Large boars like this Texas tusker are quick and agile animals with excellent hearing and sense of smell. That makes easing within good bow range a true test of stalking practice and patience.

omnivorous, opportunistic feeders with a special fondness for acorns and the fallen fruits of other mast-bearing trees. Older, larger boars tend to lead a solitary life, seeking the companionship of sows only during the breeding season. Such boars tend to develop a surly disposition and, if pressured, can be a formidable foe. Rugged and strong yet amazingly quick and lithe, huge hogs remind me of a well-conditioned heavyweight boxer, demanding both admiration and respect.

Still-hunting and stalking are common bowhunting methods for most hog hunters, but tree stands along trails and feeding areas work, too. Hogs have exceptionally keen noses, and their sense of hearing is acute. Working close enough for a killing shot can be a true challenge. A hog's eyesight comes in a distant third in sensory defense mechanisms. In open terrain, glassing for stalkable game is often time well spent. In dense woodlands and nearly impenetrable brush country jungles, taking a stand near rooting areas can sometimes pay off. In other parts of the country, hounds are commonly used to locate hogs and bring them to bay.

Whatever hunting method and hunting area you choose, realize that these big animals are quite capable of inflicting serious injury on any careless hunter. Special care is needed when trailing wounded hogs. Their thick, brushy habitat typically cuts visibility to a matter of feet. No one I know wants to suddenly be looking at the business end of an irate boar headed his way at point-blank range. Consequently, proper shot placement is an absolute must.

The older trophy-class boars rarely provide tasty table fare; however, the pork of younger animals is excellent.

Turkeys and Other Birds

"Big game with feathers." That's how one veteran hunter summed up wild turkeys. Added another, "If gobblers ever develop a sense of smell to go with their eyes, no hunter's ever going to kill one."

In truth, it's the legendary eyesight of turkeys that makes them so tough to bowhunt. Able to see in an almost complete circle, the big birds can distinguish color better, detect movement faster, and react more quickly than most hunters who pursue them. Is it any wonder that turkey hunters commonly speak of them with awe and admiration — even reverence — when asked about a wild turkey's vision? About all they lack in the optical department is good nocturnal vision, a fact that accounts for their daily search for suitable nighttime roost trees.

The hearing of turkeys is believed to be better than that of man, too. Birds are quick to pick up and pinpoint the source of sounds that pique their curiosity and suspicion. When alarmed, they can fly at speeds exceeding 50 mph or dash off at a ground-covering pace approaching 20 mph. Their sense of smell, however, is quite poor and of no concern to hunters.

There are four separate species that fascinate — and frustrate — most North American turkey hunters. These include the Eastern wild turkey, the Florida or Osceola turkey, the Rio Grande turkey, and the Merriam's turkey. There are two separate species living in Mexico, the Mexican and Gould's turkey.

Springtime hunters commonly locate a roost area the evening before a hunt and set up nearby before first light the following day. Decoys and/or calls are then used to lure lusty toms close to the carefully concealed hunters. In the fall, when gobblers are not as responsive to calls, some hunters seek to locate and scatter turkey flocks, then call in an attempt to dupe lone birds into responding and approaching to rejoin the flock.

Taking turkeys with a shotgun is challenging; pursuing gobblers with bows and broadheads is triply difficult. In the first place, shots

A well-located blind and decoy spread can be deadly effective for bowhunters wanting to tag a big gobbler. The blind hides hunter movements and the jake decoy (center) will attract the attention of approaching longbeards. It's the author's favorite turkey hunting setup.

must be close, and the gobbler's exceptional eyes are quick to pick up movements as a bowhunter attempts to draw an arrow. Second, the kill area of these birds is an unusually small target, about the size of a grapefruit or softball. Third, even mortally wounded birds have the stamina to run or fly away, leaving little or no blood to follow, making recovery an iffy proposition.

Some veteran bowhunters suggest shooting for the gaudy red, white, and blue head of a strutting tom, stating a hit will anchor the bird while anything else will result in a clean miss and uninjured bird. I've dropped gobblers in their tracks with head shots and can vouch for their effectiveness. Other hunters insist a solid broadside shot to the base of the wing is best, while some seek to break the bird's back by shooting at the center of the gobbler's fanned tail as he faces directly away. I've taken toms with these recommended shots and know they're deadly, too. Whichever you choose, it's generally a good idea to get to any arrow-hit bird as quickly as possible, pinning the turkey and preventing possible escape. However, care must be taken anytime an arrow does not completely pass through the bird's body; a broadhead-tipped shaft protruding from the flopping, thrashing bird could severely slice any careless or excited hunter.

Two devices used by some turkey hunters are string trackers and penetration limiters. Both can aid in recovery. One mounts to the bow and dispenses a thin string connected to the arrow, playing out as the bird runs or flies away. The other is fitted to the shaft or broadhead and keeps the arrow in the bird's body, making running or flying difficult, if not impossible.

Another excellent investment is a completely enclosed portable blind. Where legal, these handy devices take you to where the turkey action is, can be set up in a jiffy, and totally hide you from eagle-eyed toms as you draw your bow. Small shooting windows in the camouflaged cloth — or shoot-through mesh netting — allow point-blank shots at wary birds. And while you're at it, why not add a decoy or two and several calls — box, slate, and diaphragm — to your turkey hunting gear? Instructional how-to tapes can have you

sounding like a boss gobbler or sexy hen in no time flat.

My personal favorite setup is to stake a jake decoy 15 or so yards directly in front of my blind, with one or more hen decoys close by. I make sure the jake is always facing me. Approaching toms almost invariably head straight for the jake, fanning and strutting in front of the young tom.

This often gives me the perfect shooting opportunity and is a deadly setup. Also, I typically call sparingly, especially when birds have answered my calls and may be headed my way. An occasional cluck or purr is often ample incentive for the amorous gobbler to find that coy hen.

Trophy birds are determined by weight, length of beards — those clusters of bristly feathers sprouting from a tom's chest — and the length of the spurs found jutting from the back of each foot. The National Wild Turkey Federation, a South Carolina-based non-profit organization dedicated to the management and wise use of these big birds, does keep official records of giant gobblers taken with both gun and bow. The meat of wild turkeys is leaner and drier than that of domesticated birds; however, the breast meat is quite good when properly prepared.

Other game birds and waterfowl — pheasants, grouse, ducks, and geese — are routinely taken by bowhunters every fall. Many are arrowed by big game hunters in pursuit of deer, elk, and other species. Others are intentionally hunted by archers seeking special challenges.

Plump fowl always adds variety to any hunting camp menu and seems especially taken with a well-aimed arrow. Also, fast-flying pheasants cackling into the autumn air ahead of trembling bird dogs locked on point, and waterfowl rocking toward the decoy spread on cupped wings, provide all the shooting challenge any bowhunter could ask for. Practice shooting flu-flu arrows at airborne frisbees or plastic milk jugs to sharpen your eye prior to the hunt. Granted, you'll miss far more flying birds than you'll hit. But you'll never forget the few shots that fly true and bring a winged target tumbling to earth. Guaranteed! I know!

M. R. James arrowed this Mississippi longbeard from a portable Double Bull blind situated at the edge of a greenfield where turkeys feed.

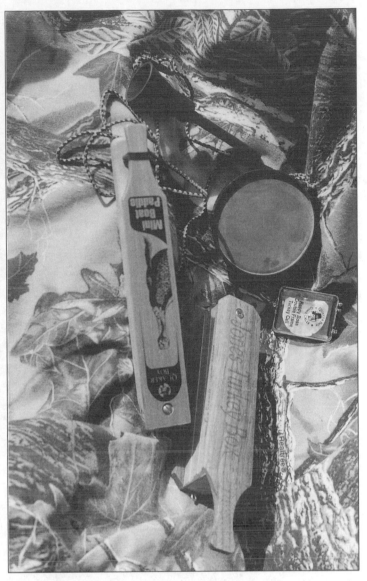

Slate, box, and diaphragm calls can be mastered with practice and instructional tapes. Learning basic turkey talk is not that difficult.

Chucks and Ground Squirrels

The ubiquitous woodchuck — and its western high country cousin the rockchuck — plus the common ground squirrel or gopher, quite likely have combined to provide bowhunters with more off-season shooting practice and small game hunting challenge than all other small critters combined.

Literally millions of woodchucks — or groundhogs — thrive throughout the eastern United States and across most of Canada, while rockchucks — or marmots — are commonly found across much of western North America. These burrowing rodents are familiar sights along farm-field fence rows and ditch banks throughout the spring, summer, and fall. Dens with freshly-dug dirt fanned at each entrance mound indicates occupancy by one or more furry tunnelers. In the Rockies, the shrill alarm whistle of keen-eyed marmots perched atop arrow-destroying rockpiles is an all-too-familiar high country sound.

Stalking close to any of these furry varmints as they feed or sun themselves is no simple chore. Seemingly ever alert, they frequently sit upright to scan their surroundings for any hint of danger. Their eyesight is excellent and quick to pick up movement, even at great distances. Hearing is well-developed, too, and I've seen some circumstantial evidence they also use their sense of smell in heavily hunted areas.

I arrowed my first 'chucks as a teenager by slipping along railroad tracks near my southern Illinois home. Later, at the request of area farmers, I honed my stalking and shooting skills on beanfield-raiding rodents. I've taken dozens of animals in a single season, but when the landowners pressed for total extinction of these troublesome farmland pests, I always made certain I left enough for seed. Later, after moving to Montana, I stalked rockchucks to keep my skills sharp during spring and summer months. There are few better ways I know of to prepare for stalking big game than to go 'chuck hunting with your bow in hand.

Active feeders early and late in the day, groundhogs can be glassed from a distance and stalked by taking advantage of terrain or any available cover. Sharp broadheads are a must to anchor these chunky rodents, which will dash headlong for their burrows at the first hint of trouble. However, care always should be taken to avoid lost arrows that might damage farm machinery or injure livestock.

Many landowners welcome responsible hunters who ask permission to lend a hand helping keep the local varmint population under control. This approach sometimes opens doors to return in the fall when big game seasons open. Surprising to some, one bonus involved in hunting chucks is the fact they make pretty good table fare.

Gophers are another matter. Largely regarded purely as pests by

Arrowing pheasants on the wing — or ground — is an ultimate bowhunting challenge.

time should be spent looking than moving. Everything you do should be done in slow motion. Use your eyes to seek out any nearby movements. Use your ears to hear a telltale rustling in the grass. "Easy does it" is always a key ingredient to most stalking and still-hunting successes. And when your arrow flies true, always handle the carcass with care. These critters sometimes carry disease that can infect humans.

Stalking gophers or prairie dogs in open pastures is my favorite way to prepare for caribou hunts on the treeless tundra where accurately judging distances can be a problem for many bowhunters. I've discovered that plenty of shooting practice at pint-sized pasture pests is a perfect tune-up. When I can consistently put my hunting arrows through or within a whisker of a gopher or prairie pup at common bowhunting yardages, I know I'm ready to draw down on any big-racked, white-maned bull that will appear huge by comparison.

Shooting gophers and prairie dogs is an excellent way to introduce youngsters and other bowhunters to archery. Most any bow and set of arrows will do nicely. While broadheads are mandatory for 'chucks and marmots, blunts, Judo points or even field points will do the job on ground squirrels. Action often is fast-paced, and the excitement generated by lots of shooting opportunities at live game can be addictive. More than one serious big game bowhunter got his or her start by slipping up on 'chucks and gophers in the budding days of a now blossoming huntin' career.

Coyotes and Foxes

Calling foxes and coyotes within bow range is often the easy part; penetrating their hides with a sharp broadhead is where the difficulty lies. I'd venture a guess that more arrows have been launched at these varmints than any other fur-bearing predator that responds to a call. I'd also speculate that far more of those airborne missiles have missed than connected.

Many songdogs and foxes taken by bowhunters are shot by chance encounters during pursuit for other game. I arrowed my first fox from an Illinois whitetail stand; my first coyote fell as I stalked Colorado mule deer. Many bowhunters I know can tell similar stories.

During a New Mexico elk hunt a few years back, a coyote trotted up and stopped broadside less than a dozen short yards from where my guide and I crouched watching a bugling bull moving through the shadows across a grassy park. As Mr. Coyote paused to check out the noisy bull, I eased to full draw — much to the horror of my elk guide who was visibly relieved when I let down and grinned over at him. As things turned out, I didn't get either the coyote or bull — but I know I could have let the air out of that critter had I taken the shot. And maybe I should have. Over the years

landowners, they can wreak havoc in and around livestock pastures, hayfields, and croplands. "Destructive" is one of the kinder terms used by many ranchers and farmers when describing these prolific little burrowers. Ditto for the less numerous prairie dogs found in certain western states and provinces.

These tiny, hyperactive bundles of energy possess tremendous reflexes and seemingly are capable of dodging arrows launched from even the fastest, flattest-shooting bows. Highly visible, gophers are rarely a problem to find. Consistently hitting them is an entirely different matter.

As with any type of successful spot-and-stalk endeavor, more

Cottontails are North America's favorite small game animal. They test shooting skills and provide some tasty eating, too.

Grouse are a tricky target for the northwoods hunter.

I've taken more called-in elk with my bow than coyotes. Ditto for foxes.

Simply stated, calling these wily, wary, arrow-ducking predators is downright thrilling. And you don't have to be all that good with a call to get the job done. Screeches of birds or small game in agony are easy to imitate. Predators have incredible hearing, and I've brought foxes and coyotes on the run from up to 50 yards simply by making kissing sounds with my lips. But each animal also has a keen nose and excellent eyesight to complement its acute auditory assets. So you'd better be at full draw and on target because you're not going to have much time to aim and release. Foxes and coyotes can swap ends and reverse direction in a nanosecond. They won't hang around long once they realize they've been fooled.

Shooting from a tree stand is rarely any more effective than getting off a shot from ground level. Believe me, these critters are quick to look up and pick up any overhead movements. Your best bet is to completely conceal yourself in a well-camouflaged portable blind and be ready to take your best shot. Another effective calling technique I've used is setting up in an open field after dark (where legal, of course) and employing a red light to illuminate any approaching target. Darkness seems to dull the senses and allay the fears of hungry predators. I've shot several foxes while sitting in plain view with a hunting partner beside me manning the light.

Candidly, you probably won't collect too many fox or coyote pelts in a season — or a lifetime, for that matter — but it's fun to try. Calling these suspicious, sagacious varmints is great practice for other game, too. Bobcats are yet another calling possibility, as are cougars and bears if you want to graduate to other game.

Rabbits and Hares

The common cottontail, as well as its larger cousins the jackrabbit and snowshoe hare, are naturals for bowhunters. They're challenging to hunt yet generally plentiful enough to provide plenty of shooting practice for any licensed hunter. A bonus is the fact their meat can provide some welcome variety to any camp menu.

Cottontails are the king of North American small game. Widely distributed and capable of multiplying like a pocket calculator, they have good eyes and even better ears, making stalking them in brush patches and weed fields no piece of cake. And since hitting a running rabbit with an arrow isn't easy, most bowhunters try to spot a rabbit huddled in its grassy form and shoot at a stationary target. A few routinely hunt with beagles and use the time-tested technique of standing atop a stump or other briar patch high point and letting the dogs do their work, taking shots at cottontails hopping past well ahead of the trailing hounds. Personally, I prefer early morning hunts on snowy days when fresh tracks lead directly to Mr. Rabbit and when cottontails hiding in clumps are easier to spot.

In northern and western areas, jacks and varying or snowshoe hares attract the attention of some bowhunters. They're ideal for honing still-hunting and stalking skills. At times, I've arrowed jackrabbits while walking back to camp after a morning's deer hunt. On other occasions, I've gone after then intentionally during midday lulls when practice shooting at paper or foam targets leaves something to be desired. Most hares I've arrowed have been taken for the pot during big game bowhunts.

I prefer judo points or broadheads for bunnies, although those large rubber blunts that kill by shock, not penetration, work quite well. And whether hunting solo or as part of a group (some bowhunting clubs make annual outings for cottontails, jacks, or hares), I always pick my shots carefully. Concentration is the key. Learn to repeatedly shoot a "good arrow" and you've learned the secret to consistent bowhunting success.

Small birds and animals of all kinds — usually living within a short drive of home — are among the best teachers available.

Chapter 28
The Future: Africa and Other Adventures

THERE'S NO SHORTAGE of bowhunting opportunities anywhere around the modern world. Australia and New Zealand have good numbers of resident bowbenders, and specialized outfitters welcome Yanks in search of new species. Hunting in Russia — for giant bears and big moose and sheep — is said to be as good as Alaska was in "the old days." The same can be said of other parts of Asia and certain areas in South America. Even Europe seems to be offering more opportunities for local and visiting archers. And keep this fact in mind: *Virtually every legal species of big game found anywhere on earth is now being pursued by adventuresome bowhunters.*

(Above) Dave Holt spends months in Africa every year, hosting bowhunts and doing some serious hunting. That's a good impala ram he's holding.

(Left) Dr. Dave Samuel has hunted Africa, helping to establish present day bowhunting opportunities in southern Africa. That's a nice kudu bull he's smiling over.

Neil Summers of Bowhunting Safari Consultants is another frequent visitor to the Dark Continent. He arrowed this Cape buffalo on one of his many adventures.

Dreaming of joining the action? Probably no overseas destination is more popular than Africa, the land that has stirred the imagination of any hunter who's ever read Hemingway, Ruark, or Capstick. Pope and Young hunted there. And Fred Bear and Howard Hill, too. It's where Bob Swinehart first took the dangerous Big Five with his longbow, setting the bar high but not out of reach for contemporary bowmen. Gary Bogner recently duplicated Swinehart's feat using a compound bow. It's also where Chuck Adams and an A-list of other noted modern bowhunters — including Fred Asbell, Dave Holt, Dave Samuel, and Dwight Schuh — have ventured in search of new archery horizons and additional big game challenges. It's also one of the best bargains around. Not only is an African adventure readily available, it's extremely affordable.

For example, an African quest for several species of plains game is less pricey than a single fly-in, fully-guided Alaskan moose hunt. Non-stop jet flights from several U.S. cities can have bowhunters and their gear in Johannesburg in less than a day. Very few who make the long journey say they don't dream of returning. In fact, most can't wait to make another African bowhunt. And another. And another. . . .

Africa offers a great variety of game animals, too. From impala to wildebeest, kudu to warthog, Cape buffalo to lion and rhino and elephant. Name it and some bowhunter has been there, done that. With planning, budgeting, and professional assistance, you can do it, too. *Note: Dave Holt spends several months in southern Africa every year and helps book bowhunts with first-rate outfitters. Contact him at DHAfrica@Juno.com.*

Now here's a brief summary of several African hunting destinations:

South Africa

Bowhunting has been legal in this country for more than two decades. Both plains and dangerous game may be hunted with archery tackle, but there are restrictions on the required foot-pounds of kinetic energy for various species. Any knowledgeable outfitter can provide equipment specifics. South Africa is likely the number one travel destination for modern bowhunters. *Note: Hunts may take place on private lands that are high-fenced.* For travel information, contact the South African Tourism Board, 747 Third Ave., New York, NY 10017.

Namibia

This dry, sparsely country is also very bowhunter-friendly and offers great hunting potential because of its variety and sheer numbers of game animals. Bowhunting has been legal there since 1997

Illinois bowhunters Ralph and Vicki Cianciarulo are both avid archers. They spent their honeymoon on an African adventure.

and equipment must meet certain basic kinetic energy standards. Archery hunting for dangerous game is not permitted. For travel info, contact Republic of Namibia, Ministry of Environment and Tourism, 4th Floor, Swabou Bldg., 7 Post St. Mail, Private Bag 13346 Windhoek, Namibia.

Botswana

Archery hunting was legalized in this southern Africa nation in 1995, but only plains game bowhunting is permitted. Tackle requirements are bows drawing at least 50 pounds and arrows weighing a minimum of 400 grains. For details, write the Republic of Botswana, Director of Wildlife and Tourism, P. O. Box 131, Gaborone, Botswana.

Mozambique

Bowhunting plains and dangerous game is legal in this east African nation. There are no specific equipment restrictions. For details, write the People's Republic of Mozambique, 1990. M St. NW, Suite 570, Washington, DC 20036.

Zimbabwe

Once a popular African bowhunting destination after archery equipment was first legalized for hunting in 1991, recent political unrest and internal warfare have made this a risky proposition for bowhunters. The State Department has occasionally issued warnings to Americans thinking of traveling to Zimbabwe. While excellent hunting opportunities still exist, it's safe to say dangers also exist. For more details, contact Zimbabwe Tourism Board, 1270 Avenue of the Americas, Suite 412, New York, NY 10020.

Zambia

Open to bowhunting since 1993, all native species may be pursued with archery tackle. Bows must meet certain poundage standards from 40 to 80 pounds, depending on the game being hunted. Note: All hunting was suspended in 2001 while the government reviewed the allocation of hunting areas, but things have now returned to normal. For info, contact Zambian National Tourist Board, 237 E. 52nd St., New York, NY 10022.

If an African safari interests you, check with experienced outfitters who can provide the details necessary to plan a quality adventure at a very reasonable cost. This singular experience can broaden any serious hunter's horizons.

Directory of Manufacturers, Organizations, & Publications

Abe & Sons, 800 Sunshine Lane, Coos Bay, OR 97420, Ace Sportswear, P. O. Box 64790, Fayetteville, NC 28306, (443) 553-1223, Clothing

O. L. Adcock, 3116 Encanto Dr., Roswell, NM 88201, (505) 625-6908, Custom Bowyer

Advantage Camouflage, P. O. Box 9638, Columbus, GA 31908, (706) 569-9101 Clothing

ACI/Ellett Brothers, 267 Columbia Ave., Chapin, SC 29036, (800) 822-8728, Wholesaler/Distributor

ADG Sports, 2080 N. Hwy. 360, Ste. 135, Grand Prairie, TX 75050, (972) 623-1674, Cases

Aftershock Archery, Inc., P. O. Box 575, Walled Lake, MI 48390, (248) 363-6622, Broadhead

AIM, 95 Milk St., Willmantic, CT, (860) 423-8609, Wholesaler/Distributor

Allen Company, P. O. Box 445, Broomfield, CO 80038, (303) 469-1857, Cases

Alpen Outdoors, 10722 Arrow Rt., Ste. 404, Rancho Cucamonga, CA 91730, (909) 987-8370, Optics

Alpine Archery, P. O. Box 319, Lewiston, ID 83501, (208) 746-4717, Bows

American Visionwear, 6812 Fairgrounds Pkwy., San Antonio, TX 78238, (210) 520-7927, Range Finders

American Whitetail, Rt. 1, Box 244 J, Ferdinand, IN 47538, (812) 937-7185, Targets

Ameristep, P. O. Box 189, Clio, MI 48420, (810) 686-4035, Blinds

AMS Bowfishing, EP1064 Hemlock Ln., Stratford, WI 54484, (715) 687-2350, Bowfishing Gear

APA Innovations, Inc., Box 1420, Biggar, SASK S0K 0M0, (306) 948-5101, Arrow Rests

Apple Archery Products, 245 Beshore School Rd., Manchester, PA 17345, (717) 266-7889, Bow Maintenance

Archer's Choice Equipment, P. O. Box 279, Dunlap, TN 37327, (423) 949-5000, Accessories

Archer's Choice Video/TV Show, 31570 Willow Rd. Lanark, IL 61046, (815) 493-8998, Accessories, Shooting/Hunting

Archery Business, 6420 Sycamore Ln., Ste. 100, Maple Grove, MN 55396, (800) 848-6247, Magazine

Archery Hall of Fame, 1555 S. 150 W., Angola, IN 46703, (260) 665-1604, Organization

Archery Interactive, 11000 E. 53rd Ave., Denver, CO 80239, (303) 375-1352, TechnoHunt Target System

Archery Research, P. O. Box 5487, Tucson, AZ 85703, (520) 884-9065, Bows

Archery Shooter Systems, 109 N. Wagner St., Endeavor, WI 53930, (608) 587-2554, Accessories

Archery Shooters Association, 1301 Shiloh Rd. #720, Kennesaw, GA 30156, (770) 795-0232, Organization

Arctic Shield, Inc., 905 S. 9th St., Ste. D, Broken Arrow, OK 74012, (918) 258-8788, Clothing

Arizona Archery Enterprises, Inc., 2781 N. Valley View Dr., Prescott Valley, AZ 86314, (520) 772-9887, Vanes

Arizona Rim Country Products, 6401 W. Chandler Blvd. #A, Chandler, AZ 85226, (480) 961-7995, Fletching Jigs

Arrow Brake Targets, 59498 270th St., Warroad, MN 56763, (218) 386-2889, Targets

Arrow Dynamics, 536 SE Jefferson , Topeka, KS 66607, (785) 233-9541, Arrows

ArrowSport, P. O. Box 258, Confrey, MN 56019, (866) 266-2776, Organization

ArrowTrade, 3479 409th Ave. NW, Braham, MN 55006, (320) 396-3473, Magazine

ARS Solutions, LTD, 940 Industrial Dr., Ste. 107, Sauk Rapids, MN 56379, (800) 547-7120 Accessories

ASAP, Inc., P. O. Box 793, Freeland, MI 48623, (989) 695-9968, Accessories

Aspen Longbow Co., W2890 Lorraine Dr., Missoula, MT 59803, (406) 251-3300, Custom Bows

Ashco Mfg., Inc., 28701 E. Broadway, Walbridge, OH 43465, (419) 838-7157, Treestands

Associated Weavers, 2670 Lakeland Rd., Dalton, GA 39721, (800) 843-1842, Accessories

Archery Trade Association, P. O. Box 258, Comfrey, MN 56019, (866) 266-2776, Organization

Atsko/Sno Seal, Inc., 2664 Russell St., Orangeburg, SC 29115, (802) 531-1820, Scents, Waterproofing

A-Way Hunting Products, P. O. Box 492, Beaverton, MI 48612, (989) 435-3879, Game Calls

Aznat, LLC, 1418 E. Marconi Ave., Phoenix, AZ 85022, (800) 632-5750, Arrow Accessories/Magnock

Backland Outdoors, 17128 240th St., Hutchinson, MN 55350, (320) 234 6192, Accessories/Camo/Clothing

Badlands Packs, 1414 S. 700 W., Salt Lake City, UT 84104. (800) 269-1875, Packs/Bags

Ballistic Archery, Inc., P. O. Box 9, Rosemont, NJ 08556, (609) 397-1990, Accessories

Barrie Archery/Rocky Mtn., P. O. Box 482, Waseca, MN 56093, (507) 835-3859, Broadheads

BBK Enterprises, 119 Bobby Lou, San Antonio, TX 78218, (210) 637-1633, Treestands

BCY, Inc., 697 Middle St., Middletown, CT 06457, (860) 632-5775, Accessories

Bass Pro Shops, 2500 E. Kearney, Springfield, MO 65898, (800) BASS PRO, Mail Order

Fred Bear Equipment Co., 4600 SW 41st Blvd., Gainesville, FL 32608, (352) 376-2327, Bows/Accessories

Bear Hunting, 2450 121st. Ave., Clear Lake, MN 55319, Magazine

Bear's Paw Bows, P. O. Box 577, Lakeside, MT 59922, (406) 844-0287, Custom Bows

Becoming an Outdoors Woman, 1900 Franklin St., Stevens Point, WI 54481, (877) BOWOMAN, Organization

Beman, 5040 W. Harold Gatty Dr., Salt Lake City, UT 84116, (801) 539-1433, Arrows

Ben Pearson Archery, P. O. Box 327, Brewton, AL 36427. (251) 867-8980, Bows

Benchmark/Pee Willie Wick, 10740 Gurney Rd. Baker, LA 70714, (225) 261-8624, Scents

Benders No-Glov, 2803 S. 22nd St., La Crosse, WI 54601, Shooter's Aid

Berne Apparel, 104 E. Main St., Berne, IN 46711, (260) 589-3136, Clothing

Big Game Products, P. O. Box 382, Windom, MN 56101, (507) 831-4350, Treestands

Bighorn Bowhunting Co., 2881 31st Ave., Greely, CO 80631, (970) 356-80611, Custom Bows

Big Oak Outdoors, 1015-B N. Court St., Montgomery, AL 36104, (334)-269-2825, Treestands/Accessories

Bingham Projects, 1350 Hickley Dr., Ogden, UT 84401, (801) 399-3470, Bow Kits

Biter Products Corp., 26585 136th St., Zimmerman, MN 55398, (612) 251-3713, Treestand Accessories

Bitzenburger, 13060 Lawson Rd., Grand Ledge, MI 48837 (517) 627-8433, Jigs/Accessories

Blackhawk Arrow Co., P. O. Box 4240, Austintown, OH 44515, (330) 793-3314, Arrows

Blackwater Creek Treestands, P. O. Box 580, Meridian, MS 39342, (601) 484-2987, Treestands

Black Widow Bows, 1201 Eaglecrest, Box 2100, Nixa, MO 65714, (417) 725-3133, Custom Bows

Blodgett Calls, 421 Park Ave., Corning, NY 14830, (607) 937-0766, Game Calls

Bodoodle, Inc., 3301 US Hwy. 84 N, Coleman, TX 76834, (915) 625-3524, Arrow Rests

Bohning Co., Ltd., 7361 N. Seven Mile Rd., Lake City, MI 49651, (231) 229-4247, Accessories

Boone & Crockett Club, 250 Station Dr., Missoula, MT 59801, (406) 542-1888, Organization

Bow & Arrow Hunting, 265 S. Anita Dr., Ste. 120, Orange, CA 92868, (714) 939-9991, Magazine

Bowhunt America, 2960 N. Adcademy Blvd. #101, Colorado Springs, CO 80917, (719) 495-9999, Magazine

Bowhunter Magazine, 6405 Flank Dr., Harrisburg, PA, 17112, (717) 540-6719, Magazine Publishing

Bowhunting Preservation Alliance, P. O. Box 258, Comfrey, MN 56019, (866) 266-2776, Organization

Bowhunting Safari Consultants, 1-800-833-9777 www.bowhuntingsafari.com, Hunt Booking Agency

Bowhunting World, 6920 Sycamore Lane N., Maple Grove, MN 55311, Magazine

The Bowsite, P. O. Box 955, Eastford, CT 06242, (860) 974-3668 Website/Web Design

BowTech, 90554 Hwy. 99 N., Eugene, OR 97402, (541) 284-4711, Bows

Bracklyn Products, 4400 Stillman Blvd., Ste. C, Tuscaloosa, AL 35401, (800) 247-2955, Accessories

Brauer Bros., 1520 Washington Ave., St. Louis, MO 63103, (314) 231-2864, Cases

Braun-Woodke Products, 8462 Section Line Rd., Harbor Beach, MI 48441, (989) 479-0280, Treestands

Brennan Industries, 2035 Riley Rd., Sparta, WI 54656, (608) 269-0832, Bows

Brownell & Co., Inc., P. O. Box 362, Moodus, CT 06469, (860) 873-8625, String/String Mate

Browning Archery, P. O. Box 5487, Tucson, AZ 85703, (520) 884-9065, Bows

Brunton, 620 E. Monroe Ave., Riverton, WY 82501, (307) 865-6559, Optics

Buck Derby Tree Slings, 14191 Frontier Rd., Camden, MI 49232, (517) 254-4636, Treestands

Buck Magnet, 84 Benedict Rd., Pittsford, NY 14534, (716) 264-9117, Scents

Buck Stop Lure Co., P. O. Box 636, Stanton, MI 48888, (989) 762-5091, Scents

Buck Wear, 2040 Lord Baltimore Dr., Baltimore, MD 21244, (410) 687-3337, Clothing

BuckShot Treestands, P. O. Box 7127, Wilmington, NC 28406, (910) 341-7900, Treestands

BuckWing Products, 2650 Lehigh St., Whitehall, PA 18052, (610) 264-1122, Accessories

Bug Out Outdoorwear, Inc., P. O. Box 185, Centerville, IA 52544, (641) 437-1936, Clothing

Bullet Archery Products, P. O. Box 965, Duncansville, PA 16635, (814) 693-6992, Broadheads

Bushnell, 5200 Cody, Overland Park, KS 66214, (913) 752-3410, Optics

C.P. Oneida Eagle Bows, 20669 30th Ave., Marion, MI 49665, (231) 743-2427, Bows

C. R. Archery Products, P. O. Box 10561, Lancaster, PA 17602, (717) 394-5769, Bow Accessories

Cabela's, One Cabela Dr., Sidney, NE 69160, (800) 237-4444, Mail Order

Carbon Impact, 2628 Garfield Rd. N., Ste. 3, Traverse City, MI 49686, (231) 929-8152, Arrows

Carbon Tech, 4751 Pell, Ste. 3, Sacramento, CA 95838, (916) 641-8088, Arrows

Carl Zeiss Sports Optics, Kingston Ave., Chester, VA 23836, (804) 530-5841, Optics

Carolina Archery Products, 620 N. Valley Forge Rd., Hillsborough, NC 27728, (919) 245-1400, Arrow Rests

Carter Enterprises, P. O. Box 19, St. Anthony, ID 83445, (208) 624-3467, Releases

Cascade Archery, 12930 228 St. NE, Arlington, WA 98223, (360) 435-4251, Custom Bows

Cavalier Equipment Co., P. O. Box 753, Gilbert, AZ 85233, (602) 497-2977, Arrow Rests

Cedar Hill Game Calls, 238 Vic Allen Rd., Downsville, LA 71234, (318) 982-5632, Calls

Champion Bow Co., 359 Johnson Ave., Winnipeg, Canada R2L 0l2, (204) 982-6000, Bows

J.K. Chastain Archery, 490 S. Queen St., Lakewood, CO 80225, (303) 989-1120, Custom Bows

Christian Bowhunters of America, 34 Ohio St., Jamestown, NY 14701, (716) 484-7046, Organization

Christian Deer Hunters Assn., 2503 St. Anthony Rd., Minneapolis, MN 55418, (612) 789-2380, Organization

Cobra Mfg. Co., Inc., P. O. Box 667, Bixby, OK 74008, (918) 366-3634, Bow Sights

Compton Traditional Archers, 18408 E. St. Rt. 2, Harrisonville, MO 64701, (816) 884-3774, Organization

Contain/V.S.I., P. O. Box 337, Shakopee, MN 55397, (612) 496-0189, Clothing

Copper John/Stanislawski Archery , 173 State St., Auburn, NY 13021, (315) 258-9269, Bow Sights

Cornhusker Archery, P. O. Box 467, Bassett, NE 68714, (888) 684-2290, Accessories

Counter Assault, 120 Industrial Ct., Kalispell, MT 59901, (406) 257-4740, Bear Spray

Cover Up Hunting Products, 1205 State Hwy. JJ, Holister, MO 65672, (417) 336-4930, Scents

Crawford Mfg., 1927 Junction Rd., Mocksville, NC 27028, (336) 284-2253, Treestand Accessories

Critters Dreams, S. 5605 Sunrise Dr., Falls Creek WI 54742, (715) 877-2230, Packs/Bags

CSS/Custom Shooting Systems, Rt. 1, Box 125A, Salt Rock, WV 25559, (304) 736-3639, Bows

Custom Tapered Arrows/Shafts, 15563 Coo. 27 Blvd., Pine Island, MN 55963, (507) 356-8857, Custom Arrows

Dakota Archery Pdts., Inc., 916 NE 6th St., Madison, SD 57042, (605) 256-2373, Holders/Stands

Dalton Archery Products, 16462 N. Saddlewood Rd., Nine Mile Falls, WA 99026, (509) 467-4042, Accessories

Darton Archery, 3540 Darton Rd., Hale, MI 48739, (989) 728-4231, Bows

Day One Camouflage, 3300 S. Knox Ct., Englewood, CO 80110, (800) 347-2979, Camo Clothing

Dead On Range Finder, P. O. Box 17633, Missoula, MT 59808, (406) 544-3076, Range Finders

Deer Me Products, Inc., 1201 Nightengale St., Braham, MN 55006, (320) 396-3735, Treestand Accessories

Deer Quest, Ltd., P. O. Box 843, Cannonsburg, MI 49317, 1-800-795-7581, Scents

Delta Industries, 117 E. Kenwood St., Reinbeck, IA 50669, (319) 345-6476, Targets

Diamond Archery, Inc., 1338 Hawn Ave., Shreveport, LA 71107, (318) 677-2600, Bows

Doc's Deer Scents, 2118 Niles-Cortland Rd., Cortland, OH, (30) 638-9507, Scents

Doinker/Leven Industries, 9025 Eton Ave., Unit A, Canoga Park, CA 91304, (818) 700-2899, Accessories

Doo Sung/Cartel, 95 Milk St., Willimantic, CT 06226, (860) 423-8609, Bows

Doskocil Mfg. Co., Inc., 4300 Barnett, Arlington, TX 76017, (817) 467-5116, Cases

Double Bull Archery, P. O. Box 923, Monticello, MN 55362, (763) 295-3664, Blinds

Double Triple Trading, P. O. Box 6073, Anaheim, CA 92816, (714) 630-5908, Cases

Drake Outdoors, 10774 Brix Hwy., Brooklyn, MI 49230, (517) 467-2561, Clothing

Drury Outdoors, P. O. Box 71, Bloomsdale, MO 63627, (573) 483-9351, Hunting Videos

Duravanes by Norway, P. O. Box 516, Myrtle Point, OR 97458, (541) 572-2950, Vanes

Mel Dutton Decoys, P. O. Box 113, Faith, SD 57626, (605) 967-2031, Game Decoys

Dwyer Longbows, P. O. Box 221, Holmen, WI 54636, (608) 526-4297, Custom Bows

E. W. Bateman & Co., P. O. Box 109, Foscher. TX 78623, (830) 935-2255, Accessories

Easton Technical Products, 5040 W. Harold Gatty Dr., Salt Lake City, UT 84116, (801) 539-1400, Arrows

Easy-Eye Archery Products, 7196 Arkansaw Rd., Allen, MI 49227, (517) 869-9727, Adhesives

Eclipse Broadheads, 10342 Ardyce St., Boise, ID 83704, (208) 322-7796, Broadheads

Edgefield Outdoor Products, 7550 O'Hara Dr., Spanish Fort, AL 36527, (251) 621-9383, Accessories

EJ Sceery Outdoors, P. O. Box 6520, Santa Fe, NM 87502, (800) 327-4322, Game Calls

Elastic Products, P. O. Box 39, Marble, NC 28905, (828) 837-9074, Clothing

Elimitrax, 3433 T. S.. Campbell, Ste. T, Springfield, MO 65807, (800) 630-7290, Outdoor Wear

Ellington & Rush, 496 Moccasin Gap Rd., Lula, GA 30554, (706) 677-2394, Accessories

EOTech, 3600 Green Ct., Ste. 400, Ann Arbor, MI 48105, (734) 741-8868, Sights

Eradicator Bow Sights, 7129 E. Pleasant Valley Rd., Shepherd, MI 48883, (800) 750-7910, Sights

Escalade Sports, 4600 SW 41st Blvd., Gainesville, FL 32608, (325) 376-2327, Bows/Broadheads

Essential Gear, Inc., 171 Wells St., Greenfield, MA 01301, (413) 772-8984, Accessories

Everywear West Camo, Inc., 1207 Alpine Ave., Cody, WY 82414, (307) 587-6567, Camo Clothing

Evolved Habitats, 2261 Morganza Hwy., New Roads, LA 70760, (225) 638-4016, Scents

Extended Exposure, 1783 Berkeley Ave., St. Paul, MN 55105, (651) 698-3333, Accessories

Extreme Archery Products, 7120 US 60, Ste. B, Ashland, KY 41102, (606) 928-9447, Sights

Extreme Dimension Wildlife Calls, P. O. Box 220, Hampden, ME 04444, (207) 862-2825, Game Calls

Extreme Shot Camera Mounts, 139 Winchester Place, Fairview Height, IL 62208, (314) 239-1305, Accessories

EZE-LAP Diamond Products, 3572 Arrowhead Dr., Carson City, NV 89706, (800) 843-4815, Sharpeners

The Fall Stopper, 3540 Otter Rd., Toddville, IA 52341, (319) 395-0676, Treestand Accessories

Feather Flex Decoys, 8575 W. 100Th St., Overland Park, KS 66210, (913) 317-9600, Decoys

Feather Visions, 6 Besemer Rd., Ithaca, NY 14850, (607) 539-3308, Optics

Fedora's Custom Bows, 115 Wintersville Rd., Richland, PA 17087, (717) 933-8862, Custom Bows

FHFH (Farmers & Hunters, Feeding the Hungry), 216 N. Cleveland Ave., Hagerstown, MD 71740, Organization

Field & Stream Licenses, P. O. Box 47366, Plymouth, MN 55447, (763) 557-8888, Clothing

Field Logic, Inc., 101 Main St., Superior, WI 54880, (715) 395-9955, Targets

Fieldline, 1919 Vineburn Ave., Los Angeles, CA 90032, (332) 226-0830, Packs & Bags

Field's Edge Concealment, P. O. Box 1205, Stone Mountain, GA 30086, (770) 465-9996, Camo Pattern

Fine Line, Inc., 11304-A Steele St., Ste. A, Lakewood, WA 98499, (253) 539-3661, Sights

Fitzgerald Hunting Corp., P. O. Box 126, Tecumseh, MI 49286, (517) 423-8124, Scents

Flex-Fletch Products, 1840 Chandler Ave., St. Paul, MN 55113, (651) 426-4882, Vanes

Follow-Thru, LLC, P. O. Box 381, Eastpoint, FL 32328, (850) 899-8834, Sights

Forge Bow Co., 2860 S. 171St St., New Berlin, WI 53151, (414) 732-7400, Bows

Fortune Products, 205 Hickory Creek Rd., Marble Falls, TX 78654, (830) 693-6111, Arrow Accessories

Foster Mfg., P. O. Box 458, Batavia, OH 45103, (513) 735-9770, Holders/Stands

G5 Outdoor LLC, P. O. Box 59, Memphis, MI 48041, (810) 392-8431, Broadheads

Game Tracker, Inc., P. O. Box 380, Flushing, MI 48433, (810) 733-6360, Arrows

Game Warning Systems, P. O. Box 226, Plymouth, WI 53073, (920) 892-2553, Hunting Accessories

Game-Hunter, 541 Bishop St. NW, Atlanta, GA 30318, (404) 352-0673, Clothing

Gatco Sharpeners &Timberline Knives, P. O. Box 600, Getzville, NY 14068, (716) 877-2200, Knives

Gateway Feathers, 1015 Lorenza Pkwy., Douglas, AZ 85607, (520) 805-0863, Arrows

Gladiator Broadheads, 325 S. Industrial Dr., Orem, UT 84058, (800) 551-0541, Broadheads

Golden Key-Futura, P. O. Box 1446, Montrose, CO 81402, (970) 749-6700, Arrow Rests

Gold Tip, Inc., 352 S. Goldtip Dr., Orem, UT 84058, (801) 229-1666, Arrows

Gorilla Treestands, P. O. Box 378, Flushing, MI 48433, (810) 733-6360, Treestands

Grayling Outdoor Products, P. O. Box 192, Grayling, MI 49738, (517) 348-2956, Arrow Rests

Great Northern Bowhunting Co., 201 N. Main, Nashville, MI 49073, (517) 852-0820, Custom Bows

Great Plains Traditional Bows, 314 W. Foster, Pampa, TX 79065, (806) 665-5463, Custom Bows

GrenTree/Lee-Park, 540 A-1 N. Main St., Manchester, CT 06040, (860) 643-7344, Bows

Grim Reaper Broadheads, 1250 N. 1750 W, Provo, UT 84604, (801) 377-6199, Broadheads

HH&H Archery Supply, P. O. Box 353, Maple Lake, MN 55358, (320) 963-6118, Accessories

Hall Interactive Solutions, 7240 W. Mexico Dr., Lakewood, CO 80232, (303) 807-4862, Interactive Targets

Hally Caller Widlife Calls, 443 Wells Rd., Doylestown, PA 18901, (215) 345-6354, Game Calls

Hawgs Ltd., P. O. Box 279, Manton, MI 49663, (231) 824-6040, Scents

Haydel's Game Calls, 5018 Hazel Jones Rd., Bossier City, LA 71111, (800) 429-3357, Game Calls

HHA Sports, Inc., 7222 Townline Rd., Wisconsin Rapids, WI 54494, (715) 424-8080, Sights

High Country Archery, P. O. Box 1269, Dunlap, TN 37327, (423) 949-5000, Bows

High Country Publishers, 10959 W. Bear Creek Dr., Lakewood, CO 80227, (303) 988-3021, Dave Holt Books

High Point Tool Co., 11355 Backus Rd., Wattsburg, PA 16442, (814) 739-8521, Treestand Accessories

High Racks, P. O. Box 201, Staples, MN 56479, (218) 894-2442, Blinds

Hind Sight, Inc., P. O. Box 482, Pickney, MI 48169, (734) 878-2842, Sights

Hi-Tec Archery, 275 N. 300 W, Koosharem, UT 84744, (435) 638-7459, Gyro-Tec Compound Bow

Hi-Tek Sports Products, 809 Holcomb St., Watertown, NY 13601, (315) 788-0107, Stabilizers

Horizon Bow, Inc., 13891 Marihugh Rd., Mount Vernon, WA 98273, (360) 757-2923, Bows

Horne's Archery, P. O. Box 318, Boyd, TX 76023, (940) 433-3044, Custom Bows

Horn's Products, Inc., 3422 Valley Rd., Marysville, PA 17053, (717) 957-4636, Holders/Stands

Hoyes Outdoor Products, P. O. Box 606, Riverside, PA 17868, (570) 257-1813, Scents

Hoyt USA, 543 N. Neil Armstrong Rd., Salt Lake City, UT 84116, Bows

HTM Precision Machining, Inc., P. O. Box 28, New Albany, PA 18833, (570) 363-2515, Sights

Hunter Safety System, 288 W. Main St., Ste. 2, Dothan, AL 36301, (334) 637-0083, Treestand Accessories

Hunter's Specialities, Inc., 6000 Huntington Ct. NE, Cedar Rapids, IA 52402, (319) 395-0321, Game Calls

Hunter's View, 8515 N. University St., Peoria, IL 61615, (309) 689-1113, Treestands

Hunt for A Cure, Dr. Arnold S. Leonard Cancer Reserach Fund, (612) 445-0565, Fundraising

Ideal Products, P. O. Box 1006, DuBois, PA 15801, (814) 894-2444, Clothing

IHUNT Communications, P. O. Box 1148, Chanhassen, MN 55317, (952) 959-2800, Book Publishing

Impact Archery, 1360 Union Hill Rd. Ste. 3C, Alpharetta, GA 30004, (770) 521-9173, Sights

In-Heat Scents, P. O. Box 515, Kosciusko, MS 39090, (662) 289-4073, Scents

Inside Archery, 2960 N. Academy Blvd. #101, Colorado Springs, CO 80917, (719) 495-9999, Magazine

International Bowhunting Org/IBO, P. O. Box 398, Vermillion, OH 44089, (440) 967-2137, Organization

Invisablind, 100 Church St., Stevensville, MT 59870, (406) 777-5818, Blinds

J&L Bow Accessories, 5522 89th St., Pleasant Prairie, WI 53158, (262) 942-9960, Stabilizers

Jackie's Deer Lures, Rt. 1, Box 306-B, Tollesboro, KY 41189, (606) 789-2256, Scents

James Valley Scents, 38853 SD Hwy. 20, Mellette, SD 57461, (605) 887-3125, Scents

JB Archery Products, 226 Hickory Knoll Dr., Bluffton, IN 46714, (260) 824-8483, Sights

Jennings Archery, N.A. Archery Group, 4600 SW 41st Blvd., Gainesville, FL 32608, (352) 376-2327, Bows

Jim Fletcher Archery, P. O. Box 218, Bodfish, CA 93205, (760) 379-2589, Releases

Jo Jan Sportsequip Co., West Pointe Dr., Bldg. 3, Washington, PA 15301, (724) 225-5582, Fletching Gear

Jones Calls, 4015 Main St., Ste. A, Springfield, OR 97478, (541) 741-0263, Game Calls

Jordan Outdoor Enterprises, Team Realtree, P. O. Box 9638, Columbus, GA 31907, (706) 569-9101, Camouflage

Juniper Mountain Longbows, 2135 Deer Park Rd., Vale, OR 97918, (541) 473-3812

King Outdoors, LLC, E10901 Railroad Dr., Fall Creek, WI 54742, (715) 877-2848, Treestand Accessories

King of the Mountain, 2709 W. Eisenhower, Loveland, CO 80537, (970) 962-9306, Wool Clothing

King's Outdoor World, P. O. Box 307, Mt. Pleasant, UT 84647, (435) 462-1334, Clothing

Knight & Hale Game Calls, P. O. Box 1587, Ft. Smith, AR 72901, (800) 531-1201, Calls

Kolpin Outdoors, Inc., P. O. Box 107, Fox Lake, WI 53933, (920) 928-3118, Cases

Kool-Dri Rainwear, P. O. Box 120, Reinholds, PA 17569, (800) 523-8025, Raingear

Kota, 3495 58th Ave., NE, Oberon, ND 58357, (701) 798-2776, Custom Bows

Kustom King, P. O. Box 11648, Merrillville, IN 46411, (219) 322-0790, Traditional Tackle

Kwikee Kwiver Co., P. O. Box 130, Acme, MI 49601, (231) 938-1609, Quivers

LaCrosse Footwear/Danner, 18550 NE Riverside Pkwy., Portland, OR 97230, (503) 766-1010, Boots

Lansky Sharpeners, P. O. Box 50830, Las Vegas, NV 89016 (702) 361-7511, Sharpeners

Ron LeClair's Traditional Archery, Box 145, Potterville, MI 48876, (517) 645-7729, Custom Bows

Leica Sports Optics, 156 Ludlow Ave., Northvale, NJ 07647, (770) 993-8197, Optics

Little Big Horn Outfitters, 1030 Mary Laidley Dr., Covington, KY 41017, (859) 356-4350, Blinds

LLD Artistic Targets, 4627 W. Good Hope Rd., Milwaukee, WI 53223, (414) 352-3238, Targets

Loggy Bayou Enterprises, P. O. Box 804, Magnolia, AR 71753, (870) 234-2260, Treestands

Lone Wolf Custom Bows, 3893 Grey St., Glennie, MI 48737, (517) 735-3358, Custom Bows

Lone Wolf, Inc., 3314 E. Grange Ave., Cudahy, WI 53110, (414) 744-4984, Treestands

M.A.D. Calls, 4500 Doniphan Dr., Neosho, MO 64850, (800) 922-9034, Game Calls

Magnus Archery Co., P. O. Box 1877, Great Bend, KS 67530, (620) 793-9141, Broadheads

Maple Leaf Press, Inc., 1215 Beechtree St., Grand Haven, MI 49417, (616) 846-8844, Target Faces

Mar-Den Vortex, P. O. Box 1037, Wilcox, AZ 85644, (520) 384-3176, Broadheads

Martin Archery, 3134 W. Hwy. 12, Walla Walla, WA 99362, (509) 529-2554, Bows

Mathews, Inc., 919 River Road, Box 367, Sparta, WI 54656, (608) 269-2728, Bows

McKenzie Targets, P. O. Box 480, Granite Quarry, NC 28072, (704) 279-8363, Targets

Micro Technology, 932 36th Ct. SW, Vero Beach, FL 32968, (772) 569-3058, Broadheads

MirTec, 100 Applewood Dr., Sparta, MI 59345, (231) 733-4173, Outdoor Wear

Modoc Broadheads, 33 S. Pit Ln., Nampa, ID 83687, (208) 466-1827, Broadheads

Monarch Bows, P. O. Box 433, Darby, MT 59829, (406) 821-1948, Custom Bows

Montana Black Gold, 34370 Frontage Road, Bozeman, MT 59715, (406) 586-1117, Sights

Montana Camo, Inc., P. O. Box 1327, Victor, MT 59875, (406) 961-6829, Camo Pattern

Montana Canvas, P. O. Box 390, Belgrade, MT 59714, (406) 388-1225, Tents

Montana Decoy, Box 2377, Colstrip, MT 59323, (406) 748-3092, Decoys

Morrell Mfg., Inc., 1721 Hwy. 71 N., Alma, AR 72921, (479) 632-5929, Targets

Mossy Oak Camo, P. O. Drawer 757, West Point, MS 39773, (662) 494-8859, Camo Clothing,

MPI Outdoors, 10 Industrial Dr., Windham, NH 03087, (603) 890-0455, Packs/Bags

Mrs. Doe Pee Buck Lure, 603 Redbud Ridge Rd., Mt. Pleasant, IA 52641, (319) 385-3875, Scents

Muck Boot Co., 3310 H St., Omaha, NE 68107, (402) 731-1662, Footwear

Multiple Product Sales, P. O. Box 104771, Jefferson City, MO 65110, (573) 635-4946, Rests, Stabilizers, Accessories

Muzzy Products, 110 Beasley Rd., Cartersville, GA 30120, (770) 387-9300, Broadheads

Mystic Longbows, 21485 N. Cameron Rd., Cuba, IL 61427, (309) 785-5109, Custom Bows

Nat'l Bowhunter Educ. Foundation, 2504 Ramsgate Way, Ft. Smith, AR 72908, (479) 649-7872, Hunter Ed Organization

Natural Gear, 5310 S. Shackleford Rd., Ste. D, Little Rock, AR 72204, (501) 228-5590, Camo Clothing

Nature Vision, 213 NW 4th St., Brainerd, MN 56401 (218) 825-0733, Cameras

Navjo Longbows, 1824 Hwy 79 S, Henderson, TX 75852, (903) 657-8780, Custom Bows

Neet Products, Inc., 5875 E. Hwy. 50, Sedalia, MO 65301, (660) 826-6762, Accessories

Nelsons Arrows, 1181 Swede Hill Rd., Greensburg, PA 15601, (724) 837-6210, Arrows

New Archery Products, 7500 Industrial Dr., Forest Park, IL 60130 (708) 488-2500, Broadheads

Nikon, 1300 Walt Whitman Rd., Melville, NY 11747, (631) 54708588, Optics

Nite Hawk Archery, 8031 11th Ave. S, Bloomington, MN 55420, (612) 866-0255, Accessories

Non-Typical, Inc., 860 Park Ln., Park Falls, WI 54552, (715) 762-2260, Cameras/Monitors

North American Whitetail, 2250 New Market Pkwy., Ste. 110, Marietta, GA 30067, (770) 953-9222, Magazine

North Starr Tree Stands, 2351 E. Bear Lake Rd., Hillsdale, MI 49242, (517) 439-1313, Treestands

No Trace by Red-On, 1500 Central Ave., Albany, NY 12205, (866) 452-4562, Scent Control Clothing

Ol' Man Treestands, 32 Raspberry Ln., Hattiesburg, MS 39402, (800) 682-7268, Treestands

Original Brite Site, 34 Kentwood Rd., Succasunna, NJ 07876, (973) 584-0637

Outback Technologies, 6726 Buena Vista Rd., Columbus, GA 31907, (706) 562-0770, Accessories

Outdoor Edge Cutlery Corp., 4699 Nautilus Court S. #503, Boulder, CO 80301, (303) 530-7667, Knives

Outdoor Technologies, 24260 Jessie St., Denim Springs, LA 70726, (225) 665-3876, Scents

Outlaw Decoys, 624 N. Fancher Rd., Spokane, WA 99212, (800) 653-3269, Decoys

Outdoors Yellow Pages, 202 Industrial Loop, Staten Island, NY 10309, (718) 689-0216, Publishing

Outland Sports, Inc., 4500 Doniphan Dr., Neosho, MO 64805, (800) 922-9034, Treestands

Owl Precision Metals, 17115 Kenton Dr., Ste. 207, Cornelius, NC 28031, (704) 655-8989, Treestands

PAMS Arrow Making Supplies, P. O. Box 52, Lyons, MI 48851, (989) 855-3035, Arrows

P. S. Olt, P. O. Box 550, Pekin, IL 61554, (309) 348-3633, Game Calls

Pacific Bow Butts , P. O. Box 108, Ilwaco, WA 98624, (877) 642-4989, Targets

Palmer Bow Co., 480 N. Center St., Sabinal, TX 78881, (830) 988-2019, Custom Bows

Pape's Inc., 250 Terry Blvd., Louisville, KY 40229, (502) 955-8118, Archery Equipment

Paradox Products, 21 Janet Ave., Strasburg, PA 17579, (717) 687-5147, Accessories

Parker Compound Bows, Inc., P. O. Box 105, Mint Springs, VA 24463, (540) 337-5426, Bows

Paullet, 280 Rue Des Carrieres , Limas, France 69400, 0033620621329, Quivers

Pella Products, 835 Broadway, Pella, IA 50219, (800) 832-6225, Clothing

Penn's Woods Game Calls, P. O. Box 306, Delmont, PA 15626, (724) 468-8311, Game Calls

Pentax USA, P. O. Box 6509, Englewood, CO 80155, (303) 728-0362, Optics

Petersen's Bowhunting, 6420 Wilshire Blvd., Los Angeles, CA 90048, Magazine

Physically Challenged Bowhunters of America, RR1 Box 470, New Alexandria, PA 15610, (724) 668-7439, Organization

Pine Ridge Archery, P. O. Box 310, Wauconda, IL 60084, (847) 526-2349, Treestands

Pioneer Hunting Products, P. O. Box 5168, Lakeland, FL 33807, (863) 648-5477, Clothing

Plano Outdoor Pdts., 431 E. So. St., Plano, IL 60545, (630) 5232-9737, Cases

Pope and Young Club, P. O. Box 548, Chatfield, MN 55923, (570) 867-4144, Organization

Port Midwest Int'l, P. O. Box 119, Burlington, IA 52601, (319) 753-5179, Blinds

Pradco Outdoor Brands, P. O. Box 130, Centerville, IA 52544, (641) 856-2626, Bowhunting Equipment

Precision Designed Pdts., 3999 CR 5200 Archery Ln., Independence, KS 67301, (316) 331-0333, Accessories

Precision Shooting Equipment (PSE), P. O. Box 5487, Tucson, AZ 85703, (877) 607-0381, Bows

Predator Products, Co., 17497 144th Ave. #1, Nunica, MI 49448, (877) 607-0381, Sights

Predator, 2605 Coulee Ave., LaCrosse, WI 54601, (608) 787-0500, Camo Clothing

Primos, Inc., 604 First St., Flora, MS 39071, (601) 366-1288, Hunting Calls

Professional Bowhunters Society, P. O. Box 246, Terrell, NC 28682, (704) 664-2534, Organization

Professional Hunting Pdts., P. O. Box 849, Marshall, MI 49068, (616) 789-1507, Treestands

Proline Archery, 2288 Bachman Rd., Hastings, MI 49058, (616) 945-3802, Bows

Promat Target, 333 Plumer St., Wausau, WI 54403, (800) 324-124, Targets

Pronghorn Custom Bows, 2491 W. 42Nd St.Casper, WY 82604, (307) 234-1824, Custom Bows

Pro Release, Inc., 33551 Giftos, Clinton Township, MI 48035, (810) 792-1410, Releases

Quaker Boy, Inc., 5455 Webster Rd., Orchard Park, NY 14127, (716) 662-3979, Game Calls

Quality Archery Designs, P. O. Box 940, Madison Hts, VA 24572, (804) 528-1044, Archery Accessories

Rack-n-Spur Archery, 4621 Coble To Only Rd., Nunnelly, TN 37137, (931) 729-1600, Sights

Ragim Archery, VIA Napoleonica 28, Forgaria, Italy 33030, (39-0427-808189), Bows

Rain Shield, Inc., 5110 A Cedar Lake Rd., Minneapolis, MN 55416, (952) 543-1894, Camo

Rancho Safari, P. O. Box 691, Ramona, CA 92065, (619)789-2094, Camo Clothing/Quivers

Raven Arrows, 993 Grays Creek Rd., Indian Valley, ID 83632, (208) 256-4341, Arrows

Pete Rickard, P. O. Box 292, Cobleskill, NY 12043, (800) 282-5663,

Razor Caps, Inc., 6 Terrapin Ln., Mercerville, NJ 08619, (609) 890-2010, Broadheads

Realtree Camo, P. O. Box 9638, Columbus, GA 31908, (800) 992-9968, Camouflage

Recover, 5520 7th St. SE, Minot, ND 58701, (701) 852-8723, Game Finders

Red Feather, Inc., P. O. Box 560, Cibolo, TX 78108, (210) 945-8552, Arrows

RedHead/Bass Pro, 2500 E. Kearney, Springfield, MO 65898, (800) 227-7776, Mail Order

Red-On, 1500 Central Ave., Albany, NY 12205, (866) 452-4562, Clothing

Reel Deer, Inc., 110 E Azalea Ave., Foley, AL 36535, (251) 943-6395, Scents

Reflex (Hoyt), 543 N. Neil Armstrong Rd., Salt Lake City, UT 84116, (801) 363-2990, Bows

Remington Footwear, 149 E. Chestnut St., Lancaster, OH 43130, (740) 654-9908, Footwear

Renegade Archery Co, 18706 Co Hwy Q, Bloomer, WI 54724, (715) 568-2730, Bows.

Ridge Outdoors/Skeeter Beater, P. O. Box 389, Eustis, FL 32727, (352) 357-2669, Accessories

Rinehart 3-D Targets, 1029 S. Jackson St., Janesville, WI 53546, (608) 757-8153, Targets

Rivers Edge Hunting Products, P. O. Box 666, Cumberland, WI 54829, (715) 822-2470, Treestands

Robertson Stykbows, Box 7, HCR 88, Forest Grove, MT 59441, (406) 538-2818, Custom Bows

Robinson Outdoors, Inc., P. O. Box 18, Cannon Falls, MN 55009, (507) 263-2885, Scents

Rocket Arrowhead Corp., 2025 Gateway Circle, Centerville, MN 55038, (651) 653-6778, Broadheads

Rock-It Outdoors, 6025 Martway, Mission, KS 66202, (208) 550-0376, String/String Mate

Rocky Mtn. Elk Foundation, 2291 W. Broadway, Missoula, MT 59802, (406) 523-4595, Organization

Rocky Shoes and Boots, 39 Canal St., Nelsonville, OH 45764, (740) 753-1951, Clothing/Footwear

Rose Plastic USA, P. O. Box 698, California, PA 15419, (724) 938-8530, Accessories

RS Bow Vise, 335 W. John St., Hicksville, NY 11801, (516) 932-5007, Accessories

SCI World Bowhunters, 4800 W. Gates Pass Rd., Tucson, AZ 85745, (520) 620-1220, Organization

Satellite Archery, N. American Archery Group, 4600 SW 41st Blvd., Gainesville, FL 32608, (352) 376-2327, Broadheads

Saunders Archery, P. O. Box 476, Columbus, NE 68601, (402) 564-7176, Arrow Accessories

Savage Systems, Inc., 110 N. Front St., Oak Grove, LA 71263, (318) 428-7733, Arrow Rests

Savora Broadheads, 1546 Bolach Ave. NW, North Bend, WA 98045,(800) 424-6737, Broadheads

Scent Sling, 1070 E. Lafayette, St., Ste. 109, Tallahassee, FL 32301, (850) 877-5003, Scents

Scent-Lok/ALS Enterprises, 1731 Wierengo Dr., Muskegon, MI 49442, (616) 725-6181, Clothing

Schafer Silvertip Bows, 312 Helena Flats Rd., Kalispell, MT 59901, (406) 357-0740, Custom Bows

Schaffer Performance Archery , 1403 E. Cliff Rd., Burnsville, MN 55337, (952) 6169, Arrow Rests

Scott Archery Mfg., Inc., 101 Tug Brnach Rd., Clay City, KY 40312, (606) 663-2734, Releases

Scrape Juice/Muzzy, 110 Beasley Rd., Cartersville, GA 30120, (770) 387-9300, Scents

Selway Archery, 802 S. 2nd, Hamilton, MT 59840, (800) 764-4770, Bow Quivers

Shelter-Pro/Underbrush, P. O. Box 337, Stearns, KY 42647, (606) 376-2004, Blinds

Shrewd Precision Archery, P. O. Box 235, Caswba. VA 24070, (540) 864-7041, Archery Accessories

Simmons System Archery, 157 Win Dre Dr., Jasper, AL 35504, (205) 387-7174, Broadheads

Sims Vibration Labratory, 301 W/ Business Park Loop, Shelton, WA 98584, (360) 427-6031, LimbSavers

SKB Corporation, 1607 N. O'Donnell Way,Orange, CA 92867, (800) 654-5992, Cases

Skyline Camo, 5225 SW Blvd., Hamsburg, NY 14075, (716) 649-2312, Camo Clothing

Snake Skin Illusions, 1020 Front St., Conway, AR 72032, (501) 327-2253, Camo Clothing

Speciality Archery Pdts., P. O. Box 889, Clear Lake, IA 60428, (641) 424-5762, Accessories

Sportchief Canada, 888 Chambly Rd., Marieville, Quebec J3M 1R2, (800) 567-1729, Clothing

Sports Sensors, Inc., 11351 Embassy Dr., Cincinnati, OH 45240, (513) 825-5745, Chronograph

Sportsman's Outdoor Products, 9352 S. 670 W., Sandy, UT 84070, (801) 562-8712, Packs and Bags

Spot-Hogg Archery Products, P. O. Box 226, Harrisburg, OR 97446, (541) 995-3702, Bow Maintenance

Stacey Archery Sales, 6866 Jennifer, Idaho Falls, ID 83401, (208) 523-7278, Bows

Stanley Hips Targets, 1211 W. Blanco, San Antonio, TX 78232, (210) 492-8774, Longhorn Targets

Stearns, Inc., 1100 Stearns Dr., Sauk Rapids, MN 56379, (320) 656-3294, Packs/Bags

Steel Force Broadheads, P. O. Box 9, Rosemont, NJ 08556, (609) 397-1990

St. Joe River Bows, 3140 Homer Rd., Jonesville, MI 49250, (517) 849-2939, Custom Bows

Stone Mtn. Bow Strings, P. O. Box 2483, Orofino, ID 83544, (208) 476-7811, String/String Mate

Stoney Wolf/BKS, 124 Columbia Ct., N. Chaska, MN 55318, (952) 556-0075, Accessories

Storm Archery, 5005 Co. Rd. 29, Auburn, IN 46706, (260) 927-8095, Bows/Accessories

Straight Shot Archery Pdts., 319 Hallie Irvine St., Richmond, KY 40475, (859) 626-3602, Accessories

Strawberry Wilderness Archery, 1031 Bridge St., Prairie City, OR 97869, (541) 820-4344, Accessories

Strong Case, Inc., 26563 Corporate Ave., Hayward, CA 94545, (866) 552-2273, Cases

Sullivan/Innerloc, 1472 Camp Creek Rd., Lakemont, GA 30552, (706) 782-5863, Broadheads

Summit Specialities, 715 Summit Dr. SE, Decatur, AL 35601, (256) 353-0634, Treestands

Super Carbon Arrows, P. B. 67, Mint Spring, VA 24463, (540) 337-3600, Arrows

Sure Foot Corp., 1401 Dyke Ave., Grand Forks, ND 58203, (701) 775-9560, Clothing/Accessories

Sure-Loc Archery Pdts., 100 Quality Ln., Versailles, IN 47042, (812) 689-9926, Sights

Sureshot Archery Pdts., 2991 St. Jude Dr., Waterford, MI 48329, (248) 980-8657, Sights

Sure Shot Archery, 476 Table Rock Rd., Beaver, WV 25813, (304) 763-4228, Releases

Swarovski Optik, 2 Slater Rd., Cranston, RI 02920, (401) 965-8474, Optics

Swift Instruments, Inc., 952 Dorchester Ave., Boston, MA 02125, (617) 436-2960, Optics

T&J Tree Stand Systems, 2211 Brookwood Ct., Joliet, IL 60435, (815) 725-7268, Treestands

T.R.U. Ball Release, P. O. Box 1180, Madison Heights, VA 24572, (804) 929-2800, Releases

Tailorrmaid Archery Pdts., 3627 11th St., Wyandotte, MI 48192, (734) 246-3182, String/String Mate

Tallahoma Industries, 1811 Old Estill Springs Rd., Tullahoma, TN 37388, (931) 455-1314, Clothing

Target Communications, 7626 W. Donges Bay, Mequon, WI 53097, (262) 242-3990, Hunting Event Shows

Tecomate Seed Co., P. O. Box 1688, McAllen, TX 78505, (888) 629-4263, Game Feed

Thistle Down Archery, Rt. 1, Box 1093 Pioneer Rd., Homedale, ID 83628, (208) 337-5966, Arrow Accessories

Tiger Tuff, #3 Custom Mill Ct., Greenville, SC 29609, (864) 370-1500, Accessories

Tim's Archery, 1201 Eagle Way, Rock Springs, WY 82901, (307) 382-9196, Bows

Tink's, P. O. Box 244, Madison, GA 30650, (706) 342-9196, Deer Scents/Lures

Tippmann, 88 Hoskins St., Hesperia, MI 49421, (231) 854-5041, Accessories

Toxonics Mfg., 1324 Wilmer Rd., Wentzville, MO 63385, (314) 639-8500, Sights

Tracer Products, Inc., 9539 Legend Isle, San Antonio, TX 78254, (210) 387-3766, Lighted Nocks

Traditional Bowhunter, 280 N. Latah, Boise, ID, 83706, (208) 383-0982, Magazine

Trail Sense Engineering, 122 Marathon Dr. , Middletown, DE 19709, (866) 222-2849, Cameras/Monitors

Trailhawk Treestands, 2605 Coulee Ave., LaCrosse, WI 54601, (608) 785-0500, Treestands

Trailtimer Co., P. O. Box 28722, St. Paul, MN 55128, (800) 328-4827, Cameras/Monitors

Trebark Camo, P. O. Drawer 757, West Point, MS 39773, (662) 494-8859, Camo Clothing

TreeSlinger, 64700 M-40, Jones, MI 49061, (269) 435-2456, Treestand Accessories

Treestand Mfg. Assn., P. O. Box 15214, Hattiesburg, MS 39404, (601) 384-7983, Organization

Trophy Ridge, 732 Cruiser Ln., Ste. 200, Belgrade, MT 59714, (406) 388-7781, Sights

Trophy Rock, 743 W. 1200 N, Ste. 200, Springville, UT 84663, (801) 368-6391, Game Attractants

Trophy Taker, P. O. Box 1137, Plains, MT 59859, (406) 826-0600, Arrow Rests

Trophyline, LLC, 1904 Philadelphia Rd., Jasper, GA 30143, (706) 629-0214, Treestand Accessories

TruAngle Broadhead Hones, 6658 S. State Rd. 13, Wabash, IN 46992, (800) 8540 8942, Sharpeners

Trueflight Feathers, Box 1000, Manitowish Waters, WI 54545, (715) 543-8451, Fletching

True-Fire Corp., N7355 State St. N., Fond du Lac, WI 54937, (920) 923-6866, Releases

Tru-Flite Archery Pdts., 5040 W. Harold Gatty Dr., Salt Lake City, UT 84116, (801) 539-1400, Arrows

TruGlo, Inc., 13745 Neutron Dr., Dallas, TX 75244, (972) 774-0300, Sights

Turbo Nock, Inc., 165 S. 4th St., Hughesville, PA 17737, (866) 814-4722, Nocks

United Foundation for Disabled Archers, P. O. Box 251, Glenwood, MN 56334, (320) 634-3660, Organization

U.S. Sportsmen's Alliance, 801 Kingsmill Pkwy., Columbus, OH 43229, (614) 888-4868, Organization

Vanguard USA, 9157 E. M-35, Whitmore Lake, MI 48176, (734) 449-1200, Cases

Vibracheck, 10003 Raymar St., Pensacola, FL 32534, (850) 857-0092, Stabilizers

VibraShine, Inc., P. O. Box 557, Taylorsville, MS 39168, (601) 785-9854, Trail Monitors

Video Hunter Camcorder, P. O. Box 203, Liberty, IL 62347, (800) 485-1508, Camera Bowmount

Vigil Game Monitor, 6291 Teller Rock Forest, Quebec City, Canada J1N 3A8, (819) 864-4637, Cameras/Monitors

Viper Archery Products, P. O. Box 506, Huntington. WV 25710 (304) 633-7131, Sights

Vital Bow Gear, P. O. Box 4013, Pocatello, ID 83201, (208) 232-2818, Arrow Rests

Vulture Treestands, 16726 150th Ave., Spring Lake, MI 49456, (616) 844-1947, Treestands

W.L. Gore & Associates, 795 Blue Ball Rd., Elton, MD 21921, (410) 392-3700, Clothing

Walls Industries, Inc., P. O. Box 98, Cleburne, TX 76033, (817) 645-4366, Clothing

Wasp Archery 707 Main St., Plymouth, CT 06782, (860) 283-0245, Broadheads

Weber's Leather Collection, 4996 39th Ave. NE, Alexandria, MN 56308, (320) 762-2816, Clothing

Wellington/Tink's, P. O. Box 244, Madison, GA 30650, (706) 342-4915, Scents

Western/National Bowhunter, P. O. Box 511, Squaw Valley, CA 93675, (559) 332-2535, Bowhunting Publications

Wheeler Archer, P. O. Box 256, Weidman, MI 48893, (989) 644-5825, Bows

Whitetail Institute of North America, 208 S. Browning St., Afton, IA 50830, (641) 347-8041, Feeds & Minerals

Whitetails Unlimited, 1715 Rhode Island St., Sturgeon Bay, WI 54235, (920) 743-6777, Organization

Whitewater Outdoors, Inc., W4228 Church St., Hingham, WI 53031, (920) 564-2674, Clothing

Wildlife Images, 1115 W. Liebau Rd., Mequon, WI 53092, (262) 243-6021, Clothing

Wildlife Research Center, 1050 McKinley St., Anoka, MN 55303, (763) 427-3350, Scents

WildTech Corporation, 1082 Tamberwood Ct., St. Paul, MN 55125, (651) 730-7333, FireTacks

Wildwood Innovations, Rt. 4, Box 286, Ashland, WI 54806, (715) 685-0020, Bow & Arrow Stands

Wiley Outdoor Products, 115-A Willie Dr., Pearl, MS 39208, (601) 664-1185, Game Calls

Winn Archery Equipment, 13757 64th St., South Haven, MI 49090, (269) 637-2658, Releases

Winner's Choice Bowstrings, 141 E. Main St., John Day, OR 97845, (541) 575-0818, Custom Bowstrings

Wolf Creek Productions, P. O. Box 904, Perry, MI 48872, (517) 625-9653, TV/Videos

WomenHunters.com, 8268 Old Jefferson Hwy., Kershaw, SC 29067, (803) 475-2250, Organization

Woods Wise Products, P. O. Box 681552, Franklin, TN 37068, (931) 364-7913, Game Calls

WRI/Vista, P. O. Box 70, Poncha Springs, CO 81242, (719) 539-1293, Accessories

Wyandotte Leather, Inc., 1811 6th St.Wyandotte, MI 48192, (734-282-3403

Xtreme Scents, 1290 Durwood Ct., Brighton, MI 48116, (810) 220-9392, Accessories

Yikes Bow Sites, 107 Dianne Dr., Brookhaven, MS 39601, (601) 833-5395, Bow Sites

Zebra Bowstrings, 919 River Rd., Sparta, WI 54656, (608) 269-2728, Bowstrings

Zenith/Britesite, 94 S. Rd., Wading River, NY 11792, (631) 929-3223, Arrow Rests

Zipper Mfg. Corp., Rt. 1, Box 147A, Ravenswood, WV 26164, (304) 273-3135, Custom Bows

2XJ Enterprises, 51 Ulmer Ln., North East, MD 21901, (443) 553-0088, Broadheads

Bibliography

Asbell, G. Fred. *Stalking and Still-Hunting: The Ground Hunter's Bible*. Self-Published; Longmont, CO, 1997.

Asbell, G. Fred. *Instinctive Shooting II*. Published by Cowles Magazines; Harrisburg, PA, 1993.

Asbell, G. Fred, Dave Holt, M. R. James, and Dwight Schuh. *The Complete Bowhunter: Bowhunting Equipment and Skills*. Published by Cowles Creative Publishing, Minnetonka, MN,1996.

Editorial Committee, M. R. James, Editor; *Bowhunting Big Game Records of North America*, First Edition. Published by Pope and Young Club, Milton, WI, 1975.

Editorial Committee, Glenn Helgeland, Editor; *Bowhunting Big Game Records of North America*, Second Edition. Published by Pope and Young Club, Salmon, ID,1981.

Editorial Committee, Lee Kline, Editor; *Bowhunting Big Game Records of North America*, Third Edition. Published by Pope and Young Club, Placerville, CA, 1987.

Editorial Committee, M. R. James, Editor; *Bowhunting Big Game Records of North America*. Fourth Edition. Published by Pope and Young Club, Chatfield, MN, 1993.

Editorial Committee, M. R. James, Editor; *Bowhunting Big Game Records of North America*. Fifth Edition. Published by Pope and Young Club, Chatfield, MN, 1999.

Fitz, Grancel. *How To Measure and Score Big Game Trophies*. A

Pope and Young Book, Published by Blue-J, Inc.; Fort Wayne, IN, 1977.

Holt, Dave. *Balanced Bowhunting: A Guide to Modern Bowhunting*, 1st and 2nd Editions, Published by High Country Publishers; Lakeside, CO, 1988 and 2004.

James, M. R. *Of Blind Pigs and Big Bucks*. Published by Blue Jay Book Publishers; Powder Springs, GA, 2003.

James, M. R. *The Bowhunter's Handbook*, 1st Edition. Published by DBI Books, Iola, WI, 1997.

James, M. R. *Successful Bowhunting*. Published by Blue-J, Inc.; Fort Wayne, IN, 1985.

James, M. R. *Bowhunting for Whitetail and Mule Deer*. Published by Jolex, Inc.; Paramus, NJ, 1976.

Marlow, Roy S. *Timeless Bowhunting — The Art, The Science, & The Spirit*. Published by Strikepoint Technologies; Bergheim,TX, 2003.

National Rifle Association of America. Bowhunting: *A Complete Guide to Bows, Gear, and Game for the Bowhunter*. NRA Hunter Skills Series; Washington, DC, 1991.

Rue, Leonard Lee, III. *Complete Guide to Game Animals*. Published by Outdoor Life Books/Van Nostrand Reinhold, Co., New York, NY, 1981.

Samuel, Dr. Dave. *Know Hunting: Truth, Lies, & Myths*. Published by Know Hunting Publications; Cheat Lake, WV, 1999.

Samuel, Dr. Dave. *The Complete Bowhunter: Understanding Whitetails*. Published by Cowles Creative Publishing, Minnetonka, MN, 1996.

Schuh, Dwight. *Fundamentals of Bowhunting*. Published by Stackpole Books, Harrisburg, PA, 1991.

Schuh, Dwight. *Bowhunter's Encyclopedia*. Published by Stackpole Books, Harrisburg, PA, 1987.

Schuh, Dwight. *Bowhunting for Mule Deer: A Detailed Guide for Hunting Open Country Bucks*. Published by Stoneydale Press Publishing Co., Stevensville, MT, 1985.

Schuh, Dwight. *Bugling for Elk: A Complete Guide to Early-Season Elk Hunting*. Published by Stoneydale Press Publishing Co., Stevensville, MT, 1983.

Statistical Summaries. 17th Recording Period, 1989-1990; 18th Recording Period, 1991-1992; 19th Recording Period, 1993-1994; 20th Recording Period, 1995-1996; 21st Recording Period, 1997-1998; 22nd Recording Period, 1999-2000; 23rd Recording Period, 2001-2002. Published by the Pope and Young Club, Chatfield, MN, 1989-2002.

Wadsworth, William H. *Bowhunting Deer*. National Bowhunter Education Manual. Published by National Bowhunter Education Foundation, Murray, KY, 1975.